The Civil War in Greenbrier County West Virginia

The Civil War in Greenbrier County West Virginia

Tim McKinney

Quarrier Press
Charleston, WV

Quarrier Press
Charleston, WV

Book and cover design:
Colleen Anderson/Mother Wit Writing and Design

ISBN: 1-891852-36-1

Library of Congress Catalog Card Number: 2004108160

10 9 8 7 6 5 4 3 2 1

Cover illustration: The Old White hotel at White Sulphur Springs depicted in the 1850s. Painting by William Grauer, 1932. *Courtesy of The Greenbrier, White Sulphur Springs*

Back cover illustration: "Anxious Moments," The Battle of Lewisburg. *Courtesy Robert Tuckwiller, Tuckwillergallery.com*

Printed in the United States of America

Distributed by:
Pictorial Histories Distribution
1125 Central Ave.
Charleston, WV 25302
www.wvbookco.com

Dedicated in memory of
Dr. Otis K. Rice
1919-2003
Friend, mentor, and first
Historian Laureate of West Virginia

Table of Contents

Acknowledgments

This endeavor would have been impossible without the generous assistance of many people. In compiling this list of people to whom I am much indebted, I have attempted to include everyone and I sincerely apologize for anyone I may have accidentally omitted.

Margaret Allen, Alderson, WV for sharing the papers of Charles Goddard, editor of the Fayette Tribune in the 1920s and 30's; Colleen Anderson, Charleston, WV did an exemplary job with the layout and design of this work; Jim Arbuckle, Charlottesville, VA for sharing the video history of his ancestor, David Creigh; The entire staff at the West Virginia Department of Archives and History, Charleston, with special notice of Fred Armstrong and Dick Fauss. Angela Beavers, Rupert, WV for her many labors over the years attempting to preserve and promote Greenbrier Civil War history; Dee Ann Blanton, National Archives and Records Administration, Washington, DC for recovering the court martial records of David Creigh; Dorothy Bodel, Blacksburg, VA for sharing her research into the activities of the Sisters of Charity at the Montgomery and Greenbrier White Sulphur Springs during the Civil War; Margaret Brennan, Wheeling, WV for her many efforts to preserve and promote West Virginia history; Marcia Wilson Cales, Organ Cave, WV for sharing her pictures of the saltpeter hoppers at Organ Cave; The Clark County Historical Society, Springfield, OH (especially Mr. & Mrs. Tiemen) for access to the cannon captured at the Battle of Lewisburg; Betty Clark, Vining Library, WVU Institute of Technology, Montgomery, for her tremendous assistance with interlibrary loan.

Nina Clark, Kanawha Falls, WV for believing in me all these years; Bill Clements, Quarrier Press, Charleston, WV for believing in me and assisting my endeavors, wherever they may lead; Wes Cochran, Parkersburg, WV. Wes makes the work of many authors easier with his publication of census and genealogical material; Robert Conte, historian for The *Greenbrier*, White Sulphur Springs, shared his expert knowledge of that famous resort's history and provided a wonderful tour of the property in 2003; Mr. & Mrs. Lewis Crawford, Rupert, WV shared the letters and papers of their Confederate ancestor, Andrew Cook; Valerie Crook, Monroe, NC Assistant State Coordinator of the West Virginia Genealogical Web Project, and coordinator of the Greenbrier County web page; Steve Cunningham, president of the Kanawha Valley Civil War Roundtable; My good friend Jack Dickinson, bibliographer of the Rosanna Blake Confederate Collection at Morrow Library, Marshall University, Huntington, WV. Jack shared my enthusiasm for this endeavor and rendered more assistance than I could ever have a right to expect. This work would be less complete without his support and suggestions along the way; Bob Driver, Brownsburg, VA shared his expert knowledge of the circumstances surrounding the hanging of David Creigh at Brownsburg in 1864; Ray Epling, Greenbrier County Historical Society, for assistance with photographs; Mary Giles, archivist for the Diocese of Charleston, Charleston, SC assisted with the recovery of the letters written at White Suplhur Springs by the Sisters of Charity in 1861-1862; Kurt Graham, webmaster of the Phillips Legion Georgia Cavalry webpage, shared his expert knowledge of that units participation in the early West Virginia campaigns.

Cheryl Keenan, Gauley Bridge, WV for exemplary service as manuscript editor; Janie Morgan, owner of Organ Cave, WV for allowing me access to her considerable files relevant to the history of that fascinating West Virginia cave; The entire staff of the Ohio Historical Society, Columbus, OH; Rev. Carl Renick (retired) Lewisburg, WV gave us an excellent tour of the John Wesley Methodist Church; Jim Talbert, archivist of the Greenbrier County Historical Society, Lewisburg. Jim shared my enthusiasm for this project and offered every possible assistance along the way; Robert Tuckwiller, owner of the Tuckwiller Gallery in Lewisburg, for permission to publish his painting, "Anxious Moments" The Battle of Lewisburg; The entire staff at the University of Virginia Library, Charlottesville; The entire staff at the Virginia Historical Society, Richmond; The entire staff in the Special Collections Department, Virginia Tech, Blacksburg; Staff of the West Virginia and Regional History Collection, WVU, Morgantown; Susan Williams, Falls View, WV for her interest in, and assistance with, my various endeavors.

To my wife Brenda, and my son Jason, for tolerating the long hours of research and writing that went into this project. When my research trips required them to become "Civil War widow and orphan" they bore my absence with resolute patience; To all my family and friends who support my work and offer their best wishes for whatever my latest endeavor may be; To the many unsung heroes of the World Wide Web who freely share their considerable knowledge of our great nation's history.

INTRODUCTION

Greenbrier County was formed by an Act of the Virginia Legislature in 1778 from parts of Montgomery and Botetourt counties. At the time of its formation, Greenbrier County extended from the top of Allegheny Mountain to the east, then westward to the Ohio River. Since 1778, 16 counties have been formed entirely or partially from land originally encompassed by Greenbrier County.

In 1769, the first permanent settlement was made in Greenbrier County near the present town of Frankford. Lewisburg, the county seat, was created by an Act of the Virginia Assembly in October 1782. It is the third oldest town in West Virginia and retains much of its antebellum charm.

Greenbrier is the second largest county in the state, comprising an area of 1,022.8 square miles. From north to south, the county spans 41 miles and from east to west, its maximum width is 51 miles. The county takes its name from the river which flows across it, and it is believed the river was named from the abundance of greenbriers that grow in the river valley.

Greenbrier is a beautifully rugged and mountainous county with a peak elevation of 4,372 feet at Grassy Knob. From its earliest days, the county's abundant hardwood forests and bluegrass valleys drew settlers primarily of Scots-Irish, English, German, Welsh, Dutch and French origin. Among this hardy stock of pioneers could be found Presbyterian, Anglican Lutheran, German Reformed Church, Quakers, Dunkards and Mennonites. By the 1850s the county was home to 39 churches that were predominately Methodist, Baptist and Presbyterian.

In 1860, on the eve of conflict, Greenbrier County consisted of 1,802 families for a total population of 12,211, which included 783 male and 742 female slaves. The county consisted of

985 farms, the majority of which were between 100 and 500 acres, with an average size of 140 acres. These farmlands were used extensively to raise prime cattle, hogs, sheep, and horses. The value of the county's livestock in 1860, adjusted for inflation to 2004, was in excess of $14 million. Greenbrier was also among the wealthiest counties in western Virginia, being home to 40 men whose estates, when adjusted for inflation to 2004, were valued in excess of $1 million each.

Though strong Union sentiments had characterized Greenbrier before the war, a majority of its citizens determined to side with the South in the political events that ultimately led to war, and the division of Virginia itself. Greenbrier sent no delegates to either the First or Second Wheeling Conventions, which gave birth to the Reorganized Government of Virginia, and began the journey toward West Virginia statehood. Her citizens not being in favor of a division of the commonwealth, it sent no delegates to the 1861-1862 session of the First West Virginia Constitutional Convention, and at no time was she represented in the Reorganized Government of Virginia.

As a staunchly pro-Southern county, the residents of Greenbrier cast no votes for Abraham Lincoln in the elections of 1860. Once Lincoln's call for 75,000 troops made war inevitable, Greenbrier County used its wealth to rapidly arm and recruit men for the Confederate military. At the beginning of the Civil War, the county had 2,474 white male residents between the ages of 18 and 55, or "military age." Of that number, roughly 2,000 served the Confederacy between 1861 and 1865. It is worth noting that some men younger than 18 and older than 55 were also recruited from Greenbrier County. The vast majority of these men enlisted during the first two years of the conflict.

Greenbrier County was strategically important to the armies of the North and South as a gateway to northwestern Virginia to the west, and the Shenandoah Valley to the east. Other factors contributing to the military value of Greenbrier County include its use as a base from which to either attack, or defend, the vital railroads of southwestern Virginia, and its proximity to the salt mines of the Kanawha Valley. The county's livestock, agricultural products, and saltpeter caves were also coveted - saltpeter being necessary in the production of gunpowder. When Organ Cave, near Ronceverte, came under control of the Confederate Mining and Nitre Bureau in the summer of 1861, it proved to be a vital source of saltpeter for the Confederacy.

Two of Greenbrier's popular antebellum tourist destinations, White Sulphur Springs and Blue Sulphur Springs, were used repeatedly during the Civil War as military hospitals and barracks. Both antebellum resorts changed hands numerous times during the war, and both bore silent witness to the heroism, sacrifice, and despair of fratricidal conflict. The "Old White" (present-day Greenbrier) at White Sulphur Springs was occupied by Confederate forces almost continuously during the first year of the war, and it was occasionally occupied by Federal and Confederate forces alike from 1862 until 1865. At Blue Sulphur Springs, where Allegheny College once stood, Confederate forces established a military hospital in 1861. The graves of dozens of men who perished in that remote mountain hospital can yet be found on a nearby hill. Some of them traveled from as far away as Georgia and Mississippi. They entered the mountains of West Virginia with youthful enthusiasm, entirely unprepared for the hard reality of mountain warfare.

Greenbrier County also played an important role in the Confederate postal system, with Confederate post offices operating at various times in Frankford, Lewisburg and White Sulphur Springs. These post offices were among the very few offices west of the Allegheny Mountains to receive Confederate stamps. Without stamps, the local postmaster would write "paid" on the envelope. The post office at White Sulphur Springs was probably the last Confederate post office operating in West Virginia at the close of the war. For nearly two years after the war, the postmaster at White Sulphur Springs tried unsuccessfully to get the Federal Government to reimburse him for more than $200 worth of stamps stolen by Union soldiers in 1864.

A careful review of the *Official Records of the War of the Rebellion*, published by the United States Government, between 1881 and 1901, reveals more than 1,400 pages of letters, orders, dispatches and other documents relevant to the Civil War in Greenbrier County. From this fact we may glean some idea how much "war" Greenbrier's residents were subjected to. The tale of David Creigh, "The Greenbrier Martyr," reminds us that it was not only the actual combatants who paid a heavy price during those four bloody years. I am very pleased to publish here, for the first time, the Official Court Martial records of David Creigh. These records are housed at the National Archives in Washington D.C., and had been considered "lost" to history. Mr. Creigh's tragic tale resonates across the years. As recently as 2002, the Greenbrier Valley Theatre staged a very successful run of "The Greenbrier Martyr," a play about the life and death of David Creigh, written by Mr. K.C. Davis.

Between 1861 and 1865, more than 60,000 warriors of the Blue and Gray traversed Greenbrier County in a long series of skirmishes, battles, and maneuvers. The county became a crossroad for armies of the North and South, and remained so throughout the conflict. Two United States soldiers became Medal of Honor recipients for combat action here, in 1862 and 1864.

Even in the years immediately after the war, Greenbrier County played a prominent role in events that shaped this nation. During the summers of 1867-1869 General Robert E. Lee visited the Greenbrier White Sulphur Springs. At a meeting there in 1868, General Lee and other prominent veterans of the Blue and Gray, signed the *Greenbrier Manifesto*, a document that called for reconciliation between the North and South. Thus Greenbrier County, crossroads of the Blue and Gray, became a conduit for lasting peace.

The research and writing necessary to produce this work has been a journey well worth taking. Remembrance is a virtue, and it is one of the great blessings of this author's life to be able to share these memories.

To the Patriots
- OF -
North Western
VIRGINIA!!

WHEREAS -- a Convention is to be held in Wheeling on the 11th. of this month, for the avowed purpose of effecting a division of the State, and attaching a portion thereof, as a miserable appendage, to one of the Republican states, or else forming the same into a new, and insignificant Free State. And believing that either change would be ruinous to our property and our social happiness. We therefore earnestly call upon the people of North Western Virginia, in their several counties, who still remain loyal to the 'Old Dominion,' and are opposed to being tacked on the 'TAIL END' of the BLACK REPUBLICAN DESPOTISM! to send Delegates to a convention to be held at Lewisburg, on the first Monday in July next, to enter their solemn PROTEST against this wicked and treasonable scheme, and also to take such action as may then be thought proper, after knowing the result of the Wheeling Convention. If a convention, gotten up as the one to be held at Wheeling has been, has the power to divide the State, then, upon the same supposition, we, in convention, by the same right and power, can annul their acts, or SEPARATE AGAIN FROM THEM!!

Lewisburg, Va. June, 1st. 1861.

CHAPTER ONE
THE PATH TO WAR

The April 17, 1861 decision of the Virginia Convention to take the road to secession was met with cautious enthusiasm in Greenbrier County. Months of public debate and indecision preceded the Convention's vote. With Virginia's course now set, at least there was some certainty as to what path the Old Dominion would follow and the citizens of Greenbrier County were quick to answer the call. One week later, on April 24, the Greenbrier County Court passed the first of several levies intended to "provide for the equipping of volunteers and the care of indigent families of those in service of the state." This levy required the citizens to pay .40 tax per $100.00 value of land, .40 per $100.00 worth of property and six and two-thirds percent on every $100.00 of interest being accrued by bonds, bank accounts, and so on.(1) For this levy, James Withrow, John W. Dunn, and Johnston E. Bell, all prominent citizens of Lewisburg, were appointed agents to oversee the acquisition of equipment and supplies for the troops then being assembled. Harvey Handley, Thomas Pare, and John Withrow were charged with forming a committee to provide for the families of these volunteer soldiers.

By late April and early May 1861 the nucleus for several companies of Confederate soldiers had already formed in Greenbrier County. These companies consisted of lawyers, clerks, printers, farmers, mechanics, clergymen, and men and boys from all walks of life. On April 21, 1861, Henry Mason Mathews wrote Governor John Letcher from Lewisburg: "Every man, young and old is ready to start at a moments warning to defend the old Commonwealth." Six days later Gov. Letcher nominated Mathews second lieutenant in the Confederate Corps of Engineers. Subsequently appointed captain, his service with the engineers ended on June 21, when he was ordered to join Gen. Wise at Lewisburg. Mathews, a 27-year-old Lewisburg attorney, was immediately assigned the rank of major in the Wise Legion Quartermaster Department.

On May 2, 1861, William F. Gordon Jr., clerk of the Virginia House of Delegates, and his business partner, S.M. Keller, proposed establishing a powder manufactory in Greenbrier and Monroe counties to mine saltpeter for the production of gunpowder. Virginia authorities asked how long it would take the men to put their plan into operation, the scale of the proposed works, and how much investment would be required. There is no record that this particular plan was ever implemented, however, Organ Cave in Greenbrier County was supplying saltpeter to the Confederacy by August 1, 1861 under direct supervision of A.W.G. Davis, another prominent citizen of Lewisburg who held the rank of general in the prewar Virginia militia.(2)

It has been documented that Greenbrier County has at least 105 caves, or one-fourth of the caves in the entire state. Several of the Greenbrier caves contain saltpeter deposits that were used in the manufacture of gunpowder as far back as the War of 1812. Today Organ Cave is one of the few commercially operated caves in West Virginia. The cavern gets its name from a very large formation of stalagmites that resemble a pipe organ. A major attraction there is the presence of several saltpeter hoppers that Confederate soldiers used during the Civil War.

On May 6, 1861, Gen. Robert E. Lee notified Lt. Col. John Echols of Union, Monroe County, that he was authorized to "call out and muster into the service of the State, volunteer companies from the counties of Pendleton, Augusta, Pocahontas, Monroe, Highland, Bath, Rockbridge, Greenbrier, and Allegheny, to rendezvous at Staunton..." Col. Echols received Lee's letter while at home on May 9, and immediately rode to Lewisburg where he penned a reply to Gen. Lee: "...I have ordered out one infantry company from Monroe County, two rifle companies from this county [Greenbrier], and three companies from Allegheny County, which will reach Staunton on the 15th instant...."(3) John Echols was a 38-year-old native of

Gen. John Echols CSA, 1823-1896. *Courtesy USAMHI*

Lynchburg, Virginia, and had been commonwealth's attorney prior to the Civil War. Standing six feet four and weighing 260 pounds, he made an imposing figure on the battlefield.

Another early Greenbrier appointment was that of John Morris to the Confederate Quartermaster Department on May 7, 1861. Lt. Col. Henry Heth of Chesterfield County, Virginia, then Acting QM General, recommended Morris to the position with the rank of captain. Morris was charged with the procurement and distribution of equipment, supplies and food, to the Confederate forces of Greenbrier and Monroe counties.

Everyone seemed caught up in the excitement of the times and few apparently paused to consider the ramifications of Civil War. The venerable John McElhenney, pastor of the Old Stone Church in Lewisburg, watched the tragedy unfold and prayed for peace. He worried about the bloodshed and suffering that he knew must surely come, as he explained to Mrs. Samuel Price of Lewisburg: "These young people, who are rushing into this conflict with so much enthusiasm, do not know what a calamity has overtaken us, or what tribulation we may have to pass through."(4)

The Federal Government was also active at this time establishing military departments to facilitate the conquest and control of Virginia. On May 9, the U.S. War Department issued General Orders Number 19: "The Department of the Ohio is extended so as to embrace so much of Western Virginia and Pennsylvania as lies north of the Great Kanawha, north and west of the Greenbrier, thence northward to the southwest corner of Maryland, thence along the Western Maryland line to the Pennsylvania line, and thence northerly to the northeast corner of McKean County, in Pennsylvania.(5)

On May 16, Dr. John A. Hunter, a 54-year-old Lewisburg physician, was nominated by Gov. John Letcher as surgeon of the Trans-Allegheny District of Virginia. Dr. Hunter served in that capacity throughout the war. He rendered valuable and efficient service at several military hospitals, including the Greenbrier White Sulphur Springs.

Also on May 16, the Greenbrier Sharpshooters, commanded by Captain Samuel W. Brown, and the Greenbrier Rifles, commanded by Captain Robert F. Dennis, departed Lewisburg in route to Staunton. These men subsequently became Companies E and F, 27th Virginia Infantry, Stonewall Brigade. At the outbreak of hostilities, Captain Samuel Brown was the 23-year-old resident physician at Frazier's Inn near present-day Rainelle, and Captain Robert Flournoy Dennis was a 37-year-old Lewisburg attorney. Many of these men were members of the Old Stone Church in Lewisburg and Rev. McElhenney was among the throng of people gathered for their sad departure: "Two companies had just been raised in old Greenbrier, and were hastening to the seat of war; the members of his congregation were buckling on their armor; the old gentleman was with them in spirit. He rode down to the village to bid them farewell. He said if he had been ten years younger, he would have gone with them to the front. His only son had joined the service; his grandsons were volunteers in the Southern army; his daughter's family had taken refuge at the parsonage; he had cast in his lot with his people."(6)

The men from Greenbrier reached Staunton on the 17th and

Captain R.F. Dennis. A pre-war Lewisburg attorney, he organized the "Greenbrier Rifles" in 1861. *Courtesy Greenbrier Historical Society*

the following day Private Andrew N. Cook, from Big Clear Creek Valley near present-day Rupert, wrote a letter home to his wife and two children: "We arrived in this place yesterday evening...We have been treated with great respect and kindness ever since we left home. The citizens of Lewisburg besides the provisions given to do us on the road, made up over a hundred and fifty dollars for the benefit of this company. The people every where promised with tears in their eyes that the wives and children of the volunteers should not suffer while there was anything in the country..." The next day he told his wife about the reputation his company had already achieved: "...they call us the Greenbrier Sharpshooters, our colonel made a speech yesterday in which he told us that our fame had spread all over the state. I fear we have been over rated..." Then on May 21st Pvt. Cook told his wife that some of the troops were ordered east: "...the Lewisburg and Allegheny companies started this morning for Harpers Ferry...there is a good deal of dissatisfaction about having to take muskets in stead of rifles...through the extravagance of some of our company we ran out of bread today. I was sent to town to buy bread, I could get but little, but the ladies of Staunton ascertaining our condition soon flooded our camps with the dainties of Staunton."(7)

Andrew Cook's complaint that his rifle company had been issued smoothbore muskets was not uncommon among Southern soldiers during the first year of the war. Large bodies of men were recruited faster than weapons and supplies could be procured and it was not unusual to have riflemen without rifles, cavalrymen without horses, artillerymen without cannon, and all branches of service lacking the basic necessities of military life.

Greenbrier County was home to two prewar militia regiments, the 79th and 135th. These regiments assembled in Lewisburg and held drills May 21-23, and on the 24th there was a general call for men to enlist which drew a large and enthusiastic crowd. The Lewisburg *Weekly Era* of May 25, stated that for the two weeks previous the ladies of Lewisburg had worked day and night making uniforms for the volunteer companies. Adam C. Snyder, editor of the *Weekly Era*, was among those who joined Captain Dennis's Rifle Company. In his final editorial statement, Snyder captured the mood of the time: "The justice of our cause insures our success; and if wickedness is punished in proportion to its enormity, Abe Lincoln, his diabolical advisers and sycophants will enjoy the superlative torments of a special and intense hell prepared as a reward for their merits."(8)

Patriotism and a desire to defend their homes from "northern fanatics" led many men from Greenbrier County to join the army. Separation from loved ones and the hardships of military life caused some men to reevaluate their decision rather quickly. On May 26, Andrew Cook wrote his wife telling her to be on the lookout for some Greenbrier men who had deserted scarcely one month after volunteering: "I am sorry to tell you that ten of our men deserted us last night....if they get to Greenbrier I want all to set their mark on them, Ben Crane, Henry Crane, Marshall Crane, P. Price, Jesse Price, Pleasant Hawkins, William Simpson, Charles Easter [actually Heister] and Johnston Easter. There has been a party of men sent after them, whether they will come out there or not I don't know."(9)

Another of the Confederate companies from Greenbrier enrolled early in the war was the Greenbrier Cavalry, later Company A, (1st) and D, 14th Virginia Cavalry under Captain Robert B. Moorman. Moorman's company departed Lewisburg for Staunton on May 24, arriving at Staunton the 26th. The Greenbrier Cavalry made a fine impression on everyone as the *Staunton Spectator* reported: "This fine company, numbering eighty...arrived at this place on Sunday evening last, bearing a beautiful banner which had been prepared and presented by the ladies of Lewisburg. It contained the Virginia coat of arms on one side, and on the other, the inscription 'God speed you.' This is one of the finest cavalry companies in the State. The soldiers are men of character and respectability, and the horses are No. 1..." Departing Staunton for northwestern Virginia in early June, the *Staunton Spectator* declared: "This company is a specimen of what Greenbrier can do, and she may well be proud of it. We can say, without being invidious, that we never saw a finer body of men and horses in our lives. Try it again, Greenbrier. We like to see such specimens."

Assigned as escort company to Gen. Robert S. Garnett at Laurel Hill, its members were involved in some of the first bloodshed of the war. On June 1, Pvt. Calvin Renick, a 25-year-old farmer from Renick's Valley, was on picket duty six miles from Philippi, Barbour County. When a scouting party of the 2nd U.S. Cavalry came near, Renick and the other pickets opened fire. Pvt. Renick killed one of the Federal cavalrymen, said to be the first man killed in the war.

On May 28, 1861, Virginia authorities discussed a proposal by A.W.G. Davis of Lewisburg to manufacture gunpowder for the use of the State. Gov. Letcher wrote to Mr. Davis telling him that Virginia would purchase all the good quality rifle and musket powder that he could deliver. By August 1, "General" Davis was supplying the promised powder from his works at Organ Cave near Lewisburg. This manufactory subsequently became part of Nitre District Number 4, Confederate Nitre and Mining Bureau, with headquarters at Union, Monroe County, and commanded by Captain James Bradford Noyes, a prewar salt maker from Kanawha County. The following day another proposal from Greenbrier County was debated, this one being an offer from

Samuel C. Luddington to operate a postal "express" on horses from Jackson River Depot (present Clifton Forge area) to Buffalo on the Kanawha River. This express service would make the 362 mile round-trip three times per week, with a strict schedule of hours and days. Luddington proposed to charge the government $154.00 per week for this service. Governor Letcher's Advisory Council referred the proposal to the Postmaster General of the Confederate States, with the recommendation that some type of mail delivery be established as demanded by the public interests. While a short-lived express service was quickly established from eastern into western Virginia, it was not operated by Mr. Luddington. In early June he became a contract beef supplier with the Confederate Quartermaster Department and worked in that capacity through the fall of 1864.(10)

On May 30, the Greenbrier Sharpshooters arrived at Harpers Ferry and quickly established their camp alongside hundreds of other troops, many from the deep south. The next day Andrew Cook told his wife about their arrival: "I landed at this place yesterday evening late in the day. I met with Captain Dennis of Lewisburg, he told me to call at his office and get a letter…it proved to be yours of the 22nd May…Harpers Ferry is one of the most romantic places I ever saw, it looks like nature carved it out for some great tragedy. It is now strongly fortified and well guarded by large forces…" After telling her about preparations for defense, he described a case of apparent early-war sabotage: "…one of the soldiers from Mississippi took a drink of liquor and immediately fell dead. Since that time the officers have ordered the heads to be knocked out of the barrels and nearly four hundred gallons of whiskey and wine poured into the river, it is supposed that some abolitionist put Strychnia in it…" During most of the Civil War, officers and physicians of the North and South believed that whiskey had medicinal purposes and thus it was not uncommon to see wagon loads of liquor trailing along with any large body of troops.(11)

Lewisburg was established in the spring of 1861 as a recruitment center for the Confederacy. This fact led many men, individually and in groups, to make the trek into Greenbrier and enlist. Numerous early-war companies of southern troops that were recruited elsewhere officially mustered into Confederate service while camped in and about Lewisburg. Being situated along the turnpike connecting western Virginia to the east, the town's people also witnessed many soldiers passing through en route to join their various commands. These visits by transient soldiers occurred early and often and continued throughout the war. An early example of this was the June 2, 1861 arrival of a few members of the Confederate "Shriver Greys," later Company G, 27th Virginia Infantry, recruited at Wheeling. They had been cut off from joining their regiment at Harpers Ferry, via the Baltimore and Ohio Railroad, and reached Lewisburg en route eastward: "It was an exciting trip. Everywhere along the route from the Red House Shoals to Meadow Bluff, we met men with muskets on their shoulders, *going to meet the Yankees!*...The wildest rumors were in the air, and our statement that there were no Yankees this side of the Ohio River was not believed. We were received with suspicion in Lewisburg. The town was in a state of great excitement; the streets were patrolled; trunks were packed for flight, and lights were kept burning in the houses. There were rumors of an uprising amongst the negroes: arms had been found hidden in a barn; the ringleader had been arrested..."(12) The uprising referred to occurred in mid-May when "Uncle Reuben," a slave belonging to James Withrow, was accused by another slave of hiding weapons for use in a servile insurrection. Obviously the episode caused a great uproar and the townspeople remained on the alert for some time afterwards. Uncle Reuben was subsequently tried and convicted of the plot. He was hanged on June 28, 1861.(13)

As if matters were not already at fever pitch in Greenbrier County, a breathless courier galloped full speed into Lewisburg on June 3, yelling "the Yankees are coming, the Yankees are coming. 1100 Federal cavalry have entered Braxton County and laid Sutton in ashes, en route to Lewisburg." Hearing the news, the citizens were nearly panic-stricken. There were at that instant only a few Confederate soldiers in Lewisburg and they would be no match for 1100 fire-breathing Yankee cavalrymen. Citizens and soldiers scrambled to sound the alarm. Women and children were told to stay home and lock their doors. Bags were packed and wagons readied, livestock and foodstuffs secreted, and valuables locked away. The nearest Southern force of any size was in Union, Monroe County, and a courier was rapidly dispatched there seeking reinforcements. Arriving at Union just after dark, the courier explained the desperate situation and all of Monroe County was soon in an uproar, as an eye-witness explained: "A man from Blue Sulphur calls for men to go immediately to Lewisburg to meet a large invading cavalry company...an attack expected this evening or tomorrow. The volunteer company collecting, ordered to march. We begin to think of removing the women and children to the retired places in the county...no sleep at all...Volunteers coming in from all quarters, some of them shouting and alarming the ladies...."(14)

A column of reinforcements several hundred strong hastened toward Lewisburg, not knowing what calamity might await them. Large numbers of these men had not been issued uniforms or weapons and their appearance was more that of a lynch mob than an army on the move. Some wore jeans and flannel shirts, others various styles of homespun garments, a few were even barefoot. Here and there among the muskets could be seen shotguns, horse pistols, homemade swords and daggers, pikes, spikes, and bayonets. What this "army" lacked in finesse however, it made up for in patriotic zeal.

Approaching Lewisburg well after midnight, the reinforcements could tell from some distance that the town was "illuminated bright as day." The surreal appearance of the village lent an eerie aspect to an already bizarre event. Arriving on the outskirts of town, the column was met with word that the Yankees were supposed to be "seven miles out," and numbered some "3,000 to 5,000." Working through the night establishing defensive positions, the rescuers hardened their resolve and awaited the contest. The beauty and peace of the June 4 sunrise seemed in stark contrast to the commotion in town. Everyone watched and waited but no Yankees came. Finally, mercifully, word spread at noon that the entire story was nothing but a false and wild rumor. Unfortunately for the Confederate forces however, a ball rolled cannot be recalled, and it was impossible to halt additional reinforcements local commanders knew were on the way. Within 12 hours nearly 3,000 Confederate soldiers from seven different Virginia counties had assembled in and near Lewisburg.

Later that same day Col. Jubal Early, commanding at Lynchburg, received by telegraph an even wilder rumor of invasion. This one claimed that "Ten thousand Northern troops and twelve hundred horse are now in Fayette County, making forced marches for the Virginia and Tennessee Railroad." Col. Early found the report incredulous, but forwarded it to the Confederate President, Jefferson Davis: "I send the dispatch for what it is worth. I cannot believe there is any truth in it. The country from which it comes has been very much stampeded with false rumors of insurrection on the line of the Virginia and Tennessee Railroad. To allay excitement, I would suggest that a special messenger be sent to Lewisburg by the Central Railroad." Receiving Col. Early's telegram, President Davis notified Gen. John B. Floyd who was then at Abingdon, Virginia: "A dispatch from Col. Early...states that...Northern troops...are pushing for the Virginia and Tennessee Railroad, and advancing through Fayette County to Lewisburg. Send reliable information as far as can be obtained. Press forward organization of brigade of riflemen, and, if report is true, call out all available force and protect railroad." Although Confederate authorities had serious doubts about the rumor's validity, they decided to err on the side of caution. Even before the rumor developed, they planned to send someone into western Virginia to coordinate Confederate efforts in the region and oversee the recruitment and training of troops. The urgency of the rumor spurred them to action. On June 6, Adjutant and Inspector General of Virginia, Samuel Cooper, appointed ex-Governor of Virginia, Henry A. Wise, Brigadier General of Provisional Forces. Wise was ordered to proceed from Richmond to the Kanawha Valley, collecting what forces he could along the way. He was told about the perceived danger to the railroad and that an "invading army" was reportedly nearing Lewisburg. Fully aware that Gen. Wise would have no time to properly organize and train his men, he was told to rely on the "valor and knowledge" of the people of the country "as a substitute for organization and discipline." He was told that if he could not defeat the enemy, he was to stop their advance and endeavor to "embarrass and delay his movements." Lastly, he was advised that Gen. John B. Floyd was charged with protection of the railroad and if their forces were to unite, Gen. Floyd would be in overall command.(15)

Henry A. Wise was born at Drummondtown, Virginia, December 3, 1806. He was a graduate of Washington College, Pennsylvania, studied law and was admitted to the bar in 1828. He served as Democratic governor of Virginia from 1856 to 1860, during John Brown's raid on Harpers Ferry. Gen. Wise had no military training at all and worse yet, he was a political nemesis of Gen. Floyd, with whom he was expected to cooperate.

On June 10, "The Greenbrier Mountain Rifles," later Company C, 46th Virginia Infantry, enlisted at Meadow Bluff. This 72-man company was led by Captain Alexis M. Buster, a 23-year-old Lewisburg hotel clerk. They were officially mustered into Confederate service at Gauley Bridge on June 30.

With Gen. Wise on the march toward Lewisburg and wild rumors flying faster than bullets, John H. Ruckman, Attorney for Pocahontas County, penned a desperate appeal for aid to Jefferson Davis on June 10. He told Davis that his county and Greenbrier were on the verge of Yankee takeover. Citing the apparent lack of any cohesive Confederate plan to retain the region, he said, "Two weeks since this thing was not half so gloomy. In less than two more we shall be overrun, unless there is a far greater force...sent us. The enemy is now within a few hours march of our county lines." He reported that Confederate forces of western Virginia were only "half armed" and did not have sufficient ammunition to supply "more than one round to the man." Declaring Pocahontas and Greenbrier counties loyal to the South, he asked for help before it was too late. "Many of our best families have their carriages in readiness to move...Nothing but destruction awaits our houses and barns. Our waving fields of grain and grass, our thousands of cattle, they will soon possess....I am done writing. I will take my rifle, shot-gun, pis-

Gen. Henry A. Wise CSA, 1806-1876. *Courtesy National Archives*

tol, and cutlass, relying upon the God of battles, and go to meet the enemy."(16)

Gen. Wise arrived at Lewisburg on June 14, and was greeted by many well-wishers and old friends. While serving as democratic congressman from Accomack County in the early 1850's, Wise had advocated political reforms and internal improvements in western Virginia that earned him a great deal of gratitude. Furthermore, he was remembered for a four-hour speech he gave at the courthouse in Lewisburg on March 24, 1855, while running for governor. In the speech he reiterated his support for internal improvements and education in western Virginia. There were some, however, who suspected that Henry Wise's interests in the west were self-serving and it was generally felt that he did not care for the mountaineers of western Virginia. His overbearing, even condescending ways, alienated many western Virginian's, especially during his tenure in the Kanawha Valley in the summer of 1861. Three days after Wise reached Lewisburg, an infantry company known as the White Sulphur Rifles was enlisted "for one year," and attached to the Wise Legion. Their captain was Zachariah F. Morris, the 31-year-old Postmaster at Alvon, Greenbrier County.(17)

With Wise in Lewisburg, Col. Christopher Q. Tompkins was busy training recruits west of Charleston, in the Kanawha Valley. Col. Tompkins was an experienced military man, having served 16 years in the United States Army. He graduated West Point in 1836, 27th in a class of 49. He owned a large estate on the top of Gauley Mountain, two miles east of Gauley Bridge, where he relocated with his family from Richmond in 1856. Prior to the war, he was a successful businessman with interests in several coal mines of Fayette and Kanawha counties. Wise wrote to him on June 17, explaining his plan of advance and telling him that 298 men would proceed the next day from Lewisburg to Gauley Bridge, Fayette County. Once there, they would be posted in various locations in and near the upper Kanawha Valley to sound the alarm should the enemy advance. Most of the troops Wise sent to Gauley had not been officially mustered into service. On the day after their arrival, the "Dixie Rifles," later Company C, 60th Virginia Infantry, were formally enrolled. A number of Greenbrier County men were in their ranks, the first of dozens from Greenbrier who would eventually join the 60th Regiment. This company elected Beuhring H. Jones their captain. Jones was well known in Greenbrier County for his services before the war as junior editor of the *Lewisburg Chronicle*. At the time of his election Captain Jones was wearing a brand new Confederate uniform jacket that he paid a Lewisburg tailor to produce for him: "I had just returned from Lewisburg, and sported a gray jacket, gotten up by a tailor of that place, who, by way of securing the job, had assured me that he was perfectly "Au fait" in all the minutiae pertaining to the decoration of military rank. I was quite proud of my up-buttoned, close-fitting 'Jacket of Gray' and felt all the importance of the commander, until I was startled from my dream of consequentiality by being addressed by an old soldier as 'Corporal Jones.' My 'Knight of the Shears,' equally ignorant with myself had braided me a corporal. My mortification was excessive, nor did I recover my usual composure until spasmodically I tore off the libelous braid, and cast it disdainfully upon the ground."(18)

Also at Gauley was a prestigious infantry company from Richmond commanded by General Wise's son, Captain Obidiah Jennings Wise. This company, the "Richmond Light Infantry Blues," assembled in Richmond and enrolled at Lewisburg while camped at the Fair Grounds. They were an elite command made up of sons from some of the most wealthy and influential families of Richmond and eastern Virginia. The "Blues" were Virginia's oldest and most distinguished company. They were formed as a militia unit in 1789 and were given their nickname upon adoption of blue uniforms in 1793. John H. Cochran, a member of the "Blues," wrote to his mother from Lewisburg the day before their advance to Gauley: "You will doubtless be surprised at receiving a letter from me at this place. Our company has been transferred to the Wise Legion....We will be mustered into service this evening for the war....We are busily engaged in drilling raw recruits and getting ready for a fight....All are well and in fine spirits...I remain as ever, your affectionate son."(19)

Gen. Wise remained at Lewisburg until June 20, attempting to arrange for additional manpower and trying to organize an efficient supply system. So early in the conflict there was a great lack not only of experienced officers to lead the men but experience was lacking in all facets of military operation. Especially critical at this juncture was a need for efficient operation of the Wise Legion Quartermaster Department. Wise knew that once his men were stationed in the Kanawha Valley they would be at least two or three days distant from their supply base at Lewisburg and White Sulphur Springs. Those supply points received their stores from the Confederate depot on the James River, another 40 miles and 2 or 3 days distant, making the entire process take upwards of one week—and that was in good weather. When the frequent rains of the summer and fall of 1861 turned the so-called turnpikes into rivers of mud, the time it took to haul supplies over the mountains increased substantially. Having been a congressman and governor of Virginia, Wise was politically well-connected and was able to get the attention from Richmond that some commanders only wished for. Nevertheless, the armies of the budding Confederacy were far-flung and all were begging for the necessities of warfare and all possessed legitimate, even urgent, needs. Wise found himself but another voice in a chorus of commanders and he grew impatient. He strutted around Lewisburg like a "game-cock," barking orders and sending dispatch after dispatch to Richmond. His entreaties finally garnered some attention when on June 21, the Confederate Assistant Adjutant General, R.H. Chilton, wrote him saying that some of his "wishes" would be granted: "Brig. Gen. H.A. Wise, Lewisburg, Greenbrier County, Virginia: Agreeable to wishes expressed...a field piece, with ammunition, has been forwarded to your command. A company of artillery...is now being enlisted here for your command...As Captain H.M. Mathews can be spared from the duty in which he is at present engaged, he will be ordered to report to you. Three other officers will be directed to join you."(20)

Gen. Wise departed Lewisburg on June 20, reached Gauley Bridge on June 22, and the next day sent another letter to Col. Tompkins. He informed the colonel that he had with him at Gauley Bridge 340 men, some of whom were not yet mustered. He said he was expecting the arrival of Captain Brock's cavalry company, 90 men, making his total force 430. "I will leave two untrained companies here, say 130, with Captain Buckholtz to be drilled in infantry and artillery practice and to guard the Gauley Bridge, and will take on with me tomorrow two of the infantry and two of the cavalry companies of my Legion to Charleston, say 300 efficient men well armed. When I see you I will be happy to interchange views upon all the topics of this command." (21)

On June 24, Colonel St. George Croghan, one of Wise's cavalry officers, told the general that he had information indicating he could acquire 500 rifled muskets from Fayetteville, North Carolina. Desperate for any and all supplies, Wise figured the trip was worth the gamble and ordered Col. Croghan to make the journey without delay. Wagons and teamsters would be necessary to haul the weapons so his order stated that "in passing Lewisburg he will obtain from the Quartermaster the necessary certificate of transportation who is required to provide means thereof."(22) Col. Croghan was an active and efficient officer who frequently paid for supplies from his own pocket and would then be reimbursed. The quartermaster at Lewisburg had already paid him several times for such transactions, most recently reimbursing him twenty dollars he paid for "7 tents and poles."

Gen. Wise arrived in Charleston on Wednesday, June 26, and established his camp near the courthouse, with headquarters at a local hotel known as the "Kanawha House." Several days later, Wise moved his troops to Camp Two Mile on Charleston's west side. The military situation Wise found at Charleston was no better than the one he left in Lewisburg. Many of the company commanders were incompetent and the need for arms and equipment severe. Col. Tompkins was still at Camp Coalsmouth (present-day St. Albans), training recruits and scouting the area. Confederate military activity in the Kanawha Valley had not escaped notice by Northern commanders and on July 2, Gen. George B. McClellan ordered Gen. Jacob D. Cox to proceed to Gallipolis, Ohio, and prepare an invasion of the Kanawha Valley. The Federal Government had reliable information concerning Confederate efforts in the region and Gen. Cox was ordered to act promptly. He was given command of approximately 3,000 soldiers from Kentucky and Ohio. Preparations for the invasion were quickly made and in a few days the Wise Legion would find itself in a very bad situation.

While Wise was on the Kanawha, additional troops for his command continued to pour into Greenbrier County. Among these was a company of infantry from Charlottesville, Virginia, known as the University Volunteers, later Company G, 49th Virginia Infantry. They were a relatively small company, numbering only 59 officers and men. This company marched into Lewisburg at 4 p.m. Saturday, July 6. The following day Private James Hamner of the University Volunteers, penned a letter to his mother: "We are now in Lewisburg...we came by the White Sulphur, the White is a beautiful place but has now only 15 or 16 guests....We are quartered here in the C.H. [courthouse]. The citizens are very kind to us, and send us plenty to eat, in the way of buttermilk, coffee and meat....Gen. Wise is at Charleston...we may have fighting to do in a week or ten days...I don't think Wise has a large enough force, he ought to be reinforced. I will try to write as often as I can, I am writing on my tin plate." The next day Pvt. Hamner wrote again to his mother telling her that a large quantity of muskets, rifles and ammunition had arrived at Lewisburg. These were the supplies that Col. Croghan was sent for on June 24. There were rumors afloat that some Union men between Lewisburg and Gauley Bridge had threatened to seize the supply train on its advance to the Wise Legion. Accordingly, a guard of 20 men was selected from the University Volunteers to ride with Col. Croghan into the Kanawha Valley. The balance of that company would remain in Lewisburg. Pvt. Hamner was among those selected for the guard. They departed Lewisburg on Tuesday, July 9, arriving at Gauley Bridge on the 12th. Gen. Wise and his staff had recently returned to Gauley Bridge and Wise received the supply train personally.(23)

Col. Croghan traveled not only to North Carolina, but also visited the Ordinance Department in Richmond attempting to obtain hand grenades. He obtained the promised 500 muskets plus a large quantity of cartridge boxes and leather pouches, as well as gun tools, 50 tents, 500 hats and 500 blankets. He stated in his report that upon his return to Lewisburg, he "obtained 13,000 musket cartridges, handed over to me by Capt. Thomas upon your requisition I believe. All the articles numerated I have brought to this point, and have handed them over to the proper officers...."(24)

A member of the University Volunteers who remained behind at Lewisburg wrote to his brother at 10:30 pm. July 12, the same day Croghan's supply train reached Gauley: "...everything is as quiet in barracks as possible, all who are here being sound asleep, many being absent visiting the ladies and hospitable people of the town. The people of this place far exceed in hospitality those of any place I know, e.g. [for example] Mr. Bell [local merchant] just opposite the C.H. where we are quartered, invariably insists on having 5 to dine with him at every meal & though he can not always get his full no. seldom has less than 2 or 3, sometimes 6." He described a prayer meeting he attended at Mr. Bell's

Postwar view of the Greenbrier County Courthouse, constructed in 1837. In the summer of 1861 the courthouse served as barracks for the "University Volunteers" from Charlottesville, Va. Some of those pictured are (left to right): #2. Charles Buster, Clerk of the County Court and a Confederate Veteran; 3. Lillian Beard; 5. Carrie B. Stratton; 6 Edward W. Sydenstricker; 8. Howard C. Skaggs, Clerk of the Circuit Court. *Courtesy Greenbrier County Historical Society*

house and went on to praise the local citizens: "The people seem so well behaved, so quiet, so generally intelligent & well educated and above all so pious. And I may add so intensely Presbyterian....And then the ladies are so pretty, so tasteful in their dress—and not a day passes but some _ dozen bouquets come into barracks with the compliments of Miss So & So, to Mr. So & So..."(25)

Several dozen hoppers used in the production of saltpeter still remain at Organ Cave. *Photo courtesy Marcia Wilson Cales*

Paddle used to scrape saltpeter off the rocks at Organ Cave during the Civil War. *Courtesy Organ Cave*

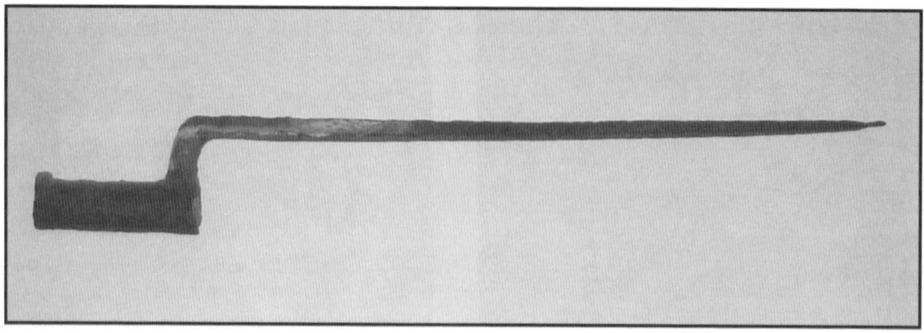

Bayonet found near Organ Cave. *Courtesy Jeff Holliday*

Above: Cannon ball found near Organ Cave several years ago.
Left: The entrance to Organ Cave in 1907.
Author's collection

Joel Morgan was a civilian worker at Organ Cave during the Civil War.
Courtesy Janie Morgan, Organ Cave, WV

Confederate monument at Lewisburg.

CHAPTER TWO
ADVANCE AND RETREAT: THE FIASCO OF WISE AND FLOYD

From April to July 1861, Southern efforts to establish a strong foothold in West Virginia were feeble at best. Early success recruiting men from areas south of the Kanawha Valley did not offset lackluster results in other areas of the state. Many of the residents of southern and central West Virginia were independent mountaineers who preferred to stay that way. Above the line of the Baltimore and Ohio Railroad which ran eastward from Parkersburg, Confederate enlistments fell far short of expectations. Further complicating matters was the area's rough topography and relative isolation, compared to the east. As a result, Southern armies in West Virginia were hampered by excessively long lines of supply and communication. Control of the B&O Railroad, the Kanawha Valley, and the region's four "turnpikes," was critical for both governments.

The Federal government was able to quickly rally men of Ohio and Pennsylvania, cross the Ohio River, and enter the "western frontier." The Union plan to "save" West Virginia was simple; advance eastward along the Parkersburg—Staunton Turnpike in the north, and the Kanawha Valley in the south. A Union victory at the "battle" of Philippi, Barbour County, on June 3, and subsequent victories in the Northwest set the stage for Federal forces to occupy the Kanawha Valley. On July 11, a Union invasion force commanded by Gen. Jacob D. Cox began making its way up the Kanawha Valley from Point Pleasant. A number of brief skirmishes developed along the way, culminating in a battle at Scary Creek, Putnam County, on July 17. Though Southern forces were victorious at Scary Creek, Gen. Wise knew he could not hold his position without reinforcements and supplies. With troops under Gen. Cox moving up the valley, and additional Union forces under orders to march from the upper Tygart Valley region, by way of Weston, Sutton, and Bulltown, to cut the Confederate lines at Gauley Bridge, Wise knew he would be caught between two jaws of a pincer movement. He sent a dispatch to Gen. Lee informing him of his situation, and on July 24, began his "retrograde movement," toward Greenbrier County.(1) That very day Gen. Lee wrote to Wise congratulating him for his victory at Scary Creek. Lee told him that with the twin defeats at Rich Mountain and Laurel Hill, Gen. George B. McClellan's forces may advance to Huntersville, Pocahontas County. If they did, Lee told Wise "...the road is open to him to Lewisburg, to turn upon you or to seize at Millborough the Virginia Central Railroad." Lee explained that a "concentration of forces" in that region would hopefully prevent an advance into Greenbrier County.(2)

Federal forces occupied Charleston just a few hours after the Wise Legion withdrew. Once there, Gen. Cox issued a statement to the citizens to ease concerns some had that his men would come as "robbers and murderers." The Confederate soldiers reached Gauley Bridge on July 26, exhausted and hungry. Many were without shoes and others were sick and broken down. Even before word of Wise's retreat reached Greenbrier County, W.H. Syme, Samuel Price, and Mason Mathews, three prominent citizens of Lewisburg, wrote to Jefferson Davis telling him that Greenbrier was open to invasion. Their concerns were exactly the same as those expressed by Gen. Lee in his letter of July 24. They said defeats in the Northwest opened the way for Federal forces to occupy Lewisburg, "with the view of arresting the supplies of men and munitions destined for Gen. Wise." Further, they stated that they were "very destitute of the means of defense...a large majority of our young men have volunteered and gone into the service....We ask, can nothing be done for our security and relief?...Our people are much excited, and whether we are in any real danger or not, our people lack a sense of security…"(3)

Their sense of security was further shaken when word reached Greenbrier that Gen. Wise's Legion was in full retreat. Furthermore, it was believed that the advancing Yankees were "murdering men, women and children," and were intent on camping at Meadow Bluff. Consequently, men and boys marched to Lewisburg from adjoining counties. An eye-witness at Blue Sulphur Springs described this rag-tag army: "they were armed with shotguns, rifles, pistols, Bowie knives made from files, and some carried pitchforks. It was a motley army indeed….It was a false rumor however and a couple days later they passed back in groups without the swagger which they had previous."(4)

The Wise Legion withdrew from Gauley Bridge on July 27, having set the covered bridge there on fire and watching it fall into the Gauley. Many of Wise's men were sick with measles and even typhoid. Insufficient means of transportation forced all but the very weakest to march as best they could and try to keep up with the column. Pvt. James Hamner, University Volunteers, was among the "marching sick," as he explained in his diary: "…they had no conveyance for the sick, so Hines and myself walked…I was very sick, I lost my knapsack & everything in it….The next day I rode in Mr. Harper's wagon." He said they spent the night—"a miserable night,"—at a church near Pigott's, which was then a mill located just east of present-day Ansted. "I had a high fever and cold chills all the time. The next morning, to the surprise of everyone, myself included, I broke out beautifully with measles….I had a companion, Burgess, who also broke out during the day with measles."(5)

Another soldier on the sick list described a ride he received as the Legion reached Sewell Mountain in eastern Fayette County. He said their regimental surgeon sent a man with a wagon to pick him up. The problem was that when the gentleman arrived he was drunk on "mountain dew." Nevertheless, the opportunity to ride to the hospital at Lewisburg, some 25 miles distant, was very appealing: "This jehu full of corn whiskey regarded not mountain gorge nor aches of man, but frequently at half speed would go down the mountain where the road was a shelf midway between the sky and the depths, the hack touching ground in high places...The man was driving his own team and drinking his own whiskey, and proposed to regulate time and speed to suit himself. But events proved he was not destined to be our destroyer, and in due course some time that night we were landed in front of the measles hospital in Lewisburg."

This "hospital" had been established in an old carpenter shop, "where lay crowded on the work bench, saw horses and floor the most filthy and poorly attended lot of men one could conceive of." Adding insult to injury was the fact that every inch of available space in the hospital was already taken: "Gaskins and I leaned against the wall picking out the cleanest looking man to lie on. It was evident we would have to lie on some of them. When it occurred to me we might find lodgings with Mr. Wetzel whose acquaintance I had made when we passed through Lewisburg on the way to Gauley....before daylight we were comfortably lodged there. There we remained until we were sent on to the White Sulphur Springs and quartered in the ten-pin alley which had been converted into a hospital."(6)

The retreat continued and the Wise Legion reached Bungers Mill, a few miles west of Lewisburg, on July 31. Here, Wise thought it best to refit and reorganize his troops. He also considered a junction between his force and that of Gen. John B. Floyd, then operating in southwest Virginia to protect the line of the Virginia and Tennessee Railroad. General William Wing Loring was commanding the Rebel army of northwest Virginia and Wise also considered a junction with him. While at Bungers Mill, the measles problem reached epidemic proportions, further demoralizing the troops. (7)

Wise sent a letter to General Lee giving his reasons for leaving the valley and offering his suggestions as to the best course of action. He told Gen. Lee that the Kanawha Valley was "disaffected and traitorous." He declared that it was "gone from Charleston to Point Pleasant before I got there." He claimed Boone and Cabell County were nearly as bad, and "the state of things in Braxton, Nicholas, and part of Greenbrier is awful."

Wise observed, quite accurately, that the militia was of no real value, adding tersely that "they are worthless who are true, and there is no telling who is true." He said the people of western Virginia were convinced that the area was lost to the Confederacy. "And let me here say," he wrote, "we have worked and scouted far and wide and fought well, and marched all the clothes and shoes off our bodies, and find our old arms do not stand service...."(8)

The Union army under Gen. Cox reached Gauley Bridge on July 29, just two days after the Rebels withdrew. The Yankees found there 1,500 smoothbore muskets, large quantities of ammunition, powder kegs broken open and their contents poured into the river, piles of bacon beside the road and every conceivable item of military equipage. All of these items were abandoned by the retreating Confederates due to a lack of transportation and to speed their flight. It was a serious loss of material for an army already chronically short of supplies.

Gen. Cox fully understood that Gauley Bridge was the gate through which all important movements from eastern into southwestern Virginia must necessarily come, and that it formed an important link in any chain of posts designed to cover the Ohio Valley from invasion. It was also the most advanced single post which could protect the Kanawha Valley and it was but two or three day's march from Lewisburg and points south. Outposts were established in the vicinity of Gauley Bridge and preparations were made for its defense. Scouting parties were sent out as far east as the western foot of Big Sewell Mountain. These scouts determined the approximate location of enemy forces from information supplied by the local inhabitants. With the Confederates no closer than Greenbrier County, Gen. Cox was free to supply and organize his command. Steamboats laden with supplies were sent to Cox from Gallipolis, Ohio. These boats were able to come within three miles of Gauley Bridge. This fact gave the United States forces a very significant advantage over their Southern adversaries, who were forced to haul supplies by wagonload over the mountains.

Following the Federal defeat at the Battle of Manassas on July 21, Gen. McClellan was ordered to Washington and Gen.

William S. Rosecrans assumed command of the Department of the Ohio, encompassing West Virginia. Gen. Rosecrans, then at Clarksburg, busied himself in developing a new plan of advance and on August 3, he ordered Gen. Cox to construct "small field works" in the vicinity of Gauley Bridge. He also ordered Col. Erastus B. Tyler to occupy Summersville, Nicholas County, with his 7th Regiment Ohio Volunteer Infantry. With Col. Tyler at Summersville, a line of direct communication was opened from the Kanawha Valley to Rosecrans' headquarters at Clarksburg. Col. Tyler could also advance toward Greenbrier County, which is exactly what his commander had in mind. Gen. Rosecrans told Tyler that within 10 days his forces should be ready to advance on Greenbrier County. Once there, he hoped to "seize Lewisburg, which is but five days' march from head of steamboat navigation on the Kanawha," and establish there "a provision depot of ample size, properly fortified."(9)

In notifying the Federal authorities at Washington of his desire to occupy Lewisburg, Rosecrans explained that once there he would prepare a "movement on Wytheville and East Tennessee." Further, he said he wanted to "seize that place, and take possession of the railroad as far down as Abingdon; break the railroad bridges down east of Wytheville, so as to prevent the enemy from coming in that direction." He said he would convert Lewisburg into a "fortified depot" for the United States Army, and would then endeavor to repair the turnpike between that point and Gauley Bridge.(10)

On August 3, Robert E. Lee wrote to Gen. Wise from his camp near Huntersville, Pocahontas County. Lee told him that if the enemy could be kept from reaching Lewisburg, they would not be able to attack the railroads further south. He asked if there were any strong positions west of Lewisburg that Wise and Gen. Floyd might be able to occupy to prevent an enemy advance.(11) Lee then wrote to Gen. Floyd at Sweet Springs, Monroe County. He told him that the enemy might advance on Lewisburg in two columns and that he wanted him to unite his forces with the Wise Legion at White Sulphur Springs and reoccupy Lewisburg.(12) Gen. Floyd had earlier written to Lee harshly criticizing Wise for his retreat from the valley. He also wrote a very acidic letter to the Confederate President, Jefferson Davis, stating that Wise's retreat was in fact a "flight from the face of the enemy." He claimed that as a result, "People from Kanawha to Wytheville are filled with alarm," and that "some people are quitting Lewisburg for safety." He said that Gen. Wise's failures had given Unionists of East Tennessee and Kentucky reason for hope and they were "becoming much excited as the war progresses."(13)

Gen. Wise received Lee's dispatch at White Sulphur Springs, to which place he had taken his command after remaining briefly at Bungers Mill. He replied that he had left behind 500 men who would be assisted by the militia of Monroe and Greenbrier counties in guarding the passes from Fayetteville, Gauley, and Summersville. He said his axmen had blocked the roads on Big and Little Sewell Mountains and in the vicinity of Bungers Mill. Wise claimed his men could defeat 5,000 Yankees even without support from Gen. Floyd. After offering his opinion as to the best course of action, he told Gen. Lee he would need "a week or ten days to organize, to refit, and refresh my very worn men, and to procure for them blankets, shoes, tents, and clothing, and to get arms fit for service." He also complained that desertions were an increasing problem and said "the people" did not want the Yankees fired upon, "lest it exasperate them." He said, "Such is one of a thousand specimens of the disloyalty in which I have been operating."(14)

Men of the Wise Legion were indeed "very worn," as their commander said. Various ailments kept dozens and eventually hundreds of men from active service in the Legion and in the brigade commanded by Gen. Floyd. When the Wise Legion moved from Bungers Mill to White Sulphur Springs, it lost more manpower to the hospitals at Lewisburg. There were so many sick soldiers there that citizens of neighboring Monroe County formed a "committee of five" to solicit "contributions for the sick."(15) By this time the town's churches, livery stables, carpenter shop, courthouse, private dwellings and the Old Lewisburg Academy, were in use as military hospital and barracks. The

Lewisburg Academy was situated near the Old Stone Church and was founded in 1810 by Rev. John McElhenney. Trustees of the academy included many prominent men of Greenbrier, Bath, Cabell, Giles, and Monroe counties. The academy was a two-story brick building and is said to have been the first brick building erected in Lewisburg. Many of the area's young men received their early education there and some, including Alex Reynolds, Samuel Reynolds, and William Procter Smith, became Confederate officers during the Civil War.

Addison B. Roler, another member of the University Volunteers, described the Wise Legion's arrival at White Sulphur Springs on August 5: "We arrived at this place early yesterday evening...the roads were dustier than any we have traveled....I have been all over the spring grounds looking for the commissary department, have not found it yet....This is a beautiful place, the waters are fine and the grounds are tastefully and delightfully laid out....our camp is on the hill back of the sulphur springs and offering a right fine view of the sulphur grounds."(16)

Not all of the soldiers slept in tents, some were allowed to occupy the hotel and cottages. William Clark Reynolds, of the 22nd Virginia Infantry, said that some of his group "quartered in the Carolina Row," and "bathed in Howard's Creek." He described the hotel as being 400 feet long, with a ballroom "50 ft. long by 90 ft. wide." And a dining room "300 ft. by 60 and parlor 50 by 90 ft."(17) Another soldier wrote simply that he "put up at the White & took room 662."(18)

On August 6, Gen. Wise and Gen. Floyd met at White Sulphur Springs. Gen. Wise, known for his long "windbag" speeches, stood up and spoke for two hours. He reviewed the history of the United States from its discovery, the Revolutionary War, the Mexican War, the causes which led to the current troubles, the fight at Scary Creek, and his retreat to the White Sulphur. Gen. Floyd, holding superior rank, received his subordinate's remarks with a patronizing air. He told Wise very firmly that he intended to reoccupy the Kanawha Valley as quickly as possible. Of course he knew any rapid movement back into the valley would give the appearance that abandoning it was unnecessary in the first place. Equally firm in his rebuke of the plan, Gen. Wise stated that he was against the move. He said it would take at least two weeks to refit his command and obtain the wagons needed for an advance. Their meeting adjourned without Gen. Floyd giving any specific orders to advance but remaining adamant that an advance would be made. This had been the two ex-governor's first "war-conference" and it was becoming increasingly obvious there would be no cooperation between them.(19)

Realizing he had been unable to dissuade Gen. Floyd from his plans and being unwilling to surrender the issue without a fight, Wise wrote to Lee early the next morning complaining of Floyd's perceived obstinate attitude. Wise took the opportunity to repeat his previous appeal that his command be separated from that of Gen. Floyd's. "Please assign to each one respective fields of operation," Wise asked. He also offered the opinion that Floyd's Brigade should guard the Fayetteville and Beckley roads, while his Legion guarded the turnpike into Lewisburg. Gen. Lee replied that it would be "contrary to the purpose of the President…and destroy the prospect of success," if their forces were divided.(20)

After their conference, Gen. Floyd returned to his brigade at Camp Arbuckle, four miles west of Lewisburg. Two days later he wrote to Wise, stating again his desire to occupy the valley and asking Wise for a list of the forces he had available for duty. This note sent the old governor's temper flying. He sent a very petulant reply, stating that at no time had his men been supplied with sufficient clothing, camp equipage, arms, shoes, and other necessities. Wise added that he was greatly in need of wagons and that 300 of his men were in the hospitals. Everything Wise wrote was true and in fact the Floyd Brigade was in similar straits, half the men being sick with measles. Gen. Floyd of course knew these facts, but did not share his reasoning with Wise, considering it his subordinate's duty to follow and not question orders. He did share his thoughts with President Davis, telling him that by combining their available forces with the militia, he could "move against the enemy." Floyd added that when they did move it would "require great circumspection, attention, and tact to mollify the temper and feelings of the people west of here, if half be true of what has reached my ears relative to their present exasperated and excited state of feeling." On that same date, Floyd admitted in a letter to L.P. Walker, Secretary of War, that he knew the Wise Legion was in no condition to render much assistance. Further, he admitted that his own cavalry was useless because most of them were unarmed, and that his brigade was decimated with measles. Seeing another opportunity to criticize Wise, he said the people of the area were greatly dispirited, and the enemy elated, by the "retrograde movement of General Wise."(21) Floyd's plan to combine his forces with the militia was not realistic at that time. The militia had already been allowed to return home and harvest their crops. When the militia was active earlier that summer, they were not issued weapons or necessary supplies because none were available and that situation had not improved. Desertion was another problem because many of these men enlisted to protect their own homes and communities. When the tide of war took them beyond their own county, many of them did not feel obligated to serve and simply went home. One of the militia brigades that Gen. Floyd expected to rely upon was the Nineteenth, commanded by Gen. A.A. Chapman. Their commander admitted in a report to Gen. Lee that of his six companies, a "strong spirit of insubordination" prevailed in three. He also stated that he did not believe he could muster enough men to meet the necessities of war unless they resorted to a draft, and he expressed his desire that a draft order may be issued at a "very early date." It was not that these men were for or against either government, instead they were independent farmers who failed to see how the war directly affected their own destiny except in the protection of their own homes. A Union army officer who had just recently arrived in the area gave his impression of the mountaineers he had encountered: "although the inhabitants were not ready to do much for the rebel cause, they would do less for ours."(22)

Gen. Floyd received a second note from the Wise Legion on August 8, this one from Wise's cavalry commander, Col. James Lucius Davis, then at Meadow Bluff. The colonel reported enemy scouts 23 miles west of his camp. He said they could ad-

Col. James L. Davis. Commander of the 10th Va Cavalry at Meadow Bluff in 1861. *Courtesy USAMHI*

vance on him by taking the Wilderness Road, a little-used side road that led to Summersville. Col. Davis' little command was part of the 500-man force Wise left behind to scout the enemy and guard the roads into Greenbrier County. The sorry condition of his command was a microcosm of the larger problem: "I have here besides guards, scouts & etc., about 100 cavalry, not well armed or equipped. Our horses are generally badly off for shoes, and the shoeing is proceeding slowly, for want of smiths and forges. About 150 militia, 50 armed and poorly equipped, are in bivouac near me; say 100 unarmed as yet. General Wise, as you are aware, is two days' march east of me." Col. Davis's information concerning enemy scouts came from Lt. Col. St. George Croghan, also of the Wise Legion, who was then scouting near Summersville. Croghan reported a rumor he heard that "General Tyler," actually Col. Tyler, "says he will go to Lewisburg, if he wades there in blood."(23)

On August 9, Gen. Floyd informed Robert E. Lee that he had gone personally as far west as Meadow Bluff, where he met with a large number of the local inhabitants. He said the citizens were "in a panic" after Wise's retreat, but his brigade's presence in the area had given them some sense of security. He said Gen. Cox had won friends among the citizens in the valley by furnishing them bacon, flour, coffee, and sugar at very low prices.

He said Cox had opened trade via the Kanawha River to Cincinnati, and that he would advance as soon as possible to prevent a union between the forces of Gen. Cox and Col. Tyler. Floyd then wrote an order to Wise telling him to bring all of his available force to Camp Arbuckle early the next morning. He said information coming in from scouts indicated that Col. Tyler was advancing from Summersville, and "these people must be met."(24)

In response to his orders, Gen. Wise sent Floyd two cannons and some additional cavalry. Wise echoed his commander's sentiments in suggesting that the militia of Gen. Beckley and Chapman be recalled from their homes. He believed they should be supplied with picks, axes, shovels and spades, to obstruct the roads, saying that Colonel McPherson, of Lewisburg, "might readily select a corps of that description to operate on the road..." Obviously, Gen. Wise understood that the militia were yet woefully armed and equipped but if they could be provided the proper tools, their work on the roads would facilitate the movement of the regular Confederate forces.

Wise then wrote to Gen. Lee asking for weapons and saying that some of their deserters were coming back in. He said they were in very desperate need of portable forges because "blacksmiths cannot be got here, nor shoes, nor iron to make them." The next day Gen. Floyd took the bold and necessary step of officially assuming command of all Confederate forces intended to operate against the Yankees in the Kanawha Valley and adjacent country. Of course this order angered Gen. Wise and he wrote again to Lee asking that their commands be separated. Wise also argued that Floyd's plan to occupy the valley was doomed to failure. He said advancing that far would force their army to haul supplies an additional 40 miles over some of the worst roads in western Virginia. Gen. Wise preferred to draw the enemy to the eastern edge of Fayette County, thereby lengthening the Yankees supply line, but not adding any burdens to their own. Lee replied to Wise on August 12, saying that he had no weapons to send other than flint-lock muskets. After reviewing the activities of the Union army in West Virginia, Lee said he thought their goal was to influence elections in favor of the "Pierpoint dynasty."(25-26)

On August 14, after growing impatient with the delaying tactics of Wise, Gen. Floyd peremptorily ordered Wise to march with all the forces under his command to join him at Meadow Bluff. Wise complied with this order the next day, after writing a letter of complaint to Gen. Lee. With reinforcements on the way, Gen. Floyd sent a scouting party westward to Big Sewell Mountain, and began moving his entire command to that point. The scouts, under Col. J.L. Davis and Col. Henry Heth, advanced 17 miles. At the western base of Big Sewell the intrepid scouts rode directly into an ambush.(27)

Earlier that day a 120-man scouting party from the 11th Ohio Infantry, commanded by Col. Joseph Frizell, rode forward from Gauley Bridge with the stated purpose of finding the enemy. These men had the distinction of being the first Federal troops to advance that far into southwest Virginia. As the Yankees rode along the winding turnpike approaching the base of Big Sewell, a lieutenant of the 11th Ohio observed Floyd's cavalry a short distance ahead. Using hand signals so as not to give their position away, the Yankees quickly dismounted and took cover in the thickets along the road. As the Rebels came near, one of them suddenly caught site of a Yankee and opened fire. Soon the entire scene was filled with smoke and the sound of gunfire. Two men of the 11th Ohio were wounded in the first volley, one in the right hand, the other his left hand. These men were just the advance of Col. Frizell's party and when the others heard the firing they came on in a rush, as one witness described: "Hearing the firing, the colonel gave the order to double-quick, and upon turning a bend in the road a squad of Rebel cavalrymen were encountered, who gave and returned a volley and then retreated. The colonel formed an ambush and sent out scouts from Company H, under Lieutenant Weller, who also encountered Rebels and received and returned a fire. After waiting for some time and no enemy appearing in the road, it was thought best to fall back..." (28)

Having withdrawn a short distance along the turnpike, Col. Heth told his men to regroup and see if the enemy came on. Their brief but exciting skirmish cost the Confederates two men killed and three wounded. Col. Frizell told his men that he would like very much to capture some Rebels. He planned to wait until later that evening and then quickly advance to surprise the enemy. After discussing the merits of the proposal with some of his officers, it was decided that their best course of action was an immediate retreat. As the Federal forces fell back to the vicinity of Gauley Bridge, Heth's men withdrew two miles to the top of the mountain. Although this skirmish was a minor affair, it was the baptism of fire for all involved. It would prove to be just the first in a series of bloody clashes to come.

When the Yankees returned to Gauley Bridge and reported their skirmish, Gen. Cox knew that the time was near at hand when his forces and Floyd's would clash in more than a brief contest. Cox wasted no time informing Gen. Rosecrans of developments and requesting additional ammunition. He said they had on hand about 45 rounds per man of musket and rifle cartridges, and five cannons with about 140 rounds per gun. He went on to ask for "at least 200,000 musket cartridges; caliber .69; 20,000 enfield cartridges, caliber .57; 10,000 ditto caliber .58; 50,000 cartridges for the Greenwood altered rifle, bright barrels; 200 rounds each James solid shot and James shells, and 300 each of grape and canister for smoothbore, with 150 solid shot, all for six pounders. Extra caps for muskets, 30,000; also 1,000 friction primers for cannon. If a persistent defense is to be made here we should want much more than above, and it should be where we could easily get it."(29)

On the day after the skirmish, the combined commands of Floyd and Wise arrived in the vicinity of Big Sewell Mountain. The Wise Legion camped in an oat field near the mountain's eastern base (present-day Rainelle golf course). From Sewell Mountain, Floyd wrote to Jefferson Davis on August 16, telling the president that the people were much dispirited after Wise abandoned the valley. Noting that Gen. Cox was busy "conciliating" the "whole population" he said the retreat was being used by Cox to the "greatest advantage." He also told Davis that Wise would "scarcely agree at all to any action," and that entering the valley without a fight would be the strongest possible condemnation of the retreat. “But,” Floyd wrote, “to remain in quarters at White Sulphur, with the whole northwestern portion of the State blazing with Civil War, is what is not long to be endured.”(30) The next day, August 17, Gen. Floyd and part of his brigade climbed up and over Big Sewell, encamping at its western base. Floyd established his headquarters at the home of Frank and Margaret Tyree. This house still stands and is known as the Old Stone House or Tyree Tavern. The Tyree's had two sons in Confederate service and Mr. Tyree occasionally volunteered as a scout for the Rebels. It was rumored that Mrs. Tyree was a Confederate spy. A Southern soldier with the 22nd Virginia Infantry recorded his impression of the Tyree family: “At the foot of [Big] Sewell on the west, pioneer Frank Tyree and his wife and children lived, influential Presbyterians, and were noted among the mountain dwellers. Mrs. Tyree was a remarkable woman—fearless as any stalwart of either company and decidedly defiant. It was said that she stood in her chicken house with an axe in her hand and defended it from marauding Federal soldiers. It was commonly known among the Dixie Boys that in the darkness of night she managed to reach Gen. Lee, riding miles alone through the mountains, and had given Lee valuable information.”(31)

After remaining at Tyree's one day, Gen. Floyd moved his headquarters back to the western top of Big Sewell. Gen. Wise was then camped on the eastern top of the same mountain, about one mile distant, and within sight of, Floyd's camp. Their combined forces were much reduced by disease and lack of supplies. Another of Floyd's cavalry commanders, Col. Albert G. Jenkins, wrote to Gov. Letcher on August 18, asking his help obtaining reinforcements and supplies. In an earlier face-to-face meeting with the governor, Col. Jenkins promised to send him a report from western Virginia. Jenkins was able to report some progress, but also cautioned the governor that letting West Virginia fall into the hands of the enemy would be “disastrous to our cause.”(32)

The animosity between Wise and Floyd also affected the opinion of men in the ranks. This caused considerable difficulty when even the simplest needs of cooperation were met with re-

Gen. Albert Gallatin Jenkins CSA. He served extensively in Greenbrier County and died in 1864 of wounds received in the Battle of Cloyd's Mountain. *Courtesy National Archives*

sistance from officers and men alike. Writing home from his camp on Big Sewell, a member of Floyd's body guard told his family that Wise and Floyd were as much opposed to each other as "fire and water." He said Wise "stoops from the dignity of a commander to discuss with his men the propriety of every petty command. Surely such a man is not fit for the post he occupies." This particular body guard was rather enamored with Floyd and considered him "something of a Napolean." He said Floyd swore he would never retreat and would fight the enemy at all odds. Further, he wrote that two days previous he heard Floyd boast that "if you ever see this force in full retreat on this road I swear my carcass will not be in it." This was rather reminiscent of an earlier pledge made by Gen. Wise when he was advancing into the Kanawha Valley. He told a young lady at whose table he had just enjoyed dinner, that he was not stopping his advance until he got to the Ohio River and "put his foot in it." When, some six weeks later, she saw him in hasty retreat she said, "well, I reckon he put his foot in it."(33)

Others were homesick and less concerned with personal politics. Capt. J.P. Sheffey told his girlfriend that they were now camped on Sewell Mountain and "we have been sleeping with our horses out in the fields and wildwoods with only the heavens or perchance the leaves of some friendly tree above us." He told her about the weather and about going on scout one night when he met "with some little fun and frolic." Turning to affairs of the heart he said, "when all other enjoyments save that of thinking and dreaming constantly of the dear ones I have left behind me are taken away from me by the wild excitement of this kind of life, I can still steal away occasionally and write to you, the dearest of them all....Do not think that I ever forget you. Morning, noon & night, always and everywhere, I think and dream of you, and the happiness that awaits me when these troubles are over."(34)

Also dreaming of home was Andrew Cook, one of the first men of Greenbrier sent east during the war. He wrote home on August 19, from Camp Harmon, near Winchester, Va.: "I have had a severe attack of remittent fever...I tried my souls best to get a furlough to come home till I would get well but all in vain. I have lain and studied, and dreamed about drinking out of some of the cold pure springs of old Greenbrier. But alas, when I awoke I found myself in this miserable low swampy badly watered badly timbered and badly peopled country. I say badly peopled because the people are so mean....But I do think hard that we must be dragged away from our own homes when so much exposed to come to this filthy unhealthy county..."(35)

Another Southern soldier, this one a patient at the measles hospital in Lewisburg, wrote to his brother: "We are among the kindest people here you ever saw for strangers. Some ladies visited our hospital a little while ago, and brought us chicken soup rice, butter & etc. and told us we should have anything we wanted if we would only make it known. One of the ladies is mistress of one of the finest hotels in Lewisburg; she said with tears in her eyes that her husband was a soldier in Gen. Lee's army and that she knew how to sympathize with the poor soldiers. God bless the ladies of Lewisburg, they seem like the people of Pine Creek."(36)

Chapter Three
This Unnatural War

The Division of a State is dreaded as a precedent. But a measure made expedient by a war, is no precedent for times of peace. It is said the admission of West Virginia is secession, and tolerated only because it is our secession. Well, if we can call it by that name, there is still difference enough between secession against the Constitution, and secession in favor of the the Constitution.

Abraham Lincoln

On August 19, Gen. Floyd notified Gen. Wise to be prepared to march toward the Kanawha Valley early the next morning. Floyd chafed for action and with his long delayed plan of advance finally reaching fruition, he was anxious for the hunt. Although Gen. Floyd lacked experience, he was never lacking in confidence, almost to the point of recklessness. The same could be said for old Governor Wise, a man who "knew little of subordination but was as stalwart as any many in the field." Gen. Wise was delayed getting under way on the 20th, due to an ammunition wagon breaking down. He notified Floyd of the delay and asked for the loan of some wagons to assist his movement. As usual there were no extra wagons available, so the Wise Legion rolled along behind the Floyd Brigade as best they could. Evening coming on, the combined forces stopped and selected campgrounds adjacent to the road. The infantry had managed to advance just nine miles after an all-day march. They were now at Locust Lane, about 20 miles from the valley. The cavalry, however, had gone 26 miles and skirmished twice with the enemy before dark. In the first fight, Floyd's cavalry attacked and quickly dispersed a small band of Federal cavalry along Sunday Road. This route branched off the turnpike in a northeastward direction toward Carnifex Ferry and Summersville and was patrolled frequently by United States Cavalry. The day's second skirmish was yet another ambush courtesy of the 11th Ohio Infantry. This one occurred along the road a few miles east of Gauley Bridge. Col. Frizell's men outnumbered the surprised Confederates five to one and when the melee was over four Confederates were emptied from their saddles. Nightfall found the Confederate forces divided, with Floyd camping along Sunday Road and Wise about two miles west of him near present-day Hawks Nest State Park.(1)(2)

The fighting of August 20 would prove to be a harbinger of events to come. On that same day, Gen. Rosecrans, still at Clarksburg, issued a proclamation to the "Loyal Citizens of West Virginia." This proclamation was an attempt by the U.S. military to pacify politicians of Virginia's "restored government," who wanted public opinion placed on an equal footing with military affairs. Rosecrans told the mountaineers that they had "a right to stand in the position you have assumed, faithful to the constitution and laws of Virginia as they were before the ordinance of secession. The Confederates…have brought war on your soil. Their tools and dupes told you you must vote for secession…that unless you did so…abolitionists would overrun you, plunder your property, steal your slaves, abuse your wives and daughters, seize upon your lands…Eastern Virginians who have been accustomed to rule you…have conspired to tie you to the desperate fortunes of the Confederacy..." Complaining about the frequent attacks by bushwhackers on messengers and sentries, Gen. Rosecrans said he was going to hold the neighborhoods where these acts occurred responsible. "Citizens of Western Virginia," he wrote, "your fate is mainly in your own hands…If you stand firm for law and order…you may dwell together peacefully and happily as in former days."(3)

On the same date that Rosecrans issued his proclamation, the Second Wheeling Convention for the Restored Government of Virginia was coming to a close. After weeks of rancorous debate, the convention agreed upon the formation of a new state with 39 counties, all west of the Allegheny Mountains. This was originally to be called the State of Kanawha.

When Gen. Floyd advanced from Sewell Mountain, he allowed

detachments from the 45th and 50th Virginia Infantry regiments to remain in Greenbrier County, at the eastern base of Big Sewell. Subsequent to the skirmishes he sent word for them to advance at 4 a.m. the next morning "in the direction of Gauley Bridge."(4) During the evening hours of August 21, Floyd's men advanced down Sunday Road, past the scene of their little fight, and crossed the Gauley River at Carnifex Ferry. Gen. Wise encamped at the junction of Sunday Road and the turnpike, present-day Hico, east of Ansted. That evening Floyd sent a courier to Meadow Bluff and Lewisburg to inform the small forces remaining there of developments and to make sure the commissary at Lewisburg remained active forwarding supplies.

With Greenbrier County nearly emptied of Confederate forces another prominent citizen of Lewisburg took pen in hand to contact the Confederate government. This time the writer was Mr. Thomas Mathews, the 56-year-old cashier at the Bank of Lewisburg. He wrote to the Confederate president on August 22, telling him that Floyd and Wise had advanced "some forty or fifty miles" toward the enemy. He noted that their forces were diminished by disease and exhaustion and that the enemy had the advantage of using the river for their supply line. He wrote that occasionally information about what the Yankees were up to reached Lewisburg "...from their rear by some one leaving the Kanawha Valley, crossing out by Coal [River] through Fayette and Raleigh, and bringing information to this place." Apparently, Mr. Mathews' information was quite accurate and current. He told President Davis that the enemy force "is larger than ours; that they have steam-boats above Charleston and over 200 wagons and teams." Mathews asked for reinforcements, reminding the president that if the enemy advanced beyond Greenbrier County they could attack the railroad. "The whole country from the Virginia and Tennessee Railroad to the Kanawha Valley is sound and loyal," he declared. In closing, Mathews offered the names of several other prominent citizens, whom he said could verify his "sincerity of purpose and conviction of judgment." Among those listed was Mr. Jeremiah Morton, president of the White Sulphur Springs Company.(5)

Civilians North and South, prominent and otherwise, involved themselves in the war effort, especially during the first months of the conflict. Some were talented "letter writers," others carried messages or organized "aid societies" for soldiers and their families. Other volunteers included nurses, clergymen, blacksmiths, wheelwrights, farmers and gunsmiths. In West Virginia, a region truly on the border of North and South, some families, churches, and entire communities were divided in their loyalties. This division of sentiment prevailed throughout the conflict and endured well beyond the war years. As a predominately Confederate leaning county, Greenbrier's few Union citizens kept to themselves until after the war. Whatever aid or information they were able to offer the Federal troops was usually kept confidential. One Greenbrier Unionists, who was outspoken against the Confederacy was Dr. John F. Caldwell. Born in Frederick County, Virginia, in 1796, Dr. Caldwell moved to Lewisburg in 1824. When the war began he was practicing dentistry at Charleston, Kanawha County. In 1860 and 1861 pro-Union articles written by Caldwell were published in several newspapers. When he sent copies to Lewisburg for distribution to the citizens, "the Rebels took them by mob force and burnt them in the streets." Dr. Caldwell described the majority sentiment at Lewisburg in the spring of 1861: "There were here at Lewisburg none that I could call Unionists certainly. I was myself a refugee from my home or rather kept away from my home on account of my adherence to the cause of the Union." Dr. Caldwell's 400-acre farm was situated on the Greenbrier River, three and one-half miles east of Lewisburg. Oddly enough, he said he was not seriously disturbed by Confederate forces during the war, but was arrested by a "Federal captain" in 1863 "for attempting to arrest my colored servant who was trying to escape."(6)

On Sunday morning, August 25, a 175-man detachment of Gen. Floyd's cavalry, commanded by Col. Albert Gallatin Jenkins rode into yet another ambush by the 11th Ohio Infantry. Leaving Carnifex Ferry and riding out close to Hawks Nest, Col. Jenkins' men ignored the advice of men from the Wise Legion who told them to go no further. They rode into their worst ambush yet, costing them 16 men wounded, one killed and two captured. Early the next morning, Gen. Floyd's forces were able to recover some of their dignity when they surprised and soundly defeated Col. Erastus B. Tyler's 7th Ohio Infantry at Cross Lanes, just beyond Carnifex Ferry. Tyler failed to post sufficient pickets and his men were attacked while eating breakfast and totally routed. His defeat cost the 7th Ohio at least two men killed, 29 wounded, and 110 captured. The Confederates lost one regimental flag and several men killed and wounded. Gen. Floyd hailed this as a great victory and no doubt looked forward to the glowing reports he knew Southern newspapers would carry, especially considering the fact that he had the editor of the *Lynchburg Republican* on his staff.

Members of the Wise Legion were less fortunate with the media and had received more than their share of negative publicity. An officer of the Legion wrote to the Richmond newspapers from Lewisburg in an attempt to answer their critics: "I find that so many improper reports are…calculated to lead the public mind astray, as to the efficiency of the Wise Legion." The writer went on to describe their march into and out of the Kanawha Valley, their enemy contacts in Greenbrier and Fayette counties, and their lack of efficient weapons. "Let the Wise Legion have its just deserts and escape calumny for a while," he wrote, "and it will silence lying and slandering.…In other places soldiers are safe unless engaged with the enemy in battle, but here almost every bush conceals a Union man with his rifle. Pickets are shot within thirty feet, and the murderer cannot be caught. Depend upon it, the Wise Legion has no easy time; nor is it inactive or useless."(7)

On August 26, Pvt. Andrew Cook wrote to his family near present-day Rupert, from his camp in Fairfax County, Virginia. Several hundred Greenbrier men were serving in the east and they grew concerned upon hearing how close the enemy came to invading Greenbrier County. Pvt. Cook said it gave him "great satisfaction to learn that you and the children were well and still out of the hands of the Yankees. You have no idea of the uneasiness it produces here to hear of the Yankees getting near Greenbrier."(8)

On August 31, 80 members of the 7th Ohio Infantry captured at Cross Lanes arrived in Lewisburg on their way to prison at Richmond. Having heard numerous rumors about Yankees, even that some had "devilish horns," many of the town's citizens came out

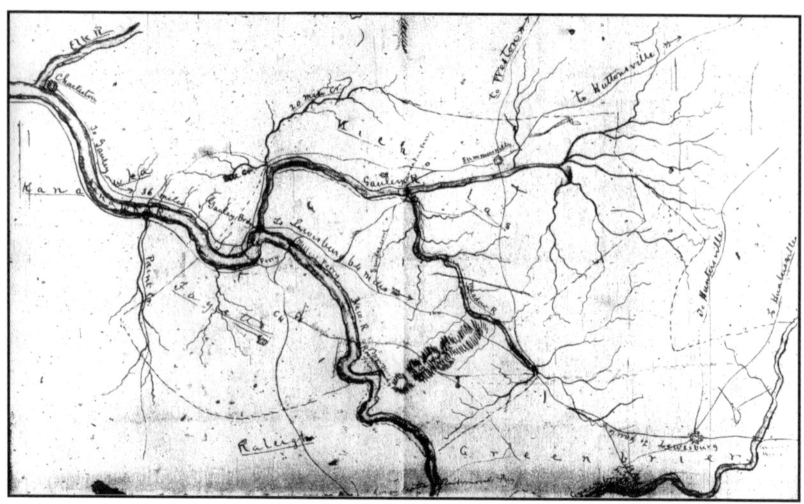

Map drawn by Confederate forces in 1861 showing area from Lewisburg to Summersville and Charleston. *Courtesy State of West Virginia*

to have a good look. Pvt. William Jeffrey, one of the prisoners, described the event: "We passed through Lewisburg—the finest place we had seen since coming to western Virginia. Here, as at other places, the people flocked out to see us. A 'Yankee' seemed to be as much of an object of curiosity to them as a live hippopotamus would have been. They stared at us civilly for the most part, only the small boys shouted 'Yankee' and 'Yankee Doodle.' A large company followed us out of town as far as the first mile. The Virginians commonly called us 'Yanks' usually with 'damned' prefixed." Early the next morning, the "Ohio Pets" reached White Sulphur Springs: "A Georgia regiment was stationed here and the soldiers followed us from the time we entered the grounds till we got out of town, hallooing and shouting, and offering various prices for a Yankee scalp....The place seemed nearly deserted of all inhabitants except soldiers."(9)

One of the Georgia soldiers at White Sulphur Springs was Pvt. W.R. Redding of the 13th Georgia Infantry, just arrived. In a letter home, Redding said the prisoners included five Union men, apparently civilians from the Kanawha Valley, who had "pointed out the secessionist in their county to the Yankees, and then would go with them and take their property. They took all the meat and flour one poor old widow had...they take everything." Pvt. Redding also said that nearly 300 men of his regiment were sick with measles, mumps and typhoid fever. He was also ill, suffering from a cold complicated by "bowell disease." In his weakened condition his hand writing was very poor. He apologized for it by saying "you must forgive me for I am very nervous this morning, and this pen is just as mean as I am nervous." Understandably homesick, he closed by asking his wife, "Lizzie," to "kiss the sweet little boys for me and write immediately and address me at Louisburg, Va."(10)

White Sulphur Springs, Lewisburg, Meadow Bluff, and Blue Sulphur Springs, became home to hundreds of sick soldiers in 1861. Lacking a sufficient number of physicians to care for them all, some soldiers were assigned as orderlies, doctor assistants, or nurses. Lt. William Smith, a 26-year-old prewar school teacher from Carroll County, Virginia, was a nurse at the Lewisburg Hotel, operated by Daniel Stalnaker. The hotel was home to 13 Southern soldiers suffering from various maladies in early September 1861. Smith worked as a nurse for Doctor D.C.B. Caldwell, a 35-year-old Greenbrier County physician, whom Smith described as an "excellent physician." Smith was also impressed with the ladies of Lewisburg, saying that they were "ever attentive to our sick boys. They prepare mouth watering soup and everything necessary for them to have, and take great pains to make them comfortable...I don't think there is another such town in the State." Lt. Smith worked as a nurse in Lewisburg from August through October, 1861. He told his family to address all mail to him in care of his good friend, Mr. Charles A. Stuart, the 26-year-old clerk of the circuit court.(11)

A member of Gen. Floyd's staff who was ordered to carry dispatches to Lewisburg wrote to his family from that town on Monday, the second of September: "I arrived here on Saturday after a long and tiresome ride of 62 miles...there is a great deal of talk about our recent engagement...our prisoners passed through this place on Saturday....My action in the engagement has been greatly complimented...Gen. Davis [A.W.G. Davis] of this county, told me that he noticed me particularly & was much pleased with my conduct while under fire....Saturday night I staid at Mr. [Samuel] Prices, took dinner at Uncle Tom's [Thomas Creigh] on Sunday & spent last night at Uncle David's [David Creigh]. At each of these places is a crowd of ladies, to whom I fear I appeared rather awkward not being a ladies man....I am now in Anderson's store writing in great haste..."(12)

Subsequent to Floyd's defeat of the 7th Ohio, Gen. Rosecrans was ordered to proceed south from Clarksburg and Sutton to attack Floyd at Carnifex Ferry. Gen. Floyd received word early in September that U.S. forces were gathering at Sutton and he correctly determined his camp was their objective. Attempting to speed reinforcements then on the march to join him, Floyd sent several couriers with orders for the men to hasten their advance. These reinforcements were from Georgia and North Carolina and began arriving in Greenbrier County during early September. Gen. Floyd's occupation of Carnifex Ferry caused some people to evacuate their homes, apparently believing they would be arrested or otherwise disturbed. In response, Gen. Floyd issued a proclamation addressed "To All Whom It May Concern." In the statement, Floyd said he came into western Virginia to vindicate the political supremacy of the State. He said Union citizens would not be disturbed as long as they did not openly oppose the Confederacy. On the other hand, he said anyone who aided or abetted the "murderous invaders" of Virginia would be arrested for treason.(13) In fact, many civilians of southern West Virginia had already been arrested by Blue and Gray alike, and sent to prisons North or South. The charge was generally suspicion of being in sympathy with the enemy. It was also not uncommon for some people to report another citizen as a spy or "sympathizer" as a means of settling an old grudge. Little or no proof of disloyalty was required and by the end of 1861 hundreds of West Virginia civilians had been incarcerated by one side or the other. An early war example of this was the case of Morris Johnson, arrested in Greenbrier County in late August 1861. Mr. Johnson was born in Monroe County, West Virginia, and moved to Illinois in 1856. Early in the war his young son, Edden, was a student at Allegheny College, Blue Sulphur Springs.

Edden Johnson was staying with his aunt, Ms. Evelyn Jarrett, a 37-year-old widow and mother of four. School was suspended because of the war and when Edden's father came from Illinois to take him home he was arrested by the Confederates and charged with being a spy. Mr. Johnson was taken to Lewisburg where he was told he would be tried by court martial. Fearing that Morris Johnson would not receive a fair trial, his relatives and friends quickly gathered up all the gold they could and rode to Lewisburg. Edden Johnson arrived in town about dark and went straight to the hotel. "On the veranda were a number of officers," he wrote, "and I soon saw that father's uncles and grandfather Ellis were among them. Father was in a room off the office under guard...Grandfather...was permitted to take me to father...they feared the result of the court martial the next morning. I learned that a large number of relatives and former neighbors had come to Lewisburg to bear witness for father." Early the next morning the court martial was held and very shortly rendered a verdict of not guilty. This verdict was no doubt helped along by the $1,500 in gold that Mr. Johnson's friends and relatives distributed here and there among the Confederate officers. Edden Johnson wrote that it took his father three years to repay the money.(14)

On September 4, Gen. Lee wrote Floyd from Valley Mountain, Randolph County, informing him that his command needed a good supply of salt. Lee wondered if Gen. Floyd's men might be able to procure salt from the Kanawha Valley, or from the salt works at Bulltown, 18 miles north of Sutton. "We could send wagons to Lewisburg if you could cause it to be delivered there," Lee wrote. Gen. Floyd replied that the enemy were in possession of Sutton and that he lacked sufficient supplies to attempt an advance into the Kanawha Valley. He told Gen. Lee that he believed salt could be obtained from Warfield, a small salt works on the border of Kentucky across the river from Logan County. Floyd said he had made arrangements with an "active, energetic man," to procure salt from Warfield as soon as possible, adding that he would send a strong escort of cavalry to make certain the delivery was made at Lewisburg.(15)

Colonel John McCausland informed Gen. Floyd on September 9 that his scouts reported a large force of the enemy advancing just 18 miles from Summersville. Realizing that these men were on the march to attack him at Camp Gauley, Gen. Floyd ordered the 14th North Carolina Infantry, recently arrived at Lewisburg, and the 13th Georgia Infantry at Meadow Bluff, to proceed at once to his location. These regiments would already have been with Gen. Floyd but disease and lack of transportation delayed their progress. The Floyd Brigade would need all the help it could get in the impending battle and their commander was frantically attempting to speed reinforcements. He also told Col. Croghan, then at Lewisburg, to "have the hospital at Lewisburg properly organized and supervised," and that in the meantime he was authorized and instructed to "gather up such of the soldiers as are parading the streets and troubling the town and bring them with your command of cavalry to this camp." Also, that he should "investigate the cases of the invalids," and send all of them that he felt might be able to render service. Gen. Floyd said he had reliable information that 6,000 Yankees were marching to attack him and he wanted Col. Croghan to hurry up with his cavalry. He also said he wanted the "Union man" who had been arrested and allowed bail, to be re-arrested and sent to Richmond with the other prisoners at Lewisburg.(16)

Gen. Wise sent the 22nd Regiment Virginia Infantry to Carnifex Ferry, but failed to reinforce that position with all the men requested by Floyd. Wise held the turnpike at the mouth of Sunday Road and in the vicinity of Hawks Nest. At about 3 p.m. on September 10, the Battle of Carnifex Ferry began when advance elements of General Rosecran's army stumbled upon the Rebels at Camp Gauley. The Yanks found the enemy waiting on them "through the opening of the woods on our left, their entrenchments in an open space beyond a deep and steep valley and crowning the crest of the opposite hill."(17)

When the battle commenced, Gen. Floyd met their 7,000-man army with fewer than 2,000 of his own troops because the Georgia and North Carolina regiments had not yet arrived. Nevertheless, the outnumbered Confederates put up a stout resistance, the initial ferocity of which caught the Yankees off guard.

A member of the 10th Ohio Infantry described the opening volleys: "They opened fire with rifle and musketry, grape and canister, shot and shell. There was not an inch of ground, a tree, nor a blade of grass that did not receive its share of fire."(18) And from Col. William Lytle, commander of the 10th Ohio, this description: "Their entire battery opened on us with grape and canister with almost paralyzing effect, my men falling around me in great numbers."(19)

The men in blue overcame their surprise and over the course of several hours made a series of determined attacks upon the Confederate line. A young Southern captain wrote that enemy artillery fire sent "large balls whistling over our heads, our men flat on the ground, then a volley of musketry…then a terrible shot of shell…the bullets fell like rain whistling and whizzing over our heads…"(20)

Nightfall put an end to the contest with both sides still holding the same ground. Surprisingly, the Confederate loss was just seven wounded, 17 captured, and no deaths. Gen. Rosecrans' men were not so lucky. His forces suffered 27 killed, 103 wounded, and four missing. Shortly after the battle ended, Gen. Floyd met with his officers and decided to retreat under cover of darkness. The Confederates were seriously outnumbered and probably would have been trapped and defeated the next day had they remained. That night they crossed the swollen Gauley River, destroying the ferry and foot bridge after they crossed. The Yankees did not discover their movement and sunrise of September 11 found them several miles from Carnifex Ferry. The commands of Floyd and Wise met at the junction of Sunday Road and the turnpike, present-day Hico. Wise said that he found Gen. Floyd "lying prostrate upon the ground," apparently in a state of confusion. Gen. Floyd was wounded in the "fleshy part" of his right arm during the fight and Wise began referring to him as "that bullet-hit son-of-a-bitch." As word of the battle spread, the more the tale was told the bigger Floyd's "victory" became. When the postmaster at Lewisburg heard about the fight, he wrote to the postmaster at Richmond saying that Floyd's men killed 600 Yankees and wounded 1,000. Another wild tale gaining circulation was that 4,000 Yankees were on the double-quick march to Greenbrier County by way of the Wilderness Road. This rumor reached Col. Croghan's cavalry at Meadow Bluff at 11 p.m. on the 11th. Fearing the report was true, Croghan asked the militia for help, saying that if he was not supported at once "Lewisburg is lost."(21)

The two Rebel armies continued their retreat until they reached the Sewell Mountain range. On the 12th, Gen. Floyd ordered the militia under Gen. Chapman to leave Raleigh County and join him at Meadow Bluff. He believed the Yankees would take advantage of his retreat by advancing on Lewisburg by way of the Wilderness Road from Summersville. This road connected with the James River and Kanawha Turnpike at Meadow Bluff and was a constant source of concern for the Confederates.

Also on the 12th, Gen. Floyd ordered that the Allegheny College at Blue Sulphur Springs be officially established as a military hospital. It was already being used in that capacity but the official designation, "Special Orders Number 73," facilitated Confederate command and control.(22) Allegheny College was established in 1859 in the buildings that formerly housed the Blue Sulphur Springs resort. It was a logical choice for use as a hospital. The main building was destroyed by fire in September 1860, but the adjacent cabins or cottages remained. These cabins were one-story brick construction, each having two bedrooms, for a total of 30 apartments. After the fire, a new dining hall and kitchen was constructed with a capacity for 175 people. The campus included about 40 acres of

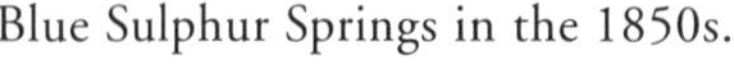
Blue Sulphur Springs in the 1850s.

This pavilion is all that remains of the once popular resort.

Above: Looking east from Blue Sulphur Springs, 2004.
Below: A section of the Blue Sulphur Turnpike between Meadow Bluff and Blue Sulphur Springs, 2004. *Photos by the author*

mostly level land. A small mountain stream ran through the campus and at the east end the famous Blue Sulphur Spring gushed out of the ground. Visitors claimed the water was so impregnated with sulphur that you could smell it several miles away. The spring was covered with a beautiful pavilion that remains today—the only remnant of a once thriving southern resort. Gushing from the spring the water appeared blue as indigo, but when put into a glass appeared crystal clear.

The Allegheny College catalogue for the 1860 term carried this vivid description of the location: "It is situated in Greenbrier County Virginia, thirteen miles from Lewisburg, twenty-two from the White Sulphur, and thirty-two from the Red Sulphur, on the great thoroughfare leading to Guyandotte. From the 1st of June to the 1st of November stages pass daily each way. No position can be more favorable to good morals. There is no place nearer than Lewisburg where liquor is sold, or any temptation to dissipation exists...Of what other school in Virginia can as much be said? The springs are located in a section unusually picturesque and healthful, and the student can scarcely fail to derive both physical and moral tone from all the surroundings of the School."(23)

On September 14, Gen. Rosecrans ordered Gen. Cox to scout the road in the direction of Sewell Mountain. Cox was told to determine where the Confederates had gone and prepare to attack them as soon as possible. He was ordered to load his wagons with food and enough ammunition to give each man 100 rounds. One Federal regiment would remain at Gauley Bridge for the protection of that post, while the others prepared an advance. Cox was also told to send his topographer forward to "report on the topographical and military features of the road to Lewisburg."(24) Two days later, Cox had advanced about 16 miles to Spy Rock, or Lookout, Fayette County. At that time Rosecrans told him to send a strong scouting party to the top of Big Sewell Mountain, unaware that the area was already occupied by Wise and Floyd. Cox was advised to push his outposts as far as possible and attempt to capture some Rebel scouts. These bold movements by the Yankees began to make matters rather hot for Gen. Floyd.

The two former governors remained at Sewell Mountain several days agreeing to disagree. After conferring with Wise for two hours the evening of the 16th, Gen. Floyd determined to fall back to Meadow Bluff, roughly 15 miles distant. Persistent rumors led him to believe the Yankees were advancing on that position. Believing the demand to be urgent, Gen. Floyd abruptly roused his men from their slumber at 10 p.m. It was raining heavily and the night was exceedingly black. Throughout the camps, many of Floyd's officers and men could be heard grumbling about the move which they felt could surely wait until dawn. The old general was undeterred, however, and before midnight his brigade was sloshing along the muddy turnpike, their column lit only by an occasional torch. Gen. Wise was against the move and to Floyd's dismay remained at Sewell against orders to the contrary. Gen. Wise very appropriately dubbed his position on Sewell "Camp Defiance." At noon of September 17, the wet, weary, and sleepless men of the Floyd Brigade stumbled into Meadow Bluff. Many of the men collapsed upon the damp ground and fell asleep. Others attempted to light fires to cook breakfast. Last to reach camp was the wagon train which had been thoroughly bogged down by the deep mud and was strung out for over a mile. Many of Floyd's men who were previously healthy were made ill by this unnecessary exposure to the elements. Others, in poor health when the move began, took a turn for the worse and were sent on to the hospitals at Lewisburg. Three of these men perished along the lonely road, more casualties of a mistaken campaign, in this "unnatural war."

Typhoid, dysentery, measles, mumps, and various other ailments raged throughout the camps. Lt. William Smith, still working as a nurse in Lewisburg, told his brother on September 18, that fully half of Floyd's and Wise's forces were sick: "They send them to Lewisburg, the White Sulphur and the Blue Sulphur Springs by wagon loads. I believe that some die every day. It is truly distressing to see them coming in, over these rough roads, on wagons."(25)

Gen. Floyd desperately wanted his brigade and the Wise Legion to be combined at Meadow Bluff, but Gen. Wise would have no part of it. Wise discounted rumors of an enemy advance along the Wilderness Road into Greenbrier County. He believed the Yankees would advance directly along the turnpike to Sewell Mountain and, if not met there, would occupy Lewisburg and other points south. Both men held stubbornly to their positions and wrote letters of complaint against the other to President Davis and Gen. Lee. Remaining convinced his brigade would battle the enemy at Meadow Bluff, Floyd ordered trenches dug along the eastern bank of Meadow River. Of course, since the trenches lined the river bank they were subject to frequent flooding, which is exactly what happened. On the 19th, Gen. Wise notified Floyd that two of his scouts had reported the enemy advancing along the turnpike at "double-quick," six miles from Camp Defiance. "I shall hold on here," Wise said, "and fight the enemy, expecting them to attack me before sunrise this morning."(26) Receiving the dispatch, Gen. Floyd was unimpressed. He said he had known for several days of the enemy advance and that he felt sure their goal was actually Meadow Bluff. "I regret exceedingly," he wrote, "that you did not think proper to bring up my rear, as directed in my order…Disastrous consequences, which may ensue from a divided force, may result from this…If you still have time, upon the receipt of this, to join my force and make a stand against the enemy at this point, I hope you will see the necessity of doing so at once…"(27)

Gen. Wise replied that he could not leave Camp Defiance if he wanted to because he lacked enough wagons for transportation. He said his wagons were hauling corn from the east and transporting sick troops to the hospitals. Wise complained that he had to deal with sick men of his command and Gen. Floyd's because surgeons of the Floyd Brigade left their sick "suffering and dying on the way," to Meadow Bluff. He claimed his wagons would have to be retrieved from Jackson's River, White Sulphur Springs, and Lewisburg, before any movement could be attempted. He also reminded his commander that the Floyd Brigade quartermaster borrowed five wagons that had not been returned. "I have a large amount of baggage, ammunition, and stores accumulated here," Wise wrote, "which I am bound to save, and will save from the enemy, who have approached within 6 miles of me in force....My position here is strong, and is much stronger than that of Meadow Bluff....As I finish, the enemy appear four miles and a half from my camp. This is certain. I shall await an attack, and leave it to your better judgment to send reinforcements or not."(28)

Gen. Wise did not give Floyd the satisfaction of knowing that he had indeed already began making preparations to leave Sewell Mountain. During the previous day Wise ordered his commissary and quartermaster departments to withhold supplies coming into his camp with the exception of corn and oats for the horses. He also directed that all available wagons be sent to him in preparation for a movement to "some point near Lewisburg." Wise told his quartermaster that these wagons should be sufficient to supply transportation for each company, and for all the ammunition and supplies at Camp Defiance. "Preferring ammunition and ordnance first," he wrote, "provisions and forage of grain next, baggage and clothing next and cooking utensils last."(29)

Frustrated with his inability to combine their commands, Gen. Floyd ordered the militia of Generals Beckley and Chapman to join him without delay. Their combined militia forces totaled, at least on paper, about 2,100 men. Unfortunately, the militia was very poorly armed and supplied, lacked discipline, and was greatly reduced by desertion. Of course Gen. Floyd knew these facts, but apparently reasoned that any reinforcements were better than none. Further, he had become convinced that the Yankees were determined to "fight a way to Lewisburg." The militia was scattered between Fayette and Raleigh counties, and several days would be required to pull them together.(30)

The "double-quick" advance of the enemy described by Gen. Wise was correct. On Thursday, September 19, Gen. Cox ordered a large detachment of his cavalry to advance from Spy Rock toward Big Sewell Mountain. Once there, they were ordered to select camping grounds suitable for the brigade and determine the exact location of the enemy. Gen. Cox had been very active from his camp at Spy Rock accumulating supplies and preparing his command of 5,000 men for an advance.

The Yankee advance so near Greenbrier County caused considerable public alarm. It did not take long for word to spread that "10,000 Yankees" were within one or two day's march of Lewisburg. In response, Mr. W.H. Syme, a 52-year-old Lewisburg physician, penned a letter to President Davis: "Your Excellency will excuse, I hope, the liberty which I have taken of addressing you a few lines relative to the apprehensions which cause much anxiety in our community and the circumstances which have given rise to them." After giving his summary of recent military events, Mr. Syme said that Confederate forces in the region were too small to defeat the enemy and prevent an invasion of Greenbrier. "...even if they acted in harmony and concert, which I am very sorry to say I fear they do not..." As a result he said, "I really fear that our county and town are in great danger of falling into the hands of the enemy, and such an event would indeed be deplorable, not only to our loyal citizens, but to our cause."(31)

Mason Mathews, Greenbrier County representative to the Virginia legislature, also wrote to Jefferson Davis. His sentiments echoed those of his friend, Mr. Syme. Referring to the animosity between the two former governors, Mathews said he was "fully satisfied that each of them would be highly gratified to see the other annihilated." He told the president that he had recently spent time in both generals' camps and there was considerable dissatisfaction with both generals among the officers and men. Mathews believed both men should be "deposed," and some "military general appointed in their stead." He said such an action would be gratifying to the various regimental commanders and would insure success. "It would be just as easy to combine oil and water," Mathews wrote, "as to expect a union of action between these gentlemen."(32)

With the advance of Gen. Cox and his 5,000-man army, the scene of action switched to the Sewell Mountain range and would be continued with the arrival of General Robert E. Lee in Greenbrier County.

Chapter Four
Robert E. Lee in Greenbrier County

Gen. Cox began establishing camps on the western top of Sewell Mountain just one mile distant from the Confederate Camp Defiance on the eastern top of Big Sewell. In these positions, the opposing forces could see one another and even hear their bands play. Both sides could make out the enemy's tents and count their unfurled flags flapping in the mountain breeze. Opposing pickets, stationed in the great ravine or defile that separated their camps, could hear the other's conversations. The frequent movement of artillery and wagons was overheard in both camps, especially in the early morning dampness that seemed somehow to carry sound among the rolling hills. On September 20, the vanguard of the Yankee army began erecting their camps on the western peak of Sewell with smaller camps out of sight in the rear. Several mountain springs supplied water for man and beast and the area's abundant hardwood forests supplied wood for fortifications, campfires, shelter, and wagon repair. A telegraph line was soon established from Sewell to Gauley Bridge, with a series of couriers posted on horseback every 10 miles. Orders were given that no civilians be allowed to travel the turnpike or its side roads without a military pass approved by either the commanding general or one of his line officers. Staging areas for ambulance wagons were established near the headquarters camp and about two miles back at the home of Frank Tyree. The Federal quartermaster depot for the Sewell Mountain campaign was established at the home of Col. George Alderson, Spy Rock, seven miles in rear of Cox's headquarters. Mr. Alderson was a

70- year-old Confederate sympathizer and prewar colonel in the Virginia militia. He operated a toll gate and inn at Spy Rock, or present-day Lookout, known as DeKalb. When Confederate forces camped on his property in July and August 1861, they paid the old colonel for seven acres of oats and hay and for more than 200 pounds of beef. It was a different story in September when the Yankees occupied his farm for several weeks. They stripped his home of numerous personal belongings, even furniture. They consumed more than seven acres of buckwheat and 20 acres of corn; ate 140 sheep; four cows; five hogs; 22 turkeys; 50 chickens; 31 ducks; and more than 100 bushels of potatoes. For these items, Col. Alderson received no payment. He was knocked out of business as an innkeeper and was nearly devoid of the means of survival. He estimated his losses to be over $4,600. The 2004 equivalent of that is just over $100,000. (1)

During the afternoon of the 20th, Gen. Wise determined to make an advance on the enemy to determine their strength and location. For several hours his men had listened to the Yankees as they prepared their own camps and brought up supplies. Wise knew this enemy advance was exactly as he predicted it would be, and was contrary to Gen. Floyd's idea that the Yankees would advance along the Wilderness Road to occupy Meadow Bluff and Lewisburg. No doubt the verbose general was happy to be proven correct, and better still, he was now presented with an opportunity to halt the enemy advance, making himself and his Legion heroes of this young campaign. Wise Legion camps were scattered from the top of the mountain eastward to the mountain's base in Greenbrier County, present-day Rainelle. His main cavalry camp was established about halfway down the mountain in the vicinity of present-day Big Sewell Baptist Church. Doctor D.B. Phillips was Wise Legion Medical Director and was in charge of their hospital at White Sulphur Springs. Two ambulance wagons were assigned to run between the hospital and Lewisburg; two more between that place and Meadow Bluff; two more with the troops west of Meadow Bluff near Big Sewell, and two kept at Sewell ready at a moment's notice. Pole litters were provided as a means of conveyance for cavalry.(2)

Gen. Wise selected five companies of infantry totaling 250 men for his advance into the ravine separating his position and the enemy's. These included the Richmond Light Infantry Blues, commanded by Wise's son, Captain Obadiah J. Wise, and the Louisiana Rangers, temporarily commanded by Captain Francis Imboden. Tackling dense underbrush and climbing over and around large boulders to enter the ravine, the anxious Confederates were soon fired upon by 200 dismounted Yankee cavalrymen. Enemy bullets combined with thickets and tangled undergrowth to slow their advance, but Wise's men were not to be deterred. The hillsides and ravines reverberated with the loud bang of musket and small arms fire. Dense smoke rose leisurely above the trees, its pungent odor drifting among the determined combatants. This Indian-style fighting continued for about two hours when suddenly the Yankees began to fall back. Sensing victory, Gen. Wise pressed the issue, driving enemy pickets from behind rocks and trees. Excited but growing tired, Wise's men pursued the fleeing enemy until nightfall required a halt. Camp was set up in the great ravine and a messenger sent back to the mountain top with word of their progress and position. In the running skirmish, one Union soldier was killed and several wounded. The Legion had two men slightly wounded, none killed.

During the time that Wise was battling the enemy in the ravines of Sewell Mountain, Gen. Robert E. Lee arrived in Greenbrier County. It was nearly dark when Lee and his small escort of cavalry reached Frankford, east of Lewisburg. Gen. Lee sent a courier to Meadow Bluff to inform Gen. Floyd of his location, saying "I will be with you tomorrow."(3)

That evening Gen. Wise notified Floyd of his skirmish and the strong enemy advance. Still believing the true intentions of the enemy were to attack his camp, Floyd wrote to the "commandant of forces which may be at the White Sulphur Springs," to reinforce him without delay. Few able-bodied men were at the Springs and there is no record that any help was sent.(4)

Early the next morning, the clatter of horsemen riding into Lewisburg announced the arrival of Robert E. Lee. Such excite-

Gen. Robert E. Lee as he appeared in the summer of 1861. *Courtesy West Virginia Department of Archives and History*

ment as then prevailed was seldom seen in that historic community. None of the citizens knew Lee was coming, thus his sudden appearance in their midst came as a complete shock. Men, women, and children poured onto the street to see this man many had heard of but never seen. Mr. W.H. Syme caught the excitement of the moment in a letter to Jefferson Davis: "Our citizens were much pleased at the arrival of General Lee in our town this morning, en route for the west. He passed through, and I suppose by this time has reached Meadow Bluff. He had with him only an escort of cavalry, and I have not heard of any reinforcements to our little army being expected from Cheat Mountain. His presence in our midst has, however, given great satisfaction, as it assures us that, should the reports of want of harmony and concert have been well founded, no ill consequence can now flow from that source....We have entire confidence in General Lee..."(5)

Gen. Lee rode into Floyd's camp during the afternoon of the 21st. His arrival in the camps was always a matter of great curiosity and excitement. Just the sight of Robert E. Lee made a lasting impression on officers and men alike. Several in Gen. Floyd's command recorded their impressions of the great chieftain: "Here I first saw Gen. Lee. He appears in some of the pictures as I saw him there. He was clean shaven except that he had a mustache..."(6) Then this, "I had never seen him...there was a kindliness in his expression most unusual in one possessing eyes so dark and brilliant. He was dignified and courtly...so courteous, so kind..."(7) And, "I saw the great Commander-in-Chief...How distinctly I remember...the fine grey head and the kindness of his face...It was such a face as one never forgets."(8)

Generals Lee and Floyd spent the day examining the camps at Meadow Bluff and discussing events up to that time. Gen. Floyd explained the strategic differences between his camp and that of Gen. Wise, and their discussion turned to the frequent skirmishing the Wise Legion found itself involved in. Gen. Floyd told Lee that Wise held a strong position, but that he firmly believed when the enemy advanced on Greenbrier County they would use the Wilderness Road. That advance would find the numerically inferior Southern forces divided because Gen. Wise ignored repeated pleas to combine their commands. Paying careful attention to Floyd's remarks, Gen. Lee decided to write a letter to Wise at Camp Defiance: "I have just arrived at this camp and regret to find the forces not united...as far as I can judge our united forces are not more than one half of the strength of the enemy....It would be the height of imprudence to submit them separately to his attack...I beg therefore, if not too late, that the troops be united, and that we conquer or die together....I expect this of your magnanimity. Consult that and the interest of our cause, and all will go well."(9)

When Gen. Wise received Lee's dispatch, he had just returned from his camp in the ravine, having had another series of encounters with the enemy. He was wet, tired, hungry, and in poor mood: "I have just returned from feeling the enemy, being out all night and driving in their pickets this morning...but fatigued as I am, your note reads so much like a rebuke, which I do not think I deserve, that I do not lose a moment without replying...In the first place, I consider my force united with that of Gen. Floyd as much as it ever has been...Floyd has about 3,800, and I about

2,200 men, of all arms, and of these at least 5,500 are efficient....The two roads and the two positions had perhaps better be examined, I respectfully submit, before my judgment is condemned." Wise went on to defend his position at Camp Defiance, telling Lee that the enemy had advanced toward his position several times. "I laugh him to scorn," Wise wrote, "as I know he wishes to retire now more than I do." Taking exception to Lee's remark that he should consider "the interest of our cause," Wise made clear his attitude, "I am ready to do, suffer, and die for it...any imputation upon my motives or intentions in that respect by my superior would make me, perhaps, no longer a military subordinate of any man who breathes. I am sure you mean to cast no such imputation, whoever else may dare. I trust all will go well, most confidently, in your hands. I am, with the highest respect and esteem, your obedient servant..."(10)

Allowing Gen. Wise the benefit of the doubt, Lee determined to inspect Camp Defiance personally. Gen. Lee and his aide, Captain Walter H. Taylor, rode forward to Big Sewell with a small cavalry escort on the 22nd. The old governor and the renowned general were then seen in earnest conversation as they walked along inspecting the camps. Gen. Lee was observed using his binoculars to view the western top of Big Sewell, another strong position and camp of the enemy cavalry. Gen. Lee was impressed with the preparations for defense at Camp Defiance and gradually began to find some merit in allowing the Wise Legion to remain there. Though the area was accessible from a series of trails and side roads, if the enemy advanced along the turnpike, which events seemed to indicate, Big Sewell was a strong position to meet them. Late that afternoon Lee rode back to Meadow Bluff, allowing the Wise Legion to remain where they were.

While Gen. Lee was inspecting Camp Defiance, Gen. Cox was at Spy Rock preparing to move his entire command to Sewell Mountain. The various skirmishes his cavalry had with the Confederates at Sewell convinced Gen. Cox that he must occupy the area in force to prevent the enemy from moving toward the Kanawha Valley. Union scouts had done effective work giving Gen. Cox quite accurate information. He knew the Wise Legion was in his front and that the Floyd Brigade occupied Meadow Bluff. He was also told about the side roads by which his men might flank Camp Defiance. Gen. Cox telegraphed Rosecrans, telling him that he would move his entire force to Sewell Mountain the next day. Gen. Rosecrans replied that he should not advance too far lest he be ambushed or compelled to fight.

Gen. Cox made his promised advance on the 23rd, occupying in force the western top of Big Sewell Mountain that afternoon. Their sudden advance in force caught the Confederates by surprise. Gen. Wise quickly notified Lee at Meadow Bluff that the enemy had advanced with infantry, cavalry, and artillery, all visible from his camp and about one mile distant. He also said the enemy had not yet opened fire, and were reported by the cavalry as fortifying.(11)

Gen. Lee worried that the enemy advance along the turnpike might be a diversion, while their true intention was to attack Meadow Bluff by way of the Wilderness Road. He told Wise to send back his baggage train and prepare for a quick retreat on the first evidence of a move against Gen. Floyd's position. Using the Wilderness Road would allow the Yankees to flank Camp Defiance and regain the turnpike at Meadow Bluff. From there an attack on Lewisburg would be easily carried out. Accordingly, Lee ordered Col. St. George Croghan to take a company of cavalry and examine both the Wilderness Road and the Old State Road to check for enemy activity.(12)

Gen. Wise received Lee's dispatch late that evening and replied at midnight: "I saw the masses crossing the top of Big Sewell, with artillery and cavalry. We could see about four regiments...I cannot retire my baggage wagons or other incumbrances..." Having grown tired of repeated assertions of an enemy advance along Wilderness Road, Wise sought to put the idea to rest: "The idea of the enemy passing from Sunday Road to the Wilderness Road by Nichols Mill is simply absurd. There is hardly a trail there. If one, no army can possibly pass it that would startle a hare." Ever defiant, Wise declared that he was "compelled to stand here and fight as long as I can endure and ammunition last. All is at stake with my command and it shall be sold dearly."(13)

Replying at 4 a.m., Gen. Lee told Wise that no reliable information had been received from the Wilderness Road. He also said he regretted to hear that Wise could not retire his baggage wagons and was compelled to remain where he was, because he was so far from support it might jeopardize the whole command. Lee wondered if Wise had sufficient ammunition for a strong defense of Camp Defiance and if Wise had any reliable information of enemy movements that "may serve to regulate the movements of Gen. Floyd."(14)

Traveling the 15 or so miles between camps in just three hours, the courier gave Wise his dispatch at 7:00 a.m. It took the old general just 15 minutes to fashion his reply. He told Gen. Lee that his men had been skirmishing with the enemy and were very active all that night. "I tell you emphatically sir," Wise wrote, "that the enemy are advancing in strong force on this turnpike....I have a good supply of ammunition and provisions; shall keep them here, and start away my baggage wagons, if I can, this morning." Wise also said several of his men had been wounded. He said if Lee ordered him to retreat he wanted to have his wagons emptied of baggage and the teamsters used to haul away his ammunition and supplies.(15)

During the early morning hours of September 24, Gen. Cox notified Gen. Rosecrans that his camps had been quiet that morning and he intended to scout the Rebel positions. When Rosecrans realized Gen. Cox had advanced nearly to Greenbrier County, he became concerned. He told Gen. Cox that his position was seven miles beyond where he thought he was and that his camp was too far from support. He also observed quite accurately that by occupying Big Sewell, Cox had made "a military declaration of our intentions to use one route." Rosecrans told his subordinate to "make up for these, if possible, and provide against everything."(16) Gen. Cox was diligently attempting to "provide against everything," but his mind wandered home. He received word that day of the death of one of his children. Gen. Cox had known the child was sick, but this news was unexpected. Taking a break from his numerous responsibilities, he wrote home expressing his grief: "I have had a very heavy heart since, but my

Volunteer workers assembled at the Dietz house, Meadow Bluff, on May 31, 1992. This house was used several times during the war as military headquarters or hospital. Robert E. Lee was here in September 1861. Through the efforts of the author this house was added to the National Register of Historic Places in 1992. Pictured fourth from left is the late R. Hal Wals, a past president of the Greenbrier County Historical Society.To his immediate left are Richard Andre and Stan Cohen. *Photo by author*

duties have been pressing...I would have given anything...to have been with you, but God's will be done." Gen. Cox told his wife that he was 35 miles beyond Gauley Bridge and his men had been skirmishing heavily with the Rebels. He said the enemy fired artillery at their position for three or four hours, but the range was too great. He also said despite everything his attention was "more than half elsewhere." He closed his letter asking his wife to "kiss all the dear babies for me."(17)

Gen. Lee decided to reinforce Camp Defiance and return there personally. Riding out of Floyd's camp at 7 a.m. on the 24th Lee took with him two Virginia regiments as well as the 13th Georgia and 14th North Carolina Infantry, and two pieces of artillery. Sending a courier ahead to inform Wise of his advance, Lee said, "In ignorance of the movements of the enemy on our flanks...I am about to advance with such portion of Gen. Floyd's brigade to your support as can be spared from this position. My object is to unite the troops...It is hazarding too much to remain where you are compelled to fight & have no option of withdrawing if you desire." Lee went on to remind Gen. Wise of the importance of making arrangements to retire his baggage wagons.(18)

Gen. Floyd remained at Meadow Bluff with an immediate command of about 1,000 men. He busied himself organizing his command into three brigades and preparing to send more men to Sewell as soon as supplies and transportation could be secured. Floyd gave orders that any man who fired his weapon in or near camp would be confined for 24 hours without food. To enforce this rule, he established a 10-man "police guard" from each of his remaining regiments. He also authorized the expenditure of up to $600.00 hundred dollars for the purchase of a wagon and four-horse team. After checking with some local citizens a wagon and team was purchased from Mr. George Ivesay.(19)

Around 9 a.m. of the 24th, Gen. Cox ordered his men to probe the enemy flanks in search of any weakness in their line. He ordered his artillery and several companies of skirmishers to occupy the enemy in front, while his scouts probed their defenses. The advance of several hundred Yankees into the deep ravine separating the camps was quickly observed. Gen. Wise ordered a strong counter-attack, and this resulted in some heavy skirmishing that went on for several hours. A Confederate officer watched the fighting unfold and thought it was a grand sight: "I can never forget the advance of Rosecranss splendid army as their bayonets flashed in the morning sun…Wise threw forward Richardson's regiment to meet them. It was a dense forest of oaks, poplars, and chestnuts, and the regiment strung out in a picket line behind trees completely checked the advance of the enemy…it was nothing but an Indian fight—Virginians behind trees fighting Ohioans behind trees…there was no ground level enough on which to place artillery in the deep gorge…"(20)

By early afternoon several men had been killed anwounded on both sides. The mountains were alive with the booming of cannon and the crack of small arms fire. As Gen. Lee and the reinforcements neared the scene they could easily hear the fighting and hastened their march. Along the way, they began to meet members of the Wise Legion hurrying to the rear. These men very excitedly told tales of pickets shot, men killed, and wounded men being dragged out of the wilderness. An officer advancing with Gen. Lee said he thought many of these men should have been going forward instead of back. The reinforcements pressed on and, near the top of Big Sewell, halted for a rest. They had just seated themselves when the loud boom of cannon beckoned them on. Arriving around 2 p.m., the reinforcements were quickly shown their place along the top of the ridge. Musket and pistol fire mingled with the booming cannons, their echo reverberating in the mountains. (21)

Shortly after Gen. Lee's arrival at Camp Defiance, the fighting stopped. At that time, Gen. Cox sent a dispatch to Gen. Rosecrans advising him of the situation: "They hold a ridge which commands the road for nearly half a mile, and have a battery of one rifled 4-pounder, one smooth sixer, and a mountain howitzer. These they used this morning....The crest they are on is thickly wooded, and I am not yet sure whether it can be reached so as to flank them."(22) Rosecrans replied that Cox had advanced too far for anything but fighting. "Nevertheless," Rosecrans wrote, "you will take every precaution not to be drawn into a fight...Report fully tonight on the nature of the country on your front and flanks and all the by-roads by which the enemy could surprise you." Cox replied later that evening, saying that the Rebels had withdrawn most of their force. "We came here in the nick of time," he said, "and are in no danger from their forces....My examination of their flanks while occupying them in front has satisfied me that they are not as strong as we, except in cannon; that they were surprised by our approach; that their flanks are accessible, and that we can whip them."(23-24)

The advance of the Yankees settled the question for Gen. Lee. Camp Defiance must be defended. To retreat now, in the face of the enemy, would risk the capture or destruction of the entire command. Lee found that many officers of the Wise Legion were ignorant of their duties, and bitter toward Gen. Floyd and his brigade. Lee's aide, Captain Walter H. Taylor, described the situation: "The bitter feeling which had been engendered between the two commanders had imparted itself, in some de-

Gen. John B. Floyd CSA, 1806-1863.
Courtesy Museum of the Confederacy

gree, to the troops, and seriously threatened to impair their efficiency. No little diplomacy was required therefore, to produce harmony and hearty cooperation, where previously had prevailed discord and contention."(25)

Many of the same problems that plagued the Confederates also existed within the camps of Gen. Cox. There was a lack of discipline and a severe shortage of experienced officers to lead the men. Though the Union forces were generally better supplied, there was considerable waste and inefficiency occasioned by the need of experienced quartermasters. Disease was also a serious problem for Blue and Gray alike. Several hundred men of Gen. Cox's command were sick with measles, diarrhea, camp fever, and other ailments. Most of the private homes between Sewell Mountain and Gauley Bridge were taken over as hospitals. Many of these homes had been abandoned by their occupants upon the advance of Federal forces. Others were "pressed" into service.

During the evening of the 24th, Gen. Floyd received some reinforcements of his own at Meadow Bluff, with the arrival of the 20th Mississippi Infantry, commanded by Col. Dan R. Russell. Gen. Floyd was very impressed with these Mississippians, later referring to them as "The flower of my command." Gen. Lee sent a courier to Floyd with word of recent developments and asking for additional supplies of food and ammunition. That night a chilling rain set in that continued on and off all night. Gen. Lee bivouacked on the mountainside, covered only by his overcoat. His tent and personal baggage did not reach him until the 26th, having been delayed by the sorry condition of the roads. Lee arose early on the morning of the 25th and wasted no time inspecting the camps of the enemy with his field glasses. As soon as he had determined all that he could from his inspection, Lee dictated a letter to Gen. Floyd: “Everything is quiet in the enemy’s camp. I can count five or six regiments, but cannot see ground in their rear where others may be....I suppose if we fall back the enemy will follow. This is a strong point if they will fight us here. The advantage is, they can get no position for their artillery, and their men, I think, will not advance without it.” Lee then asked, “how would it do to make a stand here.” Of course the advance of the enemy had already settled the question, but Gen. Lee was attempting to pacify Gen. Floyd, who was against remaining at Camp Defiance. If they were to remain there, Lee added, “We shall require provisions and forage. Of the latter there is none, and the horses are suffering...send three days rations of flour, salt, and bacon, if you have it...send also sugar and coffee.”(26)

Toward noon Gen. Cox ordered the 11th Ohio Infantry out on reconnaissance to the right of the Rebel camp. This movement resulted in another series of running skirmishes. When the picket firing intensified, Gen. Wise entered the fray, personally leading a detachment out to meet the enemy. Once again the mountains echoed with the sounds of combat. The men not engaged had little to do except watch and listen. Anxiety levels were high as no one knew when a skirmish might become a general advance of the enemy and major combat. Gen. Wise, always ready for a fight, was in the thick of things when he was handed an order from Richmond that changed everything: “You are instructed to turn over all the troops heretofore under your command, to Gen. John B. Floyd, and to report yourself in person to the Adjutant General in the city of Richmond, with the least delay...”

Gen. Wise debated whether or not to obey the order. He felt that the advance of the enemy required his presence at Camp Defiance, at least until the intentions of the enemy were made clear. In his hesitation he wrote Gen. Lee asking his opinion, "I come to you for counsel, and will abide by it, because I have been under your eye, and you are competent to judge my act and its motive, whatever it may be. I desire to delay my report in person until after the fate of this battle. Dare I do so? On the other hand, can I, in honor, leave you at this moment, though the disobedience of the order may subject me to the severest penalties? Will you please advise and instruct me?"(27)

Gen. Lee replied that Wise should comply with the order: "I will briefly state, in answer to your inquiry, appreciating, as I do, the reluctance and embarrassment you feel at leaving your Legion at this time, what I should feel compelled to do, as a military man, under like circumstances. That is, to obey the President's order. The enemy is in our presence and testing the strength of our position. What may be the result, whether he will determine to attack or whether we may retire, cannot now be foreseen. I can conceive the desire your command would have for your presence, yet they will also do justice to your position." (28)

Accepting Lee's advice, Gen. Wise decided to obey the order. That evening he issued "General Orders Number 106" announcing his recall: "By order of the President…I am instructed to turn over all the troops…to Gen. Floyd….It is not proper here to inquire into the reasons of this order….the order is imperative, requiring the least delay…though it may call for the greatest personal sacrifice. And the order is not so inopportune, when it finds my superior in every respect, General Robert E. Lee, present, in whose command I confidently leave the safety and honor of my legion."(29) Gen. Wise departed Sewell Mountain, taking with him his son, Captain Wise, and four staff officers. They arrived in Richmond on the 28th of September. Wise's departure and the circumstances surrounding it caused some controversy among his officers and men. The situation was quite different at Meadow Bluff, however, where many members of the Floyd Brigade were elated with the news. One of Gen. Floyd's

Above: 2004 view of Confederate trench remains along the Meadow River at Meadow Bluff.
Below: Looking west along the old James River and Kanawha Turnpike from the Confederate trench remains. Little Sewell Mountain is visible in the background. *Photos by author*

staff officers recorded his feelings in his diary: "Today Gen. Wise departed with his staff for Richmond in obedience to an order from the President. This, of course, was a crushing mortification to him to be compelled to leave when in sight of the enemy. However, I consider it the greatest blessing bestowed upon us during the war. Some dissatisfaction was created in his Brigade."(30)

No doubt Gen. Floyd was equally elated with the recall, but his myriad duties at Meadow Bluff kept him too busy for celebration. He issued six special orders on the 25th dealing with everything from disposition of the sick to feeding men at Camp Arbuckle who were awaiting discharge. Dr. Lucious Farnbro, 13th Georgia Infantry, was ordered to transfer the sick troops at Blue Sulphur Springs to the hospital at White Sulphur, and to attend to them there until further orders. At 8 p.m. an incident occurred at a picket post that alarmed the entire command. A member of the 51st Virginia Infantry described the event in a letter to his brother: "One of our pickets challenged a man to halt. He replied, 'what in the hell right do you have to halt me?' and busted a cap at the picket. The picket fired and retreated. We were immediately ordered to arms. Half of each company was double quicked to the scene, the remnant were left at camp under arms. We expected to be attacked every moment...."(31)

This episode with the picket near Meadow Bluff increased the anxiety within Floyd's Brigade, and left them wondering if it was a sign that the Yankees would advance in force against their position. Gen. Floyd decided to err on the side of caution and recall the militia to strengthen his camp. Earlier in the month, Gen. Floyd allowed the militia of Greenbrier County to be disbanded with the understanding that they could be recalled at a moment's notice. William Peters, Floyd's Adjutant, ordered Gen. Chapman's 19th Brigade of militia to report to Meadow Bluff. Peters told Chapman that the militia of Greenbrier County would also be ordered out because of the "great strength" of the enemy. "General Floyd has already constructed better breast-works than he had at Gauley," Peters wrote, "and if he can get men enough to man them the enemy can never pass. General Floyd is looking every day for the advance of the enemy upon him."(32)

Chapman's 19th Brigade Virginia Militia included the 79th Regiment, Greenbrier County, under Col. George F. Henry; the 108th Regiment, Monroe County, Col. John M. Rowan; the 135th Regiment, Greenbrier County, Col. John Snyder; the 151st Regiment, Mercer County, Lt. Col. John S. Carr; the 166th Regiment, Monroe County, Col. William Suttle; Infantry Company Second Class, Monroe County, town of Union, and the Second Class Infantry company from the town of Lewisburg.

When attempts were made to call out Greenbrier County's 135th Regiment of militia, the response was less than enthusiastic. These "regiments" were actually quite small, usually consisting of between 300 and 400 men. In late September, a "Circular" was published giving the names of 123 men from the 135th Regiment who were reported as having deserted. Many of these men were actually sick, either at home or in one of the makeshift hospitals. Some men abandoned the militia and had enlisted, or would enlist before the end of 1861, with regular Confederate units. The original Circular gave only the person's name and district of residence. Where the author was able to determine age, occupation, or subsequent military service, that information is included in brackets.

Headquarters 135th Regiment Va Militia
September 1861

In obedience to the orders of the General, I hereby publish the names of all men disobeying orders, when called out in the service of the country…they are regarded in the law as deserters.

Anthony's Creek Company

William B. Fewell [age 29, carpenter]
Rufus Hefner [age 27, Edgar's Battalion]
Arch M. Hefner
Jacob Waggoner [age 19]
Robert Lawson [age 40, Edgar's Battalion]
William May [age 45, possibly 14th Va Cavalry]

James H. Spitzer [age 18]
Nicholas Maloney [age 28]
George W. Waid [surname Wade, age 29, Edgar's Battalion]
Daniel Alderman [age 30]
Leonard Alderman [age 23]
Henry Busard [surname Buzzard, age 33, Edgar's Battalion]
Jesse Gum [age 35]
Abraham Jones [age 27, 14th Va Cavalry]
John Gardner [age 25, Edgar's Battalion]
Joseph Gardner [age 17]
John May [age 39, 19th Va Cavalry]
Alexander Parkins [surname Perkins, age 21, Edgar's Battalion]
John Richy
Henry H. Sevy [age 26, Edgar's Battalion]
John Thompson [age 32, 8th Va Cavalry]
Harrison Waid [surname Wade, age 26]
Cristopher Waid [surname Wade, 60th Va Infantry]
David Coulter [surname Coalter, age 20]
Josiah Richy [surname Richie, age 40]
Henry T. Busard [surname Buzzard, possibly a duplicate]

Lewisburg Company

H.F. Hunter [Henry F., age 36]
Eugene Collins [age 40]
Anthony Lany [surname may be Cary]
James Reaser [surname Reeson, age 18]
Washington Thomas [possibly Geo. Washington Thomas, 17]
G.W. Sanders
James C. Grant [age 19]
John Oiler [age 17]
James W. Branham [surname Brackman, age 20, 22nd Va Infantry]
David Wetzel
James Johnston [James A., age 18]
Thomas Sears [age 36]
Timothy Shay [age 28]
Burwell Vaughn [age 40]

Patrick Nolin [age 35]
Charles Lemon [age 29, 60th Va Infantry]

Sinking Creek, Capt. Sammons

Andrew H. Clutter [age 21]

Spring Creek, Capt. Burr

James H. Alderman [age 25]
John A. Boggs [age 40]
Jesse Cochran [age 28]
Stuart Clutter [age 25]
James Crookshanks [age 30]
Isaac McKeever
D.V. McCoy [Daniel V., age 28]
John L. McMillion
William Mathews [age 18]
William Paul
John L. Snediger [surname Snedager, age 25]
John M. Williams [age 16]
William McCoy [age 32]
Joseph A. Rapp [age 21]

Irish Corner, Capt. Humphreys

I.N. Campbell [Isaac N., 18, brother of John]
J.A. Campbell [John A., age 21, brother of Isaac]
E.H. Adwell [Enoch H., age 24, brother of Joe and John]
J.W. Adwell [Joseph W., age 15, brother of Enoch and John]
R. Robinson [age 23]
John Adwell [age 31, brother of Enoch and Joe]
Allen Dolin [surname Dolan, age 37]
G.W. Rank
J.A. Erwin [John A., age 23]
John D. Hausel
James W. Jackson [age 30]

Joseph Morgan [age 26]
Abraham Price [age 41]
J.W. Dunbar
I.M. Dunbar
I.E. Dunbar [possibly Isaac E., age 26, 22nd Va Infantry]
Joel Morgan [age 34]

White Sulphur, Capt. Dean

J.A. Sheets
Thomas Fewel [age 21]
Henry Kefer [age 52]
Thomas M. Nicholas [x2, both Sr. and Jr.]
Porterfield Rusk
William Dorsan
John Laden [age 30]
James Hanchin [surname Hanakin, age 34]
Michael Civlihan
Michael Mulvahill [surname Mulochill, age 35]
Patrick Lahey
Joseph Hoke
A.L. Gilbert [age 16]
Patrick Yeager
Peter Ferrell
Henry Hoake
Jerry Holsaple
Abraham Ewing [age 30]
Samuel Cary

Fort Spring, Capt. Fleshman

David Fry [age 19]
Madison Fry
Madison Boon [possibly Henry M., age 19, brother of James]
James H. Boon [age 28, brother of Henry Madison Boon]
John F. Coffman [age 19]
A.D. Puliam [Algeron Pulliam, age 20, brother of Thomas]

Thomas Puliam [surname Pulliam, age 18, brother of Algeron]
Allen Howard [age 42]
Caleb Knapp [age 34]
John Hedrick
George W. Stone [age 22]
James Stone [age 18]
Archibald Tuckwiller [age 28]
Thomas Shepherd
Andrew Whanger [age 29, brother of Joseph and David]
Joseph Whanger [age 21, brother of Andrew and David]
David Whanger [age 24, brother of Joseph and Andrew]

Dutch Corner, Capt. McDowell

George W. Ronk
William Tucker
James Cury
J.N. Dolin [John N. Dolan, age 22]
Napolean Plunket [surname Plunkett, age 36]
Allen Ellis [age 41]
Adam Vance [age 38]
William Wills
John Reynolds [age 26]
James Morris [James H., age 31]
E.F. Patton [Ephraim F., age 40]
William N. Hedrick [age 47]
William Perry [age 35]

Rec^d of Charles McClung esq. 7½ bushels of wheat @ $1.25 ($9.37) for the use of the 135th Reg^t Va Ma.

John T. Blake

Jan. 21st 1862 } Assistant Qr M. 135th Reg^t Va Ma

Supply receipts signed by John Blake, Assistant Quartermaster, 135th VA Militia. *Author's collection*

Rec^d of Wallace S. Rader 44½ lbs Salted pork @ 12½ cts	$5 56	
5 bushels wheat @$1.25	6 25	
For the use of The 135th Reg^t Va Ma		11 81
Sold him 16 lbs tallow @ 10 cts	1 60	1 60
Due him		$10 21

Jan 10th 1862 } John T. Blake Ast Qr M 135 Reg^t Va Ma

Chapter Five

A Stalemate in the Mountains

As Gen. Wise rode away from Sewell Mountain on the 26th, Gen. Rosecrans arrived in the camp of Gen. Cox. This was the first opportunity Rosecrans had to view the Rebel position at Sewell and he decided to scout the Confederate camp personally. He selected one company of infantry and several officers to accompany him. Their little scouting party advanced but a short distance toward their foe when a sudden and severe thunderstorm struck. This was an especially cold rain and during the evening the rain turned into sleet. This storm would last for nearly three days, further demoralizing the troops of both sides and making travel along the turnpike all but impossible. Many of the Southern soldiers at Sewell and some of the Union men were still without tents or any shelter other than what they could improvise. Man and beast suffered alike and some parts of the road washed out so deep that barely a footpath remained. The Meadow River rose so high that Gen. Floyd's entrenchments and lower camps were fully submerged. The Greenbrier River became so swollen that when Col. Croghan left Lewisburg to forward supplies from White Sulphur Springs, he had to swim his horse across the raging waters. Nevertheless, military necessity required that everything be done that could be done, and Col. Croghan was eventually able to forward 60 barrels of flour and several barrels of pork to Lewisburg and Meadow Bluff.

Despite the deluge, Gen. Floyd ordered the 20th Mississippi Infantry to reinforce Lee at Camp Defiance. These men arrived at 10 p.m., cold, wet, and hungry, having marched the last half

Gen. William S. Rosencrans, commander of US forces during the Sewell Mountain campaign. *Author's collection*

of the journey in the pelting sleet. Over in the Federal camp, Col. Rutherford B. Hayes, of the 23rd Ohio Infantry, wrote to his wife: "We are in the midst of a very cold rainstorm…rain for fifteen hours; getting colder and colder, and still raining. In leaky tents, with wornout blankets, insufficient socks and shoes, many without overcoats…"(1)

Early the next morning, Gen. Floyd notified Lee that most of Greenbrier County was "inundated by the rain of last night." He said he was forwarding more supplies to Sewell Mountain but that it would be very difficult to obtain enough feed for the animals.

Later in the day, Gen. Floyd notified Lee of the arrival in Lewisburg of Gen. William Wing Loring. Gen. Loring marched from the Cheat Mountain Range, bringing with him the 42nd and 48th Regiments Virginia Infantry. Trailing Loring's group by about 12 hours was Gen. Samuel Read Anderson, bringing the 1st, 7th, and 16th Tennessee Infantry. This was the first visit to Greenbrier County for the majority of Loring's men. A soldier with the 42nd Virginia told his sister that Lewisburg "burst upon our view just after climbing a long and rough mountain, from the top of which we had a splendid view of the large nice farms and beautiful residences....The scenery created a momentary change in the feeling of every soldier who ascended the mountain almost wornout with fatigue...and the air was made to ring for miles around with shouts...we unfurled the banner and proudly marched through the neat village...keeping up a continuous shout, and greeted everywhere by nice young ladies who waved their handkerchiefs from nearly every window. This is truly a beautiful country, one among few that I would exchange our home in old Patrick County for."(2) Another solder said, "we went to Lewisburg but provisions were scarce there and not only that, but there is so much confusion and a great many sick soldiers there, and the streets are always crowded with soldiers passing to and from the army." (3) Still more reinforcements poured into Lewisburg that same day. These men belonged to Phillips Legion Georgia Cavalry, actually a combination of riflemen and cavalry, just arrived from Lynchburg. This unit was approximately 400 men strong and was an elite Georgia Legion. During the evening, most of the troops moved several miles west of Lewisburg to Bungers Mill and encamped there for the night. The Reverend G.G. Smith served as physician for Phillips Legion. He was very cordially received in Lewisburg as he later explained: "We reached the White Sulphur and that afternoon came into Lewisburg. There had been rain, rain, rain....I found at Bell's store corner, a quiet looking gentleman whose name was Montgomery, who invited me to his house. I spent my first night in a private home in West Virginia at Mr. James Montgomery's."(4) Another member of Phillips Legion described what a relief it was to take their heavy knapsacks off: "...when I took it off I could hardly stand up my head and shoulders felt so light it was all I could do to keep from falling over on my face."(5)

During the afternoon, an incident occurred at Sewell Mountain that cast a gloom over the entire Confederate command. Lt. Col. John W. Spalding, the 34-year-old commander of the 60th Virginia Infantry, became intoxicated and decided to conduct an advance scout of the enemy. Riding out in advance of his escort, he had not gone far when suddenly he came face to face with pickets of the 30th Ohio Infantry. Surprised, Col. Spalding reined his horse, drew his pistol and fired. The pickets returned fire, several bullets ripping into the colonel's chest. His frightened horse quickly whirled and took off down the mountain, Spalding's lifeless body dangling from the saddle. Fifty yards down the road, his body flipped off onto the turnpike, landing among the escort the poor colonel had left behind. Stunned by the sudden death of their commander, four of the men managed to place his corpse on a blanket and carry it back to camp. At the spot where the colonel fell, the Union pickets found his bloodied papers and a photograph of his wife. On the back of the picture was written "Separated by this cruel and unnatural war." As word of the Rebel colonel's death passed among the Yankee camps, Rutherford Hayes thought it was more homicide than warfare: "Our pickets killed a colonel or lieutenant colonel of the enemy who rode among them. All wrong and cruel. This is too like murder."(6)

A soldier with the 13th Georgia Infantry also recorded his impression of the late colonel's death: "The price of whose life was the wine cup, which drove from his eyes the fear of death & love for life. With dauntless steps he rode forward until pierced by the shots of two enemy pickets which ended his career in the armies on earth to join the armies in heaven or the demands in H—l."(7) A Virginia officer described the deceased colonel as having been "of small stature, probably 5' 9 in. in height, 135 or 140 lbs. weight, a light, sandy colored mustache and goatee to match…a man of intellect, ambition and rash daring. His body has been taken to Lewisburg."(8)

The next day it was business as usual and Gen. Floyd notified Gen. Lee that high water had damaged the roads and bridges between Meadow Bluff and Big Sewell. He said two bridges between their camps were completely washed away and he had men out replacing them as rapidly as possible. That afternoon additional supplies reached Meadow Bluff from Col. Croghan at White Sulphur Springs. Croghan said he had discovered the reason for the delay in shipment of supplies to Camp Defiance.

Apparently, Gen. Wise failed to rescind his order of September 18, that no additional supplies be forwarded pending a movement nearer Lewisburg. Generals Lee and Floyd knew nothing of the order and, by the time it was discovered, the supply situation at Big Sewell was desperate indeed. Colonel Croghan remained at White Sulphur Springs several more days, attempting to speed the movement of supplies and organizing the quartermaster department there. He informed Gen. Floyd that he was sending five boxes of overcoats, 400 rounds of cannon ammunition, and 50,000 rounds of small arms cartridges; also that 12 barrels of floor and one entire wagon load of pork had been washed away by the flooding Greenbrier River. Croghan said the bridge one mile below him washed out and he was having it repaired.(9)

At 5 p.m. Phillips Legion of Cavalry arrived at Meadow Bluff, having laid over one night at Lewisburg, as had Gen. Loring's men, who reached Floyd's camp one hour later. It was 80 miles from their previous camp in Randolph County to Meadow Bluff and these men walked the entire distance through deep mud and high water. That evening Gen. Floyd ordered Gen. Reese T. Bowen, commander of the Tazewell County militia, 112th Regiment, to select 200 men of his command and send them on a scouting mission to Boone County. Gen. Floyd was studying the possibility of wintering in either Logan or Wyoming County. He told Bowen to have his men carefully watch the enemy in that area and report all their movements.(10) At Sewell Mountain, Gen. Lee was busy preparing for an enemy attack that he hoped would come. He issued orders requiring the commander of each regiment to send all surplus baggage to Lewisburg. Further, Lee wanted preparation of provisions done at night, and he required all baggage wagons packed and ready to go at daylight each morning. These preparations would speed their retreat should one become necessary, and would prevent the type of losses sustained in Floyd's retreat from Carnifex Ferry.(11)

Sunday, September 29, dawned clear and pleasant, a welcomed respite from cold rain and whipping winds. Over in the Federal camp at Sewell Mountain, Major Hayes penned a letter to his wife: "A beautiful bright Sunday morning after a cold, bitter, dismal storm of three days...no teams can supply us here much longer. In this state of things we shall probably be content with holding the strong points already taken without fighting for more until another campaign."(12) At 1 p.m. three additional Ohio infantry regiments reached Sewell Mountain, swelling Gen. Rosecrans command to approximately 8,200 men. Of that number a great many were sick, however, and unfit for duty. By the first of October, Federal manpower was reduced by disease to just over 5,000 men.

Camp Defiance was also reinforced on the 29th with the arrival of the 42nd and 48th Virginia Infantry and two cannons. After their arrival, Gen. Lee wrote Floyd telling him that the concentration of so large a force would require great energy on the part of the commissary and quartermaster departments. Lee said he would require 50 barrels of flour per day and provender for the animals. The concentration of Confederate forces at Meadow Bluff and Sewell Mountain left just a small command at Camp Arbuckle, four miles west of Lewisburg. This camp was a staging area and depot for the South off and on throughout the war. During September and October 1861, it was under the immediate command of Captain John P. Sheffey, of the 8th Virginia Cavalry. A 23-year-old prewar attorney and native of Smyth County, Virginia, Sheffey did not like his monotonous duties at Camp Arbuckle. He desired to be closer to the scene of action, as he explained in a letter home: "Amid the turmoil and confusion, rapid military movements and exciting preparations for battle around me, I have been condemned to a life of comparative monotone, left...commander of this post, I have many duties but they compose a dull routine to which I cannot reconcile myself..." Captain Sheffey also did not like the fact that most of the cavalry from Smyth and Tazewell counties had been turned over to the command of Col. St. George Croghan, a man he considered "eccentric, I might say insane..." He did not find fault with Gen. Lee, however, describing him as "about the size of Gen. Floyd, has a huge iron grey mustache and is the finest looking man in the army." Sheffey referred to Gen. Floyd as "The

Grey Eagle," and claimed that if Floyd had been in command of 25,000 men, they would have fought their way to the Ohio River.(13)

That evening Gen. Floyd sent Lee a dispatch telling him that he would arrive in person at Camp Defiance the next day. Lee replied that he would be happy to see him and expressed his desire to drive the enemy "over the Gauley." Gen. Lee began to worry that the enemy would not attack him and, should that be the case, he was determined to go on the offensive. He proposed to do that by reinforcing the Wise Legion with the militia from Meadow Bluff. Lee would then lead his remaining force of 7,000 men around the enemy's flank to attack their rear. Just before midnight, the three Tennessee infantry regiments that had been encamped near Meadow Bluff reached Big Sewell Mountain. These men were placed along the fortified ridge of the Confederate right flank. The movement to Camp Defiance by Gen. Floyd with another 2,000 men was completed on October 1. The force now under Lee's command was approximately 9,000 men and about 20 cannons.

With winter rapidly approaching and disease decimating troop strength, both armies knew something must be accomplished very quickly or the campaign abandoned. By October 1st, Gen. Rosecrans commanders began expressing open opposition to remaining at Sewell Mountain. The officers felt it was time to return to their supply base at Gauley Bridge. Rosecrans was against a withdrawal, saying he wanted to be patient and await Lee's attack. More and more frequently articles began to appear in newspapers of the North and South critical of the conduct of the West Virginia campaign. General Rosecrans was severely criticized in the *Cincinnatti Enquirer* for failing to advance on Staunton and Richmond. His "inspiring visions of advance," the paper wrote, "all fade away before the dull reality that the roads are becoming impassable..." Gen. Lee was similarly abused by the press, being dubbed "Granny Lee," and "The King of Spades," for his perceived "excess of caution."

On October 2, the cold rain and biting winds returned, adding substantially to the sick lists of Blue and Gray alike. Both armies kept diligent watch over the other and each day brought a new round of brief skirmishing encounters. The situation was unchanged on October 3, although there seemed to be increased activity in the Federal camps. Watching the enemy movements with his binoculars, Gen. Lee believed an enemy attack was imminent. That evening he ordered all non-essential baggage and supplies taken back toward Lewisburg, out of harm's way. Looking over at Rosecrans position, Lee told Gen. Floyd that he believed they could "whip that fellow right where he is but it will cost us 1,500 men." Contemplating the price of victory, Lee then asked, "will it pay?"(14) The next morning, Gen. Lee was told of some complaints by citizens that wagons and teams "pressed" into service had not been returned to their owners. Lee ordered his quartermaster to release all private wagons then hauling grain to Lewisburg once their delivery was made. From that time forward his quartermaster was told to rely only on wagons he could employ. Gen. Lee was also told on the 4th about some men coming into Greenbrier County claiming to have been run off from their homes. This message came from Samuel Ludington, beef supplier with Lee's quartermaster department. Mr. Ludington said men from Nicholas County were coming south by way of the Cold Knob Road into Sinking Creek Valley. He worried that

Opposite: Sewell Mountain camp of the Richmond Light Infantry Blues, 1861. The hand-lettered comments of the soldiers follow. Top row, left to right: 1. Iwish the man who got bit by this pig would have to kill him. 2. Fall in guard for guard mount. 3. Lord, God, I can eat half that bread myself. 4. Here is a chicken I want to have it cooked. 5. Oh, by George we got us plenty bread. 6. Damn this beef I wish would have a change. 7. Well Hopkins how do you feel this morning. 8. Oh, I feel sick at my stomach, headache, pain in my back and breast, got the rheumatism and I don't feel altogether well. 9. I'll be damned if I bring any more wood. 10. I wish massa Wilmore had out in dis part of da country. 11. I'm with you, give us your hand brother. 12. Well to tell the truth I didn't do no more than I can help. 13. I don't believe in cooking it is too much like work. Bottom row, left to right: 14. Fried biscuits are done. What do you put potatoes in with flour for? 15. Why the potatoes make the flour go twice as far. 16. I would like to win one of those potatoes. *Courtesy Virginia Historical Society*

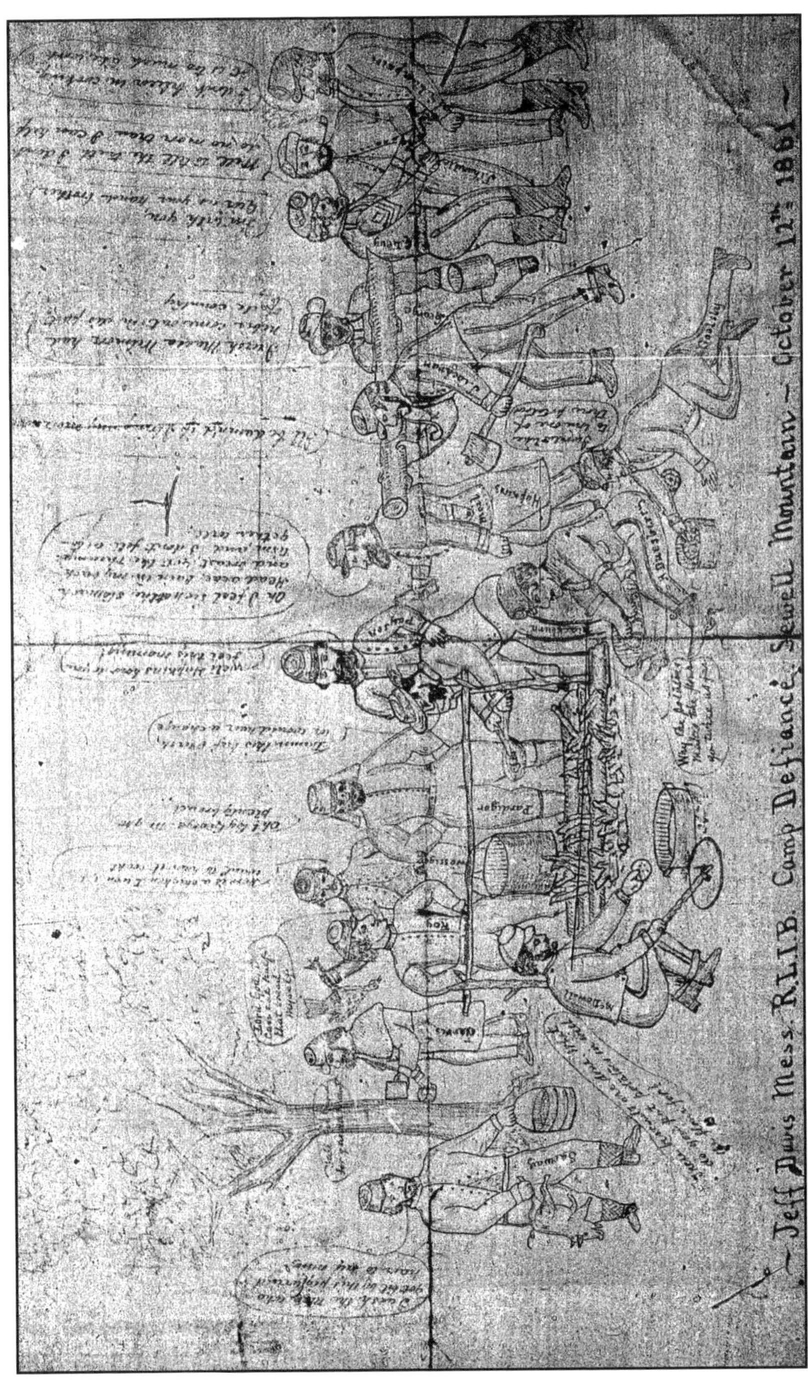
Jeff Davis Mess. R.I.I.B. Camp Defiance, Sewell Mountain — October 12th 1861

Looking west along Rt. 60 (James River and Kanawha Turnpike) at Rainelle. Sewell Mountain is visible in the background. *Photo by author*

some of these men could be spies for the North, attempting to obtain information of "all your forces and movements."(15) Indeed there was some spying taking place, but refugees had nothing to do with it. Members of the 10th Ohio Infantry were sent out at noon of the 4th on yet another Federal reconnaissance. Taking a detour of several miles around the Confederate left flank, these men came secretly upon the rear of Lee's lingering army. Once in position, they studied the movement and positions of their adversaries and as soon as darkness fell returned quietly to camp. They reported finding a "series of formidable earthworks, and a line of camps extending a distance of about five miles." This report seemed to confirm the Yankees suspicion that Lee's army vastly outnumbered their own. In fact, both armies were nearly identical in numbers and both had suffered serious loss of manpower due to disease. (16)

October 5 was a dry and pleasant day and it was spent like the previous day, in hourly expectation of a fight. Manning the breastworks all day gave soldiers the time to write letters home. One Virginia soldier told his wife that he had ridden twice along the high hills of Camp Defiance, in full view and range of Yankee cannon. He said he "looked the impudent fellows in the face," and that "with a glass you can distinguish the white men from the negroes in their camp."(17) Another soldier wrote that he enjoyed the Yankee band more than their own. Both bands played frequently, their sounds intermingling in the mountain air. "They have the best band of music that ever I heard," he wrote, adding that he was "very tired of this place."(18)

When dawn's light broke the darkness of October 6, Gen. Lee's weary men stared in disbelief toward the Federal camp. To everyone's complete surprise, the entire Federal army had secretly withdrawn from their front. During the night some of the Rebel pickets heard the rumbling of wheels and some conversation, but thought nothing of it. They thought the Yankees were just rearranging their artillery as they frequently did. By the time the Confederates realized what had happened, the Union rear guard was two or three miles beyond Sewell Mountain. Gen. Lee sent some cavalry in pursuit, but as he had anticipated, the Yankees blocked the road by chopping trees down. Disbelief and anger were prevalent in the Confederate camps. These men knew they could not go home until the Union army was defeated. Now their adversary had slyly slipped away in the night, as had Gen. Floyd from Carnifex Ferry, four weeks previous. The old adage "seeing-is-believing" applied here and Gen. Lee decided to visit Rosecrans' former camp personally. This visit was described by one of Floyd's staff officers, who went along for the tour: "Gen. Floyd, Gen. Lee, Major Glass & myself at once rode over to the recent camp of the Yankees...the whole ground for hundreds of yards was strewn with coffee, beans, soap, boxes, & all manner of camp & cooking utensils, which were of immense value. The general [Floyd] by good fortune, captured a splendid saddle. Major Glass & myself...laid up for ourselves a splendid camp chest filled with every conceivable convenience...."(19)

Indeed the Yankees did abandon a great deal of material in their retreat. In fact, the Union rear guard became so nervous with the approach of dawn that they turned entire wagon loads of supplies over into the steep mountain ravines that lined the road. Barrels of pork, flour, salt, sugar, and every item of subsistence were broken open, their contents poured out to speed their flight. The total value of abandoned property was variously estimated at between $30,000 and $50,000 dollars. Adjusted to its value in 2004, approximately $1 million dollars' worth of supplies were lost or destroyed in the rugged wilds of Sewell Mountain.

The Union army withdrew to its camps at and near Gauley Bridge. They would not seriously threaten Greenbrier County again until the spring of 1862. Once again, Gen. Lee became the object of ridicule in some Southern newspapers. Allowing the impudent Yankees to escape without a decisive battle was more than the editors of South Carolina's *Charleston Mercury* could swallow: "Poor Lee! Rosecrans has fooled him again. Are the roads any worse for Lee than Rosecrans? The people are getting mighty sick of this dilly-dally, dirt digging, scientific warfare; so much so that they will demand that the great entrencher be brought back and permitted to pay court to the ladies."

Of course the reality of the situation could not be known by someone writing from the comfort of his newspaper office. On October 7, Lee wrote to his wife, Mary, telling her of the enemy's escape and commenting on the bad press he received: "...When day appeared, the bird had flown, and the misfortune was that the reduced condition of our horses for want of provender, exposure to cold rains in these mountains, and want of provisions for the men, prevented the vigorous pursuit and follow up that was proper. We can only get up provision from day to day...I am sorry, as you say, that the movements of the armies cannot keep pace with the expectations of the editors of the papers. I know they can regulate matters satisfactorily to themselves on paper. I wish they could do so in the field...I hope something will be done to please them..."(20)

Gen. Lee quickly formed a plan of advance for the Floyd Brigade that would have them move to the south side of the Kanawha River. In that position they could cut the Union army's communications and, if reinforced, might threaten the Federal governments hold on the area. Gen. Floyd had been advocating such an advance since late September.

With those preparations under way, attention turned to repairing the turnpike toward Lewisburg and caring for the sick. The turnpike through present-day Rainelle was repaired with the help of Gen. Chapman's 19th Brigade of militia. The troops thoroughly drained the road, opened ditches and waterways, and laid timber over all the soft and muddy portions. Gen. Chapman reported his progress on October 8, and asked Lee for permission to disband his brigade: "...yesterday I had 325 of my command with 20, five wagon teams, repairing the road...and today I have 420 engaged at it. They will be able today to complete it to Meadow Bluff....I hope you may deem it prudent at the present time to disband my command, as a few days now will be important to them in seeding, after a week or two it will be too late to insure a crop. Should their services be needed after a few weeks they would be rendered with cheerfulness..."(21)

Gen. Lee also heard from Dr. O.A. Krenshaw, the physician in charge at White Sulphur Springs. Krenshaw's report was tragic and disheartening. He said he had more than 1,000 sick soldiers at the Springs and the overcrowding increased the mortality rate. "I must beg that no more sick be sent here," he wrote, adding that he would inform Gen. Lee when he was ready to accept more patients.(22) At that time, the hospital at Meadow Bluff contained over 200 patients and the Lewisburg hospitals were home to approximately 300 more. At Blue Sulphur Springs, approximately 120 patients occupied the former Allegheny College. Another 173 men occupied the hospital tents at Camp Defiance. Still other soldiers were being cared for in private homes and no estimate of their number has been found It is safe to say that in early October roughly 2,000 soldiers of Lee's command were too sick for duty. That number would nearly double within three weeks.

Of course disease was a serious problem for the Northern forces as well. By October 9, Union army physicians reported 420 patients at Spy Rock and another 1,640 between that place and Gauley Bridge. An additional 160 Union soldiers were hospitalized at Cross Lanes, near Carnifex Ferry. When strong enough to travel, many of the Union patients were loaded onto steamboats and sent to civilian hospitals in Ohio, consequently their mortality rate was generally lower than the Confederates.

William Smith, of the 50th Virginia Infantry, had been working as a hospital steward in Lewisburg for several weeks. He witnessed the slow death from typhoid and other ailments of numerous friends and fellow soldiers. When someone died with whom he had a personal acquaintance, he took it upon himself to inform the man's parents. In a letter to his brother, Smith confessed his fear that the high mortality rate would continue. He wrote about the recent passing of four friends and how distressing it was to see these young men dying almost daily. He said the men were "dropping into the grave in rapid succession," adding that there was no end in sight because the men had "undergone so much exposure."(23) Another soldier commenting on the situation in Lewisburg was Captain J.P. Sheffey, commanding at Camp Arbuckle: "The sickness in the hospitals around here is horrid. Six dead men I understand were carried out of the Lewisburg hospitals today."(24)

A soldier with Phillips Legion Georgia Cavalry, hospitalized at Meadow Bluff, informed his wife of his condition: "I am at Meadow Bluff in the hospital....Our Legion is about 16 miles from here...It is no use to try to tell you what sort of country this is. This is the damndest hole I ever saw and how people live, God only knows, for it is nothing but mountains....For four weeks we have not had but two tents with us and don't get half enough to eat. We pressed another hog yesterday....There is a good many sick here and some deaths. There was a fellow died here yesterday with typhoid fever. They are going to take his remains back to Daltare, Ga."(25)

A member of the 14th North Carolina wrote about the losses in his regiment and the removal of many patients from Camp Defiance to Blue Sulphur Springs: "A great epidemic broke out among us and nearly every one of us was sick. In a regiment of roughly 1,000 there were only 56 guns stacked at one time. The whole regiment was moved to Blue Sulphur Springs...There were barely enough well to nurse the sick. I had typhoid fever and was put into a room with seven others...They were dying all around and I could hear the salute volleys fired over the graves several times a day. Many died in the tents before coming here and were buried by the roadside."(26)

The pitiful situation with the North Carolina men was not exaggerated. Their surgeon, Bedford Brown, reported their condition to Gen. Lee after the Yankees withdrew: "We came to Virginia with 750 privates, that number has been reduced by disease to 277. Our sick men have been deposited at the various hospitals...there has been considerable fatality among our patients...the sick list has continued to increase at the rate of from ten to twelve daily....I received a note from my assistant, Dr. Wilson, stating that the fatality among the patients under his charge at Meadow Bluff, is truly alarming. The quantity of our medical supplies is now exhausted, at least so far as the special remedies are concerned..."(27)

During the fall of 1861, the situation in Lewisburg became so severe that the village was literally overflowing with sick and dying men and boys. The town's citizens did everything in their power to provide assistance but it seemed that nothing could stem the tide of death and sorrow. Ambulance wagons clogged the village streets and not a day passed without the morbid sight of burial parties passing slowly to the graveyards. Hundreds of men were lost on both sides without ever seeing an enemy combatant, slain by disease—the invisible enemy. These were the times "that tried men's souls," and these were the scenes that left indelible images upon the minds of all who witnessed it. Rose W. Fry, granddaughter of Rev. John McElhenney, published her memories of war-time Lewisburg in 1893: "The town was filled to overflowing with sick and dying men. Every public building in the place was converted to their service. The pews were taken up in the lecture-room of the church, and its aisles filled with double rows of cots. The Academy, the Masonic Hall, the hotels, offices, and private dwellings were filled to overflowing. The dead were laid out in the vestibule of the church. The long roll was heard beating the funeral march every day, as some comrade was laid to rest without the glory of the battlefield..."(28)

Gen. Lee's plan to advance Floyd's army into the Kanawha

Valley was implemented on October 12. With their departure, Lee was left at Sewell Mountain with approximately 4,000 men. Having no enemy in his front allowed Gen. Lee an opportunity to rearrange his remaining forces. He ordered the Tennessee regiments to move their camp into the valley of present-day Rainelle, two or three miles east of Camp Defiance. He also ordered the 14th North Carolina back to Meadow Bluff, where they would be better supplied and cared for. Although Gen. Lee had 54 wagons hauling supplies between the Jackson River Depot and Big Sewell, a trip that required 10 days, he found it nearly impossible to keep his command supplied. On the 13th, Lee received an inventory of supplies from his commissary officer. This report stated that 75 barrels of flour were on hand at Meadow Bluff, with 106 additional barrels expected the next day. The depot at White Sulphur Springs held 500 barrels of flour with another 500 en route from Millboro, Virginia. He was also told that horses belonging to the 8th Virginia Cavalry had been sent to Camp Arbuckle, near Lewisburg, to keep them from starving, and that one entire company from the 8th cavalry was unarmed.

Every day Lee or some of his officers received written requests for either discharge or leave of absence due to illness. To these requests would be appended a statement from the regimental physician certifying that the applicant was unfit for duty. In almost every case during the fall of 1861 typhoid was listed as the ailment. Typhoid fever is a life-threatening ailment caused by the bacteria Salmonella typhi. The illness causes sustained fever, severe headache, anorexia, slow heart rate, constipation or diarrhea, and cough. The disease is spread by drinking water or eating food contaminated with the Salmonella bacterium. Water polluted with the feces or urine of infected persons is the most common source of typhoid. Contaminated milk and milk products have also been shown as a source of infection. People can transmit the disease as long as the bacteria remain in their system. Symptoms usually occur within one to three weeks, but can appear within three days or up to three months after consumption of contaminated food or water. Historians believe that an outbreak of typhoid was responsible for the deaths of more than 6,000 settlers at Jamestown, Virginia, between 1607 and 1624. Not until 1948 was an antibiotic available to combat typhoid, and the disease still affects 17 million people worldwide every year. Even in this modern age, the mortality rate from typhoid can be as high as 20% among those who do not get proper treatment. It is therefore easy to see how and why this easily transmitted disease decimated armies of the Blue and Gray during the Civil War. Had medical science and proper camp sanitation been advanced further than it was in 1861, much of the disease problem would have been reduced. Most of the regimental surgeons and commanders in both armies were inexperienced in field sanitation. They did not realize, for example, that hilly terrain contributed to the drainage of surface water and human excrement from camps into water supplies at lower levels. Hospital facilities, segregation, and medical supply were also poor, exacerbating the problem.

On October 15, Lee wrote to Gen. Floyd explaining why he had not been able to advance toward the Kanawha Valley with his remaining forces: "I should have advanced toward Gauley, had it been possible to take the road…I sent the quartermaster and commissary on the road to see what could be procured and they report literally nothing…the men of the Wise Legion are suffering much for want of clothing. The horses of the command are without provender." Lee also indicated starvation was not a distant threat, saying, "We barely get bread from day to day. No forage." (29)

The next day Lee wrote again to Gen. Floyd, discussing the various locations of the enemy and telling his subordinate that the occupation of Cotton Hill, opposite Gauley Bridge, would put his army in position to annoy the enemy. This was merely a suggestion, however, with the final decision left to Floyd's discretion: "You must judge of the means at your disposal how you can best operate against them or whether any aid can be given you on this side…Gen. Loring thinks it important for his command to return to his line [Pocahontas County]. The reports from there indicate another attack."(30)

Gen. Lee was rapidly coming to the conclusion that the West

Gen. W.W. Loring CSA, 1818-1886. *Courtesy USAMHI*

Virginia campaigns were drawing to a close. He focused his energy on organizing matters in Greenbrier County and forwarding supplies to Floyd in the Kanawha Valley. On October 16, he issued orders intended to facilitate the transportation of mail between Big Sewell Mountain and Lewisburg: "A military express will leave these headquarters daily at 9 a.m. arriving at Lewisburg at 3 p.m. Leave Lewisburg for headquarters at 9 a.m. arriving at camp at 3 p.m. The express matter will be deposited at P.O. Lewisburg where the couriers will report daily at 9 a.m. A detail will be made of six mounted men to carry the military express between these headquarters and Lewisburg; three running each way & one reporting daily at headquarters at 8 a.m."(31)

By October 18, all but a few of the sick men at Camp Defiance had been relocated to the various hospitals in Greenbrier County. On the 19th, Gen. Lee issued orders stating that the camps at Big Sewell would be moved to the eastern base of the mountain, present-day Rainelle, the next morning. The infantry was told to march first, followed by the artillery. The cavalry was ordered to maintain their present position, keeping scouts on the turnpike and Old State Road until further orders. This movement away from Sewell Mountain was completed on schedule. With winter approaching and little prospect for any decisive military action remaining, Gen. Lee decided to return to Richmond. He notified Gen. Floyd of his decision on October 20, and also explained that military necessity required him to order Gen. Loring's command back to their old camps on the Huntersville line: "I must inform you that General Loring has received dispatches tonight from Generals Jackson and Donelson confirmatory of several previous reports indicative of attacks on both of their lines, and calling for aid. I have resisted these appeals…in the hope of uniting in an attack with your force…on General Rosecrans. I do not think it proper to retain Gen. Loring any longer…and I have not heard what time you expect to make your contemplated movement down the Kanawha…On reaching Meadow Bluff I will inform you of the probable time of my return to Richmond."(32)

Federal troops had been engaged for several days in minor activity in the direction of the Staunton and Virginia Central Railroad, and it would have been improper for Lee to maintain such a large force in an area of inactivity. He issued marching orders to Gen. Loring's command during the evening of October 20: "The dispatches from Generals Jackson [Henry R. not *Stonewall* Jackson] & Donelson…endear me to direct your return…to your former station. You will therefore commence your march without unnecessary delay. I regret the necessity that calls you from this line…& take the occasion to thank you and them for the alacrity with which you came to its support when threatened by an overwhelming force and the cheerfulness with which you have operated in its defense."(33) Over the course of the next two days Loring's men marched away from Greenbrier County. A civilian visitor in Lewisburg described their departure: "One regiment passed last evening, and another is passing while I write. It is cold and raw and showery, and some of the regiment that passed this morning came in last night, and in the dark and wet and mud, poor fellows, could get no place to sleep or anything to eat. A distant relative of mine here of the name of Wetzel provided for six of them. Many lay out in the rain all night; many drank and caroused all night, and I am really fearful that it is this unnecessary exposure that has got so many on the sick list."(34)

Early the next morning General Lee rode away from Sewell Mountain never to return. He moved the few soldiers remaining at Camp Defiance to Meadow Bluff, where he established temporary headquarters. On that same date, Gen. Floyd's command camped within five miles of the Yankees, after a difficult march of 10 days. Gen. Floyd was manifestly agitated over Lee's decision to order Loring away and return himself to Richmond. Nevertheless, within a few days, Gen. Lee and his staff would pass through Lewisburg en route to Richmond. Robert E. Lee did not return to Greenbrier County until two years after his surrender at Appomattox.

CHAPTER SIX
THE HARD HAND OF WAR

Gen. Loring's command reached Frankford, northeast of Lewisburg, on October 23. Several dozen sick soldiers were being cared for in the private homes of that village. Some of these men belonged to the 16th Tennessee Infantry and were left behind when their regiment marched to Sewell Mountain. Their captain was pleased to be reunited with them and with "Reese," his young colored servant, also left behind. The captain said that at Frankford he "fell behind the regiment to attend to some sick soldiers I left here on my way to Big Sewell. Found them doing very well....My waiting boy, Reese, whom I also left here with the soldiers, is still here, but very low, past recovering." The next day he wrote that he had given "Mrs. Scott $20.00 for her kindness to my sick." He went on alone that morning to overtake his regiment, catching up with them that night. The following day he received word that Reese had passed away: "My boy at Frankford died this p.m. at 2 o'clock. He was a faithful servant, and expressed a lively hope in the atoning blood of the Lamb of God."(1)

Gen. Lee was busy at Meadow Bluff on the 23rd tending to the minutiae of military administration. He appointed Captain J.C. Hill of the Wise Legion as Provost Marshall and ordered him to control the flow of people in and out of the camps who were not connected with the army. Citizens claiming to have business with the army were required to prove the necessity of their visit. When their business was completed, they were not allowed to leave the camps until furnished with a proper military pass by the Provost Marshall's office. This was an attempt to curtail the activities of "camp followers" and people who may intentionally or unintentionally pass military information to the enemy. Gen. Lee also ordered Dr. Krenshaw, Medical Director at White Sulphur Springs, to take under his charge the hospitals at Lewisburg. Lee told him not to send anyone to the hospitals except those who actually required medical treatment, and not to accept those who did come unless they carried an order from their regimental surgeon. When a patient became well enough to return to duty, he was not to leave the hospital without a written discharge. (2)

A private with the 60th Virginia Infantry stationed at Meadow Bluff wrote to his parents on the 23rd, telling them that out of 98 men in his company, 43 were sick.(3) A Georgia soldier, unimpressed with the mountains of West Virginia, complained bitterly that "western Virginia is not worth fighting for, it is the rag end of Hell, it is nothing but mountains."(4) Still another soldier, this one a Virginian, saw in the situation at Meadow Bluff an opportunity for free enterprise. After asking his family to send him some new boots because he was "near barefooted," he asked his wife to have the "old man" construct a box and "bring me five or ten gallons of whiskey." This box was to be of sufficient quality to keep the contents secret. He said whiskey sold for "from one to four dollars a pint, quarts sell readily at two to five dollars each. Anything that can be brought here will bring any price. I want you to send me some butter, five or ten pounds and what clothing that you can get...socks is worth seventy five cents a pair here, everything is worth four or five prices..." A few days later, this entrepreneur identified another revenue source. He told his family that three men from his company had deserted and probably gone home. If his family would locate these miscreants and return them to camp, they were worth "thirty dollars for each."(5)

Having been notified by Gen. Lee of his intention to return to Richmond, and not agreeing with that decision, Gen. Floyd wrote to the Secretary of War asking for reinforcements. Gen. Floyd believed that with 10,000 men he could defeat the enemy before winter. From his position on Cotton Hill across from Gauley Bridge, the old governor could count enemy regiments. He overestimated their strength as 13,000 when actually the number was closer to 9,000 and those were scattered out over several miles. Floyd wrote that in the position the Yankees had selected, they would always be ready to "strike Lewisburg" whenever the army at Sewell Mountain and Meadow Bluff was removed. "I have only to seize the river and roads between them and the Ohio," Floyd said, "and the base of their operations is at once destroyed." He also told the Secretary that with the departure of Generals Lee and Loring, the enemy might attempt an advance on Lewisburg. If reinforced before that happened, he said he would have "sufficient army to cross the river [and] stop him in full career by cutting his communication and supplies." The fact was the Floyd Brigade was so weakened by disease and poor supply that anything other than a very brief offensive operation was impossible. Floyd's brigade left hundreds of sick soldiers behind in Greenbrier County and the relentless progress of disease continued to erode his available manpower. In the first month after Gen. Floyd advanced from Sewell Mountain to the Kanawha Valley, his physicians discharged 52 men for disability. An additional 29 men were granted leave of absence to regain their health. More than one dozen officers of various regiments resigned their commissions while on Cotton Hill and returned home. Five of these officers belonged to the 13th Georgia Infantry. Their departure left that regiment in serious need of experienced commanders. Such was the state of affairs in the Floyd Brigade when the former governor was telling the Secretary of War about his plans of conquest.(6)

Gen. Floyd wrote again to the Secretary of War on October 27, informing him that he had artillery in position to attack the enemy at Gauley Bridge. He said the enemy force was larger than his, and asked the War Department to order Gen. Lee to support his attack. "I have done my part of this work," he wrote, "but I have not heard of Gen. Lee's movements."(7) This was a false claim on Gen. Floyd's part, because Lee told him on the 20th that he was ordering Loring away and moving his own headquarters to Meadow Bluff pending his return to Richmond. On Monday, October 28, Lee received an odd correspondence from Gen. Floyd. In it he said he was ready for active operations and that his cannon were in place to harass the enemy. He told Lee that if he would "make a decided movement in advance," it was certain they would capture the "whole of the Northern army." (8)

A military man by training, Gen. Lee of course knew that Floyd's grandiose plans were improbable. Waiting until the following day to reply, Lee told his subordinate that he had informed him on the 20th of his plans. Lee said all the sick of his command had been sent to the hospitals and that he visited the hospital at Blue Sulphur Springs personally. He said he found that hospital very poorly managed, but that the sick there were improving. Lee said the troops from North Carolina and Mississippi were still with him at Meadow Bluff, and reported by the physician as doing well. He said he failed in attempts to locate a better camping ground at Meadow Bluff and that he would be leaving that very day. "I shall visit the hospital at Lewisburg and White Sulphur," Lee wrote, "and proceed thence to Richmond." Leaving Col. James L. Davis in command at Meadow Bluff, Lee turned his horse eastward and rode away. He would not return to Greenbrier County until 1867.(9)

Writing after the war, Col. Walter H. Taylor, Lee's trusted aide, described the situation in West Virginia in 1861: "...the lateness of the season and the condition of the roads precluded the idea of earnest aggressive operations, and the campaign in Western Virginia was virtually concluded...General Lee cannot be reasonably held accountable. Disaster had befallen the Confederate arms, and the worst had been accomplished, before he reached the theatre of operations; the Alleghenies then constituted the dividing line between the hostile forces, and in this network of mountains, sterile and rendered absolutely impracticable by a prolonged season of rain, nature had provided an insurmountable barrier."(10)

Lee's departure did indeed signal the loss of western Virginia to the Confederacy. On October 24, a majority of those who voted overwhelmingly approved the new-state plan. This "secession" from the Confederacy led to the admission of West Virginia as the 35th state in the Union. Gen. Floyd remained on the Kanawha line for two more weeks. On November 1, he opened fire with artillery on the U.S. positions at and near Gauley Bridge. This was more a harassing action than a serious threat to Federal control of the area. After an artillery duel that lasted six days, Floyd's guns were silenced. He was driven completely out of the area in a series of running skirmishes that began on November 10. By November 14, there were no organized Confederate forces west of Meadow Bluff. In his running, haphazard retreat, Gen. Floyd lost several men killed and wounded. Among those killed in combat was Col. St. George Croghan, Floyd's eccentric cavalry commander. The Floyd Brigade continued its retreat until it reached the security of Dublin Depot, Virginia. After a rest and reorganization, Gen. Floyd's entire command, with the exception of the 22nd Virginia Infantry, was transferred to Bowling Green, Kentucky, to serve under Gen. Albert Sidney Johnston. With the Southern forces thus dispersed, several regiments under Gen. Rosecrans were also sent to Kentucky, and the remainder began preparing winter quarters in and near the Kanawha Valley.

The only Confederate forces of any size remaining in Greenbrier County were the cavalry under Col. James L. Davis at Meadow Bluff and two Tennessee Infantry regiments under Gen. D.S. Donelson near Caldwell. On November 13, Col. Davis wrote to the Secretary of War telling him that his camp at Meadow Bluff was one of the most important positions in the state. He proposed establishing winter quarters there so as to protect Lewisburg and restore the "wavering confidence of the community." With fewer than 2,000 Southern soldiers occupying the county, many of its citizens felt abandoned by the South. To calm the fears of the public, Davis wanted not only to remain where he was over the winter, but he also hoped to build a steam sawmill to produce planks with which the roads could be prepared for the spring campaign. Wood, coal, and good water were abundant in the area and the local people were "loyal and true to the Southern Confederacy." Within a few days, the Confederates had constructed 110 log huts or small cabins for winter quarters. Scouts were kept out on all roads the enemy might use to invade the county and efforts were made to stockpile supplies.(11)

The Tennessee regiments near Caldwell were waiting on clothing and other supplies to reach them, after which they expected to join Gen. Floyd's command in Kentucky. The Tennesseans were still in great need of blankets, clothing and shoes. Their wait for supplies had been so long and their hardships so great, the men became thoroughly disgusted. A member of the 16th Tennessee Infantry spoke for the majority, saying, "If we haven't seen Hell here, I don't know when we will." Gen. Donelson spent several days in Lewisburg preparing for the move and communicating with Richmond by telegraph. Because of persistent rumors that the enemy planned to invade Greenbrier, Col. Davis asked Donelson to delay his march to Kentucky. This was something Gen. Donelson was not at liberty to do, being under orders from Gen. Floyd to the contrary. Nevertheless, Donelson assured the colonel that in the event of an enemy advance he would assume the responsibility of coming to his aid. The following day, November 20, Donelson sent a dispatch to Gen. Floyd telling him that he was still waiting on the arrival of supplies. He also said he promised Col. Davis that he would reinforce him if attacked, adding that he hoped that promise would meet with Floyd's approval. Donelson also said applications were being made to him for medical discharge and he wanted to know if he should forward those to Gen. Floyd.(12)

Gen. Rosecrans was busy at Gauley Bridge, consolidating his command and preparing for winter. On the 19th, he telegraphed Gen. McClellan at Washington, D.C. telling him that Captain W.F. Reynolds had gone under flag of truce to within one mile of Meadow Bluff. The stated purpose of the mission was to ask Gen. Floyd to stop "kidnapping" unarmed citizens. He complained that citizens were routinely taken hostage and held pending the release of "certain hostages now in our possession." Captain Reynolds reported that the roads to Meadow Bluff were in terrible condition and that dead horses were strewn all along the way from Sewell Mountain to Meadow Bluff. It was true that dozens of horses died during the Sewell Mountain campaign. Rosecrans himself reported that 18 horses froze to death in one night. Reynolds said the Rebels he encountered wore tattered clothing and were poorly armed. As to his plans for the winter, Rosecrans said he would hold the Kanawha Valley; hold the Cheat Mountain Pass in Randolph County; hold Romney and Red-House; guard the railroads; recruit men, and put the "Mud River and Guyandotte Valleys in order." These objectives would be easier met, he said, if the army got rid of the "lazy, cowardly, slothful, and worthless officers" that infested it. Two days later he informed McClellan that a Union man who lived in Richmond had passed through the Confederate lines in Greenbrier County. This man reported just 600 Rebels at Meadow Bluff, with defensive works four miles nearer Lewisburg.(13)

Samuel Price was a 55-year-old Lewisburg attorney who spent some time in Richmond during the fall of 1861. As the military situation grew more precarious in Greenbrier County, several citizens began to write to Mr. Price asking him to intervene with the government. Accordingly, he wrote to the Secretary of War on the 23rd, telling him about the "excitement in Greenbrier." If the Yankees made it into Greenbrier and Monroe counties, he said nothing but distance would prevent their occupation of Botetourt, Rockbridge, and Augusta counties. Having a force of just 500 or 600 men at Meadow Bluff would prove insufficient to prevent their advance. "Can nothing be done," he asked, "to afford some sort of security to the people?" The Secretary of War told Mr. Price that it was absurd to believe the Federal Army would invade the Greenbrier country during the winter. He promised, however, that he would keep sufficient force in the area to protect Lewisburg from raids by forces not exceeding 100 men. This he failed to do in a timely manner and, when Mr. Price returned to Lewisburg, he found that Confederate forces were still being drained from the area with no replacements sent. (14)

Security for citizens was a valid issue, not only because of the movement of large armies, but because of the actions of soldiers alone or in small groups. Over the course of the war, hundreds of West Virginians fled their homes to the North or South. Many believed that by remaining home they risked imprisonment or conscription. With most of the able-bodied men away in the army, it was not uncommon to see women and children fleeing their homes to some place of assumed safety. In November 1861, the movement of a family out of Greenbrier County resulted in a tragic incident. Early in the war, Philip Duffy, a prominent citizen of Braxton County, moved his family to Greenbrier County. Philip Duffy was 48-years old, his wife, Sarah, was 31. The Duffy's had relatives in Nicholas County and Mrs. Duffy decided to go there, perhaps intending to return to Braxton. She packed up many of her valuables, including silverware and cash, and rode away from her temporary home near Meadow Bluff. She was accompanied by Lewis Beckner, a family friend from Nicholas County, and a young man who claimed to be 17-years old. This was probably her son, Patrick, age 22, who was on medical leave from the Braxton Blues, a Confederate company that he organized in the spring of 1861. They planned their ride so as to reach Nicholas County during the night, apparently in the mistaken hope that they would pass unnoticed by Yankee pickets. Everything progressed as planned until they came near the Nicholas County home of a Mr. Remly. Pickets of the 36th Ohio Infantry were quartered in a schoolhouse near Remly's place. While busy preparing to cook some chickens they had just "pressed" into service, the pickets heard the dull thud of approaching horses and ran outside. Staring into the coal black night, the pickets counted three riders. "Halt! Who goes there," they shouted. "Friends" came the reply. "Advance and state your business." Mrs. Duffy calmly replied that they were on their way to a house three or four miles further where they expected to spend the night. When the pickets attempted to question Mr. Beckner, he kept his eyes toward the ground and pretended to be ignorant. Mrs. Duffy spoke up, saying that he was her mulatto slave and was poorly educated. Something did not seem right. Beckner was a very large bearded man wearing a broad-rimmed hat that was pulled down well over his face. Even in the mountain darkness the suspicious pickets could tell he was not a Negro. Another curiosity was the fact that the young man with Mrs. Duffy was wearing a Confederate overcoat and, when questioned, said he was just 17-years-old. The pickets asked where he got his Rebel jacket. The boy replied that he bought it from a man in Greenbrier County. "You'll all have to go with us to see the captain," they replied. They found the captain staying in a nearby house. The captain told Mrs. Duffy to dismount while his men searched her saddlebags. They found "a quantity of silver plates, table & tea spoons, forks, butter knives, and a superbly carved silver decanter." They also found $215.00 in cash.

Apparently they planned to pass Mr. Beckner off as a slave so that his true identity would not be determined. Perhaps Beckner believed he would be jailed as a Confederate sympathizer. Whatever the reason for the attempted ruse, it soon collapsed. When the captain grew suspicious, he ordered the group into the cabin where he could question them in the light. Mrs. Duffy protested that she wanted a private meeting with the officer, saying that her mulatto slave knew nothing. Undeterred, the captain ordered Beckner off his horse and into the house. Mr. Beckner reluctantly dismounted and walked slowly toward the house. The pickets, already suspicious, kept their muskets ready. When Beckner stepped onto the porch, light from the house began to reveal his face. Suddenly he bolted past the pickets and jumped off the end of the porch. One of the pickets yelled "Halt," but he kept running and was shot in the back. Knocked down by the shock of the musket ball, he quickly "regained his feet" and started off again. By this time the picket was at his side and, using his musket for a club, "dealt him a heavy blow with might & main upon the head." Two pickets carried the bleeding man into the cabin "where after writhing in agony for an hour he died." Mrs. Duffy took the man's death very hard. She retrieved her "prayer-book" from her saddlebags and summoned Beckner's executioner to her side. The picket told the tale in his army journal: "Then kneeling close by me & by the side of the corpse she commenced reading and talking. For half an hour she lectured me. Never before, since I was born a little fellow, did I ever receive such a lecture....I considered my act justifiable....When she gave me to understand that I could go, I made my exit more willingly & with far more grace than I did my entrance."

When word of the refugee's fate reached Meadow Bluff, Col.

James L. Davis wrote a letter of protest to Gen. Rosecrans: "Meadow Bluff, Dec. 1st 1861...U.S. soldiers stationed near Summersville...arrested an unoffending female, Mrs. Duffie, while traveling on the highway...and assassinated her escort....the latter was an inoffensive citizen, the father of six small children, now destitute of subsistence...I would ask whether your sense of justice...will not suggest some punishment for the perpetrators. The officers of the Wise Legion will make some provision for the little orphans of the victim of foul murderers, wearing the uniform of US soldiers..."(15) Mrs. Duffy and her "teenage" escort were released the day after Beckner was killed.

Public confidence in the Confederate government's ability to protect Greenbrier County continued to erode. On December 7, a petition was submitted to Confederate President Jefferson Davis signed by 79 citizens of Greenbrier County. These citizens had been told that all Southern forces occupying western and northwestern Virginia were to be withdrawn to other fields of action. "Should this be the case," they wrote, "a large and vast amount of property will be left free to the incursions of the enemy, and the personal safety of many good subjects will be jeopardized by the presence of an invading army." They worried that with Greenbrier, Monroe, Pocahontas, and other counties so near enemy lines, their people would be subject to frequent abuse by the enemy. "...This section of the state," they said, "has furnished many companies of volunteers...and the additional fact of the loyalty of its people, protected only by a disorganized and poorly disciplined militia, and in view of the premises generally, your petitioners are of the opinion that this section of the State should be protected..." The first three people signing the petition were prominent citizens of Lewisburg. These were: Johnson Reynolds, a 63-year-old attorney; Daniel H. Stalnaker, a 47-year-old hotel keeper, and Floyd Estill, Lewisburg merchant, age 46. (16)

In response to this plea for protection, the War Department ordered Gen. Floyd to send one regiment to Lewisburg where it would remain during the winter. Their presence would protect the citizens of Greenbrier and Monroe counties from the "incursions of marauders," and would "prevent any panic among them." Gen. Floyd selected the 22nd Virginia Infantry. This regiment was enrolled primarily from the counties of Fayette, Greenbrier, and Kanawha and was a logical choice for the protection of that region. The 22nd Virginia arrived at White Sulphur Springs on January 8, 1862 and encamped at Lewisburg on January 12. Disease had reduced its available manpower to just 325 men.(17)

The much-feared Union raid into Greenbrier County took place in mid-December. Three companies from the 36th Ohio Infantry, about 150 men, left Nicholas County en route to Meadow Bluff on December 16. These men were guided by Riley Ramsey, a Union citizen of Nicholas County whose son was reportedly killed by guerillas sympathetic to the South. Having obtained precise information about the Rebels in Greenbrier from G.W. Shelton, a teenage deserter from the 8th Virginia Cavalry, the Yankees knew what to expect and planned accordingly. Just after daylight of the 17th, the raiding party arrived at the "plantation" of Mr. William H. McFarland, between present-day Rainelle and Little Sewell Mountain. McFarland was president of the Farmers and Mechanics Bank in Richmond. He kept a summer home in Greenbrier County that was described by the Yankees as being "a plantation of 6,000 acres with 200 slaves." They found no enemy soldiers at the farm and just 20 slaves along with their overseer, a Frenchman by the name of Dassonville. McFarland's residence was described as being of the latest style architecture, "beautiful & grand." The Ohio soldiers saw in their raid an opportunity for fun and sought to make the best of it. They determined to spend the night at the plantation. One company camped in the meadow near the house, another at a nearby bridge, and the third occupied the residence. Mr. McFarland's prized horse, valued at $1,800 and said to have taken "first premium" at the Virginia State Fair, was quickly "captured." Nine officers and men of the regiment who walked into Greenbrier County rode out on some of McFarland's best horses. Late that evening five men, newly mounted, rode out into the countryside for several miles, raiding dwellings along the way. The first home they came to belonged to Mr. Andrew Burns, a 51-year-old farmer, whose son, James, was a member of the Confederate 14th Virginia Cavalry. They also raided the home of Mr. John Valk which they found unoccupied. It may be that the Valks had "refugeed North" as they were all natives of New York and Connecticut. During this endeavor, they captured two men who were known to be scouts for the Rebels. They also captured four pistols, one musket, several cartridge and cap boxes, and three sealed letters for Rebel soldiers, found hidden in the attic of a log cabin. They returned to the residence with their "prisoners & plunder," proud of their enterprise.

Early on the 18th, the Yankees divided their force into two raiding parties and advanced on Meadow Bluff by separate routes. They burnt some wheat stacks along the way, destroyed one thrashing machine, rolled a windmill down a hill and confiscated a keg of tobacco. Descending Little Sewell Mountain into Meadow Bluff, the raiders moved to within one-half mile of the Rebel camp when they "broke pell-mell for the rebel encampment." Rushing closer to their goal, the men passed "forty-six new made graves" of Rebel soldiers. To their delight, they discovered that the Rebels fled before their approach and they were thus free to act with impunity. The men were impressed with the rows of recently completed log huts the Rebels planned to use for winter quarters. These structures were "large & commodious, running in straight rows back into a grove." The Yankees thought it was a "beautiful place." Soon the torch was introduced to the beautiful campgrounds and within minutes the entire scene was enveloped in dark swirling smoke. A separate building being used as a storehouse for commissary supplies was also looted and burned. In it, the victorious Yankees confiscated a large amount of Rebel mail, blank report and account forms, books, ink, paper, and tobacco. In the cellar they found several old uniforms, a quantity of tents, and about 1,200 spades, shovels and picks. Most of these items were thrown into some Rebel ambulance wagons nearby, and the entire treasure burned or otherwise destroyed. As the fires did their work, four officers of the 36th Ohio rode out another mile toward Lewisburg to see what plunder they might find. They raided another house and recovered two muskets, a cavalry knapsack, and a large knife. Having done all the damage they could do, and hearing that Confederate soldiers were on the way, they started back toward McFarland's plantation.

The intrepid raiders returned to McFarland's entirely unscathed and camped for the night. On the morning of the 19th, they started for Nicholas County and, after going about 12 miles, camped for the night at the home of Grigsby McClung. Mr. McClung was a 44-year-old farmer whose two sons, Andrew and Edward, were in Confederate service. At daylight of the 20th, they resumed their march. Four or five miles beyond McClung's, and now in Fayette County, they were suddenly attacked by about 70 Rebel soldiers. These men were a combination of infantry and cavalry just arrived from near White Sulphur Springs and commanded by Captain Zachariah McGruder. The Rebels took position on a hill about 120 yards distant from the raiders and opened fire. Their first volley wounded two of the raiders and scattered some others. The excited Yankees determined to take the fight to the Rebels and sped to the hilltop where the fire was coming from. Upon their arrival they found that the enemy had "taken flight" and were beyond range: "They had horses and the moment they fired they leaped upon them and were off. One in his haste left his horse, another a blanket, another a spur, another his cap, etc. They took a bridal path which led them back into the distant hills." Apparently their return fire had taken effect, as they also found at the site a pool of blood, a Rebel captain's hat, and some papers.

The proud Ohioans marched into Summersville on December 20. They brought with them two prisoners, 21 horses, four mules, 91 head of cattle, two yoke of work oxen, one wagon, 115 sheep, 17 rifles and muskets, 12 pistols, several Bowie knives and "other plunder." In his official report of the raid, Major E.B. Andrews described what he said was the mood of the citizens in Greenbrier: "The people of Greenbrier County seemed generally disposed to admit their helplessness as secessionists, and showed a disposition to make friends with the Federal authorities as the stronger power." Major Andrews added his opinion that the raid would "have a good influence, and will tend to place the people of that region on their good behavior." In a subsequent letter home, Major Andrews claimed that if they had not been burdened by their captured cattle they could have easily marched into Lewisburg: "and I have no doubt that we should have been openly welcomed by some, secretly by more, and hated and plotted against only by a few."(18-19)

All of Greenbrier County was in an uproar as word of the raid spread. On December 19, Col. Alexander Welch Reynolds wrote to the Confederate Adjutant General at Richmond. Reynolds was commander of the 50th Virginia Infantry, but he was detached from his regiment and placed in command of the post at White Sulphur Springs from September 26, 1861 until January 3, 1862. Col. Reynolds told the Adjutant General about the raid, saying that he had just received a dispatch that enemy forces were at Meadow Bluff. In response, he said he ordered all of his available force, just 25 men, to proceed to Lewisburg. Reynolds complained that his ammunition and other supplies were entirely unprotected. He then wrote to Major H.B. Davidson, Assistant Adjutant General of Floyd's Brigade, telling him that the raid was then in progress: "I have sent Major Sweeney, of Sixtieth Regiment, with a detachment forward, as far as Lewisburg, to quiet the fears of the people. They are greatly alarmed and complain bitterly of having been left entirely exposed to the enemy."(20)

On December 21, Samuel Price informed William McFarland of the raid on his farm: "On Tuesday evening last the enemy made his appearance in our county on your farm in force...One hundred of your best sheep, your two-year-old cattle, oxen, horses, and mules, including your fine young stud-horse, were

Col. Alexander Welch Reynolds. He was in charge of the Confederate camp at White Sulphur Springs in 1861. *Courtesy State of West Virginia*

carried off....Where the next raid is to be committed I cannot tell. The success of this one will inspire others. Why is the whole of Western Virginia to be given up?....A small force would have prevented this humiliating result, but now the bloodhounds have fleshed their fangs...We must move away from our homes and give up all we possess, or be subject to the invasions and insults of these robbers." (21)

Sgt. Andrew Cook of the 27th Virginia Infantry, then stationed near Winchester, received a letter from his wife telling him about the raid. Cook was from Big Clear Creek Valley, near present-day Rupert. He was among the first men of Greenbrier County sent east during the war. His reply on December 28 would prove to be his last letter home: "I seat myself, lonesome and disconsolate this morning to drop you a few lines...I am aware that the people of Greenbrier are very much dejected and downcast at the prospect of being handed over to the Yankees and I am frank to admit that they have been badly treated by the Government yet I think it will be the best policy for her to hold up till spring anyhow and try and defend the property and families of the Volunteers (as well as their own) until they get home....I have had a very lonesome Christmas..."(22)

Having repeatedly requested a short leave of absence to return home, the prayed-for respite was finally granted on January 13, 1862. Having no horse, Sgt. Cook had to walk or get whatever transportation he could from Winchester in the Shenandoah Valley to Greenbrier County. The cold winter weather slowed his travels, but he finally arrived at the banks of the swollen Greenbrier River on January 20. He stood silent and alone on the bank of the river, his woolen uniform pierced by the cold, whipping winds; his boots so worn that his feet were already numb from exposure. He knew what he had to do. He must swim the icy waters of the Greenbrier or return to Winchester. Memories of home flashed through his mind. The loving embrace of his wife and two little girls beckoned. He dove in. The icy water sent a shockwave through his body, but he swam hard, his eyes focused on the other side. Half frozen and nearly exhausted, he reached the other side and pulled himself onto the snow-covered ground. He knew he must get up and keep moving. He spent the entire day plodding along the frozen road in his wet uniform. He noticed that much of his skin had taken on a blue tint and it was all he could do to keep his teeth from chattering. Late in the day, he made it to Big Clear Creek Valley and then, home. His excited family tossed more wood on the fire and rushed to gather dry clothing for him. It was all too late. Weak and deathly ill from hypothermia, his body shivered uncontrollably and he grew confused. All that they could do was not enough. Two days later, men with shovels broke the frozen ground and laid Sgt. Andrew Cook to rest.

Sgt. Andrew Cook, 27th Virginia Infantry. Among the first to leave Greenbrier County in support of the Confederacy. *Courtesy Mr. and Mrs. Lewis Crawford, Rupert, WV*

Chapter Seven
The Greenbrier White Sulphur Springs

There is something in the prospect of visiting a watering place, which produces a wonderful elasticity of spirit. Renewed health, invigorated strength, and increased zest for life, are associated with the idea, and also escape for a time from the dull cares of life.

Godey's Lady's Book, 1842

The White Sulphur Springs resort we know today as The *Greenbrier* has a fascinating and colorful history that dates back more than 200 years. During most of its early history, including the Civil War years, it was known simply as White Sulphur Springs. When the dark hand of war swept over this region in 1861, it brought with it thousands of Confederate soldiers eager to halt any Union advance west of the Blue Ridge Mountains. Being situated along the heavily traveled James River and Kanawha Turnpike and near the railroad, the resort at White Sulphur Springs was of strategic military importance. The end of the Civil War found the famed resort but a shadow of its former self, having been used repeatedly as military hospital, campground, and cemetery.

For over half a century the White Sulphur Springs, comprising some 7,000 acres, had been widely regarded as the premier summer gathering spot of the southern aristocracy. Here, in the years before the great conflict, had gathered politicians, leading business people of the times, and wealthy travelers. In 1857, the resort was purchased from William Calwell by the White Sulphur Springs Company for $600,000. Of this amount, $200,000 was paid in cash and the balance in promissory notes. The new owners began extensive improvements on the property and, in 1858, a new hotel was completed on the site at a cost of $120,000. Known officially as the Grand Central Hotel, its name later became simply "The Old White." This new facility was over 400 feet long and was lined with wide arched porches for promenading. The upper two floors consisted of 228 guest rooms, while the first floor held the dining hall, parlors, reception rooms and ballroom. The hotel's beautiful parlor, which was advertised as being "half again as big as the celebrated East Room of the White House," occupied the eastern end of the building. An equally large and elegant ballroom occupied the other end of the hotel. By far the largest room of the hotel was the awe inspiring dining hall. Consuming nearly 300 feet of the first floor, this was the largest dining room in the United States. It could comfortably seat 1,200 guests. The Grand Central Hotel did have its faults, however. In December 1860, Mr. Joshua Humphreys, off-season manager, informed the owners that the rafters of the roof were too small and he worried that a heavy snowfall might cause a catastrophe. In 1861, a Confederate surgeon reported weakness in the buildings foundation, and also decried the complete lack of fire escapes.

Between 1857 and the beginning of the Civil War, the resort's guest capacity was further expanded with the addition of several new cottages. These were named Tansas Row (after Tensas Parish, Louisiana), Florida Row, and South Carolina Row. To add romantic flair to the grounds, the wooded hills behind Baltimore, Paradise, and Alabama rows was transformed into a series of walkways. These paths were known as Lovers Walk, Hesitancy Row, Courtship Maze, Rejection Row, Acceptance Way and Paradise Row. Lovers Leap was another well-known feature of the property, although there is no record of anyone accepting the invitation. By the summer tourist season of 1860, just months before the war, the White Sulphur Springs Company had invested $300,000 in improvements at the popular resort. This amount represented a combined investment up to that time of

White Sulphur Springs as it appeared in the 1850s. *Courtesy The Greenbrier, White Sulphur Springs*

The Old White Hotel at White Sulphur Springs in the 1870s. *Courtesy The Greenbrier, White Sulphur Springs*

$900,000, or, converted to its value in 2004, nearly $19 million. (1)

During the decade of the 1850s, debate over sectional differences that would ultimately lead to the disruption of the Union became more intense. A microcosm of the larger social picture was presented at White Sulphur Springs on August 18, 1859 with the arrival of Edmund Ruffin. The retired president of the Virginia Agricultural Society, Ruffin was an outspoken secessionist and militant defender of slavery. When the 65-year-old firebrand arrived at The Old White, he lost no time stirring up political controversy among the 1,200 guests. He found at the resort an influential crowd that included such notables as Governor Manning of South Carolina; John Winston, the ex-Governor of Alabama; Judge John Robertson of the Supreme Court of Appeals in Richmond; the Secretary of the Interior; and various Southern congressmen; businessmen; and ministers. Despite the Southern audience, Ruffin's militant ravings did not receive the response he hoped for. There was "so much bustle" and "such crowds in the parlor and ballroom" that few people would take the time to engage Mr. Ruffin in serious conversation. When he made a return visit in August 1860, Ruffin found a large number of Southern men at the resort who were "contingent or conditional disunionists," depending upon the election of Abraham Lincoln. These men he engaged in talk of secession, but nevertheless he felt alone "as an avowed dis-unionist per se, and I avow that opinion upon every occasion." (2)

Female visitors to The Old White also succumbed to sectional differences in a prewar verbal skirmish that could be called the first battle of White Sulphur Springs. When Southern writer Mary J. Windle visited The Old White, she was sternly rebuked by Northern ladies for having published the following opinion: "Pretty faces are more general in the North, but in grace, beauty and expression, the South has the superiority. In elegance of dress, the southern girl is able to beat the Parisian 'elegantes' of the North with their own weapons, when they consider it worthwhile. The New York belles, in spite of the time and money they waste upon their toilet, are the worst dressed ladies in America."

Edmund Ruffin, 1794-1865. As a visitor to White Sulphur Springs in 1859 he stirred the flames of disunion. *Courtesy National Archives.*

Needless to say, the belles of the North took exception to Windle's inflammatory remarks. Finding her strolling the grounds of the resort, they descended upon her, giving her a tongue-lashing so severe she fled to her room in tears. (3)

The summer of 1860 was a prosperous one for the resorts new owners. During July, the property manager reported that he had reduced the room rate to $2 per day for anyone staying two weeks or longer. Remaining less than two weeks cost $2.50 per day. "My administration is very popular," he wrote, "and the organization regarded by some as perfect. I receive many compliments daily...they say that the improvements are great and not one cause of complaint....We have a delightful company, 6 to 10 stages are loaded daily."(4)

A visitor during the summer of 1860 described the festive mood of the resort in a letter to her daughter: "Leland has found a great many friends from Mississippi...1,200 ate breakfast here day before yesterday...so much promenading, and so much finery....there is every kind of dress and every kind of fashion here....I have been all through the kitchen...they bake 500 pies a day, kill two beeve, 22 sheep, 300 chickens, cook 40 bushels of corn, make from ninety-five to 115 gallons of coffee twice a day besides tea and milk....I have been down to dinner, the dessert was raisin pudding, Atlantic pudding, apple pie, whortleberry pie and coffee...Tell Louisa all things have changed, but the spring and Paradise Row..."(5)

Another prewar visitor, totally charmed with the place, offered this lively description: "It is not natural scenery alone that charms one, but its reflection on surrounding objects captivate. The ladies, for instance, look more beautiful than they would elsewhere, the birds sing more sweetly, people are more natural, less affected, and enjoy life here, and all feel better for this holiday."(6)

During the winter of 1860, the resort sought to hire more help, especially carpenters and a blacksmith. It was discovered that the floor joists of the ice house needed to be replaced and that the slaughterhouse was structurally unsound. The resort was in the practice of bottling its sulphur water for sale and, in January 1861, Joshua Humphreys reported that the resort had on hand enough bottles for 1,200 boxes of two-dozen each. This water was very popular with some people for its presumed medicinal value, although its taste was said to be "almost as awful as its odor."

Despite the secession of the Southern states and the turmoil then rampant across the country, the summer season of 1861 opened at The Old White in June, as it always had. Any hopes the proprietors may have had for some semblance of normalcy, however, were soon dashed. The hotel register begins on June 6, with an entry for Mr. J. Pannell of Richmond, Virginia. No one

Col John S. Mosby in 1864. He visited White Sulphur Springs in August 1861. *Courtesy National Archives*

else registered until June 9, when Allen Caperton of Monroe County signed in, along with two members of his family. Just 41 people, an amazingly small number, registered at the hotel during the first month of the season. On June 26, the names of military personnel began to intermingle with those of civilian guests, and for the entire summer just 125 civilians visited White Sulphur Springs. This meager count stood in stark contrast to previous summers when one might expect to find more than 1,000 guests at the resort at any one time.

The guest register is an excellent primary source for confirming the early war service of hundreds of individuals and many military organizations. It is interesting to note that the entries for many of these men do not match official documents used by the U.S. Government in assembling the Compiled Service Records, or CSR. Either the military unit given in the register does not match the CSR, or the individual is not found in the CSR at all. Further, some soldiers found in the register are shown in the CSR as not having served until 1862 or even 1863. This discrepancy reflects not only poor record keeping during the war, but the intentional destruction of many Confederate records at war's end. The guest register begins on June 6, and ends abruptly on August 22, 1861, well in advance of the resort's normal closing date. For that period, the register contains 480 entries for military personnel, and 125 civilian entries, including one civilian prisoner of war. Subtracting multiple visits by the same individual leaves a total of 377 soldiers. This number includes five Union army officers captured at the Battle of Scary Creek, July 17, and quartered at The Old White pending transfer to prison in Richmond. In January 1867, Harper's Magazine carried the story of these Union prisoners as told by Captain J.R. Hurd of Kentucky. Capt. Hurd said they arrived in Lewisburg on Sunday, July 21, and were then taken to White Sulphur Springs: "It was now raining in torrents. The roads were miry, the wagons poorly covered; still, through storm and mud we were driven on, until we reached the Springs just before dark. Here [we] were happily delayed three days…Justice constrains me to say that we could not have been better treated…nor is it possible that we could have enjoyed ourselves better under similar circumstances…"

Of the 377 soldiers found in the register, 149 were officers and 228 were enlisted men. On August 4, 59 soldiers registered at White Sulphur Springs, the largest one-day total of the summer. Of course the vast majority of soldiers visiting the property pitched tents or made other arrangements and thus did not sign the register. The trickle of civilian visitors fell off as the summer progressed and, by mid-August, the resort was occupied solely by Confederate military personnel. August 22, the last day of the register, contains 55 entries. Among these is an entry for "John S. Mosby, Warrenton, Va." Known as the "Gray Ghost" of the Confederacy, Col. Mosby is remembered for his Civil War exploits as commander of Mosby's Rangers, 43rd Battalion Virginia Cavalry. What necessity drew the legendary cavalryman to Greenbrier County may never be known. Mosby himself makes no mention of the visit in his post-war memoirs. Nevertheless, the entry is there, and followed by another mysterious signature connected with Mosby's Rangers: "R.S. Rudd." The CSR lists just one person by that name in Confederate service: "Royal S. Rudd, Mosby's Rangers." Of course Mosby's famous command was not assembled until 1863, but it is apparent Mr. Rudd had some type of prior military service that is not listed in the index to the Compiled Service Records.

Confederate authorities began using The Old White and its adjacent cottages as a "field infirmary" in August 1861. It was officially designated as a military hospital in September. The cottages were taken over first, leaving the main hotel for civilian visitors. Quartermaster and commissary supplies were stockpiled at White Sulphur Springs and, by early September, the property had become an important supply depot for the Confederacy. Thousands of soldiers came to know the resort as the place where food, clothing, and medical attention could be found. Confederate cavalry were especially dependent on the resort-turned-depot as the place where huge quantities of provender for animals was kept. With so many cavalrymen in the area of Greenbrier County, it was no small task to keep the horses fed. During September 1861, the daily food allowance for each horse consisted of 12 pounds of corn, 12 pounds of oats, and 14 pounds of hay. On September 10, Col. Croghan, 10th Virginia Cavalry, signed for enough food to feed 22 horses for three days. This amounted to 792 pounds of corn, 792 pounds of oats, and 924 pounds of hay. Multiply that by the hundreds of cavalry horses in the Greenbrier region and you may get some idea what a Herculean task it was to keep cavalry on the move. (7)

Unprecedented rainfall and unseasonably cool temperatures spawned devastating disease among the soldiers in 1861. Some of the men sent to the hospital at White Sulphur Springs had known the place before the war. A young lieutenant of Floyd's Brigade told his sister in September that the army had 2,000 sick men scattered from The Old White to Meadow Bluff. "It pains me exceedingly," he wrote, "to inform you that the White Sulphur Springs, that great fashionable resort, may be called one extensive graveyard..."(8)

During early September, Pvt. Joab Smith, a 51-year-old

schoolteacher and member of the 22nd Virginia Infantry, was a patient at White Sulphur Springs suffering from dysentery. Having more or less recovered, he returned to his command on the 12th, but was soon ordered back to The Old White to serve as a nurse. In one ward of the hospital, Joab found "seventy men who were suffering various maladies, being in filth and destitute of every necessary of life, and all imploring relief which I was not able to mitigate." Late one October night, Joab confided to his journal that he feared the task of forcing the enemy out of Virginia was nearly impossible. Writing by candlelight amid the "groans and suffering of the soldiers," Joab longed to see his family: "Oh! That I could have the assurance of one day seeing my wife and children." It was not to be. Joab Smith acquired disease from the men he was trying to help. He died at White Sulphur Springs on October 27, 1861.(9)

A young Georgia soldier saw less of the suffering and more of the beauty of the place when he stopped there en route to Meadow Bluff: "White Sulphur Springs is the most beautiful place I ever saw. Besides a very large hotel, there are I suppose fifty or sixty dwelling houses for the accommodation of families who do not desire to board. Nature deemed it a beautiful place, but art has admirably performed its part. I have never seen such a display of taste and wealth." Another Georgia soldier described it as being "one of the most magnificent places, I think, in America."(10)

Dr. O.A. Krenshaw was medical director for the brigades of Wise and Floyd. On October 6, he informed Gen. Lee that he had more than 1,000 patients at White Sulphur Springs. Begging Lee to stop the flow of patients into his hospital, Dr. Krenshaw said overcrowding contributed to the spread of disease and increased the mortality rate. The hotel was overflowing with patients and all but the newest cottages had been taken over as hospital wards. Further complicating matters was the fact that the entire compound was in serious need of cooking utensils and cooks. Patients coming into the hospital arrived "without anything," and nothing could be procured nearer than Richmond. "As soon as I am prepared to receive more sick," he wrote,

"I will inform you." Dr. Krenshaw said the hotel's lower floor would contain 500 patients, and the upper floor about 600. He explained that there was a hazard to using the upper floor because if a fire broke out, it would be impossible to get very many patients out in time to save them.(11)

Lt. John D. Greever, a 24-year-old farmer from Tazewell County, Virginia, was a patient and then hospital steward at The Old White in September and October, 1861. In letters to his girlfriend, he said food was in short supply at the hospital, but that they did get plenty of coffee and molasses. He estimated the patient count at 1,000 to 1,200. Typhoid fever was the chief ailment and some days as many as four men were buried on the property. "I believe that there are no other contagious diseases in the army except fever," he said, adding that he had no idea how long he would be working at the hospital. Earlier in the summer, Lt. Greever was a patient at the Sweet Springs hospital, Monroe County, suffering with measles.(12)

On a cold November day, Col. James L. Davis received a dispatch at Meadow Bluff informing him there was a lady behind Union lines near Hawks Nest, Fayette County, waiting for an escort into "Dixie." This lady had been given a pass beyond the Union pickets by General Rosecrans and was en route to Richmond. Col. Davis selected Dr. Archibald Atkinson, as the "gallant of the regiment," to go and escort the lady into Greenbrier County. At 9 p.m. the doctor and the lady met and seated themselves upon a trunk in the crude buckboard wagon. Dr. Atkinson had no idea the lady would prove to be an old acquaintance as he later described: "Not a word was spoken for some time until the wagon gave a lurch and I said 'Madam it is rough here, suppose you lean against me.' She replied 'I thank you. I will, I know your voice this is Archie Atkinson. Oh, I am so relieved.' I replied 'Yes, and this is Miss Emily Mason.' (Her sister had married my uncle Gen. Robert Chilton) We reached headquarters about 11 o'clock, which was a log shanty. Col. Davis appeared in full uniform, the beau ideal of a gentleman of elegance and was presented. He had known Col. Mason and the two chatted pleasantly."(13)

Emily Mason. She worked as a volunteer nurse at White Sulphur Springs 1861-1862. *Courtesy National Archives*

Emily Virginia Mason was born in Lexington, Kentucky, October 15, 1815. When the war began, she was living in Fairfax County, Virginia, but soon relocated to New Jersey to help care for her invalid niece. As a southern woman just arrived in the North, Mason's movements were watched by government detectives who suspected she was a spy for the South. Her mail was frequently intercepted and, when she ventured out into public, she was harassed and ridiculed for her presumed Confederate sympathies. She was even told that if she attempted to leave the North she would be arrested. Nevertheless, after spending nearly six months away from her family in Virginia, and growing anxious as to their condition, she determined to go home. How to manage her "escape" was a problem, however. As a devout Catholic, she wrote to some Sisters of Charity who were said to be going South to work as nurses, asking if she might go with them "in any capacity." Her plea was denied by the Bishop, who feared that her presence among the nuns would jeopardize their mission. The puzzle was finally solved when some friends from Pennsylvania helped Emily slip away from "her detective." By prior arrangement, she met with some of her cousins in Newport, Kentucky on November 2nd and plotted her return to Virginia. With help from the Archbishop of Cincinnati, an "ardent Union man," Emily was able to board a steamer carrying military supplies to Federal troops in the Kanawha Valley.

This journey was a long and tedious one. It was said that Rebels infested both sides of the river, so the captain would only travel during the day. Three long weeks into their journey, the steamer ran upon a snag and had to be abandoned east of Charleston. Emily sent word of her plight to Gen. Rosecrans, a prewar acquaintance, who replied that night that he would send his "own servant and ambulance," under flag of truce, to escort her to his headquarters near Gauley Bridge. That evening Emily discovered that sick soldiers were being loaded onto the steamer and she determined to help them. She found these men in pitiful condition, "coughing, groaning and moaning. Here were men in all stages of measles, pneumonia, camp fever, and other disorders...sent in wagons over thirteen miles of mountain road, without nurses, without physician." The men told Emily that they had been sent out in the early morning without food or medicine and expected to remain without any until they reached the hospital, 20 miles below. She gathered what food, whiskey, and medicine she could and proceeded to care for the soldiers until their army physician arrived. "And this was the beginning of my ministrations among soldiers," she wrote, "which lasted to the end of the war, and which became the life of my life."

When Emily Mason arrived at Meadow Bluff with Dr. Atkinson, she found herself once again among sick soldiers, as she later described: "Every house near the camp, every barn, every cabin, was filled with sick and wounded soldiers...the stage to Richmond passed only twice a week. I must wait somewhere two days. We drove from house to house. The poor people either had their rooms filled...or they had suffered so much from disease, resulting from their hospitality, that they were afraid to take any one in...." Eventually given a bed at a local farmhouse, Emily learned that sick soldiers were being cared for in a separate building. When the family servant went to take a meal of bacon and greens to the men, she went along: "I followed the servant, to find seven East Tennesseans lying on dirty straw, in every stage of camp fever. The air was stifling; the men were suffering in every way, especially for medicine and for clean beds and clothing. With the aid of one of the least ill, we brought in clean straw, had water heated in the big iron pot...while bits of rag served for towels and toothbrushes, and we soon changed the atmosphere and the aspect of things."

When, two days later, it was time to board the eastbound stage, Emily Mason promised her sick soldiers that she would return: "I promised to come back in a week or ten days, armed with power to open a hospital and bring them into it; and here I will add that at the end of a fortnight I had the happiness to see my East Tennesseans drive up to the hospital, waving their caps to me, not one of the seven missing."

Emily's stage stopped for some time in Lewisburg and there she spoke with the Confederate Medical Director: "In this town all the women opened their houses and gave their services. The churches and courthouse were turned into hospitals. I went through one of the former to aid in giving food and medicine. In every pew lay a patient, cheerful sufferer, and into the enclosure round the altar they were constantly carrying the dead, wrapped in a single blanket. Side by side lay master and servant, rich and poor. War, like death, is a great leveler....How could I leave such scenes, where there was so much to do? Impelled by the hope of coming back with aid and comfort, I hurried away."

In Richmond, Emily told her family about the desperate situation among the soldiers in western Virginia, and explained that she would return to Greenbrier County in a few days. She met with Confederate President Jefferson Davis, who gave her work his blessing: "From him and from the surgeon general I had *carte blanche*, free transportation wherever I should go, hospital stores, and nurses *ad libitum,* could I have found any of these willing to encounter the winter's snow on the mountains, where were defeat and disaster, sickness and suffering. With one faithful man servant I set out, so full of enthusiasm as not to feel cold and fatigue, everywhere encountering that sympathy and kindness from our people which never failed me in all my wanderings....'Jim' was my protector on my journey; and when we opened the hospital at the Greenbrier White Sulphur Springs, he was my cook, nurse, maid, sympathizer, everything, and did all things well."

Emily Mason arrived at White Sulphur Springs in early December and was greeted by Dr. John A. Hunter, Confederate physician in charge. Dr. Hunter had been informed of her coming and was quite pleased to receive her assistance. His own duties took him to the various military hospitals of western Virginia and he needed someone at The Old White he could rely on. Emily found at the hospital about 200 patients, a significant drop from the number present just one month earlier. Learning that the Sisters of Charity of Our Lady of Mercy in Charleston, South Carolina, had been offered by the bishop of that state to go wherever they were needed, Emily wrote them a letter asking for their assistance in Greenbrier County. At about this same time, Confederate President Jefferson Davis asked Bishop John McGill of Richmond if he could send some nuns to White Sulphur Springs to serve as nurses. As the Sisters of the Richmond area were already overburdened with nursing duties, Bishop McGill passed the president's request to Bishop Patrick Lynch of South Carolina. (14)

Bishop Lynch informed the Sisters that the Confederate Government would pay all their travel expenses, and that he would give them $100.00 to buy winter clothing suitable for the mountain climate. Their actual labors however, were made without remuneration. Bishop Lynch selected five Sisters for the new assignment: Sister M. Ignatius (Clarke), Sister M. De Sales (Brennan), Sister M. Bernard (Frank), Sister M. Helena (Marlowe), and Sister Stanislaus (Coventry). Mother Teresa (Barry) was asked to accompany the Sisters and remain with them for several weeks. Bishop McGill asked the Confederate War Department to provide a Catholic chaplain for the hospital at White Sulphur Springs. "Our Sisters," he said, "can find plenty of work where they can practice their religion; and if they give their services for the benefit of the country...provision should be made for their having Mass and the Sacraments." Subsequently, Reverend Lawrence O'Connell was appointed as chaplain for White Sulphur Springs. (15)

Mother Theresa. She was among the volunteer nurses at White Sulphur Springs, 1861-1862. *Courtesy Archives of the Diocese of Charleston, SC*

The Sisters and Father O'Connell departed for Greenbrier County on December 19, arriving there on December 24th. Emily Mason wrote about their arrival in a series of newspaper articles in the 1880s: "They arrived at midnight Christmas Eve, in a blinding snowstorm; but they soon cleared the sky about them. Our labors were systematized, and I learned much from their teachings. The men were shy of them at first, few of them having ever seen a Catholic, much less a Sister. But very soon my pet patients confessed: 'You see, captain' (as I was called), 'they are more used to it than you are. They know how to handle a fellow when he's sick, and don't mind a bit how bad a wound smells.' It was not that they loved me less, but they loved the Sisters more—and I forgave them."

The Sisters were always keenly aware of the soldiers' sufferings and worked diligently to alleviate them. Not only did they administer the various wards, they dressed wounds, gave medication, treated various diseases, assisted surgeons, and took care of the cooking and cleaning. On December 31, Sister De Sales wrote to Bishop Lynch describing their situation: "We have not found the sick and matters in general in as bad a condition as we anticipated. The prevailing diseases are typhoid fever, pneumonia, and some few cases of consumption. I had the gratification of baptizing a few days ago a young Georgian, who died the next morning...Father O'Connell empowered me to baptize him...."(16)

Father O'Connell was also busy ministering to the spiritual needs of the hospital community. On January 11, 1862, he told Bishop Lynch of his work: "There are I suppose 2 or 300 Irish Catholics in and around this place. They keep me very busily engaged. On Sundays I have a large congregation and I have reason to believe that my ministry has already done good. Every day I teach some 40 children the rudiments of Christianity...There are over a hundred Catholics here who cannot confess in English and the consequence is that several of them have not approached the sacraments...They crowd around me and several have traveled long journeys on hearing that I could receive their confessions in their own language." Father

O'Connell also said that Mother Teresa and Sister Stanislaus had been on the sick list, but were gradually recovering.(17)

Bishop Lynch informed the Sisters in late January that he would be visiting them as soon as he could arrange it. They were anxious to see him and Sister De Sales wrote to tell him about their progress so that he might know what to expect: "You will be pleased to hear our sick are all doing well and in a fair way of recovery save three patients in my ward—two of consumption and a violent case of pneumonia. Pneumonia is not the prevailing disease. I have called my ward 'The Beauregard Ward'. I would have put it under the protection of my patron saint – St. De Sales, but was afraid of alarming the people out here – we have had and are still having pretty hard times out here – Xmas passed by without a single occurance that would remind us it was the 'Day of Days'...It has been snowing here for the last two days....This I trust will reach [you] before you start for this place....Please write—and pray for me." (18)

Sister De Sales' ward was in the resort's great ballroom, the dance program still posted at its entrance. It must have been an odd sight to have the fancy ballroom, elaborate hotel, and luxurious cottages in use as hospital wards. Where once laughter and joviality reigned supreme, were found the moans and pleading entreaties of men in various stages of life-threatening disease. The scarcity of food and basic needs was in contrast to prewar days of opulence and abundance. The resort's beautiful grounds, enlivened with paths bearing such names as Courtship Maze and Lovers Rest, were now dotted with small earthen mounds indicating where yet another mother's son was laid to rest. Thus at White Sulphur Springs was found incongruity, tragedy and despair. That bleak first winter of the war at The Old White left indelible images upon the minds of all who witnessed it. Its echo still reverberates across the years. The seldom-visited graves of those poor soldiers who perished at the resort-turned-hospital can yet be found by the modern visitor. Blessed are those who pause and remember that which a nation should never forget.

In the summer of 1889, 27 years after her departure, Emily Mason returned to the Greenbrier White Sulphur Springs. Now

73-years-old and haunted by memories of the war, she braced herself for an emotional merger of past and present:

> *I saw again, for the first time since the war, the scene of my early hospital experiences. With what emotion I found myself upon the spot sacred to such memories! Every room had its own story; and saddest of all was the place where we had laid the dead, unmarked by a single stone! I had difficulty in finding the spot. Oh, my poor fellows! Was it for this you left your Southern homes, the 'land of flowers,' Florida, Georgia, Alabama, Carolina,— to die amidst these cold mountains, and be forgotten? In the ballroom, in the dining room, where now the gay world assembled, I saw a sight they could not see, I heard a voice they could not hear. Yonder were sixty typhoid cases, there sixty wounded men. Every cottage had its quota of the eighteen hundred men we gathered in. 'Carolina Row' held the diphtheria patients, and here, in one room, on a bright, sunshiny winter's day, died four men at the same hour, while I ran in vain from one to the other, trying to tear with my fingers the white, leathery substance which spread over their mouth, and even came out upon the lips. Up to the time of the war I had seldom seen death. A merciful providence had spared me the sight of it in my own family, in the cases of my parents. And now, in this great family, I saw eighteen die daily, and could not go fast enough from one to the other, to say a last prayer and hear a 'last word.'* (19)

The 135th Virginia Militia camped at White Sulphur Springs on and off during the winter. The Sisters got to know some of the men and also some members of the 22nd Virginia Infantry. That regiment was ordered to garrison Lewisburg all winter to ease public fears of another Yankee raid. Mother Teresa's term of office expired during the winter and she returned to South Carolina in early March, leaving Sister De Sales in charge. Later that month, the Sisters re-elected Mother Teresa Superioress of the Community. In a letter written on March 11, Sister De Sales said they had just gotten word that they would be sent about 4,000 troops within the next two weeks. She also said they had enlarged their altar some three feet longer and one foot higher, much to the satisfaction of Father O'Connell. The new altar was beautifully decorated with flowers given them by the owner of the nearby millinery store. Sister De Sales said she had recently started drinking the sulphur water, which she described as "horrid." Describing the local scenery as "truly sublime," she said she had gone on a walk last Sunday with Father O'Connell and Sister Helena: "There is a walk here cut out round one of the mountains, called 'Lovers Walk.' It is just such a romantic place as you read in some romance....I wish you could have seen us scrambling up a steep mountain....when we got up you may believe we seated ourselves. I intend exploring the mountains before the hospital fills in....Kind regards to our dear Bishop, Father Sullivan, and good Dr. Corcoran—pray for me." (20)

Toward the end of March, Emily Mason left White Sulphur Springs to take charge of a hospital at Charlottesville. The Sisters now had complete control of the hospital and were solely responsible for its operation. The arrival of spring brought the resumption of active military campaigns and on April 6, Sister De Sales informed Bishop Lynch that the Confederate forces were said to be retreating toward Greenbrier Bridge, several miles away. "As I write," she said, "there are some three hundred with an immense train of wagons wending their way toward Lewisburg." That report proved to be a false alarm and nine days later she told the Bishop that everything was okay. The hospital had been filling up rapidly with new patients and Dr. Hunter telegraphed Bishop Lynch asking if another Sister could be sent. About the middle of April the Sisters received a dispatch from Confederate Gen. Henry Heth, requesting that all surplus hospital stores be moved to Union, Monroe County. Gen. Heth was not confident that his forces could hold the area of White Sulphur Springs in the coming campaigns. The Sisters were told that in that event they would be sent to Sweet Sulphur Springs, 17 miles distant. (21)

Near the end of April, Bishop Lynch was finally able to make his promised visit. As it happened, the Bishop arrived just a few days ahead of a Yankee advance into Greenbrier County in May. The Union advance and the close proximity of opposing forces made it necessary for the Sisters to abandon the hospital at White Sulphur Springs on May 10. All patients that could be moved were sent to other hospitals, leaving a small number behind under the care of local civilians. The Sisters and Dr. J. Lewis Woodville, Hunter's assistant, relocated 60 miles south, to the hospital at Montgomery White Sulphur Springs, near Christiansburg. Dr. Hunter moved first to the hospital at Salt Sulphur Springs and then to Pearisburg, Giles County. Thus ended on May 10, 1862, use of The Old White as an officially-sanctioned military hospital. It would see use several more times during the war as a field infirmary, but with far fewer patients and reduced staff. Following the Battle of White Sulphur Springs in August of 1863, Dr. Woodville and the Sisters returned, staying two days at the Greenbrier.

In Charleston, South Carolina, rumors spread that the Yankees had taken the Sisters, Father O'Connell, and Bishop Lynch prisoner. Much to everyone's relief letters were received toward the end of May from the Bishop and Sister De Sales contradicting the rumors. In reply to the Bishop's letter, Father Corcoran wrote: "The Sisters here were delighted to learn...that you were the means of saving the effects of the Sisters in Virginia at the time of their flight....Before, they were in great doubt and fear that the Sisters had left everything behind, a prey to the Yankees." (22)

The Sisters of Charity...each with their own costume of plainness and self-denial...have shown to womanhood, on the battlefield and in the hospital, a more excellent way, a beauty and nobility before which all the common graces and ornaments of the sex fade, appear like dim candles by the pure, eternal stars.

Atlantic Monthly Magazine, 1864

Rules for Hospitals

1st. Patients are not permitted to leave the hospital, except between the hours of 1 & 5 O'clock p.m.

2. Nurses will not be permitted to leave the hospital at any time without permission from the Steward; nor after 6 O'clock p.m. without permission from the surgeon.

3. Patients will not be allowed to pass through or go to the office, except on special business, or to change from one ward into another, without permission from the Steward.

4. Smoking and swearing are positively prohibited in the wards.

5. Patients are required to observe strict habits of cleanliness, & in all cases observe the orders and directions of the Stewards, ward masters and nurses.

6. Patients are not allowed to enter the dining room or kitchen except when the bell rings for dinner or other meals.

7. The Ward Master will hold the nurses strictly responsible for the cleanliness and order of their wards and all articles therein, promptly reporting any neglect of duty to the Surgeon.

8. Any hospital attendant found drinking or intoxicated will be immediately discharged from the hospital.

9. No visitor admitted at any time, except on a pass from the Surgeon, or by special permission from the Stewards.

10. The Steward will promptly report to the Surgeon any neglect in carrying out or failure to enforce the above Rules.

Rules & Regulations
to be observed by nurses and patients

Nurses will have their respective wards properly swept, arranged, and ventilated before the breakfast hour. Will carry meals to their patients in their respective wards. Will immediately after meals have tin plates, cups and saucers, knives and forks properly washed in hot water, and removed from the various rooms, after every meal the bread, meat, soup, coffee and etc. which may be remaining. Will have their respective rooms scoured, once or twice every week, as occasion may require. They will also look to the most perfect cleanliness of water pitchers, basins and chamber pots. Will communicate their wishes respecting night watches, and make all complaints of irregularities or disobedience of orders to the Stewards.

Nurses will be held responsible and punished for any neglect of duty.

Patients are expected to assist the nurses in the performance of their duties, as much as the state of their health will permit.

Patients on receiving a discharge or furlough will hand to the Steward the ticket which they received on admission to the hospital.

Patients wishing to inform the doctor of any unusual symptoms in their disease, will notify the Stewards through the nurse to that effect.

Patients are cautioned not to lie on their beds with their boots and shoes on, nor to spit on the floor, nor against the walls, nor to write, or to scratch or otherwise deface the walls of the building, under penalty of being sent to the guard house.

Patients are particularly cautioned not to use the vicinity of the hospital as a privy.

<u>The Ward Master</u> will take charge and deliver to the ordnance department all arms and accoutrements brought into the hospital, ticketing the name, company and regiment of each patient on his arms etc. He will also take charge of the clothing of the sick and be responsible for its safe keeping. He will see that the rooms are properly cleaned and ventilated and that the patients are clean in their persons and clothing. Patients should be made to wash at least once a week, their whole person. He will also see that the food is properly cooked and served.

<u>The Hospital Steward</u> will prepare the prescriptions and see that the nurses administer the medicines as directed, and that all proper attention is paid to the sick. He will receive and register the sick and exercise a general supervision and control over the sick, under the direction of the Surgeon will register all admissions and discharges and keep strict order in the hospital.

Dr. John A. Hunter
Medical Director, CSA

MILITARY PERSONNEL REGISTERED AT THE GREENBRIER WHITE SULPHUR SPRINGS JUNE TO AUGUST 1861

Guests register from the "Old White" hotel (present Greenbrier), White Sulphur Springs, June to August, 1861. Previously unpublished, this register is an excellent primary source for determining early Confederate military service of dozens of men. The popular resort opened for the summer 1861 season on June 6 and on June 26 military personnel began to mingle with the few civilian guests. The register ends abruptly on August 22, several weeks ahead of their usual closing.

Abbreviations used:

CSR – Compiled Service Records
PACS – Provisional Army Confederate States
POW – Prisoner of War
QM – Quartermaster
SGN – Surgeon
TNI – Tennessee Infantry
VAA – Virginia Artillery
VAC – Virginia Cavalry
VAI – Virginia Infantry
VAM – Virginia Militia
VASS – Virginia Sharpshooters
WL – Wise Legion

Norris, George – [Capt. 46 VAI) June 26th
Cox, W. – [Pvt. WL] June 26th
Tyndall, Mark A. Lt – [10 VAC] June 26th
Hockaday, J.F. Pvt. – [10 VAC] June 26th
Blunt, Wm. R. Pvt – [10 VAC] June 26th
Katen, A. Pvt. – [10 VAC] June 26th

Taylor, Thomas H. Pvt. – [10 VAC] June 26th
Caperton, John – [108 VAM] June 27th
Caperton, Allen – [cadet VMI to 14 VAC in 1864] June 27th
McCue, J.M. – [Lt. 59 VAI] June 28th
McComas, Wm [WLA 1861 to 16 VAC in 1863] June 28th
Spurlock, Burwell – [Pvt. WL to Pvt. 45 Btn VAI in 1863] June 28th
Blocker, John R. – CS Army [Lt. 59 VAI] June 28th
Duncan, Wm E. – [Capt. QM Dept.] June 28th
Barr, Thomas – [14 VAC] June 29th
King, John Floyd – [Wise Legion Artillery] June 30th
Douthat, Wm P. – [Sgt. Mountain Rifles, Botetourt Co. later 28 VAI] July 4th
Houston, James R. – [Graham's Rockbridge VAA, possibly early WLA] July 4th
Campbell, Parker – CSA [Gen. & Staff Major] July 4th
Ryland, Albert G. – [Capt. Wright's Co Ind. Infantry] July 4th
Favish?, Thomas L. – Wise Legion July 5th
Little, John C. – Wise Legion [Lt. 59 VAI] July 7th
Preston, Walter Creigh – University Volunteers [59 VAI] July 7th
Chilton, James Y. – University Volunteers [59 VAI] July 7th
Ludington, Sam C. – [Major WL QM and later contract beef supplier] July 7th
Liversey, S.H. – Ben McCulloch Rangers, New Orleans, July 8th
DeHart, Charles F. – Ben McCulloch Rangers, New Orleans, July 8th
Taylor, John – Ben McCulloch Rangers, New Orleans, [59 VAI] July 8th
Twells, George Lt. – Ben McCulloch Rangers, New Orleans, July 8th
Old, W.W. Lt. – University Volunteers [59 VAI] July 9th
Beale, J.M.H. Jr. Cadet – Pt. Pleasant, Va July 9th
Fell, J.P. – [Sgt. 14 VAC] July 10th
Mowry, E.S. Capt. – Goochland Infantry, [46 VAI] July 11th
Harrison, Randolph Lt. – Goochland Infantry, [46 VAI] July 11th
Wise, Peyton Lt. – Goochland Infantry, [46 VAI] July 11th
Panons?, Lt. – Sussex J. Avengers, [46 VAI] July 11th
Roney, William T. – Sussex J. Avengers, [46 VAI] July 11th
Winfield, Ben F. Capt. – Jackson Avengers, [46 VAI] July 11th
Winfield, John F. Lt. – Jackson Avengers, [46 VAI] July 11th

Thornton, Lt. – Jackson Avengers, [46 VAI]July 11th
Doak, A.V. – Wise Legion, July 12th
Davis, J. Lucius Jr. – Wise Legion, [10 VAC] July 12th
Davis, Barnhurst – Wise Legion, July 12th
Queens, John W. – Wise Legion, July 12th
Horndon, Wm – Wise Legion, July 12th
Burrows, H. Lansing – Wise Legion, July 12th
Winston, H.C. – [Wise Legion] July 13th
Crafton, Thomas H. – [Wise Legion] July 13th
Frazer, P.F. Cadet – Va Military Institute, July 13th
Summers?, A.T. Cadet – Va Military Institute, July 13th
Grasty?, S.T. Cadet – Va Military Institute, July 17th
Creigh, Thomas Dr. – [surgeon CSA] July 17th
Pate, H.A. – Wise Legion, July 18th
Jordan, Lt. – Wise Legion, July 18th
Chandler, Lt. – Wise Legion, July 18th
Bullock, Sgt. – Wise Legion, July 18th
Well, Samuel – 1st Regiment, Louisiana Volunteers, July 19th
Wise, Peyton Lt. – Goochland Infantry, [46 VAI] July 19th
Lawson, John Major – Wise Legion, [46 VAI] July 19th
Brooks, H.C. – [Col. Anderson's Regt. TNI, WL ADC] July 19th
Belcher, James R. Lt. – Wise Legion, [10 VAC] July 19th
Archer, W.S. Lt. – CS Army Wise Legion, [later 48 VAI] July 19th
Lockhart, D.B. – [Wise Legion] July 19th
McCarty, W. Page – [Lt. Wise Legion] July 20th
MacDearmon, S.D. Col. – Wise Legion, July 20th
Pallen, Montrose A. Surgeon – Wise Legion, July 20th
Gregory, Wm H.C. – [Wise Legion] July 20th
Gregory, H.C. – [Wise Legion] July 20th
Bethel, W.M. – [Wise Legion 10 VAC] July 20th
Howlett, J.B. – Richmond Lt. Infantry Blues, [46 VAI] July 20th
Butler, J.H. – Richmond Lt. Infantry Blues, [46 VAI] July 20th
Leyon, Thomas W. – Richmond Lt. Infantry Blues, [46 VAI] July 20th
Kirby, Capt. – Wise Legion Battery July 22nd
Brummel, A.O. Lt. – Wise Legion Battery July 22nd
Pairo, P.H. Lt. – Wise Legion Artillery, July 22nd

Cross, Dart? – Wise Legion Artillery, July 22nd
Duffield, C.B. Major – Wise Legion, July 22nd
McCourt, F.M. – Wise Legion, July 22nd
Brickhouse, L.L. – Wise Legion, July 22nd
Wise, Richard A. Capt. – Wise Legion, July 22nd
Woodruff, W.E. Col. – [p.o.w.] 2nd Kentucky Regiment, USA, July 22nd
Neff, G.W. Ltc. – [p.o.w.] 2nd Kentucky Regiment, USA, July 22nd
Austin, George Capt. – [p.o.w.] Company B, Kentucky, USA, July 22nd
Hurd, J.R. Capt. – [p.o.w.] Company F, Kentucky, USA, July 22nd
DeVilliers, Charles Col. (Hessian) – [p.o.w.] 11th Ohio Infantry, USA, July 22nd
Roberts, F. – Roane County, [p.o.w. note says "traitor Wheeling Convention"]
Hunter, G. Wilson Dr. – [Gen. & Staff surgeon, CSA] July 22nd
Ficklin, J.E. – [VMI Cadet and 51st Va Infantry] July 23rd
Roemer, B. Capt. – Wise Legion Artillery, July 23rd
Beleu, Wm A. – [14 VAC] July 23rd
Son, Jacob – Richmond Lt. Infantry Blues, [46 VAI] July 23rd
Hackworth, George W. – [8 VAC] July 23rd
Martins?, Henry M. – CSA, July 24th
Archer, W.S. Lt. – CSA, [possibly Wise Legion Artillery] July 25th
Brooks, W. C. – [79 VAM] July 25th
Bagwell, C.H. – Wise Legion, July 25th
Hayes, L.G. – Wise Legion, July 25th
Hanson, R.W. Col. – [2nd Kentucky Infantry, CSA] July 27th
Woolley, R.W. Major – [Gen. & Staff, Adj. Gen. Dept. PACS] July 27th
Hart, George – Jackson Guard July 27th
Barksdale, Nathaniel B. – [Wise Legion Artillery] July 28th
Andrews, T.W. Capt. – Wise Legion, July 28th
Roome, C. Lt. – Wise Legion, July 28th
Moorman, Capt. – Greenbrier Cavalry [14 VAC] July 28th
Caperton, Hugh – [27 VAI] July 30th
Atkinson, Arch Dr. – [surgeon Wise Legion] July 30th
Baldwin, Thomas S. – [60 VAI] Aug. 1st

Warwick, B. Capt. – Provisional Army, Aug. 1st
Moses, F.J. Col. – Wise Legion [assistant surgeon] Aug. 1st
Gregory, John M. Jr. – [Archibald Graham's VAA] Aug. 1st
Lewis, John – [Sgt. 8 VAC] Aug. 1st
Cook, A.B. – [Sgt. 8 VAC] Aug. 1st
Pollock, A.A. – [Lt. 46 VAI] Aug. 1st
Gillespie, Wm H. – [hospital steward Wise Legion] Aug. 1st
Boggess, A. – CSA [Wise Legion Artillery] Aug. 2nd
Ludington, Samuel C. – [Major Wise Legion QM] Aug. 2nd
Warwick, James W. – Highlanders [31 VAI not in CSR] Aug. 2nd
Stephenson, L.H. – Highlanders [31 VAI not in CSR] Aug. 2nd
Hull, Felix H. – Highlanders [surgeon 31 VAI] Aug. 2nd
Harvie, J.B. Lt. – Wise Legion, Aug. 2nd
Thomas T.L. Snead – Wise Brigade, Aug. 2nd
Bagwell, George H. – Wise Brigade [Gen. & Staff Capt.] Aug. 2nd
Coffin, W.H. M.D. – Wise Legion, Aug. 2nd
McCausland, Col. – 36 Va Vol. Infantry, Aug. 2nd
Reid, Lt. Col. – 36 Va Vol. Infantry, Aug. 2nd
Miller, S.A. – [Pvt. and Capt. 22 VAI QM] Aug. 2nd
Jefferson, Ogelsby – [Pvt. 46 VAI] Aug. 2nd
Shelton, Edward A. – [Pvt. 46 VAI] Aug. 2nd
Sherry, J.M. Capt. – 36 Va Vol. Infantry, Aug. 2nd
Loughborough, Lt. – Louisiana [1st Battalion La. Infantry] Aug. 2nd
Harden, James A. – 36 Va Vol. Infantry, Aug. 2nd
Newman, J.G. – 36 Va Vol. Infantry, Aug. 2nd
Wade, James – 36 Va Vol. Infantry, Aug. 2nd
Morgan, John - [36 VAI] Aug. 3rd
Morgan, John Jr. - [possibly 36 VAI was briefly 22 VAI] Aug. 3rd
Jackson, Wm A. Col. – [22 Va Infantry] Aug. 3rd
Cox, F.M. – [22 VAI] Aug. 3rd
Graham, E.S. M.D. – Wise Legion, Aug. 3rd
Morgan, W.S. – [36 VAI] Aug. 3rd
Jackson, L.E. Lt. – [46 Va Infantry] Aug. 3rd
Winfield, John F. Lt. – Sussex Infantry [46 VAI] Aug. 3rd
Watkins, Joseph F. – 22 Va Infantry, Aug. 3rd
Carter, Fred Lt. – Wise Brigade, [46 VAI] Aug. 3rd
Mowry, E.S. Capt. – Wise Legion, Aug. 3rd

Harrison, Randolph Lt. – Wise Legion, [46 VAI] Aug. 3rd
Weisiger, R.W. – Richmond Lt. Infantry Blues [46 VAI] Aug. 3rd
Hicks, Wm C. – [46 VAI] Aug. 3rd
Nott?, Robert – Richmond Lt. Infantry Blues [46VAI] Aug. 3rd
Harwood, Thomas – Richmond Lt. Infantry Blues [46 VAI] Aug. 3rd
Lumpkin, George T. – Richmond Lt. Inf. Blues [46 VAI] Aug. 3rd
Cochran, John – Richmond Lt. Inf. Blues [46 VAI] Aug. 3rd
Cochran, H.K. – [Capt. 14 VAC] Aug. 3rd
Duesberry, R.R. – Richmond Lt. Inf. Blues [46 VAI] Aug. 3rd
Burr, H.D. – Richmond Lt. Inf. Blues [46VAI] Aug. 3rd
Hamner, Nimrod B. – University Volunteers [59 VAI] Aug. 3rd
Caperton, I. – Va Military Institute, Aug. 3rd
Cox, Simon – Pates Rangers, Petersburg, Va [5 VAC] Aug. 3rd
Buckholtz, L. Capt. – [Chief of Ordnance WL] Aug. 3rd
Lawson, J.M. – [36 VAI] Aug. 3rd
Morgan, P.D. – [36 VAI] Aug. 3rd
Robertson, James E. – [46 VAI] Aug. 3rd
Gasry?, G. Col. – Aug. 4th
Kirby, James Capt. – [Wise Legion Artillery] Aug. 4th
Brummel, A.O. Lt. – [Wise Legion Artillery] Aug. 4th
Harrison, Charles C. – [Sgt. 46 VAI] Aug. 4th
Pardigan, J. – Richmond Lt. Inf. Blues, [46 VAI] Aug. 4th
Glenn, Peter – Richmond Lt. Inf. Blues, [46 VAI] Aug. 4th
Smith, A.D. Lt. – Wise Legion, Aug. 4th
Iaege, Fintan – Richmond Lt. Inf. Blues [46 VAI] Aug. 4th
Laidley, Rich – Kanawha Rifleman, [22 VAI] Aug. 4th
Barton, N.P. – Kanawha Rifleman, [22 VAI]Aug. 4th
Sims, J.F. – Kanawha Rifleman, [22 VAI]Aug. 4th
McMullin, John L. – Kanawha Rifleman, [22 VAI] Aug. 4th
Wise, Henry A. – [General, Wise Legion] Aug. 4th
Lucas, Daniel – [Wise Legion] Aug. 4th
Tabb, Wm B. Capt. – [AAG Wise Legion] Aug. 4th
Wise, Richard A. Capt. – Wise Legion [ADC] Aug. 4th
Harvie, Adj. Genl. – [Wise Legion] Aug. 4th
Peyton, Wm H. – [Capt. Wise Legion QM] Aug. 4th
Haskett, J.L. – [Wise Legion] Aug. 4th
Carter, Fred Lt. – Wise Brigade, Aug. 4th

Thrasher, Leroy C. Capt. – Red Sulphur Springs [59 VAI] Aug. 4th
Bigger, C. Purcell Lt. – Richmond Lt. Inf. Blues [46 VAI] Aug. 4th
Hunt, George – Wise Legion [8 VAC] Aug. 4th
Davis, James M. Lt. – [46 VAI] Aug. 4th
McComas, Wm W. – [Capt. Wise Legion Artillery] Aug. 4th
Timberlake, J.W. Capt. – [10 VAC] Aug. 4th
Brown, Joseph M. – [60 VAI] Aug. 4th
Summers, John C. – Blue Sulphur Springs [60 VAI] Aug. 4th
Tyler, Thompson – [Sgt. 46 VAI] Aug. 4th
Kinney, T.C. – Wise Legion [Lt. 59 VAI] Aug. 4th
Grasty, S. – Wise Legion, Aug. 4th
Brooks, H.C. – Col. Anderson's Regt. Nashville [WL ADC]Aug. 4th
Lowenstein, Wm – Richmond Lt. Inf. Blues [46 VAI] Aug. 4th
Rosenheim, Henry – Richmond Lt. Inf. Blues [46 VAI] Aug. 4th
Cordell, E.F. – Wise Legion, Aug. 4th
Plunkett, W.N. – Appomattox Liberty Guard [Sgt. 46 VAI] Aug. 4th
Thompson, O.D. – [8 VAC] Aug. 4th
Jenkins, Wm A. Dr. – [8 VAC] Aug. 4th
Fitzhugh, Nicholas – [Lt. 22 VAI] Aug. 4th
Moore, P.H. Major – [22 VAI] Aug. 4th
McCarty, W. Page – Wise Legion [Lt. WL Artillery] Aug. 4th
Jenkins, A.G. – Cabell County [Col. 8th Va Cavalry] Aug. 4th
Fitzhugh, H. – [8 VAC] Aug. 4th
Imboden, Francis M. – McCulloch's Rangers [Capt. 59 VAI] Aug. 4th
Buckner, Calhoun C. – McCulloch's Rangers [Lt. 59 VAI] Aug. 4th
Twells, George – McCulloch's Rangers, Aug. 4th
Anderson, Col. – Wise Legion, Aug. 4th
Deane, J.C. Capt. – Wise Legion [Capt. 59 VAI] Aug. 4th
Lawson, John Major – Wise Legion [46 VAI] Aug. 4th
Broun, Thomas L. – [Major 22 VAI] Aug. 4th
Randolph, L.C. Lt. – [46 VAI] Aug. 4th
Roemer, B. Capt. – Wise Legion Artillery, Aug. 4th
Watts, J.W. Lt. – Wise Legion Artillery, Aug. 4th
Sweeney, James W. Capt. – Wise Legion [60 VAI] Aug. 4th
Coffman, Samuel J. – University Volunteers [59 VAI] Aug. 4th
Major, Edmond P. – University Volunteers [59 VAI] Aug. 4th
Harris, Henry H. – University Volunteers [Cpl. 59 VAI] Aug. 4th

Harnsberger, John S. – University Volunteers [59 VAI] Aug. 4th
Mistear, James F. – University Volunteers [Lt. 59 VAI] Aug. 4th
Miller, E. Lt. – Jackson Guard [59 VAI] Aug. 5th
Walkup, Mathew H. – [Lt. 59 VAI] Aug. 5th
Caskie, James A. – Wise Legion, Aug. 5th
Barnes, F.J. – [Pvt. Wise Legion Artillery] Aug. 5th
Butler, W.B. – University Volunteers [59 VAI] Aug. 5th
Gay, Charles W. – University Volunteers [Sgt. 59 VAI] Aug. 5th
McPherson, Samuel M. Dr. – Wise Legion [59 VAI] Aug. 5th
Winfield, J.F. Lt. – Sussex Infantry [46 VAI] Aug. 5th
Owen, Creed W. – University Volunteers [59 VAI] Aug. 5th
Sparrow, T.W. – University Volunteers [59 VAI] Aug. 5th
McCarty, Wm T. – University Volunteers [59 VAI] Aug. 5th
Johnston, Francis – [59 VAI] Aug. 5th
Tower, Charles H. – [Pvt. 46 VAI] Aug. 5th
McFarland, James – [36 VAI] Aug. 5th
Lewis, J.W. Capt. – Wise Legion, Aug. 5th
Harrison, Charles C. Sgt. – Wise Legion [46 VAI] Aug. 5th
Randolph, L.C. Lt. – Wise Legion [46 VAI] Aug. 5th
Pardigon, Claude F. – [Lt. 46 VAI] Aug. 5th
Brock, John P. – Wise Legion [Capt. 10 VAC] Aug. 5th
Brooks, W.C. – [79 VAM] Aug. 5th
Lawson, R. B. – [8 VAC] Aug. 5th
Nighbert, James A. – [8 VAC] Aug. 5th
Ferrell, Joseph R. – [36 VAI] Aug. 5th
Leachman, W.T. – [22 VAI] Aug. 5th
Carter, Fred Lt. – Wise Legion, Aug. 5th
Bigger, C.P. Lt. – Wise Brigade, [46 VAI] Aug. 5th
Blocker, John R. – Wise Legion, [Lt. 59 VAI] Aug. 5th
Edgar, G.M. – [26 Battalion Va Infantry] Aug. 5th
Stedman, Col. – Wise Legion, Aug. 5th
Lawson, John M. – [36 VAI] Aug. 5th
Cleary, F.D. – PACS [Major, Wise Legion] Aug. 5th
Clendinen, A. – PACS, Aug. 5th
Thomas, W.H. – PACS [possibly 14 VAC] Aug. 5th
Vinney, A. – Wise Legion, Aug. 5th
Blocker, John R. – Wise Legion, [Lt. 59 VAI] Aug. 6th

Bigger, Charles P. Lt. – Wise Legion, [46 VAI] Aug. 6th
Carter, Fred Lt. – Wise Legion, [46 VAI] Aug. 6th
Sexton, Col. – [possibly "Seston" unknown] Aug. 6th
Imboden, F.M. – McCulloch's Rangers, [59 VAI] Aug. 6th
Buckner, C.C. – McCulloch's Rangers, [59 VAI] Aug. 6th
Ricketts, L.C. – [8 Va Cavalry] Aug. 6th
Fitzhugh, G.N. – [36 VAI] Aug. 6th
Major, Edmond P. – University Volunteers [59 VAI] Aug. 6th
Wolcott, Augustus – PACS [46 VAI] Aug. 6th
Cannon, Henry G. – Wise Legion, Aug. 6th
Randolph, L.C. Lt. – Green Mountain Grays [46 VAI] Aug. 6th
Harrison, Sgt. – [46 VAI] Aug. 6th
Abbitt, Wm H. – Wise Legion, [Capt. 46 VAI] Aug 6th
Abbitt, George W. – Wise Legion, [Capt. 46 VAI] Aug. 6th
Beckley, Alfred – [Gen. Va Militia] Aug. 6th
Eisenmann, Louis – Wise Legion Aug. 7th
Baldwin, James H. – Floyd Brigade, Aug. 6th
Carter, Fred Lt. – Wise Legion [46 VAI] Aug. 7th
Bigger, Charles P. Lt. – Wise Legion, [46 VAI] Aug. 7th
Bailey, James M. – [Lt. 60 VAI] Aug. 7th
Burdett, F.C. – [Wise Legion, later 26 Btn VAI] Aug. 7th
Preston, Charles G. – Greenbrier Cavalry [14 VAC] Aug. 7th
Archer, W.S. Lt. – CSA [possibly Wise Legion Artillery] Aug. 7th
Duffield, C.B. Major – Wise Legion, Aug. 7th
Hedman, Col. – Wise Legion, Aug. 7th
Fitzhugh, H.G.R. – Wise Legion, Aug. 7th
Fry, J.H. – [22 VAI] Aug. 7th
Little, J.C. – James River Rifles [46 VAI] Aug. 7th
Noel, J.R. – James River Rifles [Lt. 46 VAI] Aug. 7th
Winfield, B.F. – [Capt. 46 VAI] Aug. 7th
Ruckerd, James W. H. – Floyd Game Cocks [Capt. 51 VAI] Aug. 7th
Henley, Richardson – [Lt. 51 VAI] Aug. 7th
Phillips, George D. – [Lt. 51 VAI] Aug. 7th
Goodwin, Stanford – [Pvt. 51 VAI] Aug. 7th
Dunlap, A. – Monroe County [Thurmond's Rangers] Aug. 7th
Gilliam, Wm A. Capt. – [44 VAI] Aug. 7th
Haden, A.H. – [Lt. 60 VAI] Aug. 7th

Dickinson, Wm Col. – Kanawha, Aug. 8th
Argabrite, Jacob H. – Blue Sulphur Springs [14 VAC] Aug. 8th
Belcher, James R. Lt. – Wise Legion [10 VAC] Aug. 8th
Moorman, Capt. – [14 VAC] Aug. 8th
Dickinson, Hiram B. Capt. – [59 VAI] Aug. 8th
Preston, Charles G. – Greenbrier Cavalry [14 VAC] Aug. 8th
Pairo, T.W. Lt. – Wise Legion Artillery, Aug. 8th
Coles, Roberts Capt. – Green Mt. Grays [46VAI] Aug. 8th
Randolph, L.C. Lt. – Green Mt Grays [46 VAI] Aug. 8th
Rives, George T. Lt. – Green Mt Grays [46VAI] Aug. 8th
Harrison, Sgt. – Green Mt Grays [46 VAI] Aug. 8th
Teas, Thomas A. – [Bryan's Battery Va Artillery] Aug. 8th
Fisher, Wm Lt. – [59 VAI] Aug. 9th
Fry, Henry – [79 VAM] Aug. 9th
Fry, Joseph L. – [79 VAM] Aug. 9th
McCherry, Capt. – Wise Legion, Aug. 9th
McKendree, George – Alleghany [Lt. 27 VAI] Aug. 9th
Tucker, Julius Lt. – Meadow Bluff, [10 VAC] Aug. 9th
Barton, Henry H. Capt. – CSA [59 VAI] Aug. 9th
Wise, Richard Capt. – [Wise Legion ADC] Aug. 9th
Halliday, Edward W. – Richmond Lt. Inf. Blues [Sgt. 46 VAI] Aug. 9th
Carter, Fred Lt. – Wise Legion, [46VAI] Aug. 9th
Pate, H. – Wise Legion 1st Cavalry, Aug. 9th
Magruder, Capt. – Wise Legion 1st Cavalry, Aug. 9th
Heth, Henry Col. – Floyd Brigade [45 VAI] Aug. 10th
Dickinson, Wm – Richmond Lt. Inf. Blues [46 VAI] Aug. 10th
McDonald, J.C. – Floyd Brigade, Aug. 10th
Pate, Otho K. Lt. – "and three ladies" CSA Aug. 10th
Sheffey, John P. Lt. – Floyd Brigade [8 VAC] Aug. 10th
Randolph, L.C. Lt. – [46 VAI] Aug. 10th
Smith, Thompson L. – Chaplain 22 VAI Aug. 10th
Glover, P.I. – Wise Legion [not in CSR possibly 22 VAI] Aug. 10th
Quarrier, Joel – [22 VAI] Aug. 10th
DeCloet, Paul L. – University Volunteers [59 VAI] Aug. 11th
Old, W.W. – University Volunteers [59 VAI] Aug. 11th
Braxton, T. Dr. – CSA [Gen. and Staff Surgeon] Aug. 11th

Harvie, J.B. – Wise Brigade, Aug. 11th
Snead, Thomas T.L. – Wise Brigade, Aug. 11th
Bagwell, George H. – Wise Brigade, [Gen. & Staff Capt.] Aug. 11th
Syme, S.A.M. – Wise Brigade, [engineer and QM] Aug. 11th
Major, E.P. – University Volunteers [59 VAI] Aug. 11th
Little, J.C. – [Lt. 46 VAI] Aug. 11th
Mistear, James F. – University Volunteers [Lt. 59 VAI] Aug. 11th
Hansberger, John S. – University Volunteers [59VAI] Aug. 11th
Nounnan, James H. – Shawnee Kansas [8 VAC] Aug. 11th
Barbee, Andrew R. Capt. – Putnam, Va [22 VAI] Aug. 11th
Weisiger, Richard W. – [Pvt. 46 VAI] Aug. 11th
Bigger, C.P. Lt. – [46 VAI] Aug. 11th
Randolph, L.C. Lt. Green Mt Grays [46 VAI] Aug. 11th
Edgar, G.M. – Wise Legion, Aug. 11th
McDonald, J.C. – Floyd Brigade, Aug. 11th
Baton, Capt. – Floyd Brigade, Aug. 11th
Snider, R.B. – Smith County [Pvt. 8 VAC] Aug. 11th
Spalding, J.W. – [Col. 60 VAI] Aug. 11th
Carr, John G. – Kanawha Rifleman [Sgt. 22 VAI] Aug. 12th
Imboden, F.M. – McCulloch's Rangers, [59 VAI] Aug. 12th
Buckner, C.C. – McCulloch's Rangers, [59 VAI] Aug. 12th
Glenn?, S.C. Dr. – Floyd Brigade, Aug. 12th
Price, Samuel – Lewisburg, [Lt. Gov. of Virginia, late war] Aug. 12th
Brooks, H.C. – [Col. Anderson's Regt. TNI, WL ADC] Aug. 12th
Read, F.N. – Kanawha Rifleman [Sgt. 22 VAI] Aug. 12th
Rives, George T. Lt. – Green Mt Grays [46 VAI] Aug. 12th
Harrison, C.C. – [46 VAI] Aug. 12th
Rosenheim, Henry – Richmond Lt. Inf. Blues [46 VAI] Aug. 12th
Syme, S.A.M. – Wise Brigade, [engineer and QM] Aug. 12th
Edgar, G.M. – Wise Legion, Aug. 12th
Abbitt, Wm H. – Wise Legion, [Capt. 46 VAI] Aug. 12th
Abbitt, George W. – Wise Legion, [Capt. 46 VAI] Aug. 12th
Gibbes, W.H. – Wise Legion, [Major WL Artillery] Aug. 12th
Stalnaker, J.W. – [surgeon 14th, 16th and 23rd VAC] Aug. 13th
Thorburn, Charles C. Major – 50 Regt. Floyd's, Aug. 13th
Heth, Henry Col. – 45 Regt. Floyd's, Aug. 13th
Tucker, Julius Lt. – Wise Legion, [10 VAC] Aug. 13th

Swank, Wm A. – Wise Legion, Aug. 13th
Walkup, M.H. – Monroe, [59 VAI] Aug. 13th
Edgar, G.M. – Wise Legion, [Capt. 59 VAI/ Ltc. 26 Btn VAI] Aug. 13th
Carter, Fred Lt. – Wise Legion, [46 VAI] Aug. 13th
Bigger, Charles Lt. – Wise Legion, [46 VAI] Aug. 13th
Hill, J.C. Capt. – Wise Legion, [46 VAI] Aug. 14th
Jenkins, Wm A. Dr. – [8 VAC] Aug. 14th
Carter, Fred Lt. – Wise Legion, [46 VAI] Aug. 14th
Rosenheim, Henry – Richmond Lt. Inf. Blues, [46 VAI] Aug. 14th
Imboden, F.M. – McCulloch's Rangers, [59 VAI] Aug. 14th
Buckner, C.C. – McCulloch's Rangers, [59 VAI] Aug. 14th
Twells, George – McCulloch's Rangers, [59 VAI] Aug. 14th
Hines, Lorenzo S. – University Volunteers, [59 VAI] Aug. 14th
Bigger, Charles Lt. – Wise Legion, [46 VAI] Aug. 14th
Johnston, Frank Lt. – Wise Legion, Aug. 14th
Progler, Jules L. Lt. – 36th Regiment, [CSR says 22 VAI] Aug. 14th
Leathen?, Lt. – Wise Legion, Aug. 14th
Randolph, L.C. Lt. – Wise Legion, [46 VAI] Aug. 14th
Coles, Roberts Capt. – Green Mt Grays, [46 VAI] Aug. 14th
Rives, G. Tucker Lt. – Grays 2nd Regt., [46 VAI] Aug. 14th
Harrison, Charles Sgt. – Wise Brigade, Aug. 14th
Cox, F.M. – Tompkins Regiment [22 VAI] Aug. 15th
Davis, Wm H. – Richmond, [46 VAI] Aug. 15th
McCleery, Patrick – Lewisburg, [135 VAM and 27 VAI] Aug. 15th
Johnston, Francis – [59 VAI] Aug. 15th
Jenkins, Albert G. – Cabell County, [8 VAC] Aug. 15th
Fitzhugh, N. – [22 VAI] Aug. 15th
Wade, James – 36 Regiment Va Vols. Aug, 15th
Little, J.C. – Wise Legion, Fauquier County, [46 VAI] Aug. 15th
Stanard, W.B. – Wise Legion, Goochland Co. [CSR says engineer] Aug. 16th
Webb, Lewis – Richmond, [Wise Legion Artillery QM] Aug. 16th
Dunn, J.B. – Quartermaster, Floyd Brigade, Aug. 16th
Gray, Wm M. Capt. – Floyd Brigade, Aug. 16th
Hounshell, David S. Major – Floyd Brigade, Aug. 16th
Slade, W. Jr. Dr. – Floyd Brigade, [45 VAI assistant sgn.] Aug. 16th

Smith, T.R. Lt. – Wise Legion Artillery, Aug. 16th
Kirby, James Capt. - Wise Legion Artillery, Aug. 16th
Brummel, A.O. Lt. – Wise Legion Artillery, Aug. 16th
Casto, M.B. Dr. – Wise Legion, Aug. 16th
Ellis, Simpson – Logan County [129 VAM] Aug. 17th
Skaggs, James R. – Logan County [129 VAM and 30 Btn VASS] Aug. 17th
Hawley, Lewis J. Lt. – Caskies Rangers, [10 VAC] Aug. 17th
Lewis, W.S. – Kanawha Rangers, [22 VAI] Aug. 17th
Tompkins, Charles – Kanawha Rangers, [22 VAI] Aug. 17th
Phillips, D.B. – CSA Navy, Aug. 18th
Henningsen, Charles F. – Georgia [Col. 59 VAI] Aug. 18th
Rand, Noyes – [Cpl. 22 VAI] Aug. 18th
Ruffner, David L. Capt. – [22 VAI] Aug. 18th
McCleary, Patrick – Lewisburg [135 VAM and 27 VAI] Aug. 18th
Estill, T.M. Dr. – Floyd Brigade, [General and Staff Sgn.] Aug. 18th
Stanard, W.B. – Wise Legion, Aug. 18th
Curry, George – Monroe County [135 VAM] Aug. 18th
McCue, J.H. Capt. – Commissary Floyd Brigade, [51 VAI] Aug. 18th
Tucker, Julius Lt. – Wise Legion, [10 VAC] Aug. 19th
Hawley, Lewis J. Lt. – Wise Legion, [10 VAC] Aug. 19th
Lewis, W.S. – Kanawha Rangers, [22 VAI] Aug. 20th
Capehart, C.Carroll – Kanawha Rangers, [22 VAI] Aug. 20th
Crockett, J.A. – [8 VAC] Aug. 20th
Wasserman, Levi – Richmond Lt. Inf. Blues, [46 VAI] Aug. 20th
James, E.W. Dr. –Wise Legion, Aug. 20th
Clark, Samuel A. – Monroe County [27 VAI] Aug. 20th
Lumpkin, George T. – Wise Legion, [46 VAI] Aug. 21st
Gillespie, W.H. – Wise Legion, [hospital steward] Aug. 21st
Wallace, Gustavus A. Capt. – Wise Legion, [59 VAI] Aug. 21st
Shepperson, A.B. Lt. – Wise Legion, [59 VAI] Aug. 21st
Jordan, J.H. Dr. – Wise Legion, [59 VAI] Aug. 21st
Dunn, G.R.R. – Floyd Brigade, [Assistant QM 36 VAI] Aug. 21st
Baugh, L. – Floyd Brigade, Aug. 21st
Tompkins, Charles – Kanawha Rangers, [22 VAI] Aug. 21st
Capehart, C. Carroll – Kanawha Rangers, [22 VAI] Aug. 21st
Scott, R.T. – Monroe County [Wise Legion Artillery]

Noyes, P.H. – Kanawha Rangers, [22 VAI] Aug. 22nd
DeGruyter, M.F. – [22 VAI] Aug. 22nd
Crockett, John A. – [8 VAC] Aug. 22nd
Hawley, Lewis J. Lt. – Caskies Rangers, [10 VAC] Aug. 22nd
Rosser, Joseph T. – [Capt. 10 VAC] Aug. 22nd
Tucker, Julius Lt. – Wise Legion, [10 VAC] Aug. 22nd
Burne, C. – Meadow Bluff [108 VAM] Aug. 22nd
Hatcher, Edwin C. – [Pvt. 10 VAC] Aug. 22nd
Burwell, Wm A. Lt. – [10 VAC] Aug. 22nd
Lindsay, Capt. – Richmond, Aug. 22nd
Harbour, Joshua W. – Elamsville, Va [Cpl. 10 VAC] Aug. 22nd
McRae, Sherwin – Henrico County, [10 VAC] Aug. 22nd
Bryant, James – [Pvt. 10 VAC] Aug. 22nd
Harris, Berryman B. – [Pvt. 10 VAC] Aug. 22nd
Turner, G.A. – Union Hall, Va [Sgt. 10 VAC] Aug. 22nd
Street, John A. – Union Hall, Va [Pvt. 10 VAC] Aug. 22nd
Dickinson, James L. – Franklin County, Va [Pvt. 10 VAC] Aug. 22nd
Copeland, Wm N. – Franklin County, Va [Pvt. 10 VAC] Aug. 22nd
Holland, John H. – [Pvt. 10 VAC] Aug. 22nd
Schemerhorn, John P. - Richmond, Va [Cpl. 10 VAC] Aug. 22nd
Powell, Wm – [Cpl. 10 VAC] Aug. 22nd
Wade, John H. – [Cpl. 10 VAC] Aug. 22nd
Robbins, Thomas J. – [Pvt. 10 VAC] Aug. 22nd
Frith, Wm H. – Franklin County, Va [Cpl. 10 VAC] Aug. 22nd
Mattox, Gabriel T. – Franklin County, Va [Pvt. 10 VAC] Aug. 22nd
Rice, George W. – [Pvt. 10 VAC] Aug. 22nd
Holland, Thomas S. – Franklin County, Va [10VAC] Aug. 22nd
Preston, Stephen B. – [Sgt. 10 VAC] Aug. 22nd
Arrington, Wm S. – [Cpl. 10 VAC] Aug. 22nd
Craghead, John M. – [Sgt. 10 VAC] Aug. 22nd
Otey, Willis – [Pvt. 10 VAC] Aug. 22nd
Showalter, Jabez – [Pvt. 10 VAC] Aug. 22nd
Mattox, Wm G. – [Sgt. 10 VAC] Aug. 22nd
Lovell, James M. – Henry County, Va [Pvt. 10 VAC] Aug. 22nd
Arnold, E.S. – Kanawha, [Sgt. 22 VAI] Aug. 22nd
Dillard, W.C. – Glade Hill, Va [Pvt. 10 VAC] Aug. 22nd
Jenkins, Wm. Dr. – Green Bottom, Va [8 VAC] Aug. 22nd

Jenkins, T.J. – Green Bottom, Va [Major 8 VAC] Aug. 22nd
Bernard, W.A. – Green Bottom, Va [Pvt. 10 VAC] Aug. 22nd
Bernard, R. C. – Green Bottom, Va [Pvt. 10 VAC] Aug. 22nd
Chitwood, John H. – Green Bottom, Va [Pvt. 10 VAC] Aug. 22nd
Mosby, John S. – Warrenton, Va [Pvt. 1 VAC and Col. 43 Btn VAC] Aug. 22nd
Croghan, St. George Ltc. – 1st Cavalry [10 VAC] Aug. 22nd
Ballard, John C. – [166 VAM and later 26 Btn VAI] Aug. 22nd
Rudd, R.S. – [only one in CSR, "Royal" S. Rudd, Mosby's Rangers] Aug. 22nd

Courtesy West Virginia and Regional History Collection, West Virginia University, the R.S. Rudd papers, A&M 1162.

CHAPTER EIGHT
1862
A GRIM DETERMINATION

The occupation of Raleigh County by Union forces during December and January caused considerable alarm in nearby Greenbrier. On January 2, Virginia Governor John Letcher asked the Secretary of War to send troops to Lewisburg or else call out all available militia. The War Department replied on January 4 that a regiment had already been ordered to garrison Lewisburg and had probably arrived.(1) This regiment was the 22nd Virginia Infantry and in early January they established winter quarters in Lewisburg, much to the delight of the local populace.

Lewisburg, in that first winter of the war, was described as a pleasant town where the churches were full of soldiers every Sunday. The suspension of active campaigning left the soldiers with plenty of spare time, which many of them used to acquaint themselves with the young ladies of Lewisburg. The ladies frequently came out to witness dress parade and offer homemade goods to the troops. Some of the regiment's officers boarded in private homes for the winter and all were treated as the pets of Lewisburg. Captain William Bahlmann said they had an "altogether not unpleasant time," although "the enthusiasm of '61 was gone but a grim determination had taken its place. People had begun to realize that war was a very serious business."(2)

Captain Bahlmann acquainted himself with the family of William Graves, a 52-year-old Lewisburg carpenter with four sons in Confederate service. Mr. Graves' two daughters, ages 24 and 19, were very kind to the soldiers as Captain Bahlmann described: "I gradually introduced the men of the company into

Map of the Virginia Springs, 1870.

the Graves family and it became a sort of headquarters for us. I could go to the house at 9 o'clock at night and say, 'Miss Sallie, Miss Battie, one of our men has just walked in from Jackson's River Depot, he has walked forty miles with very little to eat.' He always got it. It wasn't roast turkey or porterhouse steak, but it would do for a soldier and the Graveses were not rich people."(3)

On January 18, the Secretary of War ordered General Henry Heth to proceed immediately to Lewisburg and assume command of all the troops in that district. Five days later, Col. Alexander Welch Reynolds informed the Secretary of War from Lewisburg that friends had told him about movements of the enemy in the Kanawha Valley. Point Pleasant, on the Ohio River, was their main supply depot. It was said that their huge supply sheds, each nearly 200 yards long, were overflowing with supplies. Federal troops were active all along the Ohio and Kanawha rivers, with detachments as far south as Raleigh Courthouse (Beckley) and Fayetteville. Col. Reynolds correctly judged that this activity was a harbinger of an early campaign by the Yankees. "The mild open winter is inviting," he said, "and I am fearful that unless something is not speedily done the enemy will be able to anticipate us in making the first move, which I think will be very unfortunate in a country like this."(4)

Several times during the winter, detachments of Union cavalry did make brief incursions in and near Greenbrier County. During the last week of January, 250 U.S. cavalry advanced out of Fayette County to within six miles of Meadow Bluff. As was usually the case, fact and fiction mingled to cause great alarm among the citizens of Greenbrier. With wild rumors afloat that the cavalry would join 1,000 infantry at Meadow Bluff, Lewisburg was thrown into a panic. Mr. A.T. Caperton, prominent citizen of Union, Monroe County, informed Confederate authorities of enemy movements on January 29, and added his belief that they would occupy Meadow Bluff. In fact, these were nothing but fact-finding missions, unsupported by infantry.(5) Similar incursions were made by troopers hunting for bushwhackers and ordered out by Col. George Crook from Summersville. Beginning in the fall of 1861, Col. Crook sent spies out as far south as the Greenbrier Valley to identify suspected bushwhackers. Once identified, soldiers were sent to arrest the suspects. It was not a well-kept secret, however, that Col. Crook had imposed a no-prisoners policy: "When an officer returned from a scout he would report that they had caught so-and-so, but in bringing him in he slipped off a log and broke his neck, or that he was killed by an accidental discharge of one of the men's guns, and many like reports. But they never brought back any more prisoners." (6)

Rumors again reached Lewisburg on February 4, stating that a Union raiding party was rapidly approaching. In response, Col. Reynolds sent an urgent plea for support to Lt. Col. William Peters of the 45th Virginia Infantry. Peters' regiment was stationed at Pack's Ferry, Monroe County, and was provided cavalry support by the 8th Virginia Cavalry. Before reinforcements could be sent, word was received that the enemy raid was actually just a "predatory party" which advanced as far as Sewell Mountain for the purpose of thrashing some wheat. (7)

Writing from "Camp Patton" at Lewisburg in early February, Captain A.R. Barbee of the 22nd Virginia Infantry, informed that regiment's former commander, Col. C.Q. Tompkins, of discontent among the men in the regiment. Many of the men and officers disliked Tompkins' replacement, Col. William Jackson, and Capt. Barbee sought authorization to form his own battalion of "400 or 600 stout cavalrymen." Barbee said he would enlist every man himself, adding that he would "have none but true—good—and brave, men." This proposed battalion was never formed, but Barbee replaced Jackson as commander of the regiment on May 2. Nevertheless, discontent among men of the 22nd would contribute to their defeat at the Battle of Lewisburg in May. Later in the war, it was alleged that quite a few soldiers of the 22nd Infantry were Union sympathizers and members of a secret society known as the Heroes of America. (8)

Gen. Heth arrived in Lewisburg on February 6, and issued General Orders Number 1, announcing his command. Having had a few days to learn the positions of the enemy and evaluate plans for the region's defense, he wrote to the Adjutant and Inspector General at Richmond. The situation Heth found was not a good one. His entire force, including the 22nd Infantry at Lewisburg and the 45th Infantry and 8th Cavalry in Monroe County, amounted to barely 1,500 men. The militia could not be relied upon and Heth knew the Yankees could easily send a superior number of troops against him and he fully expected they would do so at their earliest opportunity. He told the Adjutant General that the enemy could advance on the Virginia and Tennessee Railroad via Raleigh Courthouse, which they held, Pack's Ferry, and Peterstown to Dublin Depot. They could threaten the Virginia Central Railroad via the James River and Kanawha Turnpike to Lewisburg, White Sulphur Springs and Covington. Gen. Heth said that in his opinion the enemy would

Gen. Henry Heth CSA, 1825-1899. *Courtesy USAMHI*

move on both lines simultaneously, and in that event he did not have sufficient force to stop them. Heth also described what he said was the sentiment of the local people: "The people of this country show an indifference to its fate which amounts almost to apathy. A few weeks since, when Lewisburg was threatened by an advancing foe, with orders to burn, if they could not hold, the town, only two men of some 300 able to bear arms joined the regiment that advanced to defend their homes." Gen. Heth went on to say that he intended to construct defensive field works six or eight miles west of Lewisburg. He would order similar defensive works constructed on the approaches south from Raleigh County. "I hope that this plan will give confidence to the community," he said, "it will certainly give them the opportunity of having points on which they can rally for the defense of their hearth-stones....I shall attempt, through the influential men...to arouse the people to a sense of their danger and the necessity of aiding in defending their homes." (9)

Gen. Heth had just three artillery pieces available to him and one of those was listed as being inoperative. He requested a total of eight cannons from the Chief of Ordnance at Richmond, and was promised that he would have those by March 15. Believing that he would be able to recruit an artillery company in the Greenbrier region, Heth asked the Confederate government to send him two artillery companies from Richmond. That force would complete his artillery arm as long as they arrived already equipped and ready for service. There also existed a severe shortage of provender for the cavalry as Heth explained to the Adjutant General on March 8: "The Eighth Virginia Cavalry for two months has been guarding the approaches to Mercer County from Raleigh. This regiment must either be at once dismounted or sent to the line of the Virginia and Tennessee Railroad. All the forage in Mercer and the adjacent counties has been consumed....Not one-half of the cavalry now here...has been armed with guns of any description; consequently they never could, fight as a body on foot...I shall defer dismounting the cavalry until I hear from you....The last bushel of corn that can be bought in Mercer has been engaged, and will last only a few days..." (10-11)

Captain James G. Paxton was the Assistant Quartermaster at Jackson's River Depot responsible for sending supplies to White Sulphur Springs. He reported that the quartermaster at the Springs was hauling corn "twenty and thirty miles" from Monroe County. Finding it nearly impossible to purchase corn because the local farmers needed it themselves, the quartermaster was "impressing corn." Captain Paxton stated that, by the end of March, he believed all the corn west of the Allegheny Mountains would be consumed. If the Virginia Central Railroad was completed to Covington, Paxton said it would eliminate nine miles of wagon transportation and allow them to improve the road and supply an army as far west as Meadow Bluff.(12) The difficulty in procuring and transporting supplies was an ever-present problem for the Confederacy in southern West Virginia. On the other hand, Kanawha River navigation gave the Union army a ready chain of supply that was seldom interrupted. It was against this backdrop that the campaigns of 1862 began.

In March, President Lincoln created the Mountain Department, under Gen. John C. Fremont. Fremont divided his command of 35,000 troops into five districts, one of which, the Kanawha, included Greenbrier County. Gen. Fremont was expected to protect the line of the Baltimore and Ohio Railroad, and to destroy the Virginia and Tennessee Railroad, which connected Richmond and Knoxville. Fremont proposed attacking the Virginia and Tennessee Railroad by advancing troops along two routes. One column would march by way of Gauley Bridge and Lewisburg to Jackson River, while the other proceeded south through Beckley and Princeton. This was the very plan that Gen. Heth warned the authorities in Richmond about in February. On March 12, Gen. Rosecrans wrote to the U.S. Adjutant General from Wheeling, offering his summary of the current military situation. Among several objectives proposed by Gen. Rosecrans was a plan to occupy Lewisburg as soon as possible: "with the least practicable delay…seize Lewisburg, White Sulphur, and to strike the…Railroad at some point between Bonsack's and Salem…expel Heth, hold Greenbrier, protect the depots there, and hold the railroad with 2,000 men, a field battery, and a couple squadrons cavalry. They should establish and garrison depots at Lewisburg and Union." If successful, additional troops would threaten Lynchburg, and occupy Augusta and Rockbridge counties. (13)

In making these plans, Federal authorities had fairly accurate information as to the number and disposition of Confederate forces in southern West Virginia. Commanders at Summersville learned from a civilian recently arrived from Greenbrier County that Gen. Heth was constructing defensive field works at Brushy Ridge, west of Lewisburg. Deserters and "refugees" from the Greenbrier militia gave the Yankees in Beckley precise information as to the numbers and plans of Heth's command. (14) Indeed, there was great dissatisfaction among the militia of Greenbrier and adjacent counties because these men believed they would be ordered to some other theater of war, away from their homes. When Gen. Heth attempted to call out the militia in early March, the order was ignored by its officers. (15) Gen. Alfred Beckley resigned as commander of the 27th Brigade Virginia militia and, in response, Mr. J.W. Davis of

Lewisburg offered to take his place. (16) Worries continued to mount for Gen. Heth when he was informed that work on the fortifications at Brushy Ridge was progressing slowly because men of the 22nd Infantry worked "reluctantly."(17)

Gen. Heth and Mr. Samuel Price of Lewisburg determined to do all they could to rally the people. A petition was circulated asking the Confederate government to send additional manpower to the Greenbrier region and, on March 17, Gen. Heth and some locally prominent citizens gave a patriotic speech at the courthouse in Union, Monroe County. In consequence, the Monroe militia assembled and prepared to occupy Lewisburg. A militiaman by the name of Sherwood refused the call to service and was shot in the knee.(18) On the day after his Monroe County speech, Gen. Heth informed Robert E. Lee that he had just four "6-pounder" cannons available, and three of those were barely usable. He told Lee which approaches to the railroad the enemy would use and said he was unable to draw recruits from the Kanawha Valley because it was in Union control and the men could not get through the lines. Having failed in his earlier attempt to get the militia out, Heth tried again, as he told Gen. Lee: "I have called out the militia...of Pulaski, Montgomery, Giles and Mercer, to rendezvous at Peterstown; the militia of Greenbrier, Monroe, Craig, Allegheny, Roanoke, and Botetourt, to rendezvous at Lewisburg....The militia of Greenbrier, or a portion, has refused to obey the call..." Two days later Heth again wrote to Gen. Lee, telling him that the artillery pieces he had been promised from Richmond had not arrived. Further complicating matters was the fact that Heth's army did not include even one man who had ever served as an artillerist. Describing the long odds his army faced, Heth said, "You are perfectly aware, that 300 or 400 men, aided by 1,500 militia, cannot defend the approaches to Lewisburg against a force of 5,000 or 6,000 of the enemy...From everything that I can learn the enemy will very soon make a bold and vigorous effort to reach the Virginia and Tennessee Railroad at the same time that he menaces Lewisburg."(19-20)

Subsequent to Heth's call for the militia, a soldier with the

8th Virginia Cavalry told his sisters about their situation: "The militia of Monroe and Greenbrier have been ordered out en masse. This country has been eaten out, and is almost as barren as if the army worm or the locusts of Egypt had swept over it. It is a barren desert...The clouds are darkening above us, and God only knows what we shall see when the veil is rent. Perhaps the Goddess of Peace will spread her white wings over the land and the glorious sun again look down upon us all brightly and beautifully....For myself I laugh at the horrors and defy the tempest. We will send many a Yankee soul howling to its long home, before we yield even to overwhelming odds."(21)

Captain Thomas A. Bryan was active in Monroe County recruiting men for his artillery company, to be known as Bryan's Battery. Bryan was an 18-year-old former member of the 22nd Virginia Infantry and had received permission during the winter to organize an artillery company with recruits from Monroe and Greenbrier. Information from scouts and spies confirmed the intention of the Yankees to attack the railroads as soon as possible and, on March 26, Gen. Heth ordered Captain Bryan to bring his recruits to Lewisburg. Bryan's 110 men arrived in Lewisburg at 5 p.m. of the 26th and the following day they were officially mustered into Confederate service. The only guns available to these men were the three old smoothbore 6-pounders that Heth had earlier complained were barely serviceable. The men were told to clean and paint the cannons and prepare them for service. The following day Heth notified Gen. Lee that he had engineers at work examining the country with plans to construct additional defensive works outside of town. In the event the enemy did advance, the people of Greenbrier and Monroe counties were asked to destroy whatever grain and hay they could not move. They were also asked to drive off their livestock, thus depriving the enemy of subsistence. Heth hoped these arrangements would retard the Yankee advance, telling Lee that he would leave nothing undone to obstruct the enemy.(22)

Lower than expected Confederate enlistments, failure of the militia to report in full, and concern for the South's ability to control western Virginia prompted President Jefferson Davis to declare martial law in Greenbrier and surrounding counties on March 29, 1862. Gen. Heth proposed the declaration to the president on March 20, at the urging of Allen T. Caperton and other leading citizens of the region. The proclamation was published as General Orders No. 18: "I, Jefferson Davis...do proclaim that martial law is hereby extended over the counties of Greenbrier, Pocahontas, Bath, Allegheny, Monroe, Mercer, Raleigh, Fayette, Nicholas, and Randolph, and I do proclaim the suspension of all civil jurisdiction...and the suspension of the writ of habeas corpus in the counties aforesaid." Exceptions were made in the suspension of civil jurisdiction that would allow wills to be probated, levies to be passed and so on. The distillation and sale of "spirituous liquors" was strictly prohibited, and all persons violating the prohibition would be subject to court martial. Gen. Heth was charged with enforcing martial law and establishing a military police force for that purpose. (23)

In an attempt to deal with manpower problems, the Virginia Legislature enacted a law in March that authorized the recruiting of 10 to 20 ranger companies. These rangers were to be men whose homes were within the western parts of the state then under Union control. When operating in the same area as regular Confederate units, rangers were expected to cooperate with officers of the regular army. The companies would consist of 75 enlisted men and three officers. It quickly became apparent that passage of the ranger law had been a serious mistake. Early ranger companies were generally composed of men who had avoided regular military service, or who were, in fact, deserters. Some others were thieves and bushwhackers, loyal only to themselves and their own selfish desires. Their lawless ways rendered them infamous in a very short time, and on April 2, Gen. Heth informed Governor Letcher of the situation. Heth said the ranger companies he had encountered were "simply bands of organized robbers and plunderers...many of them...are notorious thieves and murderers, more ready to plunder friends than foes." Heth said the men were undisciplined and did whatever they wanted, whenever they wanted. "A guerilla force without being closely watched," he said, "becomes an organized and licensed band of robbers." During early April, two ranger companies were present in Lewisburg and Heth told the governor that he was seriously considering disarming them, "simply as an act of protection to the good citizens of this county." (24)

Two days later, Heth informed the governor that a committee of citizens from Pocahontas County had visited him in Lewisburg complaining about crimes committed by rangers in that county. He enclosed a letter given him by the citizens condemning the rangers and asking that they be abolished. Their letter said the rangers could not possibly benefit the Confederacy or Virginia by murdering citizens and stealing their property. The citizens forwarded their complaints through William Skeen, their Commonwealth's Attorney. Mr. Skeen's eloquent appeal included the admission that there were at least a few good men in the rangers: "Of course I do not mean to say that there are not some good men belonging to the rangers, but neither officers nor the good have power over the vicious and the bad, and the last are daily absorbing the first. A good man and loyal citizen has no more business with them than with the inmates of the penitentiary at Richmond." Gen. Heth told the governor that he would disarm the rangers at Lewisburg immediately, and added his plea that no more ranger companies be authorized. Despite the problems surrounding formation of the rangers, their organization did worry Federal officials in West Virginia. Gen. Fremont was told that Governor Letcher had authorized the men to conduct a system of guerilla warfare and that the men were robbers and murderers who were "devastating the counties of Western Virginia." The independent rangers organized under the act of March 1862 were transferred to control of the Confederate States on February 28, 1863. (25)

Gen. Heth would soon have more than rangers to worry about. On April 7, Gen. Jacob D. Cox informed Gen. Fremont from Gauley Bridge that he had received information from Colonel Crook "as to the true condition of things in Greenbrier." Refugees from Greenbrier County told the Yankees that only 300 or 400 soldiers occupied the county, and that orders had been issued to run livestock across Greenbrier River and burn their forage when the enemy advanced. Crook believed he could move south from Summersville by rapid marches and get to Lewisburg before the forage could be destroyed. Forage was already in such short supply that Union cavalry in Raleigh County imported theirs from Kanawha and Putnam. (26)

Persistent rumors of an enemy advance were frightening to the civilians of the region, who had been told that the Yankees were murdering men, women and children. Many years after the war, Mr. O.W. Kittinger recalled how his parents reacted to those rumors in the spring of 1862: "Then soon came the report that Yankees were coming...That so alarmed our parents, who knew so little about civilized warfare, that they locked up our homes and carried us children and our mothers who lived near the turnpike in the Richlands, to the big spring on the north end of Muddy Creek mountain, where we slept in the huckleberry brush under the pine trees for a whole night, while our fathers collected guns, pitchforks and axes and went out to cut trees across the James River and Kanawha Turnpike to check the Yankee army that never came at that time. We got used to the many reports that 'the Yankees are coming,' but pretty soon they did come thick and fast..."(27)

On April 16, the Confederate Congress passed an act conscripting all men aged 18 to 35 into military service, unless otherwise exempted. The following September, Congress raised the age limit to 45. Exemptions in the act that favored the upper class caused widespread discontent. Most troublesome was the exemption granted owners or overseers of 20 or more slaves. Consequently, many men sought to avoid enrollment and desertion became a serious problem among those who were called up. It was not uncommon for those who refused to serve to be branded, whipped, or even shot. Monroe County delegate Wilson Lively complained that conscripts from his district were jailed after taking their physical exams, and were then escorted under guard to training camp. Governor Letcher opposed conscription as unconstitutional and tried to provide Southwest Virginians an alternative. Less than a month after the Conscription Act was passed, Governor Letcher persuaded the General Assembly to authorize a 10,000 man state army, free from Confederate control. These men were known as the Virginia State Line, and commanded by Gen. John B. Floyd. Only men not subject to conscription were supposed to be enrolled in the State Line forces, but recruiters took anyone, even deserters from regular units. Formation of the State Line caused more problems than it solved and the legislature abolished it in February 1863.(28)

As the Union army continued making preparations for an advance on the railroad, Col. Crook complained that his men were being killed by bushwhackers who harbored themselves in Greenbrier County. Crook's forces had become quite skilled at hunting bushwhackers and seeing to it that prisoners had a fatal "accident" on the way to camp. Despite their initial successes, he grew frustrated that the problem continued seemingly unabated. Complaining to the Assistant Adjutant General on April 16, Crook said the bushwhackers would "disintegrate and hide" when approached, and when the danger had passed would reappear to commit "fresh depredations." He claimed the majority of these men were secreted in Greenbrier County and Lewisburg, and would only "sally out" from time to time. If allowed to march on Lewisburg, Crook said he would push the bushwhackers ahead of him, and those that he did not kill would not stop running until they were east of the Blue Ridge. "I am thoroughly convinced," Crook wrote, "that bushwhacking about Sutton, Bulltown & etc., will not cease until Lewisburg and Greenbrier are cleaned out, for they support these men by donation. By roads taken by these men, Bulltown, Sutton, and this place [Summersville] are nearly equidistant from Lewisburg." He also claimed the local people could stop the bushwhackers if they tried, but that they would not raise a hand to defend themselves as long as the Federal troops remained. (29)

Col. Crook's claim that bushwhackers were using Greenbrier County as a refuge was accurate. Lewisburg was used from December 1861 until May of 1862 as headquarters for the semimilitary Moccasin Rangers of Captain George Downs and Captain John S. Sprigg. The Moccasins were an informal band of about 100 men recruited primarily from Braxton and Wirt counties. Sometimes referred to as the "Western Rangers," these men targeted primarily Union citizens for retribution, but it was their raids on friend and foe alike that made them infamous. It was the Moccasin Rangers that Gen. Heth referred to as the rangers in Lewisburg that he intended to disarm. In 1863, Captains Downs and Sprigg made themselves "legitimate" by joining the Virginia State Line forces and subsequently becoming officers with the 19th Virginia Cavalry. Both men had colorful military careers and both lived to tell the tale. Captain Downs received special notice for his "brave bearing" at the Battle of Droop Mountain, November 6, 1863, and Captain Sprigg was recognized for his "distinguished conduct" in a fight at Beverly, West Virginia, July 1863.

2004 view of the Meadow Bluff campsites used by the 44th Ohio Infantry during the Civil War. *Photo by author*

Chapter Nine
They Fought Like Devils: The Battle of Lewisburg

Caught on a hook
Was Colonel Crook
So the rebel Gen. Heth concluded
A very nice trap
Without any mishap
Which the colonel wily eluded
The armies met
Most deadly set
Did the rebels make to conquer
But Colonel Crook
At the end of a hook
Soon proved the Yankees were stronger

Author unknown
Gallipolis (Ohio) *Journal*, June 5, 1862

The much-anticipated Union move against Lewisburg and the railroads began in early May. Gen. Jacob D. Cox would march with two brigades from the Kanawha Valley to strike the Virginia and Tennessee Railroad by way of Princeton. Colonel

George Crook would occupy Lewisburg and points south, while a fourth brigade under Colonel Joseph Lightburn would hold the Kanawha Valley. On May 6, Union forces under Colonel Rutherford B. Hayes occupied Giles Court House (Pearisburg), while the balance of Gen. Cox's army held Princeton. In response to the Federal advance, Gen. Heth moved on Giles Court House and defeated the enemy there on May 10. He then turned his attention on Princeton and communicated with Confederate General Humphrey Marshall, who commanded an army of approximately 2,200 men. The Yankees were subsequently defeated in a two-day battle for Princeton, ending on May 17.

With Heth occupied at Giles Court House and Princeton, Colonel Crook's forces moved on Lewisburg. The Confederate cavalry company known as the Greenbrier Swifts, commanded by Captain Benjamin F. Eakle, were camped near Handley's Hill west of Lewisburg. At 2 a.m. on May 12, these men clashed with advance elements of Crook's command consisting of Company F, 47th Ohio Infantry and companies B, H, and F, of the 2nd West Virginia Cavalry. The pre-dawn fight at Handley's Hill was brief but hotly contested. The outnumbered Confederates fled toward Lewisburg, leaving behind three of their pickets captured. Union cavalry pursued the Rebels until just outside of Lewisburg when they stopped to await daylight, fearing a trap. This delay allowed soldiers of the 47th Ohio Infantry to catch up with the cavalry. At first light Lt. Col. Elliott, commanding the 47th Ohio, advanced on Lewisburg and found about 90 Rebel cavalry drawn up in line of battle "on the hill above the town." The Yankee infantry advanced at a run and, after the first two volleys, the Rebels "broke for Dixie," pursued by the 2nd West Va Cavalry. The early morning quiet was shattered with the echo of gunfire and the thunder of 300 horses pounding the turnpike at full speed. Citizens of the town could scarcely believe their eyes, when all of a sudden, here were their defenders zipping through town at break- neck speed, hotly pursued by the Yankees. A Union soldier described the first "Battle of Lewisburg" in a letter home: "Lt. Col. Elliott ordered two companies to deploy as skirmishers, the others to advance up the road. When within 600 yards, the skirmishers opened fire. The first volley wounded the rebel captain…without further resistance they ran…They went helter-skelter, spluttering through Lewisburg, yelling like fiends, the rebels firing as they run…they would stick their guns behind and blaze away without aim….the speed of their horses saved them."(1)

The fleeing Confederates were chased to within one mile of White Sulphur Springs, losing one man killed, three baggage wagons, and six men taken prisoner. Thus had the fear of fears been realized and Lewisburg finally occupied by the dreaded Yankees: "The inhabitants were frightened to death, expecting their houses to be burned and every other calamity to befall them…It astonished them beyond measure, that we, after a forced march of two days, and having just driven the rebels from their homes, should encamp on a hillside in a drenching rain. They admit there is more quiet peace since our advent than there was before. Every store in the place is closed up….The inhabitants have a suit of clothes apiece, and don't know where the next is to come from. Silver and gold are curiosities, but everyone is rich in Confederate scrip…." The same writer went on to describe Lewisburg as having "several churches, two school houses, a bank, court-house and whipping post." He claimed the town's Irish citizens rejoiced in their arrival, as did "one true hearted patriot, J.G. Alderson." Apparently Mr. Alderson reported that he had been threatened because of his Union sympathies. When the people saw that no homes were burned down and that no looting had taken place, they began to "crawl out from their dens and cellars, where they hid themselves."(2)

The balance of Col. Crook's forces united at Lewisburg on May 14 and 15, and departed there on the 16th, en route to attack the Virginia Central Railroad at Jackson River. Passing White Sulphur Springs, a member of the 36th Ohio Infantry said he "only thought as we marched through it that I should like to read a book portraying all the intrigues, bargains and sales there of innocent daughters by ambitious mamas, during the fashionable months." (3) In the telegraph office at Jackson River Depot, the Yankees found information that Heth might be reinforced by troops from Staunton. Accordingly, Crook's brigade cut short their raid and hastened back to Greenbrier County, arriving there on the 19th. Gen. Heth's men reached Union, Monroe County, on the 21st and occupied several public buildings. A civilian witness said the men appeared to be run down and "rather raw and undisciplined." Their occupation of Union would set the stage for the second Battle of Lewisburg. (4)

On May 22, Heth's army of fewer than 2,200 men and six pieces of artillery marched away from Union en route to Lewisburg. His command left behind 30 or 40 men who were "sick and exhausted" and without supplies of any kind. The townspeople cared for the soldiers as best they could, housing 18 of them in the high school. Many of the Confederates were untrained in the science of warfare, having recently enlisted or been "pressed" into service. Lt. Col. William Finney's battalion was almost entirely made up of new recruits and former militiamen, and of the 72 men in Company I, 50th Virginia Infantry, 14 joined just four days before the Battle of Lewisburg. All of Heth's companies were also adversely affected by the recent election of new officers. Thus the Confederate army on the eve of battle consisted of many untrained men who were led by senior officers that they did not know and who did not know them. With so many new recruits and new officers, Gen. Heth led an army into combat that had little or no experience or cohesion working together. The combination of all of these factors would prove to be too high an obstacle to overcome when faced by an enemy that had trained together since the previous summer.

During the evening of the 22nd, the anxious Confederates arrived within one mile of the Greenbrier Bridge east of Lewisburg. Late that evening, several members of the 22nd Virginia Infantry, perhaps just two or three men, crept secretly into Lewisburg, going to the homes of their families and friends. Word soon spread throughout the town that the Yankees would be attacked in the morning. Anticipating an easy Confederate victory, some of the citizens prepared a great feast for the victorious Rebels to enjoy after the fight. The hopeful boys in gray spent an anxious night near the bridge, quietly contemplating the coming battle, confident of victory.

Just after 4 a.m. of the 23rd, Heth's advance, with Finney's Battalion in the lead, started out at "double quick" to surprise the Yankee pickets at the bridge, one mile distant. The bridge was guarded by 12 Union infantrymen and a half-dozen cavalry, commanded by Lt. Martin of the 36th Ohio Infantry. The sudden advance on the bridge surprised the pickets who nevertheless managed to fire a round or two before retreating across the bridge toward town. The pre-dawn quiet was shattered with the echo of gunfire as Lt. Martin's men reformed and managed to fire another volley before being overtaken and captured. The cavalry pickets made good their escape, however, and sped through the mountain darkness back toward Lewisburg. Crook's 1,400 troops were camped on the heights behind the present Greenbrier Community College and could clearly hear the fighting at the bridge. They heard just one or two rounds at first, then "in a few moments after, a round of 12 or 20 shot admonished us that our pickets were being engaged."(5) As the alarm was sounded throughout the camps, Col. Crook ordered Company D, 44th Ohio and Company G, 36th Ohio to advance as skirmishers. Without hesitation these men rushed toward the hill on the southeast side of town and began to climb the ridge opposite their camp. At that moment, two Confederate cavalrymen appeared on the eastern ridge above the pike, "wheeled their horses to the South, fired their carbines in the air, and disappeared." (6) Immediately afterward the skirmishers were surprised to see the rebels forming in line of battle along the summit of the ridge. One participant said it "appeared to me, as the sight met my gaze that moment, as though, by magic, they sprang out of the ground upon which they stood." The Rebels advanced confidently, certain they would whip the enemy for their "impudence to presume the right of our presence in Lewisburg." (7) At that instant the rebels opened a withering volley on the skirmishers, killing one and wounding three others. An officer with the 36th Ohio yelled, "Scatter and lie down!" which the men proceeded to do, "some lying down by the fence, some on the pavements, others in the middle of the streets." A soldier with the 36th Ohio would later record that he never "tried to occupy less space in my life than upon that occasion," and that "three bullets struck the earth half arm's length from my face, throwing the dirt into my face and eyes, causing them to sting smartly with pain. Looking at my watch I found it was 5:01 a.m." Amid the noise, confusion, and smoke of battle, the cry "Fall back" was heard. The boys in blue fled toward some houses where they expected to hold the enemy in check, keeping to the west of the Main Street, or pike. As the Yankees fell back, the Rebels observed their baggage wagons being moved away from town and thought the enemy was retreating. The Confederate line came alive with shouts of "Go get 'em boys," and "Run the Yanks back to Ohio." These shouts were echoed by citizens of the town who jeered the fleeing blue-bellies and shouted, "Drive the Yankees to the Ohio River."(8)

As the skirmishers fell back, the balance of Crook's force advanced and began to form on Main Street when the Southern artillery opened fire. At that instant, Heth's army advanced over the ridge toward town, screaming and yelling wildly: "It looked to me, at that moment, as if the johnnies were coming over that ridge, as numberless as grasshoppers in a stubble-field."(9) Some of the first shots fired by the Confederate artillery fell short, killing Private Charles Chewning, a 19-year-old member of the 22nd, and striking the John Wesley Methodist Church on Foster Street. Another round struck Private Adam Alt, a teenage soldier with the 44th Ohio who was standing on a rock behind his company. The shell tore into Alt's abdomen, ripping him open in "an awful way." The boy survived the injury for one hour, telling his company commander to inform his parents that he died in defense of his country.(10) Gen. Heth's artillery was placed on his left and center, and one cannon was said to be an antique captured from the British at Yorktown in 1781. Heth deployed his least experienced men, Finney's Battalion, on his left. The center was held by the 45th Virginia, and the 22nd Virginia held the right. Against the advice of his artillery officers, Heth ordered four of his cannons advanced into town and unlimbered on a small knoll. At least one cannon was placed at the current site of the General Lewis Motor Inn. Lt. Col. E.H. Harman of

Above: The John Wesley Methodist Church at Lewisburg. Constructed in 1820, it was struck by a cannon ball during the Battle of Lewisburg in 1862. Below: Signs on the John Wesley Methodist Church showing the location of the slave staircase and the location where the cannon ball struck. *Photos by author*

the 45th Virginia Infantry knew it was a serious mistake to move the artillery from the heights overlooking town. His frustration with Gen. Heth is apparent in a letter Harman sent to his wife: "A great blunder had been committed. To think of throwing the artillery in the rear of a battalion, most of which were never under fire; and to keep the guns advancing when a better position for them was on a hill in our rear, the proper place for artillery."

Now Crook's entire infantry force boldly advanced to within 200 yards of the Rebel line and engaged their visitors in a shower of lead, screaming, "Remember Ohio," and "Give the Johnnies hell." The 36th was told to attack the Rebel right while the 44th assaulted their left. Their first volley overwhelmed men of the 22nd Virginia, who fell "like ten pins in a bowling alley."(11) The 44th Ohio moved up the hill to their front, "climbing fences, breaking open gates, & marching through gardens, yards and fields." A witness said, "It would have done your heart good to see our brave boys march up that hill without once flinching. Now they pour the shot into the enemy, volley after volley, in quick succession, and onward they steadily move. The enemy are thunder struck."(12)

The 36th Ohio massed near the courthouse and moved along Randolph and Chestnut streets to form a line along present Lee Street, to meet Heth's right, while the 44th moved on up the hill through a grove of oak trees (present Van Sickler Drive) and into close contact with Finney's Battalion and the artillery on the Confederate left. Crook ordered Companies C, F, and I, of the 2nd West Virginia Cavalry to guard against any flanking movements and, in that endeavor, Company C reported they became "partially engaged" during the battle. The 45th Virginia moved north of present Lee Street, with the 22nd Virginia in a wheat field to the right, later a drill field of the Greenbrier Military School and in the path of the 36th Ohio. Finney's Battalion came within 75 yards of the 44th Ohio "when suddenly a sheet of fire gleamed from the woods, and a murderous fire was upon [them]. Most of these men had never been under fire before. At each discharge…they fell by the scores; they stood till nearly every other man lay dead or wounded…" (13)

Lewisburg's anxious citizens peered from their places of presumed safety and for a short while it appeared as if the Rebels might win the Battle of Lewisburg. Rose W. Fry, granddaughter of the Rev. John McElhenney, described what they saw: "Thus aroused, half-dressed, the children flattened their faces against the window-panes. From this position we had a good view of what was taking place on our left flank. We could see the terri-

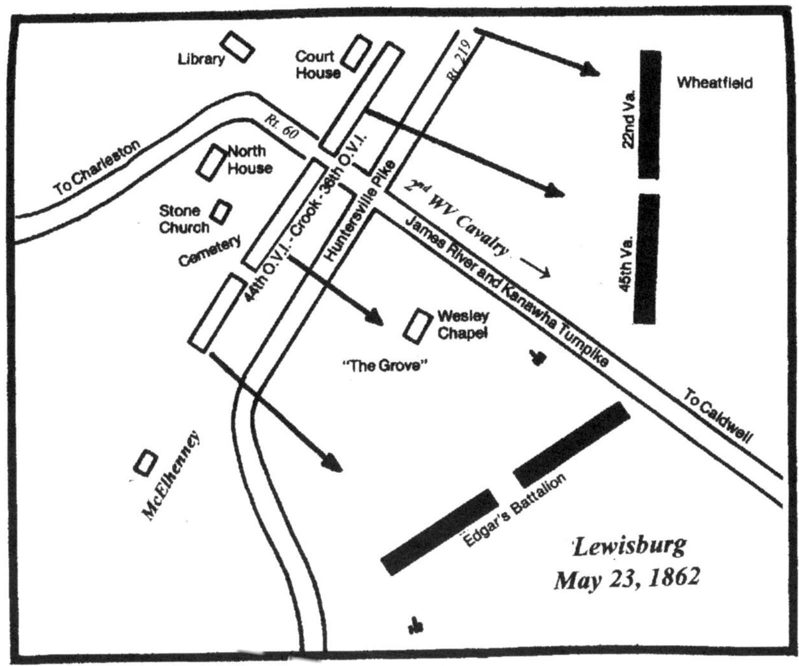

Battle map.

fied negroes running to the woods back of 'Mucklehenney's house'; we could see the puffs of smoke almost simultaneously with the rattle of musketry. We heard the discharge of artillery almost for the first time in our lives. It was an exciting, nay, even an alarming moment. The bullets whistled through the trees in the yard."(14) Indeed, it was such an alarming moment that some of the townspeople gathered their children and attempted to flee the town: "We could see many women and children, both black and white, running hither and thither; many of each class just as they had arisen from their beds—but partially dressed. They were endeavoring to make their way out of town." (15) A soldier with the 44th Ohio who remained in camp sent this account to his hometown paper, the Marietta, (Ohio), *Home News:* "To those left behind to guard prisoners, baggage, & etc., the whole affair was a splendid sight. A dense cloud of smoke hovered over our line, apparently advancing with it; sometimes hiding it entirely, and others exposing it to view....the rebels running back out of the smoke which they had made and hear us cheer...the men were compelled to laugh occasionally at the antics of the darkey cooks left behind. Whenever a shell would come squalling and cursing through the air at them, a general stampede would take place and such dodging and scrambling for shelter."(16)

As the battle raged, an artillery shell went down the chimney of the Cary house, causing a fire. This was probably the home of Orphelia Cary, a widow, whose three teenage daughters were said to be "the belles of Lewisburg." In a strange turn of events, the Methodist church was struck by an artillery shell supposedly fired by Heth's ancient Yorktown cannon. According to legend, the old gun lacked a carriage so the artillerymen chained the barrel to a slave cabin and an oak tree (behind the General Lewis Inn), using piled fence rails for support. The makeshift cannon supposedly shifted when the fence rails moved, causing a solid shot to ricochet several times before striking the church. It is unlikely, however, that the Confederates would have traveled with just a cannon barrel in tow. This gun was captured during the battle and Union forces make no mention of the gun lacking a carriage. In fact, records indicate that the captured cannon's carriage was replaced due to deterioration many years later. If the gun was chained, it was because of its position on the slope of the hill.

With Crook's infantry steadily firing and advancing, the opposing lines fought to within 75 yards of each other when the Yankees began to flank Finney's Battalion and concentrated their fire on the Southern artillery battery. Very quickly, 20 Confederates lay dead at and near the cannon emplacement while bloodied artillerymen attempted in vain to remove one gun to prevent its capture. The firing becoming so intense, the men abandoned the gun in a fence corner and made good their escape. Seeing these events unfold, Captain Charles Fudge of the 45th Virginia made a valiant attempt to remove the cannon from the fence corner, but the two horses with the gun were shot. Becoming nearly surrounded, the captain barely managed to get away. A soldier with the 44th described the intensity of the fight: "As we cleared the woods and came into a plowed field, the bullets filled the air. The rebels were falling fast and began to waiver....Captain Stough ordered Company F to direct their fire on the battery. Company K directed their fire on the caissons. Cannoneers and horses fell to the ground. Major Mitchell ordered the left to charge on the battery...the left started on a double-quick. Company F reached the guns first, and Captain Stough said...'I take this gun in the name of Company F.'" Several members of the 44th were wounded and one killed in the charge on the battery. The dead soldier was Francis Runyon, an Ohio teenager, who "behaved like an old veteran" on the battlefield. Struck twice in the chest, the boy tumbled to the ground and died within minutes. His last words were, "I die happy, tell my parents I will meet them in heaven."(17)

With Heth's artillery captured and Finney's Battalion crumbling, the Rebel center and right became caught in a deadly crossfire and began to waiver: "The rebels slowly at first yielded, yet disputed, desperately, every particle of ground, taking advantage of every fence or other cover, fancied or real, to halt, to rapidly fire, and bravely endeavor to hold." (18) Another Union soldier said they "opened on them, giving it to them on the right and left hot and heavy. When our boys got within reach of their artillery they directed their fire at them and the guns were soon silenced. After that they began to retreat but made another stand, our men never stopped but poured in such a heavy cross fire on them that they were obliged to retreat and they became confused and away they went..."(19) Lt. Col. Harman was at the Confederate center with the 45th Virginia when Finney's Battalion on his left collapsed: "I was upon the left of our regiment and saw...the regiment on my left cut to pieces, and the Yankees advance to within sixty yards of where I was, our regiment pouring the shot upon them, but they were so thick, they pressed on and passed us, firing upon us...I thought we had to fall back as a military necessity, which we did in good order, firing as we retreated."(20) Bullets pierced Harman's clothing at his right arm and left leg, but he was only bruised and managed to get away with his regiment. Capturing the cannons and "rolling up" Finney's Battalion was described by Col. Samuel Gilbert of the

44th in his official report: "I formed...in line of battle on the south side of Main Street and advanced...on emerging from a small grove we came suddenly upon a battery...which was charged...Leaving small guards over the artillery and prisoners we pushed on to the top of the hill, where the enemy had first formed...the enemy retired..."(21)

On the Confederate right, the 22nd Virginia entered the contest with 396 men. Of that number, the regiment lost 149 killed, wounded, and missing. Captain William Bahlmann's Company K of the 22nd entered the fight with 36 men and lost 21, as he later described: "Bud Sandidge was shot through the heart, Miles Johnson through the temple, C. Blake and Pat Murray through the thigh, Bill Taylor through the shoulder and I through the right arm and on the right hand....Sam Parker was killed...I was near Capt. Ben Chase who was shot through the heart and lying on his face. I bled so fast that I fainted....A bullet wound feels like the prick of a hot needle and like a marriage proposal is very sudden."(22) Bahlmann was captured and sent to prison at Camp Chase, Ohio, and was later exchanged. Lt. Col. Melvin Clarke commanded the 36th Ohio on Heth's right. In his report of the battle, Clarke says his men fought the 22nd Virginia "passing the houses" and "numerous fences" and "for a short time the fight was very sharp." He said his men closed to within 40 yards of the 22nd when "they fled in confusion...a large number of their dead and wounded lay behind the fence where they were first posted and scattered through the fields beyond."(23)

Lt. W.A. Smith of the 50th Virginia Infantry was "in the hottest of the battle...and came away without a scratch." In writing to his brother, Smith said others of his company were not so fortunate: "You will be startled when I tell you that we have 32 men killed, wounded and missing and took only 72 into the fight....Our men left the field in confusion; the rout became general, the enemy followed and fired upon us...till we had run 400 yards. Each man made his escape the best way he could..."(24)

The Rebels ran back toward the Greenbrier bridge with all possible speed, pursued by members of the 2nd West Va Cavalry. Along the way the cavalry skirmished briefly with a small rear

Washington Street (Route 60 west) in Lewisburg in the 1870s. *Courtesy Greenbrier Historical Society*

Postwar view of Washington Street (Route 60 east). *Courtesy Greenbrier Historical Society*

Left: Route 60, looking west, in 2004.
Below: Route 60, looking east, in 2004.

Opposite, top: The Second WV Cavalry charged up this Washington Street hill at the end of the Battle of Lewisburg. *Photos by author*

Right: Area between Holt and Echols Lane where severe fighting occurred during the Battle of Lewisburg. The Confederates attempted to cross an open field here and were subjected to devastating fire.

guard hastily assembled by the Confederates, who continued their retreat, burning the bridge behind them. The last of Heth's men to reach the bridge found it "blazing on both sides" and, after a moment's hesitation, ran through it without any serious burns. (25) Returning to camp, one of the Union soldiers wrote that the road back toward the bridge could be traced by "blood that had ran from the wounded," and that the "entire field and road was strewn with muskets, bayonets, cartridge and cap boxes, knapsacks and haversacks, rations, canteens...pantaloons, jackets, books, letters, paper, envelopes, and other etceteras." (26)

The defeated and demoralized men in gray reached Union, Monroe County around 4 p.m. Lt. William Smith of the 50th Infantry said they arrived "completely broken down, having marched so far with nothing to eat." Col. Alexander W. Reynolds paused during the retreat to inform Mrs. Sallie Patton at Lewisburg why his planned visit failed: "Came very near making you a visit this morning, was down as far as the second house above Mr. M's [McClung's] But unfortunately we miscalculated our strength, and were driven back with loss...Doubtless you all were very much frightened. I humbly trust that none of the citizens were hurt by our shots. Mr. M's garden seemed to be full of men at one time, in close conflict." (27)

In his official report of the battle, Gen. Heth said victory was in his grasp, but attributed their defeat to "one of those causeless panics for which there is no accounting." He declared that three of his regiments exhibited "disgraceful behavior" because they were "filled with conscripts and newly officered under the election system." Nevertheless, Gen. Heth took responsibility as commander, saying he wanted simply to give a "plain statement of facts apparent to all present."(28)

In reality, the facts were not "apparent to all present" and many of Heth's officers and men blamed him for their defeat. Some would later claim that their commander was sampling his whiskey flask before the first shot was fired, celebrating the expected victory. Others, like Lt. Col. Harman, were furious with Heth for ordering the artillery down from the ridge east of town, resulting in the loss of four cannon, at least 20 artillerymen and 38 artillery horses. While the Yankees thought the Southern infantrymen fought bravely and "disputed every inch of ground" until retreat became a necessity, Gen. Heth said their actions were "disgraceful." Certainly poor planning and an unjustifiable confidence on Heth's part contributed to the end result. Had he taken the pickets at the bridge without any shots being fired, he would have had the element of surprise on his side. As it happened, the Rebels charged the bridge, the resulting gunfire alerting Crook's army. Gen. Heth was also criticized for not sending a skirmish line out, and for ordering Finney's Battalion further left toward present Van Sickler Drive. That move stretched the manpower between the Southern left and center, weakening the line. Heth's available cavalry, the 8th Virginia, was held in reserve during the battle. Had he utilized them as either a flanking party or skirmishers, the pressure on his infantry would have been reduced. Another factor was the ferocity with which the blue coats defended their position. One captured Confederate officer commented that they would have defeated the Yankees but "they fought like devils." (29) Most of the men in the 22nd Virginia Infantry blamed Finney's Battalion for their defeat, but a majority of the officers placed the blame squarely on Gen. Heth. From start to finish, the Confederate battle plan seemed to be no plan at all, just an army of men and boys rushing headlong into a hornet's nest.

Confederate losses in the battle are difficult to ascertain due to conflicting accounts. In Gen. Heth's official report, written after they reached Union, he said he was yet to ascertain "our exact loss," but admitted a heavy loss in officers. On the day after the fight, Gen. Crook reported the enemy losses as 100 captured, 66 wounded, 38 "dead on the field," four cannons, and 300 small arms. Captain Stough of the 44th Ohio said he walked the battlefield after the fight and personally counted 45 killed, and many others wounded, "some of whom have since died swelling the number killed to 70." An amalgamation of Confederate and Union accounts gives an estimate of 70 killed, 100 wounded, and 145 taken prisoner, for a total loss of 315, or 15% of the Southern troops engaged. Federal forces reported a loss of 13 killed (actually15 because two wounded men died), 54 wounded, and seven captured, for a total of 74, or 6% of the 1,200 men engaged.

Two of Gen. Crook's wounded men, Private George Sherer of the 36th Ohio, and perhaps one other soldier, were shot and killed from nearby houses as they made their way back to camp. As the fight got under way, Crook himself was shot from one of the houses, the spent ball striking his foot. In retaliation, the houses were burned that the shots came from. The quartermaster of the 36th Ohio Infantry claimed that a total of three houses were burned down. The destruction was described in the *Point Pleasant Register*: "Mrs. Welch's dwelling in the eastern part of the town was burned last evening…because one of the wounded of the 36th was shot from it. Mrs. Welch's grand son-in-law…had returned home a few days before the battle, and too cowardly to meet the foes on the field, he murdered them when disabled. He saved his neck by skedaddling." (30) Abe Straley was the rebel soldier who shot Pvt. Sherer. He participated in the battle and at its conclusion had secretly slipped into his mother-in-law's house to get some clean clothes. Seeing Sherer pass by, and not realizing he was injured, Straley shot him. He then concealed himself in the wood shed by climbing up onto a wide plank on the rafters, remaining there until the danger had passed. The soldier instructed to burn the Welch house said they were attempting to determine how many houses the shots came from. Once that information was confirmed, he said he would "burn all the balance…I have no sympathy for any of them." (31) The editor of the Marietta, (Ohio), *Home News* offered his opinion of the bushwhacking: "We have abundant evidence that two of our men who were wounded…were shot at and killed by citizens…We learn from an officer in Company A that the houses from which the bullets proceeded have been burned. This is well. If the miscreants had been burned in them, it would have been better. We also learn that the traitors of that town…so confident were they of the defeat of the Union troops, that in many houses and the hotels ample provision had been made for feasting the victors. But instead of breakfasting on boiled secesh hams and other fixings, our boys gave them cold lead, which effectually settled their stomachs." (32) Captain James Haddow, a young soldier with the 36th Ohio Infantry, wrote his wife about the situation a few hours after the fight: "As our wounded returned…some were fired on by the citizens…A fearful day of reckoning waits those guilty of such barbarism….Many of the buildings in town were injured by the enemy's shot and shell. The whole place should be destroyed as there are no Union people in it…" Another soldier complained that with but one or two exceptions Lewisburg was "rotten secesh!"(33)

Gen. George Crook, victorious Union commander at the Battle of Lewisburg. *Courtesy State of West Virginia*

Crook's men utilized the churches, public buildings, and hotel as hospitals. Upon entering the hotel, they found that it had been secretly converted into a "banquet hall," in which Gen. Heth and his officers "were to be entertained at breakfast, after our absolute annihilation, but we did not annihilate." (34) One of the wounded rebels hospitalized at Lewisburg was Captain Bahlmann of the 22nd Virginia Infantry. He captured the experience in his journal: "After the fight was over some of the people of town came out...Miss Bettie Graves came to where I was lying...stooped over and kissed me....Pat and I were carried to private houses but on the same day were transported to the Virginia Hotel which had been taken for a hospital. Pat and I occupied the same bed while the other bed was used by Capt. John K. Thompson...whose left eye had been shot out." Several days after the fight Captain Bahlmann was among the wounded soldiers transferred to hospitals in Ohio: "Many of the ladies of the town, both married and single, gathered on the walk to see us off....The ladies I think kissed every one of these men except me. It has been a psychological puzzle to me why they didn't kiss me. My hand was bandaged and my right arm was in a sling. However, I did not go entirely without, I did my kissing in the hospital." (35)

A grotesque panorama was presented by the Lewisburg battlefield, with a combined total of approximately 85 killed and 150 wounded strewn about the village. Here and there could be seen the ghastly dead and the moaning wounded, dead horses and lost or abandoned equipment. Furrows had been plowed into the ground by the screaming artillery shells, tossing piles of earth and stone. Broken and scattered rails gave evidence where fence lines use to be and pools of blood dotted the landscape.

George Jenvy, bugler for the 2nd West Va Cavalry, inspected the battlefield a few hours after the fight: "They had been engaged in removing the dead all morning, and yet on the outskirts of the field I counted twenty dead that had not been gathered up. Behind a fallen log three dead bodies were lying just as they had been shot. They were shot in the head or breast…In a bed of clover lay a gunner…with one bullet hole through the brain and another through the jaw. He fell while in the act of discharging the largest cannon the enemy had." With ambulance wagons "in full play" and wagon loads of dead bodies passing him by, Jenvy visited the wounded men: "The first house I entered there lay on the floor twelve wounded rebels, and one of our men shot through the heart." Suffering intense pain, some of the soldiers were "supplicating God" to have mercy on their souls. "There the poor fellows lay, writhing and groaning in terrible agony. The spectacle was so sickening that I was compelled to get into the open air. I walked up the street and soon heard groans coming from another house. Looking through the window I saw several dead bodies…The next door being open, I entered and found twelve more wounded rebels. One had the back part of his head shot off leaving his brains exposed….He was still alive, moaning away the painful moments. His lamp was almost extinguished." One of the wounded Yankees complained that he was shot through the leg while marching up to the fight, by someone from behind a house, and that a citizen attempted to shoot another wounded boy but his gun misfired. "The boy coolly took note of the house and the features of the man, and in the evening took the colonel of the 36th and showed him the house – and rumor says somebody is to swing." (36)

On the day after the fight, an officer with the 44th Ohio wrote to the family of Private Adam Alt, informing them of their son's death: "It becomes my sad duty to inform you of the death of your son Adam, who fell pierced by a ten pound shell, through his body. But let it be your pride, that he died, yes, nobly died, in defense of our much loved country, and rest assured that he has been fully avenged...I have had Adam nicely washed and dressed, and he, with the rest of our glorious dead, will be buried by the regiment, in one hour from this, and his grave properly marked..." (37)

On May 24, the dead Union soldiers were buried "on a little knoll just north of the town and west of the pike. It was a delightful spot, surrounded by a very neatly made and painted picket fence, and each grave was marked with name, company, rank, and regiment of occupant." (38)

The exact location of this graveyard was not generally known until 1990, when oral history revealed the graveyard as being on the grounds of the Jack Wallace home, near the western boundary of the city. That year a plaque was placed at the sight honoring the Union soldiers. Sunken impressions in the earth at the Wallace home clearly indicate where 15 men had been buried. The event was reported in the 1991 edition of the *Journal of the Greenbrier Historical Society*. From work done by Dr. John F. Montgomery in 1984 we know that the Union soldiers remains were moved to the National Cemetery at Staunton sometime after the war. (39)

Conflicting accounts make it difficult to determine what burial arrangements were made for the Confederate soldiers. It is known that their bodies were laid out in the Old Stone Presbyterian Church until placed in a mass grave in the adjacent graveyard. Several Northern accounts state that relatives of the deceased soldiers were allowed to claim their bodies, but only a few did so. Rose W. Fry, Rev. John McElhenney's granddaughter, offered an entirely different account in 1893: "The citizens were refused permission to bury the Confederate dead. The bodies were laid out in the church until a trench, some fifty feet long, was dug, and in this enormous grave, without coffins, unknelled and unblessed, without ceremony, they were laid away." (40) Her account is corroborated somewhat by Samuel Harrison, a soldier with the 44th Ohio Infantry, who witnessed the burial and called it "the hardest sight I ever saw. They were laid in close order, side by side with their [clothes] all on and dirty, muddy, the dirt throwed in on them just like we would bury a dog." (41)

After the war the Southern soldiers were disinterred and reburied in a large common grave, mounded in the form of a cross. Since that time this has been known as the Confederate Cemetery. It is a well known and beautiful Lewisburg landmark.

On fame's eternal camping ground,
Their silent tents are spread:
While glory guards with solemn round
The bivouac of the dead

Roster of men captured at the Battle of Lewisburg

The following 115 names of prisoners taken at the Battle of Lewisburg were published in the *Wheeling Intelligencer,* May 30, 1862. Subsequent lists published in the same newspaper on July 7, and July 16, 1862 increase the total to 131. In June the *Gallipolis Journal* (Ohio) published the names of 23 Southern soldiers who were in the hospital there, having been captured at Lewisburg (see chapter 11). Of those, all but eight are duplicates from the Wheeling paper. Fourteen additional prisoners were hospitalized at Lewisburg until the surviving 12 were paroled on June 12, giving a total count of 153.

Abers, Wilson
Alderman, Marion, Bland Co.
Allen, John, Alleghany Co.
Asbury, Lorenzo D., Greenbrier Co.
Atkins, Levi, Boone Co.
Aukman, W.R., Jackson Co.
Bahlmann, Wm F., Taylor Co.
Baker, Lewis F., Nicholas Co.
Bashum, Augustus, Monroe Co.
Black, John D., Pulaski Co.
Bollis, William F.

Bowen, Edward T., Montgomery Co.
Braxton, P., King William Co.
Brooks, Leonidas L., Morgan Co. Ky.
Brown, William M., Alleghany Co.
Budon, H.V., Kanawha Co.
Burdett, George W., Monroe Co.
Bykias, James F., Fayette Co.
Caldwell, Andrew F., Mercer Co.
Campbell, J.F., Nicholas Co.
Campbell, John H., Monroe Co.
Caraco, William A., Mason Co.
Carson, W.V.B., Monroe Co.
Chandler, W.T., Monroe Co.
Chewning, Andrew J., Braxton Co.
Clendenon, R.C., Fayette Co.
Connelly, Russell F., Pulaski Co.
Covert, John, Logan Co.
Cox, Lafayette Carroll Co.
Crawford, Owens, Alleghany Co.
Crawford, William, Alleghany Co.
Creager, Calvin R., Wythe Co.
Davis, John M., Greenbrier Co.
Demsey, G.W., Fayette Co.
Dillworth, J.W., Jackson Co.
Dillworth, Josiah, Jackson Co.
Dodd, Lorenzo R., Craig Co.
Douglas, Jacob, Kanawha Co.
Dyker, Elijah, Greenbrier Co.
Eagle, William J., Greenbrier Co.
Elkins, Rafe
Ellison, Lewis A., Monroe Co.
Evans, Moab, Augustus Co.
Finney, W.W., Powhattan Co.
Firestone, Wm L., Botetourt Co.
Flint, Joseph, Greenbrier Co.
Flint, Sam D., Greenbrier Co.
Gilspear, George P. Jackson Co.

Given, Samuel, Alleghany Co.
Graham, Lanta J., Monroe Co.
Gray, Osborn W., Floyd Co.
Gray, W.T., Monroe Co.
Griffith, Isaac, Pulaski Co.
Gun, William, Pulaski Co.
Gutherie, Felix, Fayette Co.
Hall, H.G., Nicholas Co.
Hamilton, S.D., Alleghany Co.
Hansbarge, Wm T., Roanoke Co.
Harlow, Ben F., Greenbrier Co.
Harris, William, Monroe Co.
Hayes, Harlow, Fayette Co.
Hendrickson, John, Nicholas Co.
Hickman, George R., Nicholas Co.
Hill, John J., Monroe Co.
Holliday, Charles J., Greenbrier Co.
Honiker, Peter, Pulaski Co.
Hudson, Henry R., Greenbrier Co.
Humes, M.H.H., Greenbrier Co.
Humphrey, M.N., Greenbrier Co.
Johns, J.C., Jackson Co.
Johnson, H.J., Louisa Co.
Johnson, M.A., Greenbrier Co.
Keyser, Andrew J., Alleghany Co.
Kidd, John M., Bland Co.
King, Chapman, Pulaski Co.
Linthoacon, Dan A., Greenbrier Co.
Lowderbach, Josiah, Greenbrier Co.
Lowry, Sam B., Greenbrier Co.
Lufliln, Elijah, Carroll Co.
Lyons, W.H., Carroll Co.
Magan, Darius, Monroe Co.
Mahoney, John, Greenbrier Co.
McClain, Addison, Putnam Co.
McKinney, James M., Greenbrier Co.
Meadows, G.C., Monroe Co.

Miller, George W., Mercer Co.
Miller, W.F., Monroe Co.
Mitchell, John W.
Mitchell, Stephen W., Carroll Co.
Morgan, E.H., Greenbrier Co.
Morris, Augustus
Morrison, Fountain Alleghany Co.
Murry, Patrick
Neider, John T., Bland Co.
Niel, James, Monroe Co.
Niel, Wm H.H., Nicholas Co.
Oiler, John, Greenbrier Co.
Oyler, Miles P., Greenbrier Co.
Perkins, Joseph R., Greenbrier Co.
Perry, Henry E., Greenbrier Co.
Rand, N., Kanawha Co.
Remley, Mason, Nicholas Co.
Rhoads, Christopher, Greenbrier Co.
Simpson, Andrew J., Alleghany Co.
Singleton, A.R., Campbell Co. Ky.
Slowver, Wm C., Greenbrier Co.
Smith, Ballard, Greenbrier Co.
Smith, J.C.
Smith, John, Putnam Co.
Smith, Richard, Wayne Co.
Smith, Wesley, Carroll Co.
Smith, Wm L., Carroll Co.
Snow, Preston H., Carroll Co.
Spriggs, John, Jackson Co.
Sprowl, W.B., Greenbrier Co.
Stull, George L., Alleghany Co.
Suiter, M.W., Brooke Co.
Taylor, Wm J., Greenbrier Co.
Thomas, H., Jackson Co.
Thomas, Joseph B., Alleghany Co.
Triplet, M., Clay Co.
Watson, Joseph, Greenbrier Co.

Wethered, Perry B., Greenbrier Co.
Wetzel, George W., Greenbrier Co.
White, John T. Greenbrier Co.
Williams, Fred, Greenbrier Co.
Williams, James H., Greenbrier Co.
Wilson, Sam J., Fayette Co.
Winkle, George C., Monroe Co.
Workman, John W., Tazewell Co.
Wyatt, Wm H., Greenbrier Co.

CIVIL WAR RELIC Recalls Battle to Springfield Veteran On Anniversary

Memorial Hall cannon captured in Civil War by regiment of which Capt. H. E. Titus was a member, and Capt. Titus.

Famous Battle Recalled by Last Survivor

Capt. H. E. Titus Tells How Memorial Hall Cannon Was Captured

SOME of the most vivid memories of childhood include those wonderful stories of the Civil War that Granddad could tell so dramatically.

Capt. H. E. Titus of 875 W. Mulberry st., last surviving

1929 newspaper clipping showing the cannon captured at the Battle of Lewisburg in 1862, and Captain Titus, Union veteran of the battle. The gun was captured by the 44th Ohio Infantry and sent home to Springfield, Ohio.

The Lewisburg cannon in the museum of the Clark County Historical Society, Springfield, Ohio. *Photo by author, 2004*

The Confederate graveyard at Lewisburg contains the remains of at least 95 Confederate soldiers. *Photo by author, 2004*

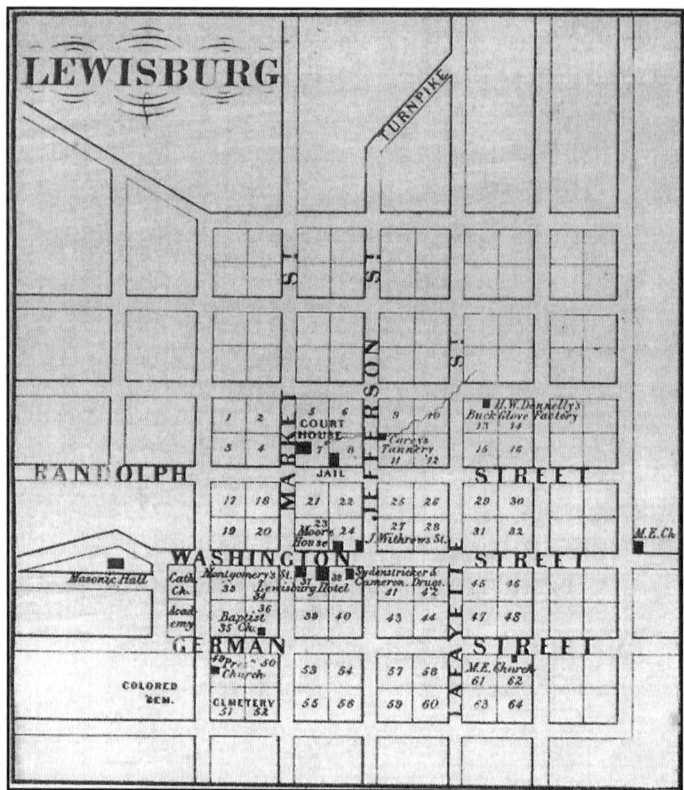

Map of Lewisburg, 1873. *Courtesy Greenbrier County Historical Society*

Chapter Ten

Civilian Prisoners of War From Greenbrier and Adjacent Counties

The following rosters list civilians from Greenbrier and adjacent counties who were held as prisoners of war. Records of civilian arrests during the Civil War are scattered and incomplete, especially as relates to arrest by Confederate authorities. These lists were compiled from a variety of sources, including the *Official Records*, (1) and numerous rolls of microfilm available from the National Archives and Records Administration as M598 *Records of Prisoners of War at the Various Military Prisons.* (2)It should also be noted that not all persons apprehended were sent to prison, some being held briefly by local military authorities, thus little, if any, record of their incarceration exists. The two most common charges against civilians were "aiding the enemy" and "bushwhacking." As a strongly divided border state during the Civil War, civilians from West Virginia were subject to arrest by authorities of the North or South, and sometimes both. When the Confederate army under Gen. Henry A. Wise retreated from the Kanawha Valley in 1861, there was a "wholesale removal" of civilian males from the area, the majority of these men being released within a few days. No comprehensive record has been found as to who was detained or for how long. In February 1862 Lt. Col. William Peters of the 45th Virginia Infantry reported that the Yankees were "carrying off citizens in large numbers" from Fayette, Raleigh, and neighboring counties. Col. Peters said he believed the prisoners were taken to exchange for Union prisoners of war. (3) The age is given for 64 prisoners out of a combined total of 232. Of these, the youngest prisoner was 16, the oldest 64, with an average all for all prisoners of 36. These lists are intended only as a guide to further research. (4)

CIVILIAN PRISONERS OF U.S. FORCES

FAYETTE COUNTY

Beckwith?, Wm. arrested for treason 1/10/1862
Call, Charles at Atheneum prison 5/3/62
Clendenin, R.C. arrested at home 5/30/1862 released from Camp Chase 12/22/1862
Corbit, Charles F. released Camp Chase 10/28/1863
Dempsey, George W. arrested at home 5/30/1862 released from Camp Chase 11/4/1862
Fisher, Lorenzo D. age 25 captured 11/9/1862 released 2/13/1863
Fisher, W.H. transferred to Ft. Delaware 7/14/1863 died 10/12/1863
Gilkerson, Isaac age 30 arrested at home 3/13/1862 transferred from Camp Chase to Johnson's Island Prison 10/24/1862 bushwhacker - sent to Vicksburg 11/22/1862
Gray, John H. age 45 arrested in Fayette County 11/4/1862 arrived Camp Chase 12/2/1862 released Camp Chase 2/13/1863
George, Tom L. captured in Fayette 10/15/63 "rebel mail carrier" to Camp Chase 11/63
George, John "justice of the peace" sent to Wheeling then Camp Chase 11/14/63
Guthrie, Felix age 30 arrested at home 5/30/1862 released from Camp Chase 11/24/1862
Hamlin?, [Hamilton] James B. age 30 arrived at Camp Chase 12/3/1862 released
Hizer, Charles W. arrived at Camp Chase 4/13/1863 released 6/3/1863
Jackson, Andrew captured in Fayette 7/20/64 to Wheeling 8/10/64 to Camp Chase 8/11/64 "Bushwhacker."

Kay, L. Dr. captured in Lexington, Ky 6/5/1862 sent to Johnson's Island Prison 9/6/1862

Kincaid, Alfred arrived at Camp Chase 4/13/1863 released 6/13/63

Lusher, Leander L. arrested in Fayette County 3/13/1862 transferred from Camp Chase to Johnson's Island Prison 10/24/1862 bushwhacker

McClung, Carroll age 52 arrived at Camp Chase 4/13/1863 released 6/3/1863

Merrill, J.W. said to belong 171 Va Militia captured Fayette Co 3/1862 sent from Camp Chase to Vicksburg 11/22/1862

Painter, Anderson age 60 arrived at Camp Chase 4/13/1863 transferred to Ft. Delaware Prison 7/14/1863 released 11/13/1863

Phillips, J.H. no charge found, released 2/65

Ruckard?, Wm. P. arrived at Camp Chase 2/24/1863 "a spy" died? 4/2/1863

Sanner, Hiram age 26 arrived at Camp Chase 6/16/1863 transferred to Ft. Delaware Prison 7/14/63

Simms, Milton age 36 released 2/5/1864

Sivey, Harmon age 36 arrested at home 1/15/1862 transferred from Camp Chase to Johnson's Island Prison 10/24/1862

Smith, W.B. arrived at Camp Chase 1/1/1862 released 11/19/1862

Smith, Wm. arrived at Camp Chase 1/11/1862 released 11/19/1862

Wood, Zachariah captured in Fayette 11/15/63 sent to Wheeling, then to Camp Chase 11/24/63 "aiding the rebels."

Cavendish, John charged with being a secessionist

Duffy, Peter charged with being a secessionist

Kious, J.C. charged with being a secessionist

Lewy, Green charged with being a secessionist

Manie, A.J. charged with being a secessionist

Martin, David charged with being a secessionist

McCutcheon, Jones charged with being a secessionist

Neal, Anderson charged with being a secessionist

Neal, Johnathan charged with being a secessionist

Rogers, Lem charged with being a secessionist
Rogers, William charged with being a secessionist
Rowsey, Kilburn charged with being a secessionist
Sevey, Herman charged with bushwhacking
Steele, Jeffrey at Atheneum prison 5/3/62
Stevens, J.J. charged with being a secessionist
Windsor, Anderson charged with being a secessionist

GREENBRIER COUNTY

Patterson, Wm. arrested in Greenbrier County 4/28/1862 died at Camp Chase 8/3/1862
Johnson, Melville S. age 41 arrested at home 3/23/1862 sent to Camp Chase released 11/19/1862
Tincher, Albert age50 arrested in Greenbrier County 3/27/1862 said to be member of 79th Virginia Militia. Transferred from Camp Chase to Johnson's Island Prison 10/24/1862 sent to Vicksburg 11/22/1862 [father of Francis and James Tincher all of Fayette County]
Tincher, Francis M. age 21 same as Albert Tincher
Tincher, James age17 listed as "guerrilla" Atheneum prison to Camp Chase 5/5/62
Ballanger, Lorenzo age 32 bushwhacker arrested at home 3/23/1862 sent to Camp Chase then to Johnson's Island Prison 10/24/1862 to Vicksburg 11/22/1862
Sprowe, Wm. Age 40 arrested at home 5/19/1862 paroled from Camp Chase 12/5/1862
Wetherall, Pierre B. arrested in Lewisburg, Va 4/11/1862 released from Camp Chase 11/4/1862 [6/28/1862 an urgent appeal for this man's release was made to Gov. Pierpont by C.P. Wolcott, Asst. Secy. Of War, Washington, D.C. Wetherall is not in 1860 census of Greenbrier County]
Carr, John age 42 released from Camp Chase 5/30/1863
Hoober, Nathan age 38 arrested in Greenbrier County 11/27/1862 arrived at Camp Chase 12/24/1862 sent to Washington, D.C. for exchange on 3/11/1863
Rusk, George W. arrested in Lewisburg, Va 6/28/1862 released

from Camp Chase 8/12/1862 another record says released 1/24/1863

Riffe, David D. age 26 arrested at home 11/27/1862 arrived at Camp Chase 12/24/1862 sent to Washington, D.C. for exchange on 3/11/1863

Williams, David arrested in Greenbrier County 11/27/1862 arrived at Camp Chase 12/24/1862 sent to Washington, D.C. for exchange on 3/11/1863

Burdett, John J. arrested 1/21/1862 transferred Camp Chase to Johnson's Island 9/6/1862 charged with sending Union men into rebel custody said to belong 79 Va Militia sent to Vicksburg 11/22/1862

Burdett, L.P. same as John J. Burdett

Smith, Ballard Jr. age 35 arrested at home 5/11/1862 released from Camp Chase 12/29/1862

Pritt, Wm. transferred from Camp Chase to Johnson's Island Prison 6/29/1862 then to Vicksburg 11/22/1862 bushwhacker

Brown, George W. arrested in Greenbrier Co 7/25/1861 said to belong 79 Va Militia transferred Camp Chase to Johnson's Island 9/6/1862 then to Vicksburg 11/22/1862

Jarrett, Joseph age 49 arrested at home 7/7/1862 released from Camp Chase 12/31/1862

Jarrett, Samuel same as Joseph Jarrett

Fox, Samuel H. age 50 released from Camp Chase 1/20/1863 another record says member 79 Va Militia who died in prison 10/21/1862

Hicks, A.J. age 16 released from Camp Chase 1/19/1863 [this is probably Andrew J. Hix listed as AWOL from the 60th Va Inf. CSA since 12/1861]

George, Thomas L. age 45 released from Camp Chase 12/29/1863 [see Fayette Co.]

George, John released from Camp Chase 1/5/1864 [see Fayette Co.]

Taylor, Silas F. age 39 said to be captain in Va Militia received at prisoner depot Sandusky, Ohio 5/1/1862 then released from Camp Chase 11/15/1864

Taylor, Garnett released from Camp Chase 11/15/1864

Barber, James bushwhacker captured in Greenbrier Co 7/30/1862 sent from Camp Chase to Johnson's Island Prison 9/29/1862 then to Vicksburg 11/22/1862

Gwinn, Augustus arrested in Greenbrier County 8/4/1862 said to be Confederate quartermaster and bushwhacker transferred Camp Chase to Vicksburg 11/22/1862

Wall, Henry age 40 arrested at home 7/15/1862 released 1/19/1863

Deshoms, John H. age 34 arrested at home 7/20/1862 on parole in Columbus, Ohio then sent to Washington, D.C. for exchange [1860 census says "physician born in France"]

Hines, C.R. age 52 ordered by Gen. Crook in 1862 to take oath of allegiance to the North and post bond or leave with his entire family.

Fox, C.R. said to belong 79 Va Militia captured in Greenbrier Co 3/23/1862 sent from Camp Chase to Vicksburg 11/22/1862

Fox, D. same as C.R. Fox

Fox, Eldridge age19 same as C.R. Fox

Fox, L.L. same as C.R. Fox

Fox, W.G. same as C.R. Fox

Garten, H. said to belong 79 Va Militia captured in Greenbrier Co 3/23/1862 sent from Camp Chase to Vicksburg 11/22/1862

Bragg, Ira said to belong 79 Va Militia captured in Greenbrier Co 3/23/1862 sent from Camp Chase to Vicksburg 11/22/1862

Riddle, J.H. age 35 guerrilla captured in Greenbrier Co 3/27/1862 sent from Camp Chase to Johnson's Island 10/26/1862 to Vicksburg 11/22/1862 resident Fayette Co

Arthur, Thomas bushwhacker captured in Greenbrier Co 3/23/1862 sent from Camp Chase to Johnson's Island 10/24/1862 to Vicksburg 11/22/1862 resident Fayette Co

Handley, Austin held by U.S. in 1862 as hostage for return of Dr. Wm P. Rucker. For the complete story see *Journal of the Greenbrier Historical Society* 1978 p. 64-85 by Robert H. Walls

McClung, Samuel same as Austin Handley

Tuckwiller, Samuel same as Austin Handley

Patterson, Henry captured in Greenbrier Co. 5/24/64 sent to Wheeling 6/10/64 "government employee" died 9/11/64

Walton, John H. said to be Greenbrier militia, age 46, 5'11" black hair, grey eyes, released at Clarksburg, WV 10/28/64

Carrol, John F. at Atheneum prison 5/31/62

Snyder, Adam C. age 31 editor of the Greenbrier *Era,* captured 8/63 confined Atheneum prison. Exchanged 1/64 for Jesse F. Phares, sheriff of Randolph Co. when released was asked if he would "call around" Wheeling again, replied: "Yes, if I can raise force enough I will pay you an early visit."

Monroe County

Johnson, G.B. arrested in Monroe County 6/22/1862 arrived at Camp Chase 7/14/1862 notation says "hospital" sent to Washington, D.C. for exchange

Mackey, Elias arrested 6/13/1863 sent to Camp Chase

Meadows, Hugh F. arrived Camp Chase 7/10/1863 sent to Ft. Delaware Prison 7/14/1863 released 11/13/1863

Rains, James P. age 57 arrived Camp Chase 4/13/1863 released 6/27/1863

Rhodes, Dickinson arrived at Camp Chase 5/8/1863 released 6/1/1863

Hornsby, Madison released from Camp Chase 12/22/1863 to remain in Ohio until end of war

Meddeus?, Patrick H. released from Camp Chase 2/5/1864 will report to Gov. Boreman

Destons, John W. Camp Chase Prison

Ingraham, S.S. Camp Chase Prison

Roach, John age 64 Camp Chase Prison

Gross, Jacob Camp Chase Prison

Foley?, Wm. Camp Chase Prison

Fornsby?, Elias released from Camp Chase Prison 6/8/1863

Hill, George W. died at Camp Chase Prison 7/28/1863

Malot, Thomas J. released from Camp Chase 12/12/1863

Hook, J.D. transferred from Camp Chase to Point Lookout,

MD Prison 3/18/1865 [this may be James D. Hooker, age 18 in 1865]

Reynolds, Thomas captured in Monroe Co. 5/24/64 sent to Wheeling 6/10/64 then to Camp Chase 10/6/64 "government employee."

Hill, William M. born in Monroe County, a resident of Iowa. Arrested January 8, 1862 in Iowa after returning from a visit to his relatives in Monroe Co. Va. Charged with writing a letter to the Monroe County newspaper sympathetic to the South. Released April 1862.

NICHOLAS COUNTY

Stover? Lucien? arrived at Camp Chase 6/6/1862 released 11/12/1862

Whitman, Andrew M. age 55 arrived at Camp Chase 2/28/1862 at Atheneum prison 5/3/62 transferred to Johnson's Island Prison 9/6/1862

Clemens, A [Ahart] T. age 28, arrived Camp Chase 10/27/1861 notation says "Floyd Brigade"

Chapman, Jacob C. age 47 arrived Camp Chase 9/15/1862 released 12/22/1862

Amick, Petry W? age 21, arrived Camp Chase 9/19/1861

McClung, George arrested 1/17/1862 either at home or in Kentucky, records conflict. Transferred from Camp Chase to Johnson's Island Prison 10/24/1862 bushwhacker

Moore, Charles S. arrived Camp Chase 7/1/1862 released 11/26/1862

Moore, Eli same as Charles S. Moore

Propps, A.W. arrived Camp Chase 12/17/1861 transferred to Johnson's Island Prison 9/6/1862

Butler, Oliver said to belong Va Militia captured in Nicholas Co 10/15/1861 sent from Camp Chase to Vicksburg 11/22/1862

Bonney, R. said to belong 77 Va Militia captured in Nicholas Co 8/26/1862 sent from Camp Chase to Vicksburg 11/22/1862

Brown, Kate captured in Nicholas Co. 6/15/63 sent to Camp Chase from Wheeling 6/63

Groynn, Wm B. Confederate conscript, captured in Nicholas Co. 10/24/63 sent to Camp Chase from Wheeling, 11/20/63

Jones, Allen K. Confederate conscript, captured in Nicholas Co. 2/3/64 sent to Wheeling and then to Camp Chase 3/5/64

Amick, Eli charged with being a secessionist

Morris, W.B. charged with being a secessionist

O'Dell, W.H. charged with aiding rebels

Props, Noah charged with being a bushwhacker

Schakelford, Cobb charged with being a secessionist

Smith, Allen charged with aiding rebels

Van Bibber, D.C. charged with being a secessionist

Van Bibber, J.C. charged with being a secessionist

White, W.T. charged with being a secessionist

Vance, George charged with being a secessionist

Clemens, E. sent from Atheneum prison to Camp Chase 5/5/62 "aiding rebels"

Pocahontas County

Black, John arrived Camp Chase 4/4/1862 transferred to Johnson's Island Prison 9/6/1862

Schneider, Addison said to belong 127 Va Militia arrived Camp Chase 4/4/1862 transferred to Johnson's Island Prison 9/6/1862 to Vicksburg 11/22/1862

Naught, Wm. released from Camp Chase Prison 1/21/1864 will report to Gov. Boreman

Sheets, John age 54 arrested at home 7/5/1862 arrived Camp Chase 7/15/1862 released 12/24/1862 posted $500.00 bond [father of Wm. R. Sheets]

Sheets, Wm. R. age16 arrested at home 7/5/1862 released from Camp Chase Prison 12/24/1862

Tucker, John S. released from Camp Chase Prison 10/28/1863 notation says from "Pocahontas County now lives Loudon County, Va."

Buzzard, Henry age 45 released from Camp Chase Prison 12/16/1863 will report to Gov. Boreman

Eagan, Charles released from Camp Chase Prison 12/29/1863

"parole of honor, British subject to report to Gov. Boreman."

Heavener, Uriah age 38 arrested in Pendleton County 4/3/1862 released 11/10/1862

McGlaughlin, John arrested at home 7/5/1862 transferred from Camp Chase to Johnson's Island Prison 9/6/1862 guerrilla

Beverage, Henry age 50 arrested 8/1/1862 in Highland County, Va released 12/27/1862

Galford, Della? arrested for disloyalty, arrived Camp Chase 2/27/1862 released 3/30/1863 [surname is probably Guilford]

Shineberry, Isaac age 20 arrested 4/4/1862 said to belong 127 Va Militia transferred from Camp Chase to Johnson's Island Prison 9/6/1862 to Vicksburg 11/22/1862

Gum, James H. age 30 arrested Pulaski River, Va 10/20/1861 said to belong 127 Va Militia transferred Camp Chase to Johnson's Island 9/6/1862 to Vicksburg 11/22/1862

McComb, Wm. W. age 32 released from Camp Chase 1/21/1864 will report to Gov. Boreman

Galford, Thomas died at Camp Chase Prison 6/19/1863

WEBSTER COUNTY

Berry, Dorsey arrived Camp Chase 6/22/1863 released 7/2/1863 posted $1,000 bond and not to leave Illinois during the war

Corbitt, Mathew guerrilla arrested in Webster County 5/20/1862 transferred from Camp Chase to Johnson's Island Prison 9/29/1862 to Vicksburg 11/22/1862

Cool, Walter age 59 sheriff, arrested 5/20/62 transferred from Camp Chase to Johnson's Island Prison 9/29/1862 [this man and four others were tried as guerrillas by US Military Commission 6/1862 and jailed in Wheeling, subsequently sent to Camp Chase]

Cool, A.A. age 21 said to be a private in the "1st Va" arrived Camp Chase 5/20/1862 transferred to Johnson's Island Prison 9/26/1862 then to Vicksburg 11/22/1862

McElwain?, George F. released from Camp Chase 2/18/1864 to remain in loyal states

Payne, Jesse W. age 29 "aiding rebels" sent to Wheeling 1/1/64 then to Camp Chase released from Camp Chase 12/5/1864

Carpenter, John L. age 41 released from Camp Chase 4/26/1865 will report to Gov. Boreman

Townsend, Eli guerrilla arrested at home 9/18/1862 transferred from Camp Chase to Johnson's Island Prison 9/29/1862 to Vicksburg 11/22/1862

Townsend, John same as Eli Townsend

Rollins, Harrison C. arrested in Webster County 5/20/1862 transferred from Camp Chase to Johnson's Island Prison 9/29/1862 [listed as Greenbrier Co resident, this man and four others were tired as guerrillas by US Military Commission 6/1862 and jailed at Wheeling, Va subsequently sent to Camp Chase then Vicksburg 11/22/1862]

Boggs, Norman said to be Confederate soldier arrested in Webster County 8/25/1862 sent to Camp Chase Prison then to Vicksburg 11/22/1862

Boggs, Wesley age 32 released from Camp Chase by oath and bond prior to 3/1862

Cool, Jesse age 25 released from Camp Chase by oath and bond prior to 3/1862

Cogar, Tunis age 48 released from Camp Chase by oath and bond prior to 3/1862

McCrea, Robert released from Camp Chase by oath and bond prior to 3/1862

Murphy, Margaret Mrs. Transferred from Camp Chase to Mass 11/19/1863

Civilians Held By Confederate Authorities

Fayette County

Anderson, Peter L. age 40, suspected Union sympathy, deserted from Col. Beckley's militia.

Armstrong, Stewart age 25, voted against secession, willing to take oath of allegiance to the South.

Bays, Isaac no record why arrested, says he is a southern man, recommend release.

Eades, Stephen voted against secession, says he has had nothing to do with Yankees. Was in Southern militia briefly, oath and release.

Fellow, Otey arrested by Caskie Rangers for aiding Yankees. Says he sent three sons to Southern army. Evidence strong against this man, hold as POW.

Flanagan, R.A. age 55, voted against secession, claims to support Confederacy. Was arrested while visiting his sick son who is in our army, oath and release.

Fox, George W. does not know why he was arrested, was taken to Camp Gauley just before battle of Carnifex Ferry. Give oath and release.

Fuller, Alexander age 22, went to see his sick brother at Charleston, arrested on trip back. Give oath and release.

Fuller, Jesse age 24, arrested along with his brother, Alexander. Give oath and release.

Gesh, A.B. arrested by Beckley's militia on suspicion. Give oath and release.

Honaker, John a youth, says his father voted for secession, and he is a Southern man. Says he was arrested when he went after his stolen horse. Oath and release.

Hunt, George voted against secession, no proof of anything. Give oath and release.

Johnson, Miles arrested by Caskie Rangers on suspicion. Oath and release.

Jones, Wm keeps a tavern near Dogwood Gap. Some Yankees got dinner at his house. Give oath and release.

Kelly, Wm arrested for suspicious activity, witnesses claim he is a spy. Should be held as prisoner of war.

Kincaid, James Jr. age 16, arrested last August [1861] held since, oath and release. [1862]

Lawrence, P. Dr. says he was arrested going to join Virginia militia. Oath and release.

Neff, Addison age 21, no cause for arrest given. Was on trip from Dogwood Gap to Greenbrier Co to see his wounded brother. Stopped for pass at Meadow Bluff and was arrested. Give oath and release.

Scarborough, Isaac age 51, says he was near his home when arrested. Says he was taking a load of beeswax and ginseng down to Kanawha to sell. Arrested by Caskie Rangers, they took his horse. Give oath and release.

Short, Samuel arrested by independent scouts. They took tow horses from him which were not returned. This man is a known secessionist, give oath and release.

White, Robert a feeble old man of seventy. Proves to be a man of good character. Give oath and release.

Williams, Isaac age 51, arrested by Caskie Rangers on suspicion. Give oath and release.

Wriston, Caleb says he gave supplies to Caskies Rangers and Jenkins Cavalry. Says the Yankees threatened men of his branch because they were secessionist. Oath and release.

Wriston, John brother of Caleb, arrested by Caskie Rangers while at the mill. Says he is a strong Southern man. Oath and release.

Greenbrier County

Wardup, William lives in Greenbrier County says he was arrested because he expressed the opinion that the Confederates would be driven out of the Kanawha Valley, which they were.

Neff, Addison [Fayette resident born in Greenbrier, see Fayette Co.]

Armstrong, Stewart [Fayette resident born in Greenbrier, see Fayette Co.]

Cornan, James [Fayette resident born in Greenbrier, see Fayette Co.]

Monroe County

Cantley, James native of Monroe County; resides in Boone; farms his own land, 100 acres. Union man, took the oath of allegiance, no charge, no proof. Recommend discharge.

Henchman, William sixty years old; born in Monroe County, has lived in Cabell, has been a magistrate and commissioner of the revenue. Union man; voted against secession; voted for a member of the Wheeling Convention and the Northern Congress. Is willing to take the oath of allegiance. Voted for establishing the revolutionary government of Virginia, ought to be tried for treason. His general character is good.

NICHOLAS CS POW

Cornan, James says the Yankees camped near his house and came to him for corn. He traded corn for coffee with Yankees. Says he served in the militia briefly and has a brother in the Wise Legion. Give oath and release.

Haywood, Thomas Is a Union man but claims no complicity with the enemy. Is willing to take oath to the south.

Kincaid, James Sr. Arrested by Wise Legion. Says he was once in the Floyd Brigade and was released because of sickness. Says he recovered and spent 18 days on Cotton Hill with the militia. Says he was going back to Floyd when arrested. Give oath and release.

McClung, Alexander Was in Wise Legion and arrested by Floyd's men without charges. Give oath and release.

McClung, M.A. brother of Alexander. Arrested by Floyd's men the day before the battle of Cross Lanes. Says he is a secessionist and was sent down with the prisoners from the battle of Cross Lanes. Says he traded the Yankees 18 pounds of butter for 9 pounds of coffee. Give oath and release.

O'Dell, Felix S. age 26, Says he was at Gen. Floyd's camp taking clothes to his father, when arrested. Claims entire loyalty to the south, has taken oath.

Rader, Anthony arrested on suspicion only. Give oath and release.

Ramsay, Samuel arrested on suspicion only. He is a Union man but professes loyalty to the Confederate Government. Give oath and release.

Siers, Isaac Says he was in Col. Tompkins regiment and was wounded in a skirmish near Charleston. Evidence suggest he is a deserter. Should be turned over to military dept.

Williams, Alexander arrested on suspicion. Says he did not vote on secession question. Give oath and release.

POCAHONTAS COUNTY CS POW

Smith, J.M. Says he was born in Alabama; moved when seven years old to Indiana. Came to Pocahontas, Va to see an uncle and was arrested....admitted his uncle was commissary in the Indiana brigade on Cheat Mountain; that he traveled in a United States Government wagon. He was arrested within the lines of the US army. Owes his allegiance to the United States....recommend he be held as a prisoner of war.

Barnes, Edward says he was born and raised in Upper Canada. Came through Pennsylvania to Virginia. Gives no account of the route he traveled. Professes great ignorance of his route. Says he worked 10 months for Mr. McLaughlin, in Pocahontas, on Tygart's Valley River. Says he was arrested in Pocahontas, and afterward said he was arrested near Meadow Bluff. I believe this man is a spy, but I have no information of the time or place of his arrest or the charges against him....I must express a regret that officers in command send prisoners here without any evidence or reports that may aid in ascertaining their true character. I would advise this man be held as a prisoner.

WEBSTER CO CS POW

Arthur, Wilson born in Randolph County, moved in 1819 to Webster. Does not know why he was arrested. He has never had anything to do with the Yankees. Says he never fought the Yankees because they did not come to his neighborhood. He is too old to go after them, but he lent his gun twice to young men to go after them. He is fifty-five years old. Says he was arrested because of malicious charges preferred by a man he sued for killing a dog....I recommend his discharge on taking the oath.

O'Brien, John an old man; says he was born in Harrison County; moved to the head of the Little Kanawha, thence to Sandy

> Fork of Elk, thence to Webster. The old man has spent his life in the woods hunting and seems to be very ignorant of what is going on in the settlements....Does not seem to know much of the difference between the United States and Confederate States, but is willing to take the oath of allegiance to the old State of Virginia...He lives remote from settlements in the woods, and makes his living by hunting and selling ginseng. Has a son in Swann's Company, Wise Legion. I recommend his discharge on taking the oath.

Total CS Prisoners: 44

Combined total US and CS: 232

CHAPTER ELEVEN
CAT AND MOUSE

The army under Gen. Heth moved in and out of Union and Salt Sulphur Springs for most of the summer. By Heth's order, the army rented a room from Mr. William Erskine, proprietor at the Salt Sulphur Springs hotel, for use as their post office. Over the course of the war, Mr. Erskine made thousands of dollars from the Confederate military, supplying lodging, quantities of beef, bacon, salt, clothing, blankets, and even buckets for use in the area's saltpeter caves.

Crook's army at Lewisburg spent the days immediately after the battle caring for the wounded and scouting the area for Confederate activity. On Sunday, May 25, a soldier with the 36th Ohio Infantry attended services at Lewisburg's Old Stone Presbyterian Church. Even though he was an "enemy" soldier, the man was somewhat surprised that he was not more cordially received. He recorded his impression of the church and its surroundings in his journal: "Just around the corner from the church is a calaboose, and, immediately by, a whipping post...stocks for neck, hands, ankles, a place where some men...had made it their occupation to whip the slaves...on that day I wore the "Blue" and as I passed out of that church but one person pressed my hand, the others looked disdainfully on as I passed by." (1) Other soldiers would record that they felt privileged to hear a sermon preached by the venerable Rev. John McElhenney.

On May 26, White Sulphur Springs was occupied by Company F of the 2nd West Va Cavalry. Other members of the 2nd Cavalry began a series of brief scouts or raids into Monroe County, resulting in a series of skirmishes that continued into June. One such skirmish occurred on May 27, when Rebel pickets were driven in from the Greenbrier River, causing Gen. Heth to place his entire force in battle array. The Shenandoah Valley successes of Gen. Stonewall Jackson caused Gen. Crook to worry that his position at Lewisburg might be at risk. Accordingly, on May 28 and 29, Crook's army relocated to Meadow Bluff, about 15 miles west of Lewisburg. The Yankees camped along the ridge lines and hills overlooking the bluffs. The *Springfield* [Ohio] *Republic* carried a description of the camps written by "Zouave," a soldier with the 44th Ohio: "We are encamped in a fine grove on the North side of the bluff; we have cleared out the brushwood and undergrowth for the purpose of giving a warm reception to all intruders. There are infantry, artillery and cavalry concentrated at this point. The most exposed flank has been protected by throwing up a breastwork one half mile in extent." (2)

Before pulling out of Lewisburg on May 29, some Union soldiers took over the newspaper office of the *Greenbrier Weekly Era*, and published their own newspaper, dubbed "The Yankee." This paper carried a variety of self-congratulatory articles, opinion, and war news. One item was a warning to the citizens of Greenbrier County: "Brothers!...the 'milk and water' policy that was pursued last summer was found ineffectual and is to be abandoned. A citizen who refuses to take the oath of allegiance to the United States is an enemy of it, and we are here to suppress these enemies. You must make up your minds...We want to know who are for us and who are against us. We had rather have a dozen open enemies than one secret foe....We feel sure that we are right, and that we will prevail....If you choose the other side, well and good. This beautiful country will be temporarily depopulated...Our surplus population will soon replace it with live Yankees...." (3)

Before Crook's army left Lewisburg, they sent most of the Rebel prisoners there to hospitals and prisons in Ohio. The largest group of these prisoners arrived at Charleston en route to Ohio on May 28, just five days after the battle. News of their arrival was carried in the *Kanawha Republican*, a Charleston newspaper: "Quite an exciting scene was presented on our wharf Wednesday afternoon, on the arrival of the secesh prisoners taken at Lewisburg...They came down the river on the steamer Victor

No. 2, and were here transferred to the steamer Glenwood, for Cincinnati. There were said to be 105 prisoners—two, Noyes Rand and Albert Singleton, were of this place—among them were also Marshall Triplett of Clay County, Joseph Dilworth of Jackson County, and J.F. Campbell of Nicholas. They report that Lewis Mahan and Charles Chewning of the Kanawha Riflemen were killed…and that Captain R.S. Laidley was wounded in the arm…." (4)

When Captain Bahlmann and 22 other soldiers wounded at Lewisburg arrived at Gallipolis, Ohio in early June, it caused quite a stir. The local newspaper published an article about their arrival, referring to the men as "bridge burners" and "picket murderers" who should have been "left on the battlefield," meaning that they should have been killed. Shortly thereafter the men's names were published in the newspaper:

> The Following is a list of the secesh prisoners now in the hospital at Gallipolis, all of whom were wounded and captured at Lewisburg. Two have died since their arrival, and one or two others are in a fair way to follow them:
>
> Ralph Elkins, Pulaski Co. Va. [50th Va Inf., exchanged 11/10/62 age 28]
> J.C. Smith, Carroll Co. Va. [50th Va Inf., exchanged 11/10/62 age 27]
> Alvers Marshall, Pulaski Co. Va. [50th Va Inf., exchanged 12/8/62 age 18]
> W.T. Chandler, Monroe Co. Va. [Edgar's Btn. exchanged 8/25/62 age 21]
> R.J. Thrasher, Botetourt Co. Va. [22nd Va Inf., died 10/1/62 age 29]
> W.F. Bahlmann, Fayette Co. Va. [22nd Va Inf., exchanged 8/25/62 age 25]
> A. Morse, Monroe Co. Va. [108th Militia, Monroe Co.]
> C. Rhodes, Greenbrier Co. Va. [22nd Va Inf., exchanged 8/25/62 age 20]
> G.L. Stull, Allegheny Co. Va. [22nd Va Inf., exchanged 8/

25/62 age 23]

W. Hansbarger, Monroe Co. Va. [Edgar's Btn. exchanged 8/25/62 age 18]

W. Neighbors, Monroe Co. Va. [22nd Va Inf., exchanged 8/25/62 age 47]

W.J. Taylor, Greenbrier Co. Va. [22nd Va Inf., exchanged 8/25/62 age 20]

J. White, Greenbrier Co. Va. [Edgar's Btn. exchanged 8/25/62 age 19]

P.H. Snow, Carroll Co. Va. [50th Va Inf., exchanged 11/10/62 age 18]

J. Smith, Putnam Co. Va. [22nd Va Inf., released 8/25/62 age 34]

A.S. Rader, Botetourt Co. Va. [22nd Va Inf., died 7/17/62]

P. Murray, Lynchburg, Va. [22nd Va Inf., exchanged 8/25/62 age 25]

J. Nichols, Pulaski Co. Va. [50th Va Inf., exchanged 12/8/62 age 22]

J.W. Mitchell, Carroll Co. Va. [45th Va Inf., exchanged 8/25/62]

W.L. Smith, Carroll Co. Va. [50th Va Inf., exchanged 11/10/62 age 18]

N. Marshall, Carroll Co. Va. [50th Va Inf., exchanged 12/8/62 age 26]

W.F. Wickline, died of wound. [Monroe Co. 50th Va Inf., died 6/15/62]

James H. McKinney [Greenbrier Co. 22nd Va Inf., died 6/19/62] (5)

On May 29, Company F of the 2nd West Va Cavalry abandoned White Sulphur Springs, returning to Meadow Bluff. The following day members of Company I rode out to Lewisburg as an escort for some wagons. They were surprised to find the town occupied by scouts of the 8th Virginia Cavalry, and in a running skirmish, lost one man captured. On June 1, Gen. Crook asked Captain Bascom of the Adjutant General's office, if he should

The Old Stone Church in Lewisburg. Constructed in 1796, it saw use as a hospital, barracks, and stable during the Civil War. *Photo by author*

remove the wounded Rebels remaining in Lewisburg, stating that "some 25" remained. Crook's estimate was high however, because on that same date a lieutenant with the 2nd Cavalry reported 14 wounded rebels still hospitalized at Lewisburg. He said all the wounded men lacked "proper surgical attendance," and two were "in a dying state." The lieutenant and 53 men from Companies F and C of the 2nd West Va Cavalry returned to the hospital on June 9 and paroled 12 men, the other two having died. They also reported that members of the Greenbrier Cavalry had been in the town, saying "3 to 10 of this band make daily visits to Lewisburg, remaining overnight, when they rejoin their companies..." (6)

Confederate General William Wing Loring was in overall command of the Department of Southwestern Virginia, which encompassed the commands of Heth in Monroe County, and Humphrey Marshall at Giles Court House. Writing from Salt Sulphur Springs on June 9, Loring informed the Adjutant General's office that the enemy occupied Flat Top Mountain and

Grave of the Rev. John McElhenney, pastor of the Old Stone Presbyterian Church for 62 years. *Photo by author*

Meadow Bluff, and that his combined manpower was too weak to protect the railroads from invasion. (7) Passage of the Conscription Act had not produced the desired result and had in fact alienated many of the young men embraced by its order. When conscription agents combed the mountains searching for men to draft, they were frequently met with shotguns, and many of those who were drafted quickly deserted. The Confederate draft also prompted some men to join the Virginia State Line forces under Gen. John B. Floyd. In that capacity their service was limited to one year, as opposed to three years in the regular Confederate service. The mountains were nearly drained of men loyal to the South well before Gen. Loring arrived, leaving little hope that he could strengthen his army with men from that region. Loring's task was huge. He was charged with protecting western Virginia to the Kentucky border and he was expected to block any hostile move toward the Virginia and Tennessee Railroad. Between the Southern armies of Virginia and Tennessee lay many miles of open country, principally covered by the Allegheny and Cumberland Mountains.

The tax-in-kind act and the policy of impressment were two other Confederate policies that angered civilians. The tax-in-kind act required farmers to contribute one-tenth of everything they produced to the Richmond government. This was especially burdensome in western Virginia, a region already hurt by a shortage of horses, mules, farming implements, and manpower. By the summer of 1862, many of the region's rural families were barely able to feed themselves, much less save a percentage for Richmond.

The policy of impressment, used by North and South alike, allowed authorities to seize food, animals, tools, wagons, anything they deemed a military necessity. Compensation was not always forthcoming, many people being simply robbed of their property. It was amid all this hardship and turmoil that war was waged in the Virginia mountains, the future of the Confederacy hanging in the balance.

Growing frustrated with failure of the draft, Gen. Heth issued a proclamation on June 9, in which he said all men between the ages of 18 and 35 who had not responded to the Conscription Act should do so within five days. Those failing to comply "will be shot as deserters wherever they may be found." (8) The proclamation had not been approved by the War Department and Gen. Loring wrote Heth advising him to revoke it: "I differ with you in the policy of shooting conscripts…Let a single man be shot as stated, unless in the act of resistance, and…we would not get another conscript—our time would be employed in hunting them down….I do not wish to sway my authority against yours, but I beg you will suppress the proclamation…I am sure that after a further reflection you will agree with me." (9)

The only real victim of the proclamation was Gen. Heth, who was disliked for several reasons, including his loss at Lewisburg and destruction of the bridge at Caldwell during his retreat. The threat to shoot civilian men was the last straw. Two weeks later, Heth was transferred to Chattanooga.

Fourteen members of the Greenbrier Cavalry on picket duty near Palestine (north of Alderson) were surprised on June 9 by a detachment of the 2nd West Va Cavalry. The pickets were pursued to Muddy Creek with a loss of three killed and one captured. The captured man was Graves, a citizen of Lewisburg. The next day Confederate cavalry at Alderson's Ferry were attacked by two companies of the 2nd Cavalry with a loss of four killed in action, two wounded, and two taken prisoner. No U.S. losses were reported. Matters began to heat up considerably for the boys in gray as Crook's cavalry remained active and vigilant throughout the month of June. They roamed the countryside with impunity, going where they pleased when they pleased. Their foraging expeditions toward Brushy Ridge, north of Lewisburg, and into White Sulphur Springs, kept the war- weary public in a constant state of alarm. On June 12, the citizens of Frankford witnessed the Union cavalry search their community, looking for Rebels and stolen cattle. Finding neither, the cavalry sped back toward Meadow Bluff. Every foraging expedition brought the loss of beef and other property to the citizens of Greenbrier and Monroe counties. During the month of June, Gen. Crook's cavalry "captured" more than 300 head of Greenbrier County cattle, 51 wagon loads of hay, and 100 bushels of corn. For the 60 day period from May 1 to June 30, the 2nd West Va Cavalry traveled 571 miles and were never more than 18 miles from their camp. (10)

On June 22, Gen. Crook made a raid toward Salt Sulphur Springs in the hope of engaging the enemy in battle. Crook had with him 1,600 infantry, 150 cavalry, and a battery of artillery. Their first stop was the John Maddy saltpeter cave in Monroe County, where they "took all our goods and chattels, broke up the kettles and burned the shanty and all the saltpeter." They also stole money, jewelry, and clothing from some of the civilian workers. (11) When the Confederates got word of the Union advance, they declined to give battle and retired over Peters Mountain, leaving the inhabitants to the mercy of the Yankees. A civilian at Union said the Federal army remained in that community just three hours. They also burned the mill at Centerville, and "carried off 22 negroes" and 80 cattle. Returning to Meadow Bluff on June 25, Gen. Crook reported his raid and declared it a complete success: "The first day I marched two miles beyond Alderson's Ferry, capturing five prisoners. The next morning I started to Salt Sulphur via Centreville, sending part of my cavalry via Union to make a feint from that direction....On my arrival at Salt Sulphur I learned that the enemy had fled in great confusion...Although the enemy fled without giving us battle, I regard the expedition as having a very important effect of not only demoralizing their force, keeping hundreds out of their ranks...but in case of a movement on the Narrows [of New River] our left flank will be entirely free." (12)

Gen. Heth arrived in Chattanooga on July 1, and three days later wrote to Jefferson Davis, giving his opinion of the situation in western Virginia. He complained that "bad, bold, and disappointed men" were trying in every way possible to break down the Confederate army in that region. He believed Gen. Floyd was "at the head of this organization," as he was attempting to build up his State Line forces at the expense of the regular military. Heth said Gen. Floyd's agents and friends convinced people that the conscript law was never intended to be carried into effect. They were also active in the camps of the regular army, boldly recruiting men who were already obligated. Gen. Floyd kept on his staff two newspaper editors, using the power of the press to undermine the authority of Generals Heth and Humphrey Marshall. "The simplest official act of a commander in Southwestern Virginia is censured by the newspapers in the pay of this party," Heth wrote, and "the utmost done to break down his influence." He also offered the opinion that if the State Line forces were ever fully organized, it would consist principally of conscripts and deserters. (13)

The Confederate President received this letter at the same time he received one from two prominent men of Monroe County. Mr. A.A. Chapman and Mr. Oliver Beirne wrote the president complaining bitterly about Gen. Heth's perceived lack of "energy and capacity." They did not believe that he should be entrusted with any large, independent command. The president did not concur in their opinion and retained confidence in his beleaguered general. Problems the Confederacy faced in the Greenbrier region were beyond the control of any one man, and Jefferson Davis fully understood that. "The character as a soldier of Brigadier General Heth is well established by long and arduous service," he wrote, adding that "criticism should not impair the confidence of the War Department, but judgment should rest on the official reports." (14)

Opposing forces played a game of cat and mouse during July with several brief skirmishes being the result. A fight at Alderson's Ferry on July 10 left seven Rebels killed and wounded. Confederate cavalry advanced from Monroe County and flanked the U.S. camp at Meadow Bluff during the night of July 12. Crook's men heard of the movement and sent Company F of the 44th Ohio Infantry and a detachment of cavalry to ambush the enemy one mile northwest of camp. Their ambush faltered in the mountain darkness with tragic results. Captain John Sheffey of the 8th Virginia Cavalry was among the intrepid Rebels operating within enemy lines. He described the events of that night in a letter to his fiancé: "They laid an ambuscade for us through which Captain Everett and I with our companies passed unscathed. They did not fire upon us thinking that we were their own cavalry whom they had sent around to intercept us. Shortly after we passed through...their own cavalry came into the ambuscade supposing in the darkness that these were we, the infantry fired into them immediately. The cavalry thinking on the other hand that we had ambuscaded them returned the fire and thus they battled it out among themselves." A "Mrs. Hannah" [Leann Hannah], who lived nearby, sent word to the Southern cavalrymen that "eleven wagonloads of dead and wounded" were hauled to Meadow Bluff. While that report was probably exaggerated, the fight itself was corroborated in the *Springfield Republic* by a soldier with the 44th Ohio: "Company F was out the other day...but failed to accomplish much, owing to West's Cavalry mistaking them for secesh and firing into them...." As this communication was for the hometown crowd, the writer skillfully omitted any casualty count and claimed the cavalry fired first. (15)

Rumors that the U.S. camp at Meadow Bluff would be attacked prompted Crook to ask Gen. Jacob Cox at Gauley Bridge for reinforcements. Gen. Crook seemed anxious for the test, saying "I will fight right here." Cox replied that his scouts had also been involved in several skirmishes and he wanted to await "better information of the rebel plans." He also asked Gen. Crook if it was true that an enemy scouting party had intercepted his mail after "passing your right." This may have been a reference to the rebel advance of July 12. (16) On Tuesday, July 15, several local citizens entered the U.S. camp at Meadow Bluff and reported Southern cavalry at the Greenbrier River looking for men to draft. In response, Gen. Crook ordered out a strong detachment of the 44th Ohio with instructions to proceed without delay. The men left camp at 8:30 p.m. and marched all night, stopping just two hours for sleep. Late the next afternoon they reached their destination, but found nary a rebel in sight. Getting under way early the next morning, the Ohioans marched several miles toward Meadow Bluff and encamped. At dusk, Yankee pickets reported spotting enemy cavalry 150 strong. Surprised at finding the bluecoats, the Rebels withdrew toward Greenbrier River pursued by the infantry. This pursuit resulted in a brief skirmish with no casualties reported on either side. (17)

Problems with disease that hit the armies so hard in the summer of 1861 reappeared on a somewhat smaller scale in 1862. Writing from Meadow Bluff, a Union soldier reported the problem to his hometown newspaper: "The general health of the brigade is bad. Our hospitals are full of sufferers from measles, diarrhea and other diseases. There are a few cases of fevers, one of which, William C. Elliott, has terminated fatally....He was modest as true merit always is, but brave as a lion....There are some others I fear who will soon join him....This is the post where the Southern troops suffered so severely. Whole regiments of them are buried around the bluffs..." The same writer complained that some men in Ohio who could enlist were avoiding service: "Young men without wives, a mother, or families depending on them...should step out cheerily and fill up the ranks, and help close the struggle. Let the men of wealth and property look into their own home circles and see who ought to go from them...Let those who wished the whole South to secede, we could whip them so easily, who filled the air with boasts of Northern superiority, but who took good care to stay at home themselves, let them step out. Surely this last call is loud and distressing enough." (18)

With Blue and Gray forces scouting Greenbrier and Monroe counties daily and skirmishing frequently, a soldier with the 36th Ohio Infantry felt like a traveling aristocrat: "Our Brigade has become quite aristocratic of late. We have visited White Sulphur, Blue Sulphur and Salt Sulphur Springs, all fashionable and somewhat noted summer resorts." He said they heard that Confederate Colonel John McCausland was now commanding in Monroe County and that his captain had seen Mr. McCausland at Gallipolis, Ohio, before the war. McCausland was on a hunt for fugitive slaves. "If he will come over to Meadow Bluff he can find more fugitives that the entire State of Virginia has lost in the last ten years." (19)

Fugitive slaves became more of a problem after the war began. Mr. Robert Dickson was a prominent Greenbrier citizen who lived two miles west of White Sulphur Springs. In the summer of 1862, he was notified by the jailer of Mason County, at Point Pleasant, that several of his slaves were being held there: "I hold in the jail of this county four negroes that is said to belong to [you] the man gives his name as George Washington…I suppose him to be about forty…he has with him his wife, Mary, she is…I suppose about forty years of age, their children Susannah and Charles the former about fifteen, Charles about twelve….also a negro man taken with them by the name of James Brown that says he is free…he is about forty…[with] crooked legs so as to make him very lame." Other slave owners complained that Northern military officials were allowing slaves to pass beyond the lines and go north. One such complaint came from Dr. J.F. Caldwell, a Lewisburg dentist and Union sympathizer. Dr. Caldwell's pro-Union sympathies made him so unpopular in Greenbrier County that he spent most of the war working in Charleston, Point Pleasant, and Gallipolis, Ohio. Writing from Charleston in early September 1862, Dr. Caldwell complained about the loss of his slaves to F.H. Pierpont, governor of the "restored" government of Virginia, at Wheeling: "Numerous negro slaves have received passes from officers of the Army in this valley to go beyond the territory of this State. Men loyal to the Union, its constitution and government, have been in this way *robbed* of their slaves, and this work of aiding slaves to escape is constantly going on…I myself have lost no less than six young negro men…Now, Sir, I ask you as the Governor of the State if there is no protection from such robberies?" (20)

Gen. Crook requested permission to attack the enemy headquarters in Monroe County on July 26. He told Gen. Cox that three deserters came into camp from Union, giving him up-to-date information. He believed that continually skirmishing with the Rebels at their outposts "only makes them worse," and he needed to move quickly while his information was current. Gen. Cox was surprised by the request and replied on July 28, saying "You have very lately asked for reinforcements in the expectation of being attacked by a superior force. You now speak of your ability to clear out Monroe County…I am not sure that I understand your dispatch." (21)

Although Crook's large-scale attack was postponed, he did send 155 men of the 44th Ohio toward the Greenbrier River on August 2. They received information that a band of Rebels would "take dinner" near Alderson's Ferry on the 3rd and they hoped to intercept them. Commanded by Captain Isreal Stough, the detachment arrived at the designated place but found "not a single rebel." Captain Stough decided to hide and wait, in the hope that enemy pickets would come along. Four hours later, two pickets made their appearance and were captured without firing a shot. These were William B. Hensley and Charles McAllister of the 8th Va Cavalry. Hensley had been in Confederate service since 1861, but McCallister served only three months, having enlisted in Giles County on April 30. Both men were sent to Camp Chase prison and subsequently exchanged. McCallister eventually returned to service and, after the close of the war, was paroled at Lewisburg on April 20, 1865. (22)

Serious manpower shortages prompted Virginia Governor John Letcher to issue a proclamation on August 4, 1862 asking men between the ages of 35 and 45 to join the militia without delay:

> The force which has been placed in the field having proved inadequate to the defense of the State, many portions of which are invaded by marauding bands of the enemy, who insult, oppress, and rob our people; and the Northern Government, smarting under their recent defeats around Richmond and elsewhere, having called for an additional force of 300,000 men, with the purpose of continuing their aggressions upon Virginia and the other States of the Confederacy, the Governor, feeling it to be his solemn duty to call upon the militia not now in service to unite with him in a prompt and vigorous effort to repel the enemy, to rescue the soil of the State and our people from the pollution and tyranny of a detestable foe, now appeals to the men of the following named counties from thirty-five to forty-five years of age, to wit: The counties of Washington, Smyth, Grayson, Carroll, Floyd,

> Pulaski, Wythe, Montgomery, Roanoke, Botetourt, Craig, Allegheny, Greenbrier, Monroe, Giles, Mercer, Bland, Tazewell, McDowell, Wise, Buchanan, Lee, Scott, Russell, Raleigh, Wyoming, Logan, Boone, Wayne, Cabell, Putnam, Kanawha, Mason, Clay, Nicholas, Fayette, Braxton, Webster, Pocahontas, and Randolph.

All men responding to this call were ordered to proceed to the salt-works at Smyth County, and report to Gen. John Floyd. In closing, the proclamation urged men to "be prompt and vigorous in action," because there was "not a day to spare." Gov. Letcher's plea for support did not produce the desired result however, and he repeated it in a second proclamation on August 30. (23)

In early August, the 44th Ohio at Meadow Bluff was presented with a beautiful blue banner that had "Lewisburg" inscribed on its folds. The banner was said to be the "handsomest one in the Division." The men were so impressed by the banner that they "swore a solemn oath, that it shall never bow its crest to a conqueror." Disease was claiming more members of the 44th than enemy bullets and presentation of the banner gave the men a morale boost. Their regimental surgeon, Dr. Steele, resigned in late July amid complaints that he was incompetent. Dr. Steele was an experienced physician and a graduate of the University of New York Medical School. That his regiment seemed to suffer more cases of disease than others assigned with it was nothing more than chance, but he was blamed by many of the officers and men. Between late July and early August, four more members of the 44th perished in the hospital at Meadow Bluff. The 36th Ohio was nearly as bad off, having recently suffered through an outbreak of typhoid. (24)

Writing from Camp Caperton, Monroe County, on August 15, Captain John Sheffey told his fiancé about a grand review of the troops that Gen. Loring held at Union in late July. Gen. John S. Williams and Col. Albert Gallatin Jenkins were also present. The captain had recently returned to camp, having being on picket duty near Alderson's Ferry for several days. He said the citizens of the area were as patriotic and enthusiastic as any he had known anywhere. "The ladies constantly supplied our pickets with food," he said, "and more than once brought it from a distance of a mile or two." He said the women also kept them informed of enemy movements and "the Yankees in consequence hated them with the most malignant hatred." The captain had been a visitor at the home of a local physician by the name of Clay. At the nearby community of Palestine, he was told that the Yankees were forcing many local families to abandon their homes. He met one such family of refugees, by the name of Dyer, and helped them save some of their property when their wagon overturned in the swollen creek: "The women had packed all their little household wealth in an ox-wagon which a little boy was driving. Just as the team entered the ford, the wagon was overturned into the water. Almost everything was ruined....I entered the stream and by hard labor succeeded in saving everything that could be saved. But bonnets and beds, silks and soft soaps, laces, and dye-stuffs, china-ware and hard-ware were mingled together in weeping, dripping, inseparable confusion."

Earlier in the summer the Confederates had a skirmish at the Johnston place on the Greenbrier River. Captain Sheffey said one of their men was severely wounded, but that the tale had a "romantic" ending, after the soldier was found "in a meadow with three balls through him, by Miss Virginia Alderson, a noble-hearted girl of Greenbrier. She had never seen or heard of him before, but he was a southern soldier. She had him taken to a house, dressed his wounds. Each of which was supposed to be mortal. Deserting her own home, she took up her abode at his bedside. Day after day, night after night, week after week, she watched as a ministering angel there, and contrary to the expectation of all he began to recover. He is now well, a man of handsome face, of noble form, of good head and gallant heart." It was thus agreed that after the war, "Miss Alderson will become Mrs. [Alex] Robinson, and I intend to dance at their wedding. She has promised that I should be there, if I am in the land of the living, which however is doubtful." Captain Sheffey did survive the war, dying in 1905. Perhaps he got his dance after all. (25)

The man Ms. Alderson nursed back to health was 25-year-old Alex Robinson, a private in the 8th Va Cavalry. Robinson claimed he was shot after he surrendered and his shooting occasioned a flurry of charge and counter-charge between officers of the Blue and Gray. Several pages of the *Official Records* are devoted to his case, and include his statement as to what occurred:

> I was in an apple orchard and the enemy came up within twenty steps of me before I saw them, and I remained perfectly still, being on my horse. One told me to surrender, which I did immediately, at the same time dropping my gun and saber. Another told me to surrender. I told him I had surrendered (having then no arms) and asked him not to shoot me. Another said, 'Damn you, why didn't you surrender before when you were shooting at us last night?' They all exclaimed, 'Damn him, shoot him!' Upon which all fired at me. Two balls passed through my body. I then fell off my horse, and while I was lying on the ground one came up saying, 'Damn him, let me ride over him and smash his damn brains out.' Another said, 'No, let me shoot him again' A third said, 'He will die anyhow; let him alone.' (26)

When Alex Robinson gave his statement, it was supposed he was dying. The military doctor that examined him declared his wounds fatal, and no doubt he would have perished without the loving care of "a noble-hearted girl of Greenbrier." The demands of several Confederate officers, including Col. McCausland and Gen. John S. Williams, prompted Gen. Crook to have the matter investigated. In his reply, Gen. Crook said the investigation revealed that Robinson raised his gun to fire and was shot. This scenario seems very unlikely given the fact that Pvt. Robinson was outnumbered and at close proximity to the enemy. It was well known within the opposing armies that Gen. Crook wanted no prisoners taken, although the policy supposedly applied only to bushwhackers. When Gen. Loring heard the result of the investigation, he was furious: "There is no doubt but that the [enemy] is guilty as alleged. The examination into the fact by the enemy is evidently evasive, but I know of no way of reaching a redress of the case, the wrongdoer being in the enemy's camp and sheltered by their uncandid search for evidence."

During early August, persistent rumors of a Union withdrawal from Greenbrier County prompted Gen. Williams to send a spy to Meadow Bluff on August 14. The spy reported that the Yankees had burned their breastworks and were in the process of falling back toward the Kanawha Valley. Two days later, Williams sent two of his scouts to Meadow Bluff dressed in civilian clothing. The movement these men reported had been ordered on August 11. The U.S. Government directed that 5,000 men be retained in the Kanawha district and that the remainder be brought to Washington, to be used in the more active eastern theater of war. This movement began on August 14. During the ensuing days, light draft steamers transported 5,000 men, 1,100 horses, and 270 wagons from the Kanawha Valley. On August 17, Gen. Cox transferred command of the Kanawha district to Col. Joseph A.J. Lightburn with headquarters at Gauley Bridge. Col. Lightburn's command consisted of two infantry regiments and six cannon at Raleigh Court House (Beckley), with two companies of infantry as a guard for wagon trains at Fayetteville; two infantry regiments with a detachment of cavalry ten miles east of Gauley Bridge; two companies each of infantry and cavalry at Summersville; and small detachments of infantry and cavalry at various posts from Gauley Bridge to Charleston, including an outpost at Coal River in Boone County. Lightburn had no forces in Greenbrier or Monroe. (27)

On August 18, Gen. Loring notified the Secretary of War that the enemy had abandoned Greenbrier County and that he was pushing his scouts to both sides of the New River. The big break came for the Confederates on August 22, when Gen. John Pope's letter-book was captured: "While there was skirmishing between Lee's and Pope's armies along the Rappahannock, Jeb Stuart made a daring raid on Catlett's Station, to the rear of the Federal army, and captured General Pope's baggage train. Included in this prize was Pope's current letter-book." (28) Gen.

Lee examined the letter-book and sent a dispatch to the Secretary of War: "I call your attention particularly to a letter in the book of August 10th from General Cox to General Pope, and the reply of the latter on the 11th, directing General Cox to remain in Western Virginia with 5,000 men, and send the rest to General Pope…I deem it important that General Loring should be informed of the force opposed to him and directed to clear the valley of the Kanawha and then operate northwardly, so as to *join me* in the valley of Virginia." (29)

Before receiving word of the letter-book, Gen. Loring sought to take advantage of the Union withdrawal. He ordered General Albert G. Jenkins to take his cavalry on an extensive sweep through the area north of the Kanawha Valley. Starting from Salt Sulphur Springs in Monroe County, Jenkins and his 550-man raiding party swept boldly into central West Virginia. On September 4, they crossed the Ohio River and became the first Southern troops to raise the Confederate flag on Ohio soil.

When news of the raid reached Col. Lightburn, he became concerned for the safety of his flanks and rear, which were unprotected. He ordered his forces at Raleigh Court House to fall back and also ordered six companies of the 47th Ohio Infantry to reinforce Summersville, fearing that Jenkins would attack that post. These movements left open all of West Virginia south of the Kanawha Valley. In the meantime, the Secretary of War told Gen. Loring about the letter-book and ordered him to "clear the valley of the Kanawha, and operate northwardly to a junction with our army in the valley." (30)

Gen. Loring's army of approximately 5,000 soldiers advanced from the vicinity of Giles Court House toward the Kanawha Valley on September 6. Moving by way of Princeton and Flat Top Mountain, Loring reached Fayetteville on September 10, and pushed the Yankees back in a series of running battles that culminated in a fight at Charleston on September 13. Col. Lightburn's entire command retreated back into Ohio in the worst set-back of the war in western Virginia for U.S. forces. This defeat coincided with similar disasters in Kentucky and Tennessee, causing Federal authorities to scramble for a plan to recover the lost territory. Gen. Loring's army accomplished a great deal with relatively little loss. He reported just 25 killed, 95 wounded, and 190 missing. Not only were the Yankees defeated, but they also destroyed or abandoned more than $1 million worth of supplies. The speed of their retreat kept the bluecoats from destroying the valuable Kanawha saline works. The sudden availability of salt at reasonable prices was welcomed relief for the citizens of Greenbrier, Monroe, and other southern counties.

Citizens of Greenbrier County rejoiced in the Confederate occupation of the Kanawha Valley. Many of Loring's men were from the local area and this was a sort of homecoming for them, the only one they would receive during the war. The victory stopped Yankee raids on Greenbrier cattle and other livestock and enabled citizens to travel freely within the county. "Floyd's Guerillas," a cavalry company of the Virginia State Line, occupied Lewisburg during part of September. These men were commanded by Captain Peachy Gilmer Breckinridge, a former Virginia Military Institute cadet with prior service in the 28th Virginia Infantry. (31)

When Federal forces threatened Staunton in April 1862, the editor of the Staunton *Spectator* took his wife to her father's home in Lewisburg, believing she would be safe there. The area very rapidly came under Federal control and the editor was delayed five months returning to Staunton. On September 23, the *Spectator* carried this notice of his return and of the events he witnessed in Greenbrier County: "For the space of three consecutive months they [his relatives] were so situated as to be the victims of alarm almost every day and night. During that time two fights occurred in the town...one on the 12th and the other on the 23rd of May last....the latter, the battle between...Heth and...Crook, in which the enemy was successful...After the battle, the enemy were infuriated to such a degree that they acted more like demons than men—they threatened to lay the town in ashes, and it was thought they would do so." (32)

On September 25, Gen. Lee wrote to Loring at Charleston telling him that if he could advance northward into the Monongahela Valley and destroy bridges of the Baltimore and

Ohio Railroad, "great benefit would be derived." Loring could then move into Washington County, Pennsylvania, and supply his army. Another proposal was that Loring's army could use the Potomac River to unite with Gen. Lee: "Probably a combined movement into Pennsylvania may be concerted." (33) Five days later, the Secretary of War told Gen. Loring that with recovery of the Kanawha Valley, his next objective was to break up the insurrectionary government in Northwestern Virginia. Gen. Loring was left considerable discretion in how to accomplish these objectives. The Secretary told him to march by way of Clarksburg, Grafton, and Romney, to some point from which he could communicate with Gen. Lee. (34) Loring replied on October 7, indicating his desire to comply with Gen. Lee's plan. He stated that if he should march down the Monongahela River, the route was so long and short of subsistence, the enemy could "destroy my army and train." He then proposed a much shorter route by which he might unite his army with Gen. Lee's: "I will, therefore, unless halted or ordered otherwise, proceed to comply with Gen. Lee's orders by moving my infantry and trains to rear and thence through Monterey & etc., while with my cavalry I will sweep through the northwest." (35)

The following day Gen. Loring began a movement out of the Kanawha Valley toward Greenbrier County. He divided his army, sending Gen. Jenkins's cavalry, 1,500 strong, to move into northwestern Virginia as Secretary Randolph had proposed. Gen. Lee was somehow delayed learning of Loring's movements and, on October 15, wrote him, saying that if he could retain possession of the Kanawha Salt Works it might be "the best service your army can perform." Lee added his opinion that the season was now too far advanced for a movement into Pennsylvania. (36) When Gen. Loring received this dispatch, his army had already passed into, and partially beyond, Greenbrier County. On the same date as Lee's communication, the Adjutant and Inspector General ordered Gen. Loring to "turn over your command, together with the orders and instructions heretofore communicated to you, to General [John] Echols, after which you will, with the least delay practicable, report in person to this office." (37)

Over the years, numerous historians have concluded that Gen. Loring was relieved of command as punishment for "disregarding Lee's orders." In a biography of Gen. Loring's life published in 1996, the author makes it clear that Loring requested a transfer because of a long-standing feud between himself and Gov. Letcher, and because of Secretary Randolph's interference with his command. At the heart of their trouble was Letcher's call for 10,000 Virginia State Line troops, the result being that regular Confederate enlistments, already weak, fell off sharply. Loring's repeated complaints about the State Line forces, echoed by Gen. Heth and others, prompted Gov. Letcher to accuse Loring of exceeding his authority. Writing from Charleston on September 22, Gen. Loring told Secretary Randolph that it was a misstatement for the governor to claim that he "issued orders to stop the enrollment in Monroe, Giles, and perhaps other counties." Loring said tactics used by officers of the State Line had seriously impaired his own efforts at recruiting. "I deeply regret," Loring wrote, "that the libel of the Governor on my conduct and motives constrains me now to depart from the preferable policy of silence..." He went on to ask the Secretary to publish his letter in the newspapers or present it to the Virginia Legislature, for his "justification." (38)

Gen. Loring resigned his command during the movement out of the valley and was subsequently transferred to Mississippi: "Maj. Gen. W.W. Loring, having been relieved from the command of the Department of Western Virginia at his own request, will proceed to Jackson, Miss., and report for duty to Lieut. Gen. John C. Pemberton, commanding." (39) Gen. Loring related the facts of his removal in a December letter to his friend, Dr. Charles Todd Quintard: "I had a brilliant campaign in Western Virginia as long as it lasted; we took the Kanawha Valley...but for the interference of Randolph with matters of which he was ignorant...[I] would have had a campaign which would have been of great service. As it was I saw no prospect in Western Virginia this winter but monotonous inactivity—I applied to be relieved and ordered to an army in the field. It resulted in me coming here [Mississippi]. (40)

Gen. John Echols assumed command of the Army of Southwestern Virginia at Lewisburg. Ordered to regain control of the valuable Kanawha Salt Works, Echols acted swiftly to reoccupy the valley, moving out of Lewisburg on October 16. Fatigued from marching and counter-marching, the Confederate army was strung out for several miles, with some troops remaining in Lewisburg until October 20. Echols reoccupied Charleston, but in the meantime, Federal authorities determined to retake the valley. On October 27, Echols notified the Richmond authorities that an enemy army of 12,000 soldiers were advancing on his position from Clarksburg and Point Pleasant. He also stated that he believed another 3,000 Yankees were moving south to attack Gen. Floyd and his State Line forces. At 2:00 a.m. October 28, Echols began a forced march out of the valley, splashing along the turnpike in a combination of rain and snow. The Yankees under Gen. Cox reached Charleston on October 29, and by November 1, the valley and adjacent territory was firmly in Federal control. Withdrawing toward the Narrows of New River by way of Raleigh County, Echols ordered his cavalry, recently returned from their raid, to operate in the counties of Greenbrier, Pocahontas, and Nicholas. He left 900 men at Mercer Court House to guard against an enemy advance on the railroad, and dispatched a small brigade into Monroe and Greenbrier to "check any advance upon…Lewisburg." Echols informed Richmond that good weather might prompt the enemy to advance into Greenbrier County, and it would require 12,000 to 15,000 men to retain control of the region. He reported the entire country all the way back to the Kanawha Valley as being "little better than a desert, having been heretofore pillaged and laid waste by the enemy." (41) Bryan's Battery Virginia Artillery occupied Lewisburg on October 29, and the following day tried out some new cannons they received to replace those lost in the battle for Lewisburg in May. Bryan's men moved into Monroe County on the 31st, camping near Union.

Chapter Twelve
To Sinking Creek and the Medal of Honor

On November 3, Secretary Randolph notified Gen. Echols that he was authorized to call on Gen. Humphrey Marshall at Abingdon for assistance. He was to request help only for the safety of the railroad, the Secretary preferring to leave Marshall's army of 2,500 at Abingdon as long as possible. By November 7, part of the 8th Va Cavalry occupied Alderson, with the 14th Cavalry at Williamsburg and Meadow Bluff. A small detachment of Confederate cavalry occupied White Sulphur Springs, with another group under Gen. Jenkins at Muddy Creek. On the 10th, the 37th Battalion Va Cavalry entered Greenbrier County from Dublin, camping between Lewisburg and Frankford. The cavalry found it difficult to remain in the Greenbrier region due to a severe lack of food for man and beast alike. With winter rapidly approaching, Gen. Echols ordered the majority of his cavalry horses into North Carolina where food was yet plentiful. Due to persistent health problems, Gen. Echols was succeeded in command on November 10 by Gen. John S. Williams. Echols returned to his home in Union to regain his health. Rev. S.R. Houston said Echols spoke "discouragingly of the state of our country." (1)

Constantly on the watch for an opportunity to disrupt rebel activities in Greenbrier County, Gen. Crook ordered another raid toward Lewisburg. Yankee cavalry commanded by Captain G.W. Gilmore rode out of Summersville on November 9. Late on the 10th the U.S. cavalry surprised and captured a wagon train belonging to Gen. Jenkins' command near Williamsburg. They captured Captain J.L. Evans and three other members of Jenkins' command, along with seven civilians, including two negro wagon drivers. They also set fire to seven wagon loads of wheat, took 23 horses, four mules, and 24 sets of harness. The raiding party returned to Summersville with their prisoners and property at 5 p.m. November 11, having traveled a total of 100 miles.

Writing from Logan County on November 19, Gen. John B. Floyd told Secretary Randolph that he believed all of western Virginia, from the Cumberland Gap to Cheat Mountain, could be protected from invasion by fortifying all the mountain passes. Ignoring the abuses of his Virginia State Line recruiters, Floyd complained that enforcement of conscription had been "injudicious and wholly ineffectual," and was "repulsive to the community." He also claimed the army in western Virginia would benefit greatly from dismounting the cavalry. Except for scouts and pickets, cavalry in the mountains were "worse than useless," and "100 horse will consume in a day" more corn than would feed an entire regiment of infantry for the same period. "I advance it as my opinion," he wrote, "that with a few passes fortified, by a judicious and efficient system of collecting conscripts, and the disbanding or removal of the cavalry force from this country, you may safely rely upon the ability of the mountain region to defend and support itself from Cumberland Gap to Lewisburg." (2)

Shortly after assuming command from Echols, Gen. Williams conducted an inspection of the Confederate army in and near Greenbrier County. He found his forces disorganized and in need of food and other supplies: "I found Gen. Jenkins' mounted men at Lewisburg in a perfect state of chaos, but the general is not to blame, as he had no chance to organize or discipline his men...." Williams had 42 cavalry companies, and 4,869 infantry and artillery, with 2,707 "absent with and without leave." Diligent efforts were being made to round up "absentees, deserters, and conscripts." More cavalry was being dismounted, the horses sent into North Carolina, and Gen. Jenkins was to visit Richmond "in a day or two." Attempting to acquire forage in Greenbrier and Monroe was a losing proposition, as they had "a surplus of nothing except a little hay and beef cattle." Williams said he had sent an agent south of the railroad to make arrangements to feed cattle there when all the local grass gave out. It was very clear from this report that with winter already at hand the boys in grey were in for a rough time.

At Charleston on November 20, Gen. Cox received a proposal to advance on Staunton by way of Beverly, Warm Springs, and Lewisburg. A strong detachment commanded by Cox would make a demonstration against Lewisburg, threatening the railroad to the south. It was hoped this ploy would cause the Rebels at Warm Springs to reinforce those at Lewisburg, thereby opening the route to Staunton. If the Lewisburg force was not reinforced, the Union army would still be strong enough to "open a double way" to Staunton and the railroad. It was this type planning that would make matters very difficult for Gen. Williams' command, especially so late in the season when the Confederates were praying for a lull in enemy activity. (3)

Regardless of the season, Gen. Crook was not interested in sitting by the fire and waiting for spring. When he got word that the 14th Va Cavalry was recruiting in the Sinking Creek Valley of Greenbrier County, he determined to attack. It was hoped Crook's men could disrupt the enemy activity and move on to Covington, where they might release Dr. J.P. Rucker, who was on trial there. Crook ordered Col. John C. Paxton to leave Camp Piatt, near Charleston, for Cold Knob in Greenbrier County on November 24. He also ordered 500 infantrymen of the 11th Ohio under Col. Philander P. Lane to march out of Summersville for Cold Knob, where they would rendezvous with Paxton and 475 troopers of the 2nd West Va Cavalry. Leaving Camp Piatt early on the 24th., Paxton's veteran cavalrymen rode hard for Summersville, arriving there at 10 p.m., having traveled 53 miles in one day. Col. Lane's infantry strike force marched away from Summersville that same morning and camped for the night 17 miles south of Summersville. Resuming their march at 6 a.m. of the 25th., the infantry encamped near Cranberry Road, on the top of Cold Knob. The 2nd Cavalry left Summersville at 7 a.m., and encamped at the Hinkle Farm in Fayette County, having gone 35 miles. Snow and blowing winds delayed the cavalry on the 25th., and that night the storm became so severe that near white-out conditions prevailed. Lane's infantry resumed their advance at 6 a.m. in the midst of a furious snow storm, driven by sharp and whipping winds. At 10 a.m., the infantrymen were relieved by the arrival of Paxton's cavalry on the top of Cold Knob Mountain, elevation 4,280 feet.

Col. Lane was to assist the cavalry in breaking up the enemy camps at Sinking Creek, but due to the severity of the weather and fatigue of his men, Lane asked Col. Paxton if he could return his force to Summersville. Paxton proposed a compromise and it was agreed that the infantry would take the advance until contact was made with enemy pickets. At that time the cavalry would take over and Lane could return to Summersville. Snow and ice caused the men's clothing and boots to freeze to their bodies, and many of their guns became useless as ice formed between the hammer and lock plate. Nevertheless, the determined Yankees pressed onward, unable to warm themselves or find shelter. The snow was eight inches deep with mountain drifts two and three feet high. Moving down the mountain, the frozen raiders suddenly came upon six Rebel pickets. A brief fight ensued in which two of the pickets were wounded and the others scattered. No doubt the equally frozen pickets found it hard to believe that they were being attacked in such inclement weather. With this skirmish, the infantry had performed their duty and turned back toward Nicholas County, arriving in camp on November 29. Col. Lane reported that it snowed for 36 hours of their journey. He said their clothing became thoroughly wet and then "frozen fast."

Col. Paxton gave Major William H. Powell permission to take an advance party of 21 men toward the main Confederate camp, some five miles distant. The advance party had not gone far when they encountered four enemy scouts. Two were taken prisoner, the other two escaped but for some reason did not rush to alert their main camp of the approaching danger. The two captives gave valuable information as to the strength and locations of the Rebels and Powell pressed onward. In a short time, the main camp of the Rebel cavalry was located, three miles from

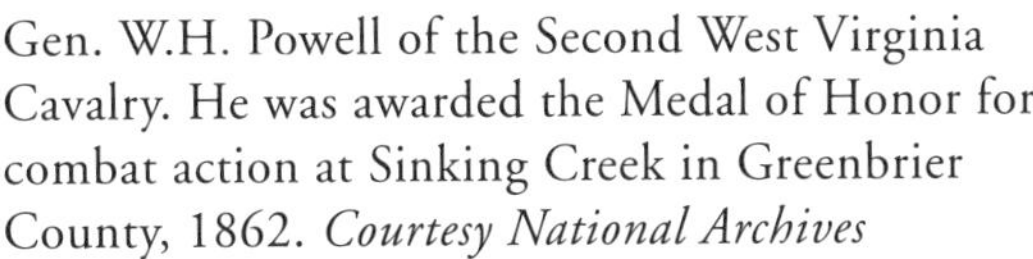

Gen. W.H. Powell of the Second West Virginia Cavalry. He was awarded the Medal of Honor for combat action at Sinking Creek in Greenbrier County, 1862. *Courtesy National Archives*

the foot of Cold Knob Mountain, at Lewis' Mill on Sinking Creek. Working entirely undetected, Major Powell used his binoculars to observe the camp, less than one mile distant. The enemy camp was 500 strong and included men from the Braxton Dragoons, Churchville Cavalry, the Nighthawk Rangers, Rockbridge Cavalry, and the Valley Cavalry.

William H. Powell was born in South Wales in 1825, his parents immigrating to America when he was five years old. An iron and nail manufacturer, Powell superintended the building of the Benwood Iron and Nail Works near Wheeling. An Ohio resident and ardent Union man, William Powell entered the U.S. Army in August 1861. He immediately began recruiting men from several Ohio and West Virginia counties to form a company of cavalry. These men subsequently became Company B, 2nd West Va Cavalry. Standing 6' 2" tall and weighing over 200 pounds, Powell was a bold and fearless man, brave to the point of recklessness. Fate and William Powell's personality came together at Sinking Creek in 1862. Peering at the unsuspecting Rebels, Powell turned and asked his little band of 21 men if they were willing to ride straight into the enemy camp and capture all they could. Col. Paxton and the other 453 troopers would not catch up for some time and Powell feared his position would be discovered. If they were to surprise the enemy, the time was now:

> Appreciating the golden opportunity, I decided to promptly charge the camp. Announcing the situation to my heroic little command of Lieut. Davidson and his twenty men, they answered 'We will follow where you

lead.' At this moment I turned my head toward the head of the valley to see if our regiment was in sight, discovering it had not reached the foot of the mountain and not having a moment to lose, I wheeled my command into line, facing the camp and charged my handful of men on a full run of a half mile down the Sinking Creek Valley into the very center of the enemy's camp, 500 strong. We were each armed with a saber and a brace of Colt's .54 caliber navy revolvers giving us 220 shots, without cessation, which we held in reserve to avoid alarming the other camp, or to be used in case of absolute necessity.

It was soon made evident that the camp was surprised and that their firearms were unloaded. A brief and very exciting hand to hand encounter ensued, in their confusion, some few of their number run up to us grasping us by the legs and claiming us as their prisoners. To such daring and undignified assaults and claims, we simply responded politely by tapping them on top of their heads with our revolvers which we held in our hands, felling several of the rudest of them to the ground, the effect of which caused them to loosen their grasp upon our exposed extremities. After thus dealing with them but for a moment, I demanded the surrender of the camp, on the condition of the protection of their lives, which demand Lt. Col. John A. Gibson and Major B.F. Eakle and Capt. W.A. Lackey of the 14th Regiment Virginia Rebel Cavalry promptly accepted and surrendered the command to me, without reservation.

Thus I captured the camp…in the Sinking Creek Valley, in Greenbrier County, Virginia, with Lieut. Davidson and twenty men at noon on the 26th day of November, 1862, without the loss of a life, or the firing of a gun or revolver." (4)

Shortly after the camp surrendered, Col. Paxton and his men arrived. In the melee, two Confederates were killed, two wounded, one paroled, and 113 officers and men captured. They also took 106 horses, five mules, 200 rifles, 50 sabers, various stores, supplies, and tents. The Yankees had two horses killed in the enemy camp and lost 10 on the march from fatigue and exhaustion. They returned to Summersville at noon on the 27th, having traveled 120 miles without food or rest, except one feed of hay for the horses. The 2nd West Va Cavalry left Nicholas County en route to Camp Piatt on November 29. They left two men in the hospital at Summersville, "whose boots we cut from their feet." All of the raiders had been "more or less frozen," and were fortunate indeed to have survived the greatest cavalry raid of the war in West Virginia. (5)

News of the great raid spread rapidly among newspapers of the North and South. From New York to Georgia and points west, Powell's charge gained lasting fame. When the prisoners taken at Sinking Creek arrived at Gallipolis, Ohio, the local newspaper reveled in the tale: "The B.C. Levi brought down from the Kanawha, 112 secesh prisoners taken by…the 2nd Virginia Cavalry….Colonel Paxton's cavalry came in on them whilst their horses were in pasture and they quite unprepared….Though ragged and badly clothed, they seemed jubilant and full of hope of final success….several expressed themselves tired of the war…It is enough to say that the expedition was entirely successful…" (6)

Not unexpectedly, Southern newspapers such as the Lexington, Virginia, *Gazette* found nothing in the raid to be happy about: "It is stated upon what seems to be reliable authority…that a force of Confederate cavalry…suffered themselves to be surprised and captured a few days ago. They seemed to have turned their horses out to grass…and themselves out some distance from their horses. A force of Abolition Cavalry dashed in upon their camp, killed their pickets, and took both horses and men without a fight….This is not the first time our forces in Western Virginia have been surprised. It is time somebody who has the authority would enquire into the causes which lead to such disasters." (7)

In 1889, Gen. George Crook wrote to the United States Congress recommending William H. Powell for the Congressional Medal of Honor for his valor on that bitter winter day in

Greenbrier County. Crook regarded the Sinking Creek raid as one of the most brilliant expeditions of the entire war. The U.S. Congress agreed with Crook's assessment and, in July 1890, Gen. William H. Powell was awarded this nation's highest military honor. The citation read: "Distinguished services in a raid, where, with 20 men he charged and captured the enemy's camp, 500 strong, without the loss of man or gun."

Gen. Powell returned to the iron and nail business after the war and eventually worked for the Internal Revenue Service in Illinois. In 1875, he applied for and received an invalid pension, based upon an injury he received at Wytheville, Virginia, in 1863. This pension was only $7.50 per month and in 1889 he was granted an increase to $30.00 monthly. This amount was increased by Congressional order to $72.00 per month in 1891. William H. Powell died at Belleville, Illinois on December 26, 1904. He was 79-years-old. His wife collected his pension at the reduced rate of $30.00 per month until her death in 1928.

The Medal of Honor.

Chapter Thirteen
Tuckwiller Hill, White Sulphur Springs, and Droop Mountain

No official report was made by the Confederates subsequent to the fiasco at Sinking Creek. Southern forces in the Greenbrier region began to construct winter quarters in the hope that calm would prevail for the foreseeable future. In early December, enemy activity in the Shenandoah Valley prompted Gen. Lee to ask whether or not the forces at and near Lewisburg could be dispatched to Staunton. If rumors were true that Gen. Cox had withdrawn most of his men from the Kanawha Valley, then the immediate threat to Lewisburg and the railroad was alleviated. From the 6th to the 16th of December, Secretary of War J.A. Seddon, Gen. Lee, and Gen. W.E. Jones, speculated as to the possibility of removing most, if not all, Southern forces from Greenbrier County. On December 11, Secretary Seddon wrote that he met in Richmond with Gen. Echols to review the military situation in southwestern Virginia. Echols complained once again that Gen. Floyd's Virginia State Line conducted themselves in ways detrimental to the regular Confederate military. The Secretary counseled patience, saying that discretion and forbearance would be necessary to avoid any embarrassment between the armies. "Few things," Seddon wrote, "would more grieve all true friends, or more rejoice all enemies of our cause," than a clash between the forces. (1)

Gen. Sam Jones was in overall command of the Department of Southwestern Virginia, with headquarters at Giles Court

House. He stated on December 11 that his cavalry force at Lewisburg was disorganized and in no condition for efficient service. To remedy this situation he had Gen. Jenkins send most of his remaining horses "to the rear," where they might obtain forage. Jenkins was ordered to have the men instructed and disciplined on foot. (2) Yankee activity along the lines of the Baltimore and Ohio Railroad and in the area of Martinsburg, Harpers Ferry, and Fredericksburg prompted Gen. Lee to reiterate his desire to consolidate manpower in the Shenandoah. Gen. Sam Jones met at Wytheville on December 15 with Gen. Humphrey Marshall in an attempt to determine which regiments might be spared from western Virginia. As a result of their conference, Gen. Jones sent five regiments into Richmond, none of these coming from Greenbrier or Monroe. It was determined the enemy still occupied the Kanawha Valley with sufficient force to threaten the railroad, thus Gen. Jones would be risking disaster if he reduced his manpower further. He told Secretary Seddon that it was impossible to forage cavalry in Greenbrier County and that it may become necessary to "withdraw all troops from that country."

The 3rd Regiment Virginia State Line, 290 infantry with 230 cavalry, occupied Greenbrier County. Their presence in the area placed an additional burden on the availability of subsistence, while at the same time offering little or no cooperation with the regular military command. Gen. Sam Jones added his voice to the chorus of those opposed to the State Line: "The presence in this department of the troops of the State Line, as an independent command, is embarrassing, and, I think, injurious. The agents of the State Line are paying much higher prices for supplies than the Confederate agents are permitted to pay for the same articles. To procure corn at the prices now allowed, I shall probably be obliged to impress it, which is very objectionable..." (3)

Writing from Charleston on December 29, Gen. George Crook said he was certain that enemy forces in the Greenbrier region would content themselves with protecting the railroad and would not attempt to retake the valley. He reported the Rebels as being between 3,000 and 5,000 strong, and stretched out along a line from Princeton and the Narrows to Lewisburg. (4)

Barely two weeks after sending five regiments to Richmond, Gen. Jones asked for their return. In a letter to Secretary Seddon on December 31, he said the Union defeat at Fredericksburg earlier in the month, and the failure of a Yankee expedition into North Carolina, would deter the enemy from advancing on Richmond this winter. Jones worried that the bluecoats would turn their attention to the Virginia and Tennessee Railroad, and would attack the salt works in Wythe and Smyth counties. Should they succeed, they would advance their lines so as to control a larger portion of western Virginia. Jones said his supposition was strengthened by the passage of a bill to admit West Virginia to the Union as a separate state. Having recently visited his forces in Greenbrier and Monroe, Jones said he was reluctant to leave those counties "as exposed" as he found them. He also reasoned that it would be advantageous to have possession of the area's "rich lands" when spring returned. (5)

From December 30 to January 1, Gen. Jones reinforced the Department of East Tennessee with the command of Humphrey Marshall. The men were to rendezvous at Bristol with Gen. Henry Heth, and pursue enemy raiders who had seriously damaged the railroad. The frequent dispatch of men and material out of the Greenbrier region gave evidence just how overburdened Confederate forces were in western Virginia. Bullets and ballots became equally important in 1863, with the pending rise of West Virginia as the 35th State in the Union. Robert E. Lee told Secretary Seddon on January 3 that the Yankees would likely make an "earnest effort" to possess every county within the proposed new state. (6)

In early January, Union forces at Camp Piatt, Kanawha County, decided to make a raid on the railroad. In the early evening hours of January 8, 300 horsemen of the 2nd West Va Cavalry rode south toward Greenbrier County, by way of Fayette. Commanded by Colonels Paxton and Powell, the men were not told of their destination until they crossed the Sewell Mountain range and stopped at a tannery two miles from Meadow Bluff after sunset of January 9. Here the command was assembled and

Col. Paxton revealed the purpose of the raid, calling for volunteers: "He told them that he wanted them for a very hard and trying march; he wanted them to keep their mouths closed, and he had no doubt that with a little prudence and their tried courage that we would accomplish what we were about to undertake...the burning of a bridge on the railroad." One hundred volunteers were selected for the daring raid. The remaining forces under Col. Powell were told to create a diversion in Greenbrier County. It was hoped Powell's diversion would draw the Rebels out of Monroe County, thereby clearing the route south.

As Paxton's men rode toward Monroe County, Col. Powell's command moved to within one mile of Lewisburg, stopping at the home of Austin Handley. The Yankees roused Handley's family from their slumber, giving Mr. and Mrs. Handley and their children just minutes to evacuate the house. It was Handley's misfortune that his home was constructed on elevated ground. Col. Powell knew that if he set the home on fire the roaring blaze would be visible for miles around. It was hoped the sight would draw enemy forces out of Monroe County, thus clearing the route for Paxton to the railroad. The weather was cold, the ground snow-covered. The Yankees must act quickly for the ploy to have any prospect of success. Some accounts claim Powell gave the Handley's 15 or 20 minutes to save what they could. Others claim he torched the home as soon as the family came out into the yard. Whatever the case, the family lost everything they had, including their stables and barn, even their horses, which the raiders ran off. They also set fire to the nearby barn of the Feamster family. In a further attempt to attract the rebels from Monroe, the raiders told their victims and others in the area that they would also burn Lewisburg.

Lt. Col. George M. Edgar was in charge of the Southern forces in Lewisburg. When he received word of the raid, the fires were already raging and a "terrific snow storm" blanketed the area. He quickly assembled his men and rode out of town, passing the Handley inferno in search of the enemy. Just beyond Handley's, his men found Powell's crew and, in a brief skirmish, chased the raiders out of Greenbrier County. In the meantime,

Col. Paxton's men, disguised as Rebels, rode into Monroe County by way of Blue Sulphur Springs. At dawn, the intrepid bluecoats passed directly through the camp of Thurmond's Rangers. Riding confidently through the camp, a few of Thurmond's men shouted questions which were calmly answered by the raiders and they were allowed to pass. The next challenge they had was just outside Centerville (Greenville), where they were halted by a Rebel patrol. Once again, a few simple questions were answered satisfactorily and off the raiders went. The Yankees found Centerville "full of rebels and citizens" because there was an election going on that day. Suddenly someone in the crowd called Col. Paxton by name and several enemy soldiers gathered around, evidently having noticed the "U.S." on the horses. Apparently the rebels were dumbfounded, because they did not challenge their visitors: "the soldiers that gathered around us saw that we were disguised, and the only wonder to me is that we were not attacked then and there, for they were as many as we." (7) With their hearts thumping in their chests and their pistols cocked and ready beneath their blankets, the anxious cavalrymen rode slowly out of Centerville. Two Confederate soldiers began following them, remaining at the rear of the column, not a word spoken between them. As had been the case during the Sinking Creek raid, rain and sleet began to fall in torrents, adding misery to danger. At the foot of Peters Mountain, their guide took a wrong turn, riding almost two miles before the error was discovered. The raiders, now half-frozen, backtracked and thought they were on the right course, but became lost again. Frustrated, the men dismounted in some woods to discuss their situation and decided to abandon the mission. Apparently, their rebel escorts had already given up and headed back to Centerville. Realizing it would be risking too much to retrace their route, the Yankees returned by way of New River and Raleigh Court House, reaching Camp Piatt on January 14.

Citizens of the Greenbrier region were outraged with the destruction of Mr. Handley's home. Numerous complaints were made with Confederate military authorities and, on January 16, Gen. Sam Jones sent a scathing condemnation of the act to the

"Officer Commanding U.S. forces in the Valley of the Kanawha." Had the mission succeeded and the railroad bridge been destroyed, the reason for burning the home may have been more apparent. The entire episode returned to haunt Col. Powell in July 1863 when he was wounded and captured at Wytheville. He was charged with war crimes and placed in the dungeon at Richmond's Libby Prison. Gen. Jones asked the War Department to deny Powell an exchange, saying he was "a bold daring man and one of the most dangerous officers we have to contend with." After an investigation revealed the true purpose of the raid and the fact that Powell was acting under orders, he was exchanged. (8)

The Yankees remained determined to destroy the New River railroad bridge, eight miles east of Dublin, and on February 17, Gen. E.P. Scammon asked Gen. Cox for permission to make another raid. Scammon was under the mistaken impression that no enemy troops were in the Lewisburg area. He wanted to attack the railroad and the iron furnaces near Fincastle, Virginia, simultaneously. Having arrived at the bridge, his men would cross the track at a point above the bridge and then float down the river, apply explosives to the bridge supports, and get back by "any way that may seem best." (9) The 22nd Virginia Infantry and the 3rd Regiment Virginia State Line were stationed at and near Lewisburg. Their presence may have been a factor in the rejection of Scammon's plan.

In March, the 3rd Virginia State Line was camped at Williamsburg and Frankford. The State of Virginia grew tired of having its own independent army and, on April 1, 1863, the State Line forces were disbanded. Although the State forces had been authorized to recruit up to 10,000 men, it totaled just over 4,000 at its zenith. An embarrassingly small number of those men entered regular Confederate service. The others simply walked away. Those remaining in service were scattered among various regiments, including the 19th and 21st Virginia Cavalry; the 23rd and 45th Battalion Infantry; Levi's Artillery Battery; the 7th Battalion Confederate Cavalry; the 10th Kentucky Cavalry, and the 39th Kentucky (Federal) forces. An officer of the State

Line who hoped to avoid conscription described their dilemma: "What shall we [officers] do to escape the Confederate Dog Catchers? This is the all absorbing question among gentleman with braid on their sleeves. These conscript catchers are ever in their mind's eye and their thoughts are constantly harassed by gloomy forebodings of the future when they will be confined to the gentle clutches of those privilege officials who will generously tender them a private's berth in the Confederate Army." (10)

In early April, Edgar's Battalion, 26th Virginia Infantry occupied Lewisburg. The 22nd Virginia Infantry found itself detached to support Gen. William E. "Grumble" Jones in a raid on northern West Virginia. Gen. W.E. Jones' men would work in conjunction with another strike force commanded by Gen. John D. Imboden. This large-scale Confederate offensive into the heart of West Virginia, a rare occurrence, was intended to destroy the Baltimore and Ohio Railroad between Oakland and Grafton. It was also expected to defeat and disburse various Federal detachments and enlist men for the Confederacy, while at the same time threatening the "restored government" of Virginia based at Wheeling.

Of course it was nearly impossible to keep an offensive of this magnitude secret and Federal commanders knew something was in the planning stages. For two weeks before the raid got under way, a flurry of dispatches and scouting reports passed between various Federal commanders in the region. On April 11, four Yankee scouts wearing Confederate uniforms were dispatched toward Lewisburg from Sutton, with orders to determine the intentions of the enemy. (11)

The Jones – Imboden raid began on April 13, and the removal of some Southern forces from the Greenbrier region to participate in the raid caused alarm for the safety of Greenbrier and Monroe. Gen. John Echols expressed these concerns in a dispatch to Gen. Sam Jones, asking if men might be sent from Princeton or the Narrows. Jones replied that he would shift some additional forces into Greenbrier and Monroe counties at his earliest opportunity. Echols was also told that some government cattle had been ordered removed from Greenbrier County, because having them there might tempt the Yankees to make a raid for the purpose of running them off. There were concerns that this movement might cause a panic among the people in the area who would assume it to mean a general withdrawal of Confederate forces. To prevent any misunderstanding, Echols was asked to reassure the people in his talks with them. (12)

From April 13 to May 22, the Jones – Imboden raid struck fear into the hearts of enemy soldiers and Union citizens of West Virginia. Gen. "Grumble" Jones, with 2,100 men, advanced from Lacy Springs in Rockingham County, and struck Oakland, Rowlesburg, Kingwood, Morgantown, Fairmont. Philippi, and Buckhannon, where he united with Gen. Imboden's command of nearly 3,400. Imboden's raiders had advanced from Shenandoah Mountain by way of the Staunton and Parkersburg Turnpike. Their plan to capture Clarksburg had to be abandoned, so the forces separated again. Gen. Jones struck at Cairo and the Burning Springs oil district, then rejoined Imboden at Summersville by way of Glenville and Sutton. When the raid was over, Jones had covered 700 miles; killed approximately 30 of the enemy and wounded upward of 60; taken nearly 700 prisoners, one cannon, and two trains of cars; burned 16 railroad bridges and wrecked one tunnel; destroyed 150,000 barrels of oil; and seized about 1,000 cattle and 1,200 horses. He accomplished this with an amazingly small loss of just 10 killed, 42 wounded, and about 15 missing. Gen. Imboden's journey covered 400 miles, during which he seized more than $100,000 worth of horses, mules, wagons, and guns. They also set fire to several railroad bridges west of Fairmont, and purchased or seized more than 3,100 head of cattle. Imboden reported a relatively trivial loss of two killed and 14 captured.

The raiders hoped to extend their ride into the Kanawha Valley, but the idea was abandoned due to the condition of the men, and the necessity of their presence in the Shenandoah Valley. Gen. Imboden left Summersville by way of Gauley River, crossed over to the Cherry River, and entered Greenbrier County along the Cold Knob road. His forces remained in Greenbrier County for two days, camping just above Meadow Bluff, at

Lewisburg, and at White Sulphur Springs. Upon leaving, they left behind 1,250 head of cattle captured during the raid. Jones crossed the Gauley at Hughes Ferry and reached Lewisburg by way of the Wilderness Road and the James River and Kanawha Turnpike. His command then divided and advanced on Warm Springs by separate routes.

While the Jones – Imboden forces wreaked havoc across northern West Virginia, Federal authorities realized that few enemy soldiers occupied Greenbrier County. The door was thus open for a Union invasion and if the Rebels in Greenbrier were defeated, it would allow the Yankees to block a likely escape route for the raiders. Col. John C. Paxton, 2nd West Va Cavalry, received orders at Camp Piatt to take his men and Captain H.H. Hagan's Company A, 1st West Va Cavalry, and defeat the enemy at Lewisburg. A force of approximately 700 mounted men rode out of Camp Piatt, arriving at the base of Big Sewell Mountain at 1 a.m. of May 1. The bluecoats lost the element of surprise, however, because citizens sent word of the Yankee advance to Edgar at Lewisburg. In response, Edgar hastily sent all sick or disabled men and prisoners to the rear. He also sent Lieutenant J.A. Feamster and 28 men of the 14th Virginia Cavalry to check enemy strength and location. Edgar's actions were just in the nick of time because Feamster's scouting party encountered the enemy advance under Captain David Dove at Brushy Ridge, 12 miles west of Lewisburg. Surprised, both parties opened fire, with no injuries reported on either side. Following orders, Feamster retired slowly, delaying the Yankee advance without giving battle. He also sent a rider to Edgar at Lewisburg, to inform him that Col. Paxton was nearing the village. Because of the skirmish, Captain Dove knew the opportunity for surprise was lost. He cautioned Col. Paxton, recommending that the advance guard take the brunt of any enemy attack, rather than subjecting the entire regiment to an uncertain fate. Paxton would have no part of it and foolishly rode directly into an ambush.

Col. Edgar received Feamster's warning at 11 p.m. and, in response, he very quickly assembled a force of approximately 250 men and marched them out to Handley's Hill (Tuckwiller

Hill), two miles west of Lewisburg. Edgar positioned five companies on either side of the turnpike, with two companies on his far right to act as a reserve. Two hundred yards to the right of his reserve, he placed 20 men where they would have a good view of the enemy, with orders to report any attempt to turn their flank. Edgar's men had scarcely finished their preparations when they heard the Yankee cavalry riding up the hill in a column of four. The men were laughing and speaking in a normal voice, totally unaware of the imminent danger. Orders had been given to allow the head of the Federal column to pass and then open fire. Unfortunately for Edgar, one of his men became excited and fired his gun earlier than expected. This caused the entire line to fire. Paxton's men were thrown into confusion, several being emptied from their saddles. The bluecoats struggled to assemble and withdrew around a bend in the road, firing as they went. Within a few minutes, a quick volley on the Confederate right told Edgar that the Yankees were attempting to turn his right flank. The 1 a.m. sky came alive with the bright flash of gunfire as Edgar's two reserve companies hastened in the direction of the firing. Col. Edgar led the men in person, going just 150 yards when suddenly they met the Yankees charging in line through the woods. The boys in gray occupied the woods in the enemy's path and opened fire. Paxton's determined troopers engaged the Rebels in a spirited fight. Realizing that the safety of his entire force depended upon the repulse of the Yankees, Edgar ordered two rifle companies from the front into the woods. Before the riflemen were fully in position, the raiders began to fall back. Just as they did, another detachment sped boldly up the turnpike directly into Edgar's barricade. When 100 Rebel defenders opened fire, it took just one volley to defeat the charge. This was the last volley fired, the stunned bluecoats retiring from the Confederate front and right. As they withdrew, Edgar sent squads of cavalry and infantry out to watch their movements. Within minutes these men reported the enemy assembling in a field for the apparent purpose of another flank attack. At the same time, Edgar heard noise on his left that led him to believe the enemy had dismounted part of their force and would attack from both directions at once. He immediately withdrew his entire force within a fenced area to the left of the turnpike. His rifle companies rested their guns on the fence rails to await the next attack, while the other men were disposed to cover an attack from both directions. No attack came and at early dawn it could be plainly seen that, with the exception of a picket, the Yankees had withdrawn beyond the hill in front. At 6 a.m., the Confederate line was approached by an enemy courier with written correspondence, asking for a truce until 11 a.m. Col. Paxton asked for "the privilege of burying his dead and taking care of his wounded." Col. Edgar ordered the bodies of Paxton's dead men conveyed to him, at the same time sending his surgeons forward to assist with the care of enemy wounded. To Col. Edgar's surprise, the Yankees took advantage of the truce to cover their retreat. By the time the truce expired, the defeated raiders were 10 miles from the battlefield. Paxton left a surgeon and one sergeant to take care of four men whose injuries were so severe they could not be moved. It was later determined that in their retreat, the Yankees seized a number of wagons and carriages to transport other killed and wounded. Conflicting accounts make it difficult to determine Federal losses, but they amount to at least six men killed, eight wounded, and four captured. Two of the wounded later died at Tuckwiller Tavern. The Confederates were more fortunate, suffering no casualties and having just four men captured. (13)

Citizens of Lewisburg were so grateful to Col. Edgar for his defense of the town that they presented him with a fine sword. Edgar's commanders and the authorities at Richmond were also elated with the victory. Gen. Sam Jones congratulated the men, describing their conduct as "judicious and gallant." Secretary Seddon praised the enemy defeat and noted that it occurred during the same week as the great Confederate victory at Chancellorsville.

Col. Paxton made no official report of his defeat, and in fact, he was dismissed from service on May 8, just six days later. A dispatch from Union General Robert C. Schenck explains his sudden dismissal: "Brigadier General Scammon telegraphs me

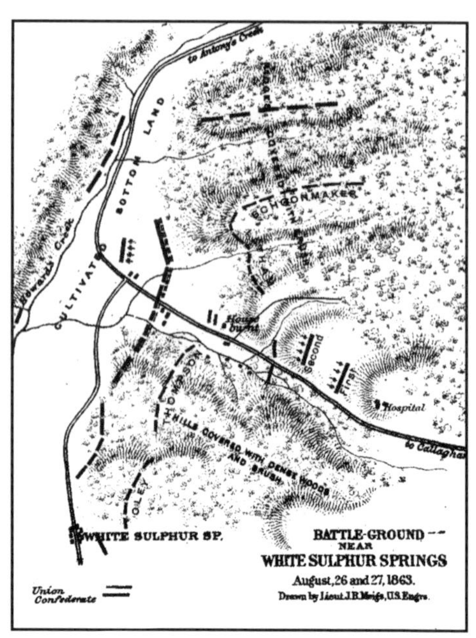

Col. George M. Edgar CSA, 1837-1913. *Courtesy State of West Virginia* Right: Map of the Battle of White Sulphur Springs from the *Official Records.*

that he sent Col. J.C. Paxton, of Second Virginia Volunteer Cavalry, to Lewisburg, to attack the enemy and create a diversion. He got drunk, and failed, and Gen. Scammon asks his immediate dismissal. In this request I urgently concur." That Col. Paxton was drunk was substantiated in a post-war article written by R.N. Sanders, a veteran of the 2nd West Va Cavalry: "We had gone to Lewisburg to clean out a force of rebels…It was…at night, and though the moon was shining brightly, we felt like it was a very hazardous thing to advance; but Col. Paxton was somewhat worse for liquor…we kept moving forward not knowing who or what was before us. Then we ran into the rebs, and a brisk fight began. There was no order or system in the fighting and we soon got all mixed up, and didn't know who was who, but we kept popping away…it was a very mean fix to get into right in the dark woods….I tell you it was enough to scare the best of us…" (14)

The *Marietta Register* (Ohio) of June 12, 1863 published a letter from George K. Jenvey of the 2nd West Va Cavalry. Jenvey was among those captured at Handley's Hill. He was released on parole in Richmond, and then sent to Camp Chase, Ohio. In his letter, Jenvey described the men of Edgar's Battalion as comparing well with Union troops in "drill and looks." He was less impressed with the 45th Virginia Infantry, saying they were the "dirtiest men I ever saw." He said Southern Home Guards were not as kind to the prisoners as regular troops. Arriving at Richmond, Jenvey's heart sank to see some U.S. flags flying upside down: "When we arrived at Libby Prison, the first thing I saw was several Union flags turned upside down. Some of them were stained with blood and rent in a manner that told a tale of the struggle by which they were taken. It looked too bad to see our national flag, stained with the life blood of its brave defenders, and hung up to ornament the entrance of a prison..."

On June 20, 1863 West Virginia became the 35th State in the Union. It was said that the western counties of the Old Dominion "seceded from secession." President Lincoln said if it was secession, it was better to secede in favor of the Constitution than against it.

The Birth of West Virginia

And on that day no loving arms
Reached forth the new-born child to take,
Mid cannon's roar and war's alarms,
Did West Virginia's soul awake.
Behold her face is stern and wild...
Grim mother of hard mountain men.
We hail the day, we pledge anew,
Our hearts, our hands, our lives to you!

By Andrew Price
West Virginia Blue Book, 1926

Southern forces in the Greenbrier region enjoyed several weeks of relative calm subsequent to the fight at Handley's Hill. In early June, several members of Bryan's Battery Virginia Artillery visited Lewisburg for the court martial of Thomas Andrew Bryan, their 19-year-old captain. Bryan was subsequently acquitted on charges of insubordination and conduct unbecoming an officer. The 23rd Battalion Virginia Infantry occupied Lewisburg until June 2, when they moved to Meadow Bluff. They returned to Lewisburg on June 19. A detachment of the 8th Virginia Cavalry occupied Frankford, and Edgar's Battalion occupied Lewisburg the entire month of July, moving to White Sulphur Springs in August. The 45th Virginia Infantry camped at Alderson during July, moving to Lewisburg in August. The entire command available to Gen. Samuel Jones totaled just 7,351 men. With this small army, he was charged with protecting the approaches to the Virginia and Tennessee Railroad and with maintaining possession of the salt works at Saltville, Washington County. To accomplish this, he had Echols's Brigade of 2,765 men at various camps in Greenbrier County. The brigade of Gen. John S. Williams, 962 men, held Saltville. A third brigade under Col. G.C. Wharton held Glade Spring and the line of the railroad with 868 troops. Col. John McCausland's Fourth Brigade, 1,546 men, occupied Raleigh County, two miles below present-day Beckley. Col. W.L. Jackson occupied Huntersville, Pocahontas County, with a cavalry force 1,210 strong.

On June 29, President Davis asked Gen. Jones if his command could assist Gen. Lee's movement into Pennsylvania by creating a diversion. If Jones could make an attack into northwestern West Virginia, it would prevent the enemy from detaching additional troops to pursue Lee's Army of Northern Virginia. Gen. Jones replied that the force of the enemy in the Kanawha Valley was equal, if not superior to, his own. If he abandoned the lines he held at that time, it would open the railroad and the salt works to invasion. If he defeated the Yankees in the Kanawha Valley, he could not hold the area very long because of his inability to supply his command. (15) Gen. Jones did not move to support Lee's invasion of Pennsylvania, but one week later, several hundred of his men were ordered to Winchester to relieve enemy pressure on Richmond. The weakening of Confederate defenses in the Greenbrier region prompted Mr. Samuel Price of Lewisburg to write Secretary Seddon on July 15. Price said the citizens were "greatly exercised" because they felt the reduction

Gen William W. Averell, 1832-1900. His army was defeated at the Battle of White Sulphur Springs. *Courtesy National Archives*

in manpower would render the region "easy prey to the enemy." Mr. Price believed it was imperative for the Confederacy to control the Greenbrier Valley. "Give it up," he said, and "every part of the new state is gone." (16)

Gen. William W. Averell received orders on August 12 to advance from his position in Hardy County and raid Lewisburg. The purpose of the raid was to confiscate the law library of the Virginia Court of Appeals. This order set the stage for the battle of White Sulphur Springs, or Rocky Gap. Averell was told that reinforcements would join him at Huntersville, Pocahontas County, where Southern forces under Col. William L. Jackson were stationed. His men would carry hard bread, sugar, and coffee. Beef and forage would be taken from the country through which they had to pass. Having seized the law books, Averell was told to take "great care" that they were not lost or damaged. The law library had been purchased for the western part of the State and it was reasoned that it now belonged to the new State of West Virginia. (17)

With a command of 1,300 men, Gen. Averell rode through

the counties of Hardy, Pendleton, Highland, Bath, Pocahontas, and into Greenbrier. In a series of skirmishes, his men forced the Rebels out of Pocahontas County toward Warm Springs. They set fire to Camp Northwest, near Huntersville, destroying all of its shops, wagons, weapons, and a nearby mill, with a quantity of wheat and flour. The Confederate saltpeter works near Franklin, Pendleton County, and at Covington, were also destroyed. At Monterey, he forced the quaterly court to abandon their session, then in progress.

Confederate authorities believed Averell's goal was to attack their position at Staunton, or even to destroy the Virginia and Tennessee Railroad. In an attempt to intercept the Yankees, Gen. Samuel Jones ordered the 22nd Virginia Infantry and four cavalry companies to Little Levels and Marlin's Bottom, present-day Marlinton, in Pocahontas County. Col. George S. Patton was ordered to march the First Brigade by way of Anthony's Creek Road to Warm Springs. Anticipating the need for more manpower, Jones asked Secretary Seddon to have the brigades of Gen. Jenkins and Col. Wharton sent to Warm Springs. (18)

Gen. Averell's command reached Callahan's, 13 miles east of White Sulphur Springs, on August 25, continuing toward Lewisburg by way of the James River and Kanawha Turnpike. His column was led by two companies each from the 2nd and 8th West Virginia Mounted Infantry, under Captain Paul Von Koenig. These men were followed by the remainder of the 2nd and 8th Mounted Infantry; Major Thomas Gibson's Independent Cavalry Battalion; Captain C.T. Ewing's Battery G, 1st West Virginia Light Artillery, with six guns; the 14th Pennsylvania Cavalry; and the 3rd West Virginia Mounted Infantry.

Opposing Gen. Averell's advance was Col. George S. Patton with 1,900 men. These included the 22nd and 45th Virginia Infantry; the 26th Battalion Virginia Infantry; the 8th Virginia Cavalry; and Captain G.B. Chapman's battery of four guns. The 23rd Battalion Virginia Infantry and the 37th Battalion Virginia Cavalry were posted at Greenbrier Bridge, present-day Caldwell. Gen. Jones met with Patton on August 25, between Huntersville and Warm Springs on the Anthony's Creek Road. Realizing the urgency of the situation, Patton's forces marched nearly non-stop for 24 hours, arriving about one mile east of White Sulphur Springs at 9:00 a.m. August 26. Their arrival came just after the arrival of Averell's men at the intersection of Anthony's Creek Road and the turnpike. The battle began immediately, with Edgar's Battalion checking the Yankee advance until their remaining forces could get into the fight. Edgar's men formed a line facing southeasterly, across the junction of the two roads, deploying skirmishers left and right. The home of Mr. Henry Miller had the misfortune of being situated between the opposing lines and Edgar's men were told to move their line up to the residence. The Southern skirmishers opened a very heavy fire on Averell's advance units, checking their progress.

As the fighting raged, Col. Patton ordered up the 22nd Virginia Infantry, placing them to the left and front of Chapman's Battery, who were on a knoll to the left of the Anthony's Creek Road. The determined rebels knew the center of their line must be held and fought stubbornly. Noyes Rand, of the 22nd Virginia, described the Confederate battle line as a "stone wall." (19) Five companies of the 22nd Virginia were deployed as skirmishers on a ridge about 400 yards to the left and front of four other companies under Major Robert A. Bailey. Averell's men engaged the enemy confidently and, in a very short time, formed for their first cavalry charge of the battle. Col. Edgar realized a charge was imminent and ordered his men to tear down the split-rail fence that lined the road and use it as a barricade. Just as this work was nearly completed, the determined bluecoats came roaring down the road, firing and screaming wildly. A heavy volley from the Southern line broke the charge, but Major Patrick McNally of the 5th West Virginia Cavalry, U.S., passed beyond the Rebel barricade and squatted down behind a tree stump. Looking around amid the chaos of battle, the major suddenly jumped up and drew his sword on a member of the 45th Virginia Infantry, demanding his surrender. The demand was complied with, but as the bold Yankee officer attempted to get back into his own lines, he was shot and killed. Several Federal thrusts were made and repulsed on Col. Edgar's line, with considerable

Col. George S. Patton, 1833-1864, the grandfather of Gen. George S. Patton of World War II fame. He fought for the Confederacy in Greenbrier County. USAMHI. *Courtesy USAMHI*

loss of life on the Union side. Just beyond the Rebel barricade, the road became littered with the bodies of dead and wounded Yankees. A member of the 45th Virginia noticed an enemy captain lying 30 yards outside their line. The man was seriously wounded and begging for water. (20) The hot August sun made the struggle more intense for Blue and Grey alike. Forty-year-old James McNeill, a captain with the 22nd Virginia Infantry, became so parched that he put two small bullets in his mouth hoping the lead would induce the flow of saliva. (21) Standing on a small hill to the right of the turnpike, Col. Patton's heart soared as he witnessed Edgar's dogged defense. "Glorious!" he shouted, "Hurrah for the gallant Edgar."

Smoke, flame, and the sounds of combat inundated the area as the battle gained in ferocity. The artillery under Chapman worked feverishly, firing nearly non-stop. The 22nd and 45th Virginia Infantry formed a line of battle to the left and right of Chapman. In response to the Confederate firepower, Averell's forces moved six cannons into position, supported to the left and right by two infantry companies. In the heat of combat, one of the Federal cannons exploded. As that occurred, the remaining five guns were moved under a murderous fire of small arms and artillery to within 500 yards of the enemy lines. The horses pulling one of the guns became frightened and ran off the road, lodging the cannon on a tree stump. With great effort, the artillery drivers extricated the gun but when one of the drivers got shot and tumbled from his horse, the frightened team jumped onto the road, the cannon turning upside down. Dodging enemy fire and grape shot from U.S. artillery firing behind them, the men eventually corrected the gun and put it into service. A subsequent infantry charge led by Captain Paul Von Koenig resulted in his death, the charge being repulsed. The battle raged unabated and, by mid-afternoon, the opposing forces were seriously low on ammunition. Just then the 23rd and 37th Virginia Battalions arrived from nearby Greenbrier Bridge. Their timely arrival and the lack of Federal reinforcements turned the tide in Col. Patton's favor.

Braving shot and shell, five companies of the 22nd Virginia moved into position to the left of Col. Derrick's 23rd Virginia. Gen. Averell ordered fresh troops to the front and endeavored to strengthen his entire line. Damaged but undeterred, Averell ordered another cavalry charge against the line held by Major R.A. Bailey. This was followed immediately by a charge against Col. Edgar's position, and then, a hopeless and final charge to the right of Patton's line. A soldier with the 5th West Virginia Cavalry described a charge he participated in: "We advanced through the cornfield, meeting with a murderous fire from the enemy, safely posted behind their breastworks. We pressed onward, however, almost up to the fortifications, but were there met with such a withering fire that human endurance could stand it no longer, and we fell back a short distance, taking position in a gully, or dry creek bed, where we were partially sheltered. In that severe charge some of our bravest officers and men fell." (22) After nine hours of murderous combat, the Yankees had been turned away in repeated attempts to take the Confederate line.

Nevertheless, Gen. Averell ordered one more charge, which also failed. Exhausted and bloodied, the opposing forces rested for the night, scarcely 300 yards apart.

During the night, Averell's officers recommended a withdrawal, but the general was against it. He believed that by waiting the Rebels might retreat, or that reinforcements could reach his command from the Kanawha Valley. When dawn broke, it was apparent that neither was going to happen and the fighting began anew. When Gen. Averell ordered another charge, it was obvious his men had all but given up the contest. According to Col. Patton, the charge proceeded "with so little spirit that it was evident that the enemy had lost confidence." Although he was for continuing the fight, Gen. Averell made every possible arrangement during the night for a fast withdrawal. His ambulances were loaded, his caissons and wagons placed in proper order, and dozens of trees were prepared to fall across the road after they passed. Col. Patton reported that the Yankees maintained a "brisk fire" of small arms and "replied" to the Confederate artillery until mid-morning.

Averell's command to retire came at about 10:30 a.m. and, in less than an hour, his long column began to move away from the bloody field. Col. Patton ordered pursuit by a detachment of the 8th Virginia Cavalry, the 37th Battalion Cavalry, and one cannon, with light infantry support. It was quickly determined, however, that the retreating bluecoats blocked the road so completely with fallen trees that pursuit was nearly impossible. The thoroughness of their work was described by a member of the 5th West Va Cavalry: "The corps of pioneers plied their axes with good effect upon many large trees near the road, cutting them nearly in two. As the troops were withdrawn, Battery G, with their guns double shotted with the last canister they had, grimly waited the expected advance of the exultant foe. As they came on with their usual yell, the battery boys let them have it red hot, and then...pulled out in a trot. The pioneers make their final cuts and the trees fell across the road...as the Confederate cavalry dashed up they were greeted with a volley from the rear guard lying behind the fallen trees...." (23) Averell's command withdrew to Beverly, arriving there on August 31.

In the two-day battle, Gen. Averell lost approximately 268 men killed, wounded, and captured. Col. Patton's total loss was approximately 167. The 22nd Virginia Infantry sustained the heaviest loss among the Southern forces, with approximately 85 men killed, wounded, and missing. Col. Patton wrote his official report of the battle while at Lewisburg on August 31st. He said his men were under fire 12 hours the first day and five the next. Subsequent to the victory, Patton's men settled into the relative ease of camp life at and near Lewisburg. During the fall, Confederate forces in Greenbrier and Monroe were harassed by Captain Richard Blazer's Independent Union Scouts, riding into

The White Sulphur Springs battlefield in 1906.

Another view of the battlefield in 1906. *Photos courtesy State of West Virginia*

The battlefield is now "Battlefield Crossing," a shopping center. *Photo by author, 2004*

Monument to Captain Paul Von Koenig, killed in the Battle of White Sulphur Springs. Originally in the center of a pasture, it is now adjacent to the Hardee's Restaurant parking lot. *Photo by author*

the area from the Kanwaha Valley. Clashing repeatedly with Thurmond's Partisan Rangers, Blazer's men set fire to two buildings at Blue Sulphur Springs in late October, capturing three rebel pickets. They also kept Thurmond's men engaged in the Sewell Mountain range and arrested citizens suspected of disloyalty. (24-25)

Wounded soldiers from both sides were cared for at the Old White hotel at White Sulphur Springs. Having been officially designated a Confederate military hospital in 1861 and abandoned prior to the battle of Lewisburg, the resort stood nearly silent until August 1863. At that time, Dr. John A. Hunter, Confederate Medical Director, designated the resort as a field infirmary for the care of those wounded in the nearby battle. The occasion proved to be a sort of homecoming for the Sisters of Charity, who had labored at the resort-turned-hospital from December 1861 until May 1862. The Sisters arrived at the battlefield on August 27, just in time to see the victorious boys in grey marching out to Lewisburg. They traveled up from Montgomery County with Dr. Archer, remaining at the hospital for three days. Dr. Archer strolled along the battlefield collecting "trophies" and gathering personal belongings of some of the wounded men. (26) Dr. Samuel C. Beard, a civilian physician, was also present, and rendered valuable service to the military during the battle and afterwards. Use of the resort as a field infirmary continued until November 7, under the direction of Dr. S.H. Austin and Dr. A.S. Patrick. At that time, most of the patients housed at White Sulphur Springs and Lewisburg were transferred to the Montgomery County White Sulphur Springs.

Charles A. Mestrezat of the 14th Pennsylvania Cavalry was a Union prisoner of war who helped care for the wounded at White Sulphur Springs. Several days after the battle, he let his wife know he was among the living: "I suppose you have heard before this that I am a prisoner of war in the land of Dixie…We had a very hard fight…Many of our boys were killed and wounded. I, through God's kind providence escaped unhurt…I feel truly thankful…I have been very kindly treated as well as all the rest of the prisoners.…you must not fret or grieve about me…I can not tell you when I will be sent into our lines…I have been sleeping with 2 Confederate soldiers part of the time, hence you will see that we are quite friendly.…Direct [letters] to White Sulphur Hospital, Green Brier Co. Va." (27) Corporal Mestrezat was eventually sent to Belle Island Prison near Richmond, Virginia. He died there on March 7, 1864, age 29.

Delayed but undeterred in their desire to control the Greenbrier Valley, Gen. B.F. Kelley ordered Gen. Averell to make another move on Lewisburg. On October 26, Averell, then at Beverly, was told to run the enemy out of the Greenbrier region and, if possible, attempt to destroy the Virginia and Tennessee Railroad. His well-equipped army of 4,000 men would be joined by a force of 970 troops under Gen. Alfred N. Duffie, who would march south from the Kanawha Valley. Averell moved by way of Camp Bartow and Green Bank to Huntersville, arriving there at noon on November 4. Duffie began his move from Charleston to Lewisburg on November 3. Averell's men reached Mill Point, near Hillsboro, on November 5, having engaged in several brief skirmishes along their route. To intercept the Yankee advance, Gen. John Echols arrived at Droop Mountain, 28 miles northeast of Lewisburg, on November 6. His little army of fewer than 1,900 men would prove to be no match for Averell's veterans who advanced in force about 10 a.m.

Echols deployed his men as best he could, and although he held a superior position, it was readily apparent that he needed more manpower. The outnumbered Rebels resisted the initial attacks, but at 2:30 p.m. their left flank was turned in a surprise move by the 28th Ohio Infantry, the 10th West Va Mounted Infantry, and part of the 14th Pennsylvania Cavalry. Heavy combat ensued, both sides suffering considerable loss. The Confederate line was eventually routed, the men running through the woods in all directions. Upon reaching the main road, the extent of the disaster became apparent with infantry, cavalry, and artillery crowding together, rushing haphazardly away from the battlefield. One of the fleeing Confederates told his father that they covered the entire distance from Droop Mountain to the Greenbrier Bridge, 32 miles, at "a full trot and often at a full run." (28) Averell did not vigorously pursue the fleeing rebels and, when they reached Frankford, they learned that Gen. Duffie's men where at Meadow Bluff, en route to Lewisburg. Echols rested his men at Frankford for two hours, passing through Lewisburg before dawn of November 7. His rear guard left the village just prior to Duffie's early morning arrival. The Confederates withdrew all the way to Union, Monroe County, their route of retreat littered with lost and abandoned equipment. When Duffie's men charged into Lewisburg, they discovered the enemy had escaped and took possession without a fight. Duffie sent a detachment of the 2nd West Va Cavalry in pursuit. These men caught up with Patton's rear guard a few miles from town, capturing some cattle, two caissons, and a few prisoners. The 22nd Virginia was forced to abandon their knapsacks and a large quantity of supplies in Lewisburg, which the Yankees captured and burned. Some accounts also claimed that the Federal troops behaved terribly toward the citizens of Lewisburg, setting fire to the Southern

Methodist Church and several dwellings. They also ransacked a number of homes looking for food and valuables. James Ireland, a soldier with the 12th Ohio Infantry, condemned the conduct of his comrades in a letter home: "The town of Lewisburg [was] ransacked by the soldiers for forage….Some soldiers act very disgracefully taking things which do them no good. The disgraceful plunder of the Caldwell or North House—burning of barn etc." (29) Gen. Averell's column reached the village at 4:00 p.m. and bivouacked on the outskirts of town.

The Yankees defeated and nearly destroyed many of the same men who had defeated them at White Sulphur Springs. Gen. Averell's command accomplished a great deal with a loss of just 30 killed, 98 wounded, and one missing. The stunned Confederates were less fortunate, suffering a loss of 275 killed, wounded, and missing.

A severe snow storm struck Greenbrier County on November 8, and the next day Gen. Duffie moved his command to Meadow Bluff. Finding it difficult to obtain provisions, he was back in Charleston by November 11. On November 9, Mr. S.W. Hall, the Appeals Court Clerk at Wheeling, inquired if the law library at Lewisburg could be seized and sent to him: "I see from the dispatches…that troops have taken possession of Lewisburg….there is, if not before this removed, a State Library, which now belongs to the State of W.Va. I hope you will have the Library and all the court records…that may remain at that place, removed to Charleston, so that I can receive them, which I am required to do by the act of the Legislature." Apparently some, if not all of the library remained, because the clerk was informed on November 11 that Gen. Averell had been instructed to "remove the library to a place of security where it could be had by the proper authorities." (30)

By November 17, Gen. Averell's army was safely back at Beverly, Randolph County. The damage they had inflicted upon the soldiers and citizens of the Greenbrier Valley destroyed any pretense of security the people may have had. The Union victory pleased Gen. Kelley immensely. He telegraphed Washington on the 19th, boasting that Averell's victory "has cleared the new state of West Virginia of any organized form of rebels." (31) Less happy was Commander-in-Chief Henry W. Halleck. The fact that Averell did not accomplish the primary goal of his mission, destruction of the Virginia and Tennessee Railroad, displeased Halleck. The benefit derived from driving the enemy out of the Greenbrier Valley was temporary. Severance of the V&T Railroad, which ran for 204 miles from Lynchburg to Bristol, and then to Knoxville, would cripple a vital Confederate link between two major theaters of war. When Knoxville came under siege on November 17 by Southern forces supplied by the Virginia and Tennessee, Averell's failure became painfully obvious.

Confederate forces lost no time reoccupying the Greenbrier Valley. Echols' Brigade of approximately 1,500 men returned to Greenbrier County. Col. John McCausland's brigade, 1,700 strong, occupied the Narrows in Giles County, about 30 miles southwest of Union, and Col. W.L. Jackson had 950 men scattered from Warm Springs to Mill Point and Huntersville. Gen. John D. Imboden's Northwest Brigade was near Harrisonburg in the Shenandoah. They were outside Gen. Jones' authority, but near enough to offer support.

It was now early December and troops on both sides of the conflict settled in for the winter, or so they thought. In an attempt to break the Confederate grip on Knoxville, Gen. Kelley proposed a new raid on the V&T Railroad. The mounted portion of Averell's brigade, approximately 2,000 men, would leave New Creek, Hampshire County (now Keyser in Mineral County) on December 8, and surge 200 miles south to strike the railroad in either Roanoke or Botetourt County. (32) To increase the daring raid's chances of success, Averell's rear and both flanks would be covered. Gen. E.P. Scammon was told to march from Charleston to Lewisburg with a brigade from his own Third Division. His advance would be led by Gen. Duffie and Blazer's Scouts. He would seize Lewisburg on December 12, and remain there until the 18th. His men were expected to detain the enemy by also threatening Union. Two infantry regiments would march from Beverly to Marlin's Bottom (present Marlinton) and then to Frankford, also remaining until the 18th. Col. Joseph Thoburn of the 1st West Va Infantry would march with 700 men from Beverly to Monterey, where he would guard Averell's train and pose threats to Staunton. A brigade of infantry and cavalry would march south from Harpers Ferry, take Harrisonburg, then threaten Staunton on December 20 and 21. It was hoped that this complex plan of protection and diversion would allow the raid to succeed.

Everything proceeded according to plan with Gen. Scammon occupying Lewisburg on December 12. Not realizing this move was part of a larger plan, Gen. Jones had Echols abandon Lewisburg without a fight. Several brief skirmishes occurred at Lewisburg and Meadow Bluff, but for the most part the Federal advance was not contested. (33) Despite his easy occupation of Lewisburg, Gen. Scammon convinced himself that guerilla activity in his rear might endanger his command. Early on the morning of the 13th, he learned that two Confederate regiments were coming up from the Narrows to assist Echols. Scammon lost his nerve and withdrew back toward the Kanawha Valley at 2 p.m. of December 13, five days before his designated departure date. (34) Gen. Averell had set his sights on Salem, and was yet 87 miles from his goal when Scammon withdrew. This, of course, left Averell's right flank fully exposed. When Col. Augustus Moor and the two infantry regiments assigned to occupy Frankford discovered that Scammon had gone, they also withdrew. (35) Riding hard for Salem, Gen. Averell had no way to know that vital parts of the plan had already collapsed. Nevertheless, with luck, skill, and unbelievable human endurance, Averell's men reached Salem at 10 a.m. on December 16. They had ridden 219 miles in eight days, eluded the enemy, and braved snow, sleet, rain, ice, and swollen streams.

Averell's men seriously damaged the railroad and destroyed millions of dollars' worth of supplies at Salem, before heading back toward the Greenbrier Valley. Aided by Confederate confusion and blind luck, the Salem raiders eluded all pursuers and, on December 20, arrived at the foot of Rucker's Gap, between Little Allegheny and Meadow Creek Mountains on the Greenbrier County line. Passing over Rucker's Gap and entering Greenbrier County, Averell arrived at the sight of present-day Neola on Anthony's Creek. His men were half-frozen, half-starved, and totally worn out. Searching for a pass through the mountains, Averell turned south, riding six miles down Anthony's Creek. That night they camped in the mountains but got little rest, having been 48 hours without food. At 4 a.m., they rode north up Little Creek and eventually entered Pocahontas County. Pursued by Echols from White Sulphur Springs and Col. Jackson from Covington, the weary raiders made good their escape once again, camping the night of the 21st at Hillsboro. On Christmas Day, Averell's exhausted band of intrepid raiders reached Beverly and safety. They had ridden 400 miles in 17 days, deep into enemy territory, through terrible winter weather, across high mountain ranges, and into the annals of military history. (36)

Echols' Brigade, consisting of the 22nd Virginia Infantry and the 23rd and 26th Battalions, along with Thurmond's Rangers and the 14th Virginia Cavalry, went into winter quarters at Lewisburg and present-day Caldwell. Desertions increased during December, but most of Echols' men seemed to be in good cheer. On Christmas eve, officers of the 22nd Infantry were in Lewisburg drinking egg nog with the ladies. (37)

1863–COMMEMORATION–1963
SERVICES

OF THE BATTLE OF DRY CREEK
At White Sulphur Springs, W. Va.

......on the 100th anniversary of the event when Union and Confederate forces met in mortal combat on August 26 - 27, 1863, we gather to dedicate this field of honor.

Battle of Dry Creek
Commemoration Committee
August 25, 1963

From the centennial booklet commemorating the Battle of White Sulphur Springs, 1863-1963. *Courtesy Greenbrier Historical Society*

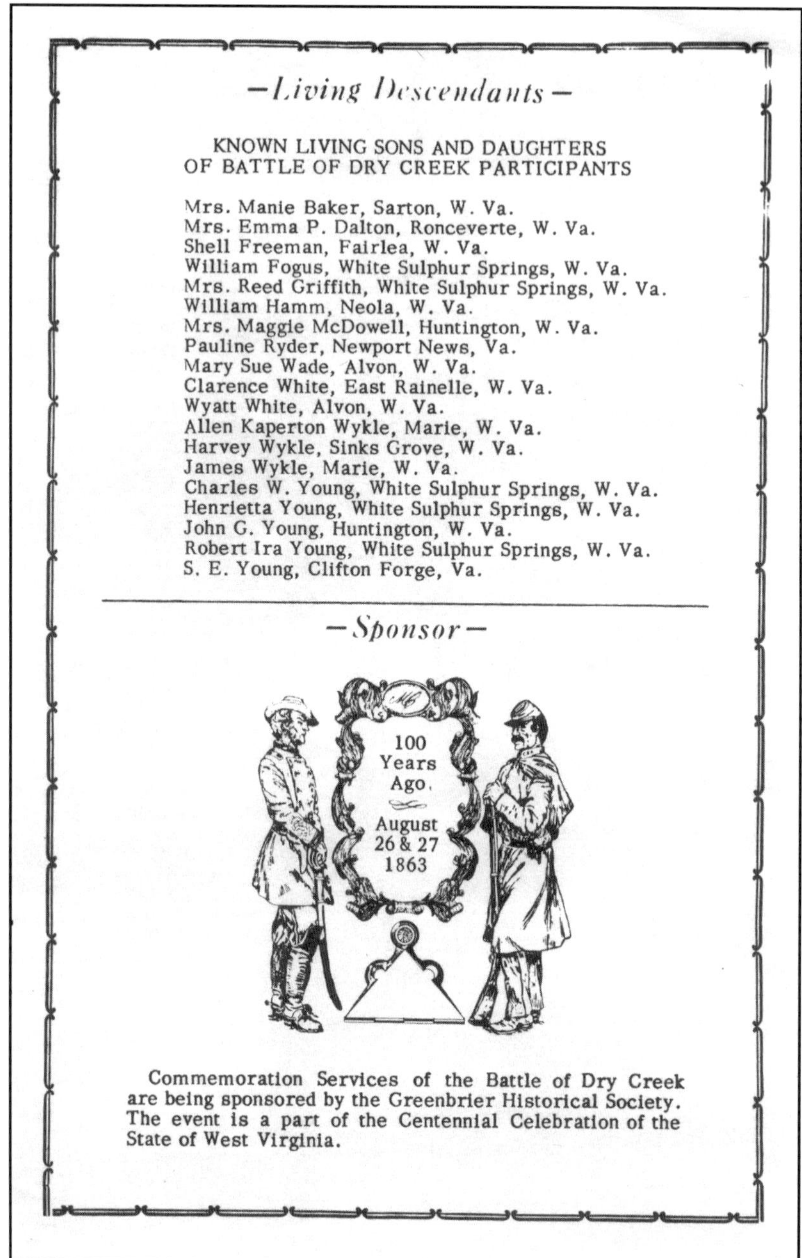

—Living Descendants—

KNOWN LIVING SONS AND DAUGHTERS
OF BATTLE OF DRY CREEK PARTICIPANTS

Mrs. Manie Baker, Sarton, W. Va.
Mrs. Emma P. Dalton, Ronceverte, W. Va.
Shell Freeman, Fairlea, W. Va.
William Fogus, White Sulphur Springs, W. Va.
Mrs. Reed Griffith, White Sulphur Springs, W. Va.
William Hamm, Neola, W. Va.
Mrs. Maggie McDowell, Huntington, W. Va.
Pauline Ryder, Newport News, Va.
Mary Sue Wade, Alvon, W. Va.
Clarence White, East Rainelle, W. Va.
Wyatt White, Alvon, W. Va.
Allen Kaperton Wykle, Marie, W. Va.
Harvey Wykle, Sinks Grove, W. Va.
James Wykle, Marie, W. Va.
Charles W. Young, White Sulphur Springs, W. Va.
Henrietta Young, White Sulphur Springs, W. Va.
John G. Young, Huntington, W. Va.
Robert Ira Young, White Sulphur Springs, W. Va.
S. E. Young, Clifton Forge, Va.

—Sponsor—

Commemoration Services of the Battle of Dry Creek are being sponsored by the Greenbrier Historical Society. The event is a part of the Centennial Celebration of the State of West Virginia.

Another page from the centennial booklet commemorating the Battle of White Sulphur Springs, 1863-1963. *Courtesy Greenbrier Historical Society*

Chapter Fourteen
1864

During January, the men of Echols' Brigade completed the construction of cabins at Camp Gauley, present-day Caldwell. A camp church and theater were also built, with breastworks and fortifications to protect both ends of the camp. Artillery emplacements were located on the top of Bunches Hill, arranged so as to command all approaches. This was also known as Camp Monroe Draft, named after a long hollow nearby that comes into the Greenbrier River from Monroe County.

Companies A, D, and K of the 14th Virginia Cavalry were stationed at Frankford, scouting and picketing under the command of Major Eakle. On January 16, Pvt. George Wilson was sent to get a wagonload of hay which was always in short supply: "I was detailed to go with a wagon for a load of hay below Gap Mills 25 miles from camp. It took us three days to make the trip. It was a very pleasant trip as the weather had moderated and I wanted to forage some anyhow. I bought a piece of bacon at one dollar per pound some lard at the same price and some potatoes at the rate of $4 per bushel and 23 pounds of coarse flour for nothing." (1)

On January 20, a petition was sent to Jefferson Davis from the various delegates and senators of western Virginia. These men expressed concern that the success of Averell's raid had made the enemy more aggressive and increased the likelihood of yet another foray into the region. They believed that there were not enough troops in western Virginia to protect the region, a theme repeated since prior to the Battle of Lewisburg in 1862. The signatories included Mason Mathews, delegate from Greenbrier County, and I.A. Alderson, senator from the Greenbrier district. Samuel Price, Lt. Governor of Virginia and Lewisburg native, forwarded the petition to the president. President Davis referred the petition to Gen. Robert E. Lee for his consideration. On January 26, Lee replied, stating that he thought it was more important "that the troops now in West Virginia should be more thoroughly organized and disciplined than increased." Lee agreed that the enemy was "much emboldened," and would probably advance in the spring. (2)

Writing from Charleston on January 25, Gen. E.P. Scammon informed Gen. Jones that he was sending Mr. C.W. Maupin into the Rebel lines at Lewisburg. Maupin was arrested by U.S. forces and held as a hostage for the sheriff of Putnam County, a Mr. Shaw, who was held "some place within the Confederate lines." It was common practice throughout the war for Blue and Gray alike to jail civilians as hostages for the safe return of other prisoners. In this way, various civilians of the Greenbrier region were jailed, having committed no offense. It was also not uncommon for two or more persons to be picked up as hostages for the return of one prominent prisoner. (3)

Persistent rumors of another enemy raid into southwestern Virginia prompted Gen. Jones to telegraph Lee on January 31, asking for support. Gen. Jones had complied more than once with requests for help from Gen. Longstreet in Tennesee, and from Gen. Lee in eastern Virginia. Thus he felt it only reasonable that temporary assistance might be sent his command for the protection of the Virginia and Tennessee Railroad. Lee replied that Gen. Jones should make an aggressive move against the enemy to "lighten" his labors. Lee also offered the opinion that the successes of Averell's raids had unduly alarmed the troops in Jones' department. This, of course, infuriated Gen. Jones, who did not attempt to conceal his anger when he replied from Dublin on February 10: "I knew my department was beyond your command, but did not think [of] any reason why you should not give me a little temporary aid...If I had declined to allow any of my troops to go beyond my department my command would now be much larger than it is....I have not observed the terror with which you seem to think Averell has inspired the troops in his front....You suggest...throwing the enemy on the defensive,

[to] lighten my labors....I am sure that if you knew the strength of my command...you would not advise me to make an aggressive movement..." (4)

The Confederate Congress approved a joint resolution of thanks to the men of the 22nd Virginia Infantry on February 15. The resolution fell upon deaf ears, however, as many of the regiment's men had grown tired of the war. Desertions were an increasing problem for the Confederacy, with some men absconding to enlist in the Union army. A soldier with the 23rd Ohio Infantry reported from Charleston on February 20 that 50 members of the 22nd Virginia had surrendered that day and were anxious to take the oath of allegiance. The men told a tale of suffering and privation and said they had "grown tired of the Confederacy." (5)

If some of the boys in gray were losing interest in the Confederate ideal, it was no real comfort to Northerners who just wanted the war to end. The Gallipolis, Ohio *Journal* published a complaint about Rebel sentiment in West Virginia on February 18, 1864: "...the State of West Virginia was not so intensely loyal as some persons wish it to be considered. The fact is that region of the country is just as well stocked with rebels, both armed and unarmed as any other portion of the South...." General John C. Breckinridge, former United States Vice President, assumed command of Confederate forces in trans-Allegheny Virginia on February 25. He inspected Echols' Brigade in Greenbrier County on March 15. After a short speech, "Three rousing cheers were then called for by Gen. Echols, and three rousing cheers made...in honor of the great hero of Murfreesboro. Everybody is favorably impressed by the new commander..." (6) Echols' Brigade reported a total of 91 officers and 1,257 men present for duty on March 31. The total present and absent was 2,343.

Secretary Seddon informed General Breckinridge on March 21 that he had information from various sources that Gen. Averell was preparing another raid. Breckinridge replied the same day that he was receiving similar reports, and asked if reinforcements might be sent from Rockbridge or Augusta County. He explained that Gen. Echols would be unable to leave the line he held as long as he was threatened from the Kanawha Valley. (7) At that time, Breckinridge had one brigade at Camp Gauley, constructing a line of defensive works along the left bank of Howard's Creek, covering the roads from Lewisburg and White Sulphur Springs; another brigade was at the Narrows of New River, Giles County; four companies of cavalry occupied Meadow Bluff; and Thurmond's Rangers held Alderson's Ferry.

Gen. Echols wrote to Gen. Breckinridge on April 1, saying that he had spent the last two or three days trying to determine what the movements of the enemy in the Kanawha Valley might indicate. He very correctly concluded that another raid on the railroad was being planned. During early April, a flurry of dispatches between Gen. Franz Sigel and Gen. U.S. Grant resulted in plans that would lead not only to destruction of the Virginia and Tennessee, but to the bloody battles of Cloyd's Mountain and New Market, Virginia.

In an effort to stem desertions and give the troops a morale boost, Lt. Governor Samuel Price gave a speech to Echols' Brigade at Monroe Draft on April 12. Price thanked the men for their service, praising their participation in engagements from Scary Creek to Droop Mountain. Gen. Echols was then called upon to speak, which he did, delivering an oratory worthy of a politician. At the end of April, Echols had 107 officers and 1,339 men present for duty, and an aggregate present and absent of 2,182. His command was inspected on May 6, and found to be well-equipped. The inspector said that the brigade was in a "thorough state of discipline and efficiency, and their military bearing and appearance was soldierly and imposing." The accuracy of the inspector's remarks would be tested immediately. On that very day, Echols' Brigade was marched off to Staunton to help resist a Federal invasion of the Shenandoah Valley by Gen. Franz Sigel. This movement was exactly what Gen. Breckinridge had tried desperately to prevent. A few days prior to their march, he informed Echols that the enemy might move aggressively from two directions at once, thus requiring a "fatal separation" of the troops. "It is hard work with the troops we have," he wrote, "to

View of the entrance to Monroe Draft (Route 63) at Caldwell. This route was traveled extensively by soldiers of the Blue and Gray. *Photo by author*

defend the salt-works, the lead mines, the railroad, the iron-works, & etc., dotted over an extended country accessible to attack from many quarters....An advance by us at this moment is impossible...We must expect feints to accompany the real movements of the enemy....I don't want to give up Greenbrier, Monroe, etc." (8)

Breckinridge would have no choice but to "give up" the Greenbrier region. Gen. Grant's strategy for western Virginia employed two pincer movements to penetrate the region. While Gen. Sigel moved on Staunton, a vital Confederate supply depot, Gen. George Crook's forces would move from the Kanawha Valley to threaten the New River bridge at present-day Radford. A simultaneous move would be made by Averell's cavalry against Wytheville and Saltville, by way of Logan County, in an attempt to destroy the lead mines and salt works there. If these operations were successful, it would sever communication and supply between Confederate forces in Tennessee and Virginia, and it might even lead to the evacuation of Richmond, capital of the Confederacy.

On May 6, the 5th West Va Infantry and Blazer's Scouts entered Greenbrier County by way of the James River and Kanawha Turnpike. These men were a decoy intended to mask the movement of Crook's main force against Dublin. Marching by way of Fayetteville and Princeton, Gen. Crook's army of 6,155 men encountered the enemy under Gen. Jenkins on May 9. They clashed in a bloody battle at Cloyd's Mountain, four miles from the railroad. Gen. Jenkins was wounded and captured in the fight, his army defeated. The Yankees then marched to within two miles of Dublin, where they encountered approximately 500 of Gen. John Hunt Morgan's men who had just arrived on the train minutes before. These men were soon dispersed, Crook's army proceeding to Dublin. Arriving at New River bridge on May 10, the Yankees discovered that the outnumbered Rebels had fled across the river and established a line of defense. After an artillery duel of two hour's duration, the boys in gray were forced to retire, after which the Yankees destroyed the bridge and other property in the vicinity. Crook's command then moved down and crossed the river at Pepper's Ferry, skirmishing along the way. Early the next morning, word was received that Gen. Averell's command of 2,479 men had failed to reach Saltville, but would attempt a move on Wytheville. That advance also failed and Gen. Crook started back toward Union on May 12. They skirmished along the way with 1,500 men under Gen. "Mudwall" Jackson, who fled rapidly toward the Narrows. Averell's men destroyed the railroad tracks, shops and depot at Christiansburg, uniting with Crook's command at Union on May 15. Averell reported his men marched 350 miles "over a region almost impassable and destitute of supplies." (9)

The Reverend S.R. Houston reported that it took the bluecoats six and one-half hours to pass through Union. The Yankees stopped on the north side of town, their camps extending four miles into the countryside. He said they desolated several local farms, killing all the sheep and cattle, and taking over the estate of Oliver Beirne as a hospital. Their combined force arrived at Meadow Bluff on May 19, hungry and worn out, many of the men being barefoot. A soldier with the 15th West Va Infantry would later record that they reached Greenbrier County "in a pitiful plight and in a state of semi-starvation." (10) Gen. Duffie reported from Meadow Bluff on May 20 that his men were "entirely broken down" from lack of rations. They were also "disorganized and demoralized, many being without clothes or shoes, [and] the horses worn down." Most of Averell's men settled into camp at Bunger's Mill, while other troops were detached to Lewisburg, Frankford, and Monroe Draft at Caldwell. When the U.S. cavalry encamped near one Lewisburg resident's home, they were "half-starved" and "drank the well dry." They also cut up the fence rails, killed hogs, and brought a great deal of suffering to the citizens. "Everything some of them had was taken, grain, sugar, bacon, and even fruits, plates, knives and forks." (11)

The occupation of Greenbrier County by 10,000 enemy soldiers was unprecedented and disastrous. A captain with the Night Hawk Rangers reported the Yankees were "taking all the flour, meal, meat, and grain they can find, leaving the citizens in a destitute condition." (12) The validity of that statement was verified by a Yankee soldier with the 1st West Va Infantry, "…every article that could be eaten was taken; and not satisfied with this, the soldiers in many instances broke up the furniture, glass, and crockery, tore up the bedding…and even at times destroyed the children's clothing; women and children, with rare exceptions, were in charge of the premises. The route of march…was followed by the grief of these poor people….Starvation almost stared these people in the face, which many of them said they would welcome rather than submit to the government." (13) Another witness said Lewisburg "looks like a dead carcass. Nobody there but women and old men and they look scared." (14) A boy of 14 who survived the ordeal said the people "had to live between hawk and buzzard." (15) A soldier with the 34th Ohio Infantry described the hardships the soldiers endured in his diary, complaining that "this is Sunday at home but not here in Virginia." (16)

At Meadow Bluff, Gen. Crook learned that Franz Sigel had been defeated at the battle of New Market on May 15, thus his command and Averell's enjoyed the only successes of the entire mission. Because of his defeat, Gen. Sigel was replaced by Gen. David Hunter, a 62-year-old, mean-spirited, humorless man, who would change the way warfare was conducted in the two Virginias. Even before Hunter assumed command in Virginia, the Confederate government had declared him a felon for his use of Negro troops and his enfranchisement of the Negro in North Carolina. Southern newspapers referred to Hunter as "Black Dave," and "brutal bandit chief," among other epithets. Even his own chief of artillery, Captain Henry A. DuPont, acknowledged Hunter's odd character, writing that his expression was "stern and severe," and that "he was free from affectation and his manner was tranquil except when disturbed by fits of sudden anger, which were by no means infrequent. Unfortunately, his mentality was largely dominated by prejudices and antipathies so intense and so violent as to render him at times quite incapable of taking a fair and unbiased view of many military and political situations...." (17) To another soldier, Hunter was "a dark visaged stern man of severe aspect; a man not at all of a sympathetic genial disposition, who was calculated to win the personal attachment of men generally. He was not only severe in appearance but he was really so." (18)

Seriously outnumbered, the only thing Confederate forces in the Greenbrier region could do about the enemy occupation was harass them. They attacked their pickets and small camps in Greenbrier and Monroe, capturing supplies and prisoners. On May 20, Col. Jackson reported that he skirmished at Greenbrier bridge with some Union cavalry, "drowning and killing 15 or 20." (19) Other brief encounters were reported all the way from Alderson's Ferry and Palestine to Frankford. Heavy skirmishing at Greenbrier bridge on May 22, between the 14th Virginia Cavalry and the 1st West Va Cavalry, resulted in Col. Henry Capehart, commander of the 1st West Virginia, being awarded the Congressional Medal of Honor. His heroic deed is described in an affidavit filed in support of the award: "The regiment was under heavy skirmishing... Watson Karr, a private in B Co. was fording the river with their horses in order to bring over some dismounted men who were on the other side. The river was high and swift and Karr was washed from his horse into the river and being swept down the river with the current. Col. Capehart...seeing the peril of Private Karr, plunged into the river on his horse, and under a galling fire of the enemy, rescued the private from drowning and brought him to shore. Every moment he was in the water under the enemies fire and at the risk of being killed. It was the bravest act we ever witnessed..." Col. Capehart received the award in February 1895 for "gallantry at Greenbrier River, W.Va. May 22, 1864." (20)

Above: The prewar Elmhurst Estate at Caldwell in the 1920s. The covered bridge was built to replace the one destroyed by Confederate soldiers after the Battle of Lewisburg. *Author's collection*
Below: Route 60 east at Caldwell and the bridge over the Greenbrier River. Col. Henry Capehart was awarded the Congressional Medal of Honor for combat action here on May 22, 1864. *Photo by author, 2004*

Union soldiers traveling alone or in small groups were easy prey to bushwhackers, home guards, and partisan rangers. While at Meadow Bluff some soldiers with the 5th West Va Infantry were told to ride with Blazer's Scouts temporarily to allow some of the scouts to recuperate from hard service. Blazer's men had recently executed six bushwhackers (a term they also used for partisan rangers) and it was understood that any of Blazer's men who might fall into the hands of the enemy would suffer the same fate. When Tom Charlton was selected to ride with the scouts, he had a feeling something would go wrong, and it did. The story of his brush with death appeared in the *Ironton Register* (Ohio) on July 28, 1887. Riding with the scouts on a foraging expedition toward Lewisburg, they came to the Tuckwiller farm at Handley's Hill. "Three of us went down to poke around in his barn to see if we could scare up any provisions. It was then after dark. There being none, we returned…" Private Charlton then decided to grab a bucket and get some water at a nearby spring. Stopping in an orchard, he was challenged by "bushwhackers" who accused him of being a member of Blazer's Scouts. One of the Rebels raised his rifle to execute Charlton but another intervened, having some doubt that he was indeed one of the hated Yankees. The men took Charlton prisoner, walking along some paths in the mountain darkness: "on this little march, I was terribly scared my spurs would give me away. If the rebs would only discover those spurs, then they'd know I belonged to Blazer's scouts, and nothing would save me. I thought as I walked they would certainly hear the noise of the spurs; and when we climbed a fence, I felt sure the spurs would give me away. At last we stopped to rest, and all sat down, and then was my chance. When we arose from there, my spurs didn't get up with me." The men spent the night in a large farmhouse and went to Muddy Creek Mountain the next morning. From there, Private Charlton could see Lewisburg and the camps of his comrades. The bushwhackers came and went in squads and companies. Some made fun of their prisoner, others threatening him. The house was occupied by an old woman and four children. "Here my captors would take turns guarding me. By this time, I had learned their names; the big fellow was Bumgarner, and the little fellow, Walker. I was left with Bumgarner…he sat in a chair before the fireplace. Directly he went to sleep, his revolver lying across his lap. There was an iron shovel…by the fireplace…I drew back the shovel and aimed a blow at him. The woman looked on with horrified eyes, but did not utter a shriek. Somehow, I couldn't strike, the shovel trembled in my hands and I laid it down. And well I did, for just then six bushwhackers appeared at the door." They then moved to another house, not very distant. At this house, the men left their Yankee pet alone with the old lady who lived there. She told him that he was in the company of some very bad men, that Bumgarner had murdered four men. That evening the prisoner was left alone with Walker. When the guard grew sleepy, Pvt. Charlton grabbed his gun and took him as his prisoner to Lewisburg. "I met Dr. Myers, our regimental surgeon, who gave me fits for not shooting the rebel. Afterward, when the doctor found out that my prisoner was a brother of the girl he was engaged to, he wasn't half so bloodthirsty." It is very likely that Pvt. Charlton's "bushwhackers" were Captain James Bumgardner and Sgt. John W. Walker of Thurmond's Rangers.

Just a few days after taking command from Sigel, General Hunter ordered Crook's division to join him at Staunton. Hunter's objective was Lynchburg, where he hoped to destroy the railroad and canal. On May 31, after 12 days in Greenbrier and Monroe, Crook's army of 10,000 men marched into the Shenandoah Valley. Due to incompetent operation of the Federal commissary and quartermaster departments, his command entered the ordeal poorly clothed and supplied, and many of the men were still without shoes. A report filed by Gen. Averell offers some insight into the condition of the Federal forces on the eve of the Lynchburg campaign: "The detachments and supplies…failed to arrive. I followed Crook's division on the 3rd [June] to White Sulphur Springs with 3,200 mounted and 1,200 dismounted men; 600 men were without shoes, and many other articles of clothing…From the 18th of May until this day we had waited near Lewisburg upon half rations, [waited] for supplies of horseshoes, nails, and clothing; but owing to the miserable, inadequate, and insufficient transportation furnished from the Kanawha we were obliged to set out again almost as destitute as when we arrived…"

General Crook reported that his men left Meadow Bluff "in a very low state.…Owing to the miserable transportation sent me…" He was determined to have an investigation and "have guilty parties punished." (21)

An infantry soldier claimed that as the men marched out of Greenbrier County "a thousand men were without arms and two thousand were without shoes." He added that it was pitiful to see the shoeless men "marching along, leaving marks of blood on the ground." (22) Reaching Lewisburg on June 1, a sergeant with the 11th West Va Infantry said the village was "a town once of some note, but now in a dilapidated condition." White Sulphur Springs was "a noted watering place, and is most beautiful. The grounds are elegantly laid out, and the buildings are in good condition." (23) An Ohio soldier thought the famous resort was "splendidly arranged," with "beautiful white cottages, all of the same size and style." The Old White hotel was "well furnished," and had the benefit of "beautiful shade trees and drives." (24)

General Crook's division made the march to Staunton in nine days, skirmishing with guerillas along the way. The troops tore up the railroad and destroyed forges, furnaces, and saltpeter works as they went. Hunter's men were already at Staunton, having defeated the Confederates in the Battle of Piedmont. Staunton's factories, shops, and supplies met the torch after Hunter arrived. Hunter's ravenous army of 18,000, with Crook's men as one division, departed Staunton on June 10, arriving at Lexington the next day. After a three-hour skirmish, Lexington was taken, with the brigade of Rutherford B. Hayes in the advance. Gen. Hunter used his army to smite not only the Confederate military, but also the southern people. The two and a half days Hunter's army remained in Lexington left indelible images of fire, theft, murder, and wanton destruction upon the minds of her people. His army burned the arsenal, warehouses, canal boats, mills, wagons, and every building except one at the renowned Virginia Military Institute. With feverish delight, his men destroyed the

Washington College library with its collection of rare and one-of-a-kind books. They ransacked and set ablaze the barracks, professors quarters, mess hall and hospital. Acting under Hunter's orders, they also burned the home of former Virginia Governor John Letcher, giving his wife and children only 10 minutes' notice. The Virginia Military Institute's bronze statue of George Washington was loaded into a wagon and hauled away.

Hunter vented his prejudices and hatreds everywhere. Even non-military targets such as private dwellings and churches met the torch on his march to Lynchburg. Riding up to the home of Major William Gilham, a VMI professor, Hunter personally told Gilham's wife to remove her furniture because he was going to burn her house. A group of Union soldiers including William McKinley, a future United States president, helped Mrs. Gilham carry her possessions out onto the parade ground. (25) She sat out in the field amidst her possessions and watched her home burn to the ground. Converted to its value in 2004, it was estimated that by the time Hunter's army left Lexington, they had destroyed nearly $70 million worth of property.

Advancing to Buchanan, they destroyed the Tredegar Iron Works and other furnaces and foundries, and then crossed the Blue Ridge at Peaks of Otter. At Liberty (now Bedford), they destroyed the railroad and burned some homes from which they were reportedly fired at. Approaching Lynchburg, they skirmished with the city's defenders at an old Quaker meetinghouse, three miles outside the city. During the night of June 17, Hunter's men could hear trains coming and going, the sounds of troops moving, and Rebel soldiers cheering. This was actually an elaborate ruse, designed to make Hunter believe the city's defenders were stronger than they were. The battle resumed the next day, but Hunter worried that he was outnumbered. Late that day, realizing he was in need of food and ammunition, Hunter ordered a retreat back into West Virginia.

The Yankee army began their retreat, pursued by enemy cavalry and followed by the ever-present "contraband," or fugitive slaves and their families. After the Dublin raid in May, Crook's army arrived at Meadow Bluff with more than 200 contrabands that had joined their march out of Giles County. The Yankees marched through Liberty and Salem, finally entering West Virginia at White Sulphur Springs. The first men to reach Greenbrier County were a detachment sent out in advance to escort 141 prisoners and 130 sick and wounded back to Charleston. Arriving at the Greenbrier River ford at Caldwell on June 22, the escort was attacked by Thurmond's Rangers. The Yankees lost four men and 20 horses in the two-hour fight. Hunter's men ransacked homes and gardens along their line of march, some of the men and animals literally starving to death. Hundreds of horses and mules that became too weak to travel were shot to prevent the enemy from taking them. Dozens of wagons were burned between Lynchburg and White Sulphur for the same reason. William McKinley recalled the hardships and the hunger, saying they marched "… without sleep or rest, part of the time wholly without food; fighting and marching and suffering, it seems to me, as I recall it, almost unreal and incredible that men could or would suffer such discomforts or hardships." (26)

For two days beginning June 24, the bulk of Hunter's army

The North House is in the center of this postwar picture, with the library building to the left. Constructed in 1820, the North House was ransacked by U.S. soldiers in the summer of 1864. *Courtesy Greenbrier Historical Society.*

Above: 2004 view of the North House and library building. Right: Soldiers wrote their names and other graffiti on the plaster walls of the present library building. Constructed in 1834, the Greenbrier County Library was home to the Virginia Court of Appeals during the Civil War. *Photographs by author, 2004*

returned to Greenbrier County, "foot-sore, tired, and hungry." Some men of the 18th Connecticut Volunteers desperately searched the area of White Sulphur Springs, looking for anything to eat. Many of the troops in their ranks were so weak from lack of food that they fainted along the march and fell behind. The men passed "many horses and mules that were down and out." They walked, stumbled, and practically crawled through Lewisburg the next day, with "nothing to eat except a cup of hot black coffee." (27) Soldiers of the 34th Massachusetts Infantry found a grist mill near the Old White hotel which they "scraped from top to bottom" in search of food. Finding none, they proceeded to scrape "the flour boxes and barrels and made cakes of the scrapings. Some of them got some sour bran which was full of worms and baked it in the ashes and ate it." Crazy with hunger, "weak and dispirited," the men decided they must "leave this place or starve." Moving slowly on toward Lewisburg, they came to the Greenbrier River, which they had to wade across. Their crossing was described by Colonel William S. Lincoln: "The scene while fording, was magnificent beyond description. The waters were spread out near two hundred yards wide, and were about two feet deep. For a distance of near a quarter of a mile, the river was fairly crowded with men....Cavalry men were mingled here and there in the crowd, many of the horses made to carry double. The artillery and wagons crossed more by themselves. Over this scene, the sun shone clear, its beams glancing brightly from our bayonets...." When they finally reached Lewisburg, "hundreds if not thousands of our troops strayed off and stayed" in and about the town all night. (28)

A soldier with the 21st New York Cavalry said the army's route of march was marked with "abandoned equipment and emaciated dead horses, put down by their riders with a shot to the head." Arriving at White Sulphur Springs at 6 a.m. of June 24, the New Yorkers were "suffering from heat exhaustion, foot trouble and fatigue." They passed beyond Lewisburg late the next afternoon. As they did, some of the local citizens "took pot shots" at their column, shouting "vile names" against the troops and General Hunter. The men "fell out" west of Lewisburg, "long after sundown." (29) Another member of their ranks recalled that they broke small branches off of birch trees as they rode along, eating the bark. One of their officers captured a frog, which he placed upon the tip of his sword and roasted over a fire. (30)

The arrival of the 22nd Pennsylvania Cavalry at the Old White hotel was described by Samuel Farrar: "We marched slowly all night and at sunrise [June 25] camped at White Sulphur Springs. Here we had good water and a delightful rest. This was a beautiful place and well equipped to entertain guests, having good hotel buildings, extensive pleasure grounds, fine lawns, bath houses, etc., but it might as well have been a howling wilderness so far as affording any food relief for our hungry army. The place was deserted, except by a half-dozen people, who were left as caretakers of the buildings....The suffering of our troops had now become alarming, after five days' marching, most of the time without any food." (31)

David Hunter Strother, also known by his pen-name "Porte Crayon," was one of General Hunter's staff officers. He recalled that on the morning of Saturday, June 25, he "took breakfast with the General on the green near the great hotel." Strother found that despite the resort's grand buildings, the place had a desolate and forlorn appearance. The Old White hotel was "entirely dismantled," having been used for some time as a Confederate hospital. (32) While the majority of Union soldiers saw in the place the grandeur of former days, General Hunter saw it as an opportunity for another inferno. When rumors began to spread that the resort was to be burned, Captain Henry A. DuPont decided he would attempt to change the general's mind. The captain knew what type of man Hunter was, and he knew he must choose his words carefully. Destruction of so much private property would be a violation of the rules of civilized warfare, and would be against specific instructions of the U.S. government. Being required to give the general a progress report at noon of June 25, Captain DuPont used the opportunity to inquire about the resort: "I remarked...General, I hear that you intend to burn the buildings here when we leave. He replied, 'Yes, I intend to burn them all down.' After a short pause, I said,

Gen. David Hunter, 1802-1886. A controversial Union commander despised throughout the South. It was during his infamous Lynchburg Raid in 1864 that Hunter signed the order for David Creigh's execution. He also ordered the burning of the resort at White Sulphur Springs but subsequently rescinded the order. *Courtesy National Archives*

don't you think, General, that the burning of these structures would be a military mistake? This seemed to arouse him, and, raising his voice a little, he at once asked, 'What do you mean, Captain, by that inquiry?' Looking him squarely in the eyes, my response was as follows: I mean this, General—if we have later to occupy and hold this country, the White Sulphur Springs will be the natural point for our principle station, as so many roads converge here. Such being the case, the buildings as they stand would furnish excellent winter quarters...In a few seconds…he quietly remarked, 'Well, I had not thought of that,' he instantly called…for the adjutant-general…Hunter said at once, 'Colonel, I have changed my mind about burning the buildings here…' (33) Thus the famed resort was saved from total destruction. The Old White Hotel was supplanted by the present *Greenbrier* Hotel in 1922.

Hunter divided his command at White Sulphur Springs, about one-half going northeast into Beverly, the balance continuing along the James River and Kanawha Turnpike toward Charleston. Reverend John McElhenney's granddaughter recalled the Union army's time at Lewisburg in 1893: "They were literally starving when they halted two days in Lewisburg for rest and food. Every half-hour through that long day an orderly would ride up with a requisition for *one-half* of the contents of the granary—wheat, corn-meal, and flour. Sadly we felt our stores lawfully despoiled. My grandmother cut generous slices of bread and ham for the starving foe, when one fellow, more desperate than the others, snatched the ham out of her hands, and ran off with it. The loaf was treated in like manner. One regiment was encamped in the brier-field, and my grandfather surmised, from the squealing in that quarter, that they were destroying his fine herd of yearling hogs....His cows were driven off, his meadows ruined...." (34)

Supplies had been expected to meet the troops at Lewisburg or Meadow Bluff, but that failed to happen. The Ohio National Guard escorted the supply wagons from Gauley Bridge and Fayetteville, but got scared off by local "guerillas" before Hunter's haggard army arrived. Upon reaching Meadow Bluff, the men discovered they must drag themselves closer to Gauley Bridge to meet the supply wagons. This required them to march over the Sewell Mountain range, an area infested with bushwhackers and totally devoid of sustenance. One soldier recalled seeing "a dollar offered for a cup of coffee, and a five dollar greenback for a single hard tack" [similar to a large cracker]. The next day he "saw fifty cents offered, in vain, for a narrow strip of bacon, not two inches long," and later, "I saw two dollars offered and refused for *one small griddle cake.*" (35)

The climb up and over Sewell Mountain was more than many of the men could endure and numbers of them fell by the roadside. One infantryman recalled that it was "8 or 10 miles up this mountain, and about the same distance down. We were very ravenous and weak." Finding along the road the carcass of a cow that had been slaughtered days before, he "managed to get some meat from the carcase...[it] was not inhabited by bees, neither was there any honey found in it, yet it was virtually the same, for swarms of living creeping worms were there and yet the meat was sweet to the taste. Had a splendid meal. A few others shared with me." Some soldiers literally starved to death, a fact General Hunter vehemently denied. The truth was acknowledged, however, by many of Hunter's officers and men: "Some men were sent back...after those that had given out by the way. Many were brought in in most pitiable condition. Some were in a dying state. Others with the flesh gnawed from their arms and other parts. Some died soon after. They were starved! Starved to death!" (36)

James Comley, an officer with the 23rd Ohio Infantry, wrote that on June 26 just 100 men were still in the ranks of his regiment, the others being too weak to continue. They began the ascent of Sewell Mountain at 3 a.m. the following day, with "only forty haggard, hollow-eyed men in the ranks." At 11 a.m., they met the supply train heading their way from Gauley Bridge: "Reached supply train…everybody crazy. All the hardships of the march had been borne with little complaint, but there were three fights among the men within five minutes after we met the supply train, and everybody quarreling like wolves." Reporting from Charleston on July 2, Captain R. Hastings gave the names of several men in the 23rd Ohio who died from starvation, and the names of others who were missing and presumed captured or dead "from hunger and fatigue."

In General Duffie's official report, filed at Camp Piatt, Kanawha County on June 30, he makes this statement: "Many of the men of my command have perished by the roadside from hunger and fatigue, whilst their horses fell from the same cause." (37)

Articles published in the *Point Pleasant Weekly* during July 1864 confirmed the starvation death of some soldiers and spoke of men who perished in the hospital at Charleston, having been "broken down by the raid."

In 1878, General William B. Tibbits described their Lynchburg retreat: "The flight of Hunter with the Confederates in close pursuit, his army without rations for man or beast…are fact written in history, if written at all…Many men died by the road side from starvation and fatigue while a large part of the cavalry became dismounted, owing to the horses giving out…." Another officer condemned the retreat in a speech he gave in the 1880s: "After leaving Meadow Bluffs, and while crossing Big Sewell Mountain, 2,000 horses either died or were shot…hunger and fatigue kept them from going any further. Hundreds of men daily dropped by the roadside and famished…hard marching and want of proper food had done the work…The writer…having been ordered back from Gauley Bridge with his regiment to succor the sick and bury the dead along the line of retreat. The spectacle of men dead by the roadside with the inner bark of the birch tree clutched in their stiffened hands, proved conclusively that hunger was real and not imaginary." (38)

Upon arriving at the Loup Creek steamboat landing on June 28, several miles west of Gauley Bridge, Hunter sent a report of his command's location and condition. He stated that their expedition had been extremely successful, "inflicting great injury upon the enemy." They withdrew from Lynchburg "short of ammunition," and reached the Kanawha Valley "without serious loss." Then, Hunter made a claim that alienated him from much of his command: "The command is in excellent heart and hearth, and ready, after a few days' rest, for service in any direction." Of course his command was not in "excellent heart," having been nearly defeated by "General Starvation." Hunter's lie resonated with his men for years beyond the war, and they never forgave him for it. A soldier with the 12th West Va Infantry spoke for all the men when he wrote: "Gen. Hunter, who had kept up during the raid a rather luxuriant table, comparatively sumptuously supplied, was perhaps himself in pretty good health and heart; but his troops in general—who had suffered much deprivation and hardship…would agree [his] opinion is hardly to be believed." (39)

By mid-July, General Hunter's army was back in eastern Virginia, having traveled by way of Parkersburg and the B&O Railroad. When the army arrived in Parkersburg, the publisher of the *Parkersburg Gazette* wrote an article stating that the soldiers were "completely worn out," and "many in the division had died of starvation."

For his honesty, General Hunter had him arrested, his newspaper shut down. The uproar over his arrest prompted West Virginia Governor Arthur I. Boreman to ask Hunter about the case. Replying from Cumberland, Maryland, on July 13, Hunter said he had ordered Mr. Wharton's release before receiving the governor's letter. He arrested Wharton, he said, because he published "contraband news," concerning the movements of Hunter's command, and the facts of his story were "utterly untrue." Hunter said there had been some "suffering" among his men, which comes with "the business of the soldier," but that after careful inquiry, he had failed to learn "even a report of any one case of death from hunger." He said they had expected supplies at

Meadow Bluff, but they had been removed without authority, because "of a stampede created by a few guerillas operating against tenfold their own force of State militia." (40) David Hunter was replaced in August 1864 by General Philip H. Sheridan. (41)

With "General Orders No. 5," General Crook ordered food given to civilians in Greenbrier County: "Charleston, W.Va., July 7, 1864 - Owing to the fact that citizens between Meadow Bluff and this place were necessarily stripped of all subsistence by our troops in passing on their late march, and are now in a destitute condition, the commissaries of this command may issue subsistence to all such persons." (42)

The Lexington, Virginia *Gazette* of July 19, 1864 published a letter written by "a lady of Lewisburg" concerning the arrival of Hunter's army: "I suppose you have heard that the Yankee army...passed through Lewisburg. Such a sight was never before witnessed by mortals. Large numbers of them were without shoes or hats, and the dirtiest raggedest set of brutes you ever saw. A majority of them were almost starved to death...No sooner here, than the vandals broke into houses and robbed the citizens of every mouthful they had to eat; carried off every blanket, quilt, pillow, bucket, cup, and cooking utensils of every kind and description. They searched our house at least fifty times...It was for two days we had nothing to eat. Every house in town shared alike. They...destroyed all the orchards and all the lots of potatoes....Some fell dead in our streets from fatigue, prostration and starvation."

CHAPTER FIFTEEN
THE HANGING OF DAVID CREIGH: A TRAGEDY OF THE LYNCHBURG RAID

David S. Creigh, pronounced "Cree," was born in Lewisburg, Greenbrier County, May 1, 1809. He was the fourth child of Thomas and Margaret Williams Creigh. Thomas Creigh immigrated to the United States from Ireland and settled in Lewisburg in 1792. Margaret Williams Creigh's father was Captain Samuel Williams, himself a native of Ireland who came to Greenbrier County in 1795. The Creigh and Williams families were related to some of the most prominent people in Virginia and, as such, were well known and respected families. Thomas Creigh was a staunch Presbyterian who engaged in the mercantile trade after settling in Greenbrier County and in that work he amassed a sizeable fortune which passed to his family upon his death in 1847.

Following his father's example, David S. Creigh became a very successful merchant and in later life was active as an elder in the Presbyterian Church at Lewisburg. Subsequent to his marriage on October 10, 1833, he worked as a farmer, bank director and Greenbrier County Magistrate. David Creigh's wife, Emily Arbuckle Creigh, was the daughter of Captain Charles Arbuckle. The Arbuckle family was one of Greenbrier's oldest and most respected families. Eleven children—eight boys and three girls—were born to David and Emily Creigh. The last of these was Egbert Creigh, who was born in 1858. By 1860, David Creigh was one of 40 millionaires living in Greenbrier County, Virginia. The United States Census for 1860 lists his estate as having a value of $39,265 which, converted to its value in 2004, comes in just under $1 million. In 1863, David Creigh paid $53.71 in taxes on his estate, which included two slaves, 11 horses and mules, one "pleasure carriage" coach, or wagon, 66 head of cattle, 29 sheep, nine hogs, two clocks, one piano, and household furniture valued at $500.00. A politically conservative man, David Creigh hoped that war could be avoided, but once it did come, his sympathies were with the South. Early in the conflict, three of Mr. Creigh's sons joined the Confederate 14th Virginia Cavalry. This unit was enrolled largely from men of Greenbrier County and it performed valuable service to the Southern Confederacy during those long and bloody four years of conflict.

On October 26, 1863 General William W. Averell, U.S. cavalry commander, received the following order which set in motion a series of events that would culminate in the hanging of David S. Creigh in 1864: "You are directed to move, with all the troops of your brigade...as soon as you can possibly get ready, on Lewisburg, in Greenbrier County, and attack and capture, or drive away, the rebel force stationed at that place or in the neighborhood....you will move on with the cavalry force...to Union in Monroe County, and thence to the bridge on the Virginia and Tennessee railroad across New River, and destroy the same...."

Destruction of the New River bridge would interrupt a vital link in the Confederate line of supply connecting the industrial and agricultural centers of Virginia with Tennessee. The subsequent movement of Averell's cavalry toward Lewisburg resulted in a fierce battle at nearby Droop Mountain, Pocahontas County, on November 6, 1863. This battle was a bloody defeat for the Confederates and it opened the way for Averell's men to occupy Lewisburg the following day. At Lewisburg, the commands of Gen. Averell and Gen. Alfred Duffie combined. The citizens of southern West Virginia knew that with the movement of so many

The David Creigh home near Lewisburg in 2004. *Photo by author*

troops through their area there always came stragglers and men who found in every occasion an opportunity to "live off the land" and "requisition supplies," or steal, from the local inhabitants. It would be the actions of one such straggler that eventually cost David Creigh his life.

This account of the events which transpired at the Creigh home is drawn from the previously unpublished official Court Martial records of David S. Creigh. These records were obtained from the National Archives and are reprinted in their entirety later in this work. Much has been written over the years about these tragic events that conflicts in several significant ways with the testimony provided at Mr. Creigh's court martial. The few people who actually witnessed these events, and thus knew all the facts, have long since passed beyond this life. This version of what transpired, based on official documents, is not intended to refute other accounts. Rather, it is hoped these records will augment the existing tales, which have gained the status of legend, and add a new dimension to our understanding of what actually

Stairway in the Creigh home that David Creigh and the soldier tumbled down during their fight. *Courtesy Jim Arbuckle*

took place. This version of events and any others are now, and shall forever be, bound together by the common thread of man's inhumanity to man. (1)

In the early evening hours of Sunday, November 8, 1863, David Creigh was visiting at the home of John W. Dunn, about one-quarter mile from the Creigh home. The men discussed the Confederate defeat at Droop Mountain two days prior and the subsequent occupation of the Lewisburg area by Federal forces. Suddenly and without knocking, a young man in the uniform of a U.S. cavalry soldier stepped into the house. "Where are your horses?" he asked.

Mr. Dunn calmly replied, "Some are at one place and some another."

Not put off by Dunn's evasive reply, the man said very firmly, "Sir, I will search your house." With that remark, Mr. Dunn quickly rose from his seat and began to follow the would-be robber through his home.

Realizing that this thief in soldier's uniform would probably visit his home next, David Creigh determined to alert his family. Exiting the front door, he walked home at a brisk pace and informed his wife, "There will be a soldier here in a few minutes to search the house. Do not be alarmed, I don't have any arms in the house but I'm going to go get one." With that, he sped back outside and down the road a short distance to Mr. Arbuckle's house where he quickly explained the situation and borrowed a pistol which he hoped he would not need. Along the way there, he met Mr. Arbuckle's wife and her son on their way to Creigh's home to assist with the care of his daughter who was sick. He told them of the developments and added, "Do not be alarmed, I shall return directly."

Returning home as fast as his feet would carry him, David Creigh entered the front door and heard a ruckus upstairs. Just as he suspected, the soldier came straight to his house after robbing the Dunn's of some watches and jewelry. Dashing up the stairs, he heard his wife remark, "I'll take those things out myself." The soldier was in the east room, violently tossing things out of a trunk searching for something valuable that he might steal.

Not satisfied with his finds, the man suddenly whirled around and stepped out into the hall where David Creigh had just arrived. Surprised but undeterred, the soldier asked in a loud voice, "Sir, have you got the key of that trunk?" while at the same time pointing to a trunk nearby that he had already attempted to open.

Mr. Creigh replied, "No, I do not have the key as that trunk belongs to Ms. Lewis who is a teacher for my children."

"Very well," the man said, "I shall break it open."

When the commotion began, Mr. Creigh's 13-year-old daughter, Elizabeth, had been lying sick in bed. When she heard the soldier threaten to break open her teacher's trunk, she pointed down the long hall and said, "Here are some trunks at the far end of the passage."

The man then moved down the hall and jerked open the first trunk he came to, examining its contents. Quickly finding two epaulettes [military uniform decoration], he gave the Creighs a hateful glance and shoved the epaulettes into his pants pocket. "These belong to Rebels," he said.

"No," said Mrs. Creigh, "they belonged to my brother, who died thirty years ago."

Ignoring the Creigh family, the soldier walked to yet another trunk to continue his rampage. Having seen and heard enough, David Creigh secretly cocked his pistol and approached the vandal. Holding up some cards from the trunk, the man asked "What are these?"

The Creighs young daughter quickly replied, "They are cards from school."

"No," the man said, "they are not."

"Yes, they are children's merit cards," said Mr. Creigh. As the man continued his search, David Creigh demanded in a firm tone, "I want you to leave my house." As he spoke those fateful words, David Creigh drew his already cocked pistol and aimed it at the intruder.

Bang! The weapon fired prematurely, the ball lodging harmlessly in the wall as the deafening noise echoed throughout the home.

No sooner had the weapon fired than the soldier sprang at David Creigh. With one swift motion, Mr. Creigh struck the man on his head with the gun crushing him downward. Now began a chaotic life-or-death struggle as the man raised himself and came up with his neck under Mr. Creigh's arm. As the two men struggled like upright wrestlers, the desperate soldier managed to raise his pistol and point it at Creigh's head.

At that very instant, Mrs. Creigh leapt forward and jerked the pistol down toward the floor. For a split second the gun was aimed at her husband's body.

Bang! The weapon fired, but the round missed its intended target and quite possibly struck the soldier himself. The smell of gunpowder and sounds of struggle filled the house as the soldier fought to free himself from Mr. Creigh's tight grip.

Their scuffle taking them near the stairwell, the man determined to throw Mr. Creigh over the railing, hoping at the same instant to break his grip. Mrs. Creigh was then standing near the head of the stairs and in one great motion the soldier managed to slam David Creigh's body against that of his wife. With that, all three of them fell down the long stairway. Mrs. Creigh went first, tumbling head over heels to the bottom, followed immediately by the men, who fell only halfway down. Unable to break the others' hold, they quickly reached the foot of the stairs and began to struggle across the entry.

At that time Mr. Creigh noticed the soldier was bleeding, but from where and by what cause he did not know. Amid the chaos, Mrs. Creigh and Mrs. Arbuckle were down on the floor attempting to grab the pistol when suddenly the weapon fired.

The bullet struck the marauding soldier, who slumped and ceased to struggle. Holding the wounded man upright, Mr. Creigh pulled him to within about 10 feet of the portico where he let him go. Exhausted and nearly panic stricken, the Creighs and Mrs. Arbuckle attempted to gather their thoughts. Just then some movement from the soldier told them their horror was not concluded and something further must be done. Seeing an axe lying nearby, David Creigh picked it up and struck the man once in the head.

Believing it unlikely that he could get a fair hearing from the U.S. military authorities, the decision was made to conceal the body before it could be discovered by Union patrols that frequently passed by. With the help of his son, an Irishman employed at the place, and two others, the body was placed into a cart partially filled with hay. As soon as it could be determined there were no soldiers in the immediate vicinity, the men took the cart about three-fourths mile from the house to an abandoned well situated between the Edgars Ferry road and the river, and about 20 feet in front of a log building. They moved the cart in close to the well, then carefully removed the body and placed it into the well. With nightfall rapidly approaching, the men tossed hay on top of the body and rode back home.

Whatever thoughts the burial party had must have been kept to themselves as no letters or other written records from them have been found. No doubt the tragic events of November 8, 1863 left an indelible impression upon the minds of all involved and it was hoped the entire episode would pass into history never to be resurrected. From David Creigh's testimony at his court martial, we see that he returned to John W. Dunn's home the next evening and, during that somber visit, told his friend his amazing tale of life-or-death struggle.

As autumn turned to winter and winter to spring, everything seemed to be about as normal as wartime Greenbrier County would allow. With the war entering its fourth spring, everyone knew that the return of warm weather would signal the resumption of active military campaigns. They could not have known that this spring's campaigns would cost Greenbrier County the life of one of its most loved and respected citizens.

After the May 1864 raid on the New River bridge at Central Depot, the troops of Gen. George Crook and Gen. William Averell encamped at and near Meadow Bluff. These forces combined with those of Gen. David Hunter to attack Lynchburg. It was during the preparations for the Lynchburg campaign that a male slave approached some of the Union forces and told them about the dead soldier in the well. On the morning of June 1 1864, Captain S.B. Howe of the First West Virginia Cavalry was ordered to use the slave's information to locate and search the well. Captain Howe reported that with the information from the "Darkey," he "readily found the well." He said that upon going down into the well about 15 feet, he found the body of a man dressed in cavalry uniform. Captain Howe examined the body, and finding it too decomposed to be removed, he left it there and returned to camp.

As word of Captain Howe's discovery spread among the officers and men, a rush to judgment prevailed and a thirst for vengeance radiated from the camps. Everywhere men were heard offering their opinion of the matter and cursing the "damned rebels." Unfortunately, no one in the Union army knew all the facts of the case and the perceived wickedness of David Creigh grew with each retelling of the tale. One U.S. cavalryman wrote that the dead man was "a member of the 34th Ohio, who, having lost his horse, went with bridle in hand to search for him. He inquired at the home of a rebel and was murdered for it."

During the night of June 1st, U.S. soldiers escorted Mrs. Creigh, Mrs. Arbuckle, and two of David Creigh's daughters to Bungers Mill, four miles from Lewisburg, where a court martial convened early the next morning. John W. Dunn was present, along with four civilians who were allowed to witness the proceedings. These civilians included George L. Knapp, a teacher, age 44; Samuel S. Hern, a millright, age 40; George W. Kittinger, a manufacturer, age 38; and O.W. Kittinger, teenage son of George Kittinger.

The court martial was presided over by six officers of the United States Military. These were: Captain J.A. Crawford, 14th Pennsylvania Cavalry, serving as Judge Advocate; Col. W.H. Powell, 2nd WV Cavalry; Lt. Col. John W. Shaw, 34th Ohio Infantry; Major William C. Carmon, 1st WV Cavalry; and Capt. W.A. Powell, 1st WV Cavalry.

With the Court fully assembled, Mr. Creigh was asked if he objected to any member of the Court. He replied that he did not and was then arraigned for trial. A total of two witnesses appeared for the prosecution and one, John W. Dunn, for the defense. Mr. Dunn was asked six questions about the case, after which the defendant was allowed to speak in his own behalf. Believing that the truth was his best defense, Mr. Creigh proceeded to explain in detail the events of November 8, 1863. Tragically, the defendant's belief that he would not receive a fair hearing from the U.S. authorities was accurate. His words fell upon deaf ears, as the records show that upon completing his statement, the defendant was not asked a single question by the Court. Instead, the "evidence" was declared closed and the hearing room cleared so that the Court could "maturely" consider the evidence. In a very short time, and to no one's surprise, the defendant was pronounced guilty. Years afterward, Mr. O.W. Kittinger wrote about the event in The *Fayette Tribune*:

They court-martialed him up stairs in the home of ex-sheriff Wallace Robinson...He made a clean breast of all the facts in the case and was very careful to give all the details as they occurred. I shall never forget how this good man looked when he came down in the yard to tell us all goodbye. He was very much agitated and great beads of perspiration stood out on every feature of his face. I was the last one he said goodbye to, and perhaps the last who he ever spoke to in Greenbrier, for it was then 20 Yankee cavalrymen marched him up the hill towards Lewisburg and little did I think as a boy that that would be the last time I would see David S. Creigh until I met him at the bar of God....Mr. Creigh was one of the most law abiding gentlemen that ever lived in the county of Greenbrier, and General Hunter did a great sin when he had this innocent man hung for trying to protect the peace and dignity of his happy home. I give these facts from memory, which has been kept fresh by hearing my father tell so many times, long after the war, what we heard on the day of the trial. Cyrus, the oldest son, gave me the same facts before his death, [Cyrus Creigh died in Baltimore, Maryland in 1927] which he had received from the lips of his mother when he returned from the war.

The next day the Union army withdrew from Greenbrier County and began an advance that would result in the Battle of Lynchburg two weeks later. They took David Creigh with them, on foot, and left his wife and daughters at Bungers Mill without transportation back to Lewisburg. At this time, their prisoner only knew that he had been found guilty of murdering a Union soldier; he did not yet know his sentence, which read as follows: "...therefore sentence the accused, David S. Creigh, a citizen of Greenbrier Co. West Virginia, to be hanged by his neck to a tree until he is dead and left hanging with an inscription 'Murderer of a Union Soldier.' And suggest it to Commanding General that the building in which the murder was committed be burned to the ground." At Staunton, Virginia on June 9, 1864, General William Averell and General George Crook approved the findings of the "military commission" and, having signed the documents, forwarded them to General David Hunter for review. If David Creigh hoped to have an impartial review of his case, it would not come from the pen of "Black Dave" Hunter. General Hunter possessed a strong dislike for the South and its people and he lost no time accepting the recommendations of the commission:

Headquarters, Dept. of West Va
Staunton, Va June 9th 1864

The proceedings, findings and sentence in the case of David S. Creigh have been approved by intermediate commanders and forwarded for the action of the Major General commanding department who directs that the sentence be at once carried into execution by Brig. Genl. Averell commanding 2nd Cavalry Division Department of West Va.

D. Hunter
Major Genl
Commanding

When Gen. Averell received Hunter's order directing that the execution be carried out, he halted his command near Brownsburg, Virginia in Rockbridge County, at the home of the Rev. James Morrison. Shortly after their arrival there, David Creigh was taken into the house and told that he was to be hanged. He was then permitted to write the following letter to his wife:

June 10th 1864

Dear Emily: I arrived this evening at the Rev. James Morrison's in Rockbridge County. After eating my supper I was taken into a house, and the sentence pronounced that I was to be hung. I was not permitted any counsel in my case.

I wish you, my dear beloved wife, to bear up under this dreadful bereavement; you and all the children bear up under this as well as you can, and all try to meet me in heaven. I am meeting death with calmness, believing and trusting in the Lord Jesus Christ the Saviour of sinners. My sincere wish is that all my brothers and sisters may meet me in heaven.

In my sentence it was read, that the house was to be burned to the ground, but the gentlemen that brought me this paper said that part of the sentence would not be carried out. I hoped that I would once more see you all on earth, but it is decreed otherwise, and I have to submit. I wish my remains to be removed and laid by the side of our father's and mother's, as soon as convenient.

The execution will take place in a few minutes. The Rev. A.G. Osborn has prayed for me before I commenced writing....I sent for him this minute, and he and Provost Marshal came in together, and Provost Marshal was authorized to say the execution, if I wished, should not take place until daylight, which I accepted: that much more time to offer up prayers to God, for myself and dear beloved wife, and children to meet me in heaven.

My dear brother Lewis, I know how this will affect you. You know all about my business....I wish my beloved son Cyrus, if he is spared through this dreadful war, to manage my business with your assistance; as dutiful a son as ever lived, and I must say so for all my sons and daughters. I now leave you, Cyrus, Thomas, Charles, Rufus, David, Christopher, Lockhart, Egbert, Margaret, Mary and Elizabeth; leave you with your Christian mother. God be your stay and support, trusting in God, and preparing to meet me in heaven.

David S. Creigh (2)

Home of Rev. James Morrison near Brownsburg, VA. It was here that David Creigh was told his fate. He was buried temporarily on this property, eventually being moved to The Old Stone Church graveyard at :ewisburg. *Photo by author, 2003*

Just after sunrise the next morning, several guards called their prisoner out of the little slave cabin where he had been jailed. He was put into a wagon and taken across the yard, up a little vale to a large tree about one-quarter mile from the Morrison home. Apparently uncomfortable with the thought of hanging the prisoner for defense of his home, no one on Gen. Averell's staff would agree to serve as hangman. The puzzle was solved by deception and the task placed upon the young shoulders of Archibald Rowand, a 19-year-old scout with the 1st West Virginia Cavalry. Mr. Rowand described the incident more than 40 years after the war closed:

To begin with, I hanged a man. It was this way: ...a citizen named Creigh had, with an axe, killed a Union soldier and thrown his body into a well. The scouts now discovered this; Creigh was captured, tried by a drumhead court martial, and sentenced to be hanged. As I was going up to headquarters the next morning I met Captain Jack Crawford, of Averell's staff, who said to me, 'Rowand, you hang the prisoner.' I indignantly told him I would do nothing of the sort—I hadn't enlisted for an executioner. It was the General's order, he told me angrily; and of course that settled it. I sent a couple of the boys for some rope from a bed (have you ever seen the beds of that day?—with an interlacing of rope in lieu of bed-springs), and put the rope around the prisoner's neck, tied the other end to the limb of a tree, mounted him on the scouts wagon, and drove the wagon from under him. I have seen civil executions since, but then I didn't know enough to tie the hands and feet of the condemned.

Private Rowand later discovered that Gen. Averell had never ordered him to be the hangman. It was all a ruse by Captain Crawford to get out of doing it himself. (3)

By nine o'clock that morning, the army was again on the move. As they departed, Rev. A.G. Osborn, Union Army chaplain from Pennsylvania, called at the Morrison home to inform them that the execution had been carried out and the body left hanging in the tree on their property. The army chaplain and some of the private soldiers were very much distressed by what

Archibald Rowand of the First WV Cavalry. As a 19-year-old scout and spy, he was deceived into hanging David Creigh. When no one else wanted to be the hangman, an officer told Rowand that the general ordered him to do it, but that was not true. Pvt. Rowand won the Medal of Honor for his intrepid exploits as scout and spy for the North. He is depicted here in the uniform of a Confederate soldier. From *On Hazardous Service* by W.G. Beymer, 1912.

they saw as the hanging of an innocent man. Rev. Osborn told the Morrison's of the "...strong impressions he had received of Mr. Creigh being a good man, and bore testimony to the perfect composure and Christian spirit with which he met his death."

As soon as the army left, Mrs. Morrison recruited a few friends to help remove Creigh's body from the tree. No coffin being readily available, the body was placed in a blanket and buried at the scene in a shallow grave. Six days later, a coffin was procured and the body disinterred and removed to the graveyard of the nearby New Providence Church. This was accomplished with the help of Cyrus Creigh, who had been given leave from his service in the Confederate Army to take care of his father's remains.

Although David Creigh was hanged on June 11th, the first word his family received of his fate was two weeks later when Gen. Hunter's army retreated back into West Virginia. With the return of hungry soldiers to Greenbrier County, the Creigh home was visited again, this time by a group of mean-spirited soldiers in search of food. Thomas Creigh described the Yankees' return in a letter to a family friend:

You are rightly informed in regard to the treatment of my brother's family by the soldiers—no, not soldiers—but fiends in the shape of men, belonging to Hunters and Crook's bandits retreating from Lynchburg. As they passed through Greenbrier—perfectly demoralized—wandering in every direction, without any discipline or order; starving and famished for something to eat; stealing, robbing and plundering every house and farm in ten miles of the turnpike, a company of fifteen or twenty went to my brother's house—half starved, filthy, dirty looking, creatures—alighted from their horses, stalked into the hall, opened a press, containing books, saw my brother's name in one of them, and then in a loud, fiendish tone of voice, inquired of each other: 'Do you know David S. Creigh? Do you know where he is? "Yes," was the reply, in louder tones of voice, 'I saw him hanging on a tree.' This reply was repeated several times whilst running up and down stairs plundering every room in the house and kitchen.

This was the first intimation of the death of my brother. My sister ventured to inquire of one who seemed more quiet than the rest, if it was really true, that her husband was killed, and he replied, with an oath, that it was true, and if she did not give them something to eat, they would burn down the house over her head. They took everything they could find to eat, stole all the jewelry from the young ladies, broke and destroyed several pieces of furniture, and for a day and a half annoyed the family in various ways always accompanied with disgusting profanity. They left almost nothing for the family to live on. It is impossible to give an adequate description of their cruelties.

The man that was killed did not belong to their army; they neither knew his name, his company or his regiment; he was never on their muster roll, and they never missed him.

I am proud that my brother died in vindicating the eternal principles of truth, and right, and faith, and trust in God. I have not told you half.

P.S. – The citizens here say that there was not a gentleman among the officers or men—all low bred, debased creatures.

The soldiers who stopped at the Creigh home first raided the home of David Creigh's sister-in-law, Mrs. J.C. Preston. On

June 29 1864, three days after their visit, Mrs. Preston wrote about the event in a letter to another of her sisters:

Our dear & noble brother has indeed joined the band of martyred heroes who have shed their blood on the scaffold & field in defence of their country & its domestic alters. But as a Christian patriot and martyr he had with unfaltering faith, unequalled composure met & suffered the malice & hatred of the war hounds of an army whose deeds are but a record at which the heart of the stoutest shrink from hearing.

Last Sabbath the infuriated soldiers with jeers and taunts brought the news to me & then went on to brothers. The very ones who had taken her [Mary Creigh] into camp & laughed at her grief, threatening to burn the house into ashes. Although shocked & crushed I would not allow myself to admit the truth until I should hear it officially & about 10 o'clock Davidella & myself walked down to sisters & Alas! Alas! It was too true. I met poor Mary at the door in all her grief. Mr. Barr & the Elders of the church had brought the official information from the chaplain [Rev. Osborn] who wrote a letter in town not being allowed to come down & Mr. Barr & the Elders brought it to her. Poor sister is crushed, overwhelmed, but there is much in the letter of the chaplain to sooth our smitten hearts. He says in this letter brother met the sentence with the greatest composure trusting in the merits of our Lord & Saviour Jesus Christ....he asked for a candle & paper to write to his family this was refused but the paper & ink were brought & he wrote but the chaplain not knowing he was coming this way was directed by brother to leave it with Mr. Myers of Lexington, which he did & we hear Cyrus is coming on with his remains....

I walked down to poor sisters early this morning & met dear Cyrus at the door. He could not bring on the remains with him...Poor sister is better today for oh I thought she could not live. Monday Cyrus brought her much comfort for he brought her the letter brother wrote just before his execution, as glorious & consolitary a testimony to his faith in God & his blessed hope through grace of a glorious immortality....

Mrs. Morrison as well as some of the Yankee officers say his calm-

ness made such an impression on the hardened soldiery that among the 300 who witnessed it there was not a dry cheek… Yet their malice was not satiated & they proclaimed they would shoot down any man who would take the body and bury it….

On July 4th, 1864, the Lewisburg Presbyterian Church passed "resolutions of respect" to honor David Creigh. The same was done by the Greenbrier County Court on July 25th. Word of the hanging resonated across the South and even garnered the attention of the Confederate Secretary of War. On July 13th, the Secretary wrote to Gen. Lee about the execution of Creigh and a Captain White who was summarily executed in Lexington, Virginia during Hunter's advance on Lynchburg. Gen. Lee replied on July 18th: "I have the honor to acknowledge…papers relative to the murder by the enemy of Mr. Creigh and Captain White….I think…something should be done, if possible, to put a stop to the barbarities of the enemy. I can see no remedy except in refusing to make prisoners of any soldiers belonging to commands in which these outrages are perpetrated…." (4)

It is significant to note that Gen. Lee proposed an unprecedented policy of retaliation in answer to the "barbarities of the enemy." The idea of taking no prisoners from commands involved in these acts was never implemented. The very fact that it was suggested illustrates the desperation and outrage felt across the South for these acts.

With the aid of some family friends, Cyrus Creigh was finally able to return his father's body to Greenbrier County on July 28, where his devoted family watched over the remains for three days. On July 31, a funeral cortege more than one mile long slowly wound its way to Lewisburg and the Presbyterian Church. Rev. McElhenney spoke of his long acquaintance with the deceased and of his many virtues. The funeral was then preached by Rev. J.C. Barr, associate minister of the Old Stone Church. Rev. Barr chose **The Christian Martyr** as the subject for his sermon. Following the services, the throng of mourners moved slowly out into the adjacent graveyard where the remains of David S. Creigh were laid to rest for the third and final time.

His tombstone bears this inscription:

Sacred to the Memory of David Creigh
Died as a Martyr in Defense of his
Rights and in the performance of his
duties as a husband and father.
Born May 1, 1809 and yielded to his
unjust fate June 11, 1864 near
Brownsburg, Virginia.

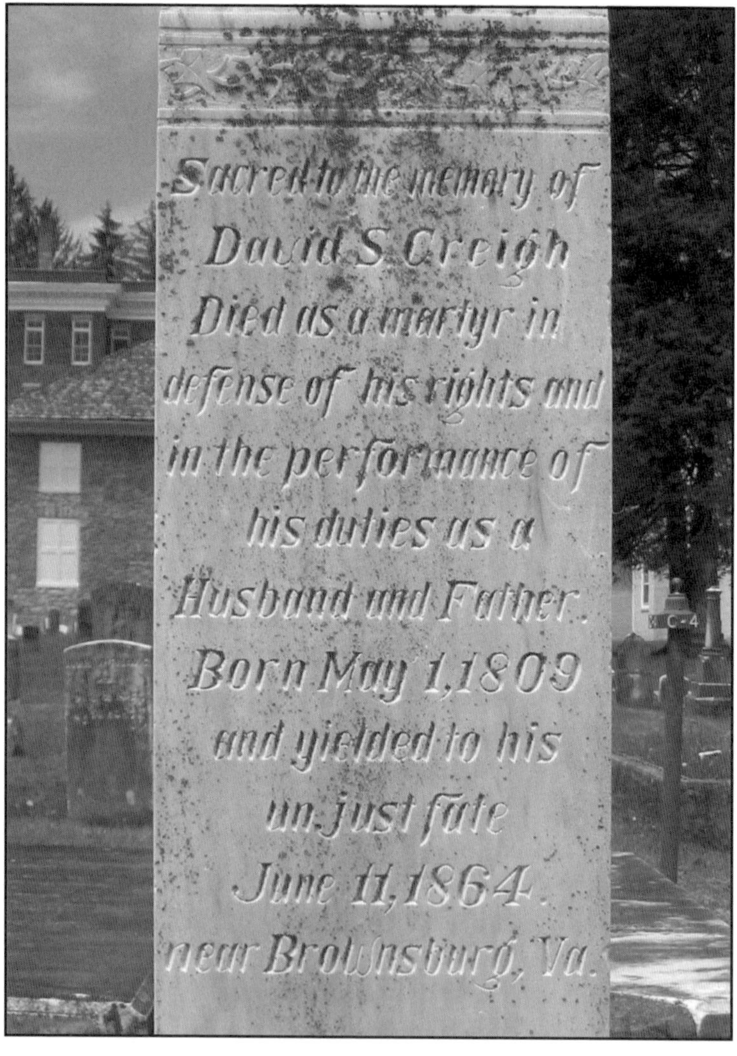

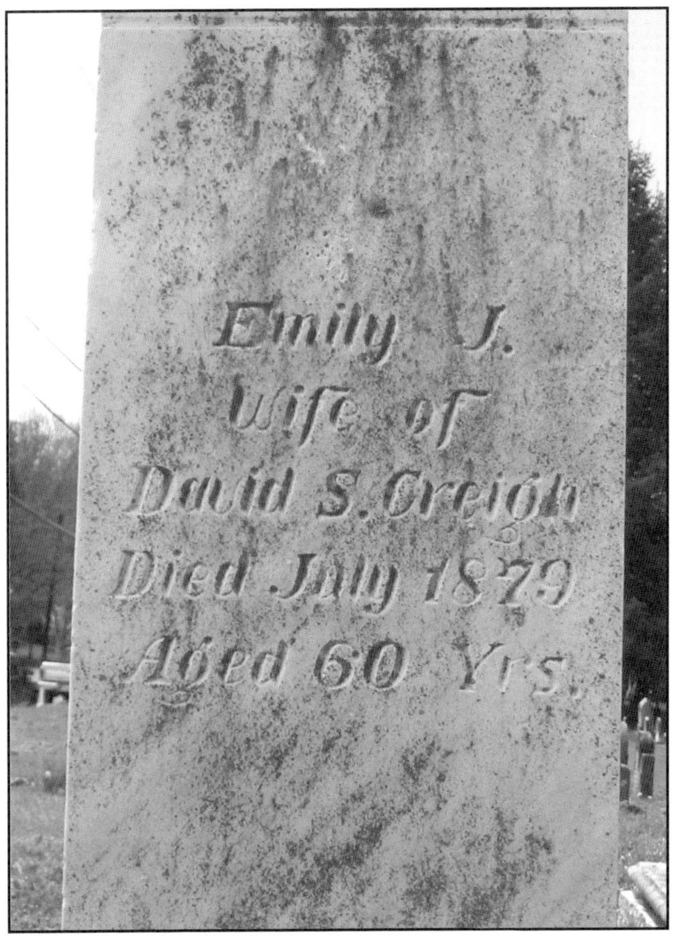

Opposite: The grave of David Creigh at Lewisburg.
Above: The grave of Emily Creigh at Lewisburg. *Photos by author*

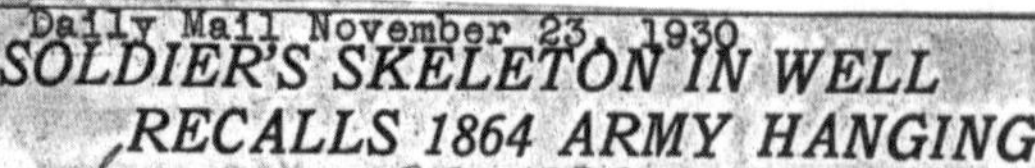

Daily Mail November 23, 1930

SOLDIER'S SKELETON IN WELL RECALLS 1864 ARMY HANGING

One Lewisburg Account is That Home Owner, Who Attacked Civil War Veteran Looting Residence, Died Rather Than Tell of Woman Slayer Who Aided Him With Axe

LEWISBURG, Nov. 22. — Last summer's unprecedented drought served to reveal an almost forgotten tragedy of the Civil war which, because of the scarcity of facts at hand, had come to be regarded locally as hardly more substantial than a tradition.

With the recent finding of a Union soldier's skeleton, the penalty paid by his supposed slayer and fragments of the story of the manner of his death again were being told.

In November, 1864, the soldier, who belonged to a detachment commanded by General Crook, is supposed to have come to the home of David Creigh, 4 miles south of Lewisburg, during the absence of Mr. Creigh, and to have confiscated some things for his own use.

Returning, Creigh was informed of the situation and gained entrance to his own home only after exchanging several shots with the intruder. He and the stranger then are said to have engaged in a fierce hand-to-hand struggle, with the soldier getting the best of the fight up to the time when both fell down a stairway.

To Deserted Well

At this point, a Negro servant brought Creigh an axe and either he or someone else in the household is said to have killed the soldier. The body, according to the story, was loaded secretly into a cart, transported across some fields and deposited in a deserted well.

Learning of the incident, Creigh was arrested by orders of General Crook, taken to Brownsburg, Va., for a court martial trial and was hanged. His body was brought back to Lewisburg and buried in the cemetery adjacent to the Old Stone Presbyterian church.

After the lapse of 67 years, the land on which the well is located now, is owned by Mrs. Lucinda Moore. During the drouth and owing the scarsity of water, Mrs. Moore decided to clean out the well with the hope of replenishing her scant supply. Her son, Leslie, was set at the task and, after getting down about 30 feet, the skeleton of

(Continued on Page Thirteen)

DEATH RECALLED BY SKELETON IN WELL

(Continued From Page One)

the Union soldier was found. The skeleton is in a good state of preservation, and was identified beyond a doubt by a belt buckle upon which was engraved an American eagle and the words "E Pluribus Unum." The metal frame of a purse and the remains of a watch also were found. The shoe soles were intact and were filled with hob-nails.

Thought To Be Buried

But few are living now who recall the circumstances of the killing and the execution of David Creigh. It had been presumed that General Crook had the soldier's body removed from the well and buried.

One story is that when Creigh fell down the stairway a woman dealt the blow with the axe and Mr. Creigh suffered himself to be hanged rather than endanger the woman.

The home where the soldier was killed still stands, in a good state of preservation, and is now the property of William Francis Boone, who with his family lives there.

The skeletal remains of the U.S. soldier killed by David Creigh in 1864 were accidentally uncovered in 1930.

Chapter Sixteen

Court Martial Records of David S. Creigh

These records were obtained from the National Archives, Washington D.C. They are a part of Record Group 153, *Records of the Office of the Judge Advocate General* (Army) and comprise case file LL 2540. The file is transcribed verbatim with a few changes to grammar and punctuation for clarity.

Proceedings of a Military Commission convened at Bungers Mills, West Va June 2nd 1864, by virtue of the following order:

Head Quarters, 2nd Cavalry Division
Department of West Virginia,
Bungers Mills, W.Va. June 2nd 1864

Special Orders
No. 6

A Military Commission is hereby appointed to convene at this place at once, for the trial of such prisoners as may be brought before it.

Detail for the Commission:

1. Col. W.H. Powell, 2nd WV Cavalry
2. Lt. Col. Shaw, 34th Ohio Vol. M. Infty.
3. Major Carmon, 1st WV Veteran Cav.
4. Capt. Elias Powell, 7th WV Veteran Cav.
5. Capt. W.A. Powell, 1st WV Vet. Cav.

Capt. J.A. Crawford, 14th Pa Cav. Judge Advocate.
No other officers than those named can be convened without injury to the service.

The Commission will sit without regard to hours.

By Command of

Brig. Genl. W.W. Averell
(signed) Will Ramsey
A.A.G

The Court met pursuant to the above order, present all the members. The prisoner, David S. Creigh, a citizen of Greenbrier County West Va. being introduced, was asked if he had any objection to any member of the Court, to which he replied in the negative. The Court was then duly sworn by the Judge Advocate, and the Judge Advocate by the President, in the presence of the accused. The prisoner was then arraigned for trial by the following charge and specifications:

Charge: "Murder"

Specification:

In this, that he the said David S. Creigh, a citizen of Greenbrier County W. Virginia, on or about the eight day of November, A.D. eighteen hundred and sixty three, at his residence in the County and State aforesaid, with an axe or other weapon, did murder a man dressed in the uniform of a United States Cavalry soldier, whose name is unknown.

(Signed) Louis A. Myers
Capt. and Provost Marshal
2nd Cav. Div. Dept. of W. Va.

To which charge and specification the prisoner pleaded as follows:

To the Specification: "Not Guilty"
To the Charge: "Guilty"

Capt. Ricker, Asst. Insp. Genl. 1st Brig. A witness for the prosecution, being sworn, testified and said:

Question by the Judge Advocate: State what you know regarding to the confession of Mr. Creigh.

Answer: I was sent for by Mr. Creigh yesterday evening, he introduced himself as being acquainted with a young lady acquaintance and heard her speak of me. His first remark to me was "I am a prisoner and I suppose you know the circumstance of the case." I told him I did not, and he asked me if he might be permitted to go home under guard. I told him I would speak to the General and if I could I would do so. I was then told by the General what the charge was. I then called on Mr. Creigh in going back from the Generals Head Quarters.
Mr. Creigh stated sometime in November 1863, a soldier called at the house of Mr. Dunn and demanded his horses. Mr. Creigh stated that he then started for home and borrowed a pistol from Mr. Arbuckle, and that he determined that no man should ransack his house, he would allow neither Northern or Southern soldier to go about his premises. On going home he found the soldier at some trunks in a hall up stairs, the soldier taking out a pair of Epauletts and accused him of belonging to the Southern army, he also took out some cards, asking him what they were, the soldier contradicted his daughter, thereupon Mr. Creigh cocked his pistol and the weapon went off in a scuffle that immediately took place, he at the same time catching the soldier around the neck under his arm holding him in that position, the soldier still struggled and drew his own revolver, in the scuffle the revolver was fired the ball passing through the soldiers breast, and he still held the soldier until he dragged him down stairs, the soldier fell on the porch. He was expecting other soldiers about and he called on his children to bring some hay and cover him up, that he then saw the soldier work his fingers and that he

got an axe and knocked him in the head, putting him in the well and covering him up with rocks.

Question by the Court: What reason did the accused give for having the soldier covered with hay after he was dying upon the porch or ground.

Answer: I think he said he expected other soldiers.

Question by the Court: Did the accused state that the soldier with whom he had had the difficulty in his house, used any violence toward his family or attempt to carry off any property out of his house.

Answer: He did not state that the soldier used any violence whatever, nor touched other property than the Epauletts and cards.

Capt. S.B. Howe, 1st W.Va. Vet. Cavalry a witness for the prosecution being sworn, testified and said:

Question by the Judge Advocate: State what you know in reference to finding the body of an unknown soldier in a well near the house of Mr. Creigh.

Answer: I was directed when I went on picket yesterday morning to make search for the body of a soldier said to have been killed by Mr. Creigh at the time Genl. Averell's forces were here the last time. I was informed in the first place that the body was in an old well near the river, I asked the Darkey if he could show me the well, he described the place so that I very readily found the well. On going down in the well and examining I found the body of the man, he was dressed in cavalry uniform. I removed the rock off the body but the body was too much decomposed to remove it.

Question by the Court: State the situates of the well and how far from Mr. Creigh's house.

Answer: I think it was on Mr. Creigh's place about three quarters of a mile from the house, between the Edgars Ferry road and the river about twenty feet in front of a log building.

Question by the Court: Was there many rocks and stones on the body.

Answer: No, not many, not sufficient to hide the body when you were down in the well.

Question by the Court: How deep was the well.

Answer: About 15 feet.

Question by the prisoner: Was there any hay in the well.

Answer: The man in the well said there was hay in the well. [an apparent reference to the "Darkey" who directed Captain Howe to the well.]

Mr. John W. Dunn, a citizen of Greenbrier County a witness for the defense, being duly sworn testified and said:

Question by the Judge Advocate: What do you know in reference to the murder of an unknown cavalry soldier last fall.

Answer: I know nothing upon earth about the murder of the man, to my own knowledge further than Mr. Creigh's own statement.

Question by Judge Advocate: What was Mr. Creigh's statement to you to regard to the murder.

Answer: Mr. Creigh stated that upon going home he found the soldier up stairs in his house, the soldier was looking at children's cards. Mr. Creigh was armed and when he approached the soldier he [the soldier] either drew or attempted to draw his pistol.

Mr. Creigh upon that presented his pistol and aimed to fire but the cap exploded. Mr. Creigh then struck him with the pistol he had in his hand, after striking him he grabbed the hand that had the pistol in it and a scuffle took place. Mrs. Creigh came in about that time and she attempted to take the pistol from the soldier and the pistol went off. This was up stairs, in the scuffle they approached the stairway and then the soldier made a wonderful effort to throw them both over the banister and Mrs. Creigh was thrown over and fell upon the floor below. Mr. Creigh and the soldier got down stairs and at the foot of the stairway he first discovered the blood upon the soldier. On arrival at the foot of the stairs the revolver was fired two or three times and was taken from the soldier by Mrs. Creigh and Mrs. Arbuckle. Mr. Creigh still held the man until they came to the portico or pavement the man then sank and died in a few minutes. He was then put into a cart and hauled away by Mr. Creigh and an Irishman employed at the place.

Question by the Court: Did the accused say anything to you as to his striking the soldier in the head with an axe, upon discovering that the soldier shows signs of life, by moving his fingers after having been covered with hay, while lying on the pavement near the house.

Answer: No sir, he did not.

Question by the Court: How long after the murder of the soldier did Mr. Creigh make the statement to you.
Answer: The night after the thing occured, the time that General Averell came in, in November 1863.

Question by the Court: Did you witness any altercation or words between the soldier and Mr. Creigh.

Answer: No.

Question by the Court: Did Mr. Creigh in his statement of this difficulty give you to understand that he had ordered the soldier out of his house before striking him with his pistol.

Answer: My recollection is that he was ordered out but whether before or after he was struck I do not know.

Statement of the prisoner:

On the Sunday evening that Genl. Averell had possession of Lewisburg, I was at Mr. Dunn's, a soldier stepped in and asked him where his horses were. Mr. Dunn remarked that some were at one place and some another. He remarked, "Sir, I will search your house." When they left the room I left and started home. I went home and told my wife there would be a soldier in a few minutes to search the house. I told her not to be alarmed and as I had no arms about the house I would go and get one. I went to Mr. Arbuckle and borrowed a pistol and as I was going there I met Mrs. Arbuckle and her son and told them not to be alarmed as I would be back directly. Mr. Arbuckle gave me the pistol and I returned to my house. The soldier was upstairs searching the trunks in the East room and tearing up things in the trunk and my wife remarked that she would take the things out herself. He came out of the room into the passage when I met him. He asked me "Sir, have you got the key of that trunk." I remarked that I had not as it belonged to a Miss Lewis, who was teaching in the family. He replied that he would break it open. My little daughter remarked, here are trunks at the far end of the passage. He went to the back window and jerked open the trunk and commenced examining & found two Epaulettes and put them into his pocket, saying they belonged to rebels. My wife remarked no they belonged to my brother-in-law, who was dead thirty years ago. As the soldier walked to the back part of the house I cocked my pistol and went up while he was examining some cards. He disputed my daughters word and said they were not cards. I remarked they were children's merit cards. I told him I wanted him to leave the house, with that I drew my pistol and aimed it at him but the cap exploded. I was standing near the ceiling and he sprang at me and I struck him with the pistol, and this crushed him down and he raised with his neck under my arm. He got his pistol and raised it over and leveled it at my head. My wife jerked his arm down and in aiming at my body the pistol went off. He made great exertion until he got to the head of the stairs when he dashed me against my wife knocking her down stairs, and me half way down, still holding onto him. At the foot of the stairs I discovered the blood. Mrs. Arbuckle and my wife both on the floor and trying to rescue the pistol. It went off, he fell then and I caught him and took him down the steps about ten feet from the portico. He fell dead, as it were, there was an axe lying near and I struck him on the head. An Irishman, my son, and myself and two others took the body of the soldier to the well, put him in the well, threw the hay in the cart into the well. Never was there a rock thrown in by me or by the party with me.

The evidence being closed the Court was cleared and having maturely considered the evidence addressed to find the accused as follows:

Of the Specification: **Guilty**

Of the Charge: **Guilty**

And do therefore sentence the accused, David S. Creigh, a citizen of Greenbrier Co. West Virginia, to be hanged by his neck to a tree until he is dead and left hanging with an inscription "Murderer of a Union soldier." And suggest it to Commanding General that the building in which the murder was committed be burned to the ground.

The Court unanimously concurring therein. Their being no further business the Commission adjourned.

James A. Crawford
Capt. Co H 14th Pa Cavalry
Judge Advocate

W.H. Powell
Col. 2nd Regt. W.Va Cavalry
President of the Military Commission (1)

Bungers Mill in the 1800s. David Creigh's court martial hearing was held on the second floor of this house. *Courtesy Greenbrier Historical Society*

Chapter Seventeen
To Appomattox and Beyond

In mid-July 1864, West Virginia Governor A.I. Boreman authorized the formation of Union Home Guard companies in the counties of Monroe, Greenbrier, Fayette, Giles, Mercer, and Raleigh. Gen. Crook implemented the governor's plan with "Special Orders No. 21," stating that these companies would be formed for the purpose of protecting the "loyal people" in those counties, and for "any other service as the Governor may require." (1) On July 21, authority was given for a company of independent Union scouts to be formed in Greenbrier County, and commanded by Captain A.W. Mann. This company was officially mustered into service in December 1864, several months having been required for its formation.

Mr. Mason Mathews, a politician and prominent citizen of Lewisburg, informed one of his sons on August 31 that everything had been quiet in Greenbrier County since June 26, "when Hunter's force retreated." Mercifully, military activity subsided in Greenbrier County in that fourth summer of the war. Never again would her citizens be subjected to large-scale invasion by forces of the Blue or Gray. (2)

In September, Confederate authorities decided to send a well-mounted cavalry force into Northwestern Virginia to interrupt Union communications. They also hoped to return with a large number of beef-cattle and horses. To accomplish this mission, the 34th Battalion Virginia Cavalry left their camp in Tazewell County on September 17, and met at Lewisburg with Thurmond's Rangers. Also at Lewisburg was Company H, 37th

Battalion Cavalry and the independent companies of J. Bumgard and J.W. Amick. Their combined manpower was 523, with 267 men being infantry. This force departed Lewisburg on September 22, passing over the mountain by the Cold Knob route toward Bulltown in Braxton County. By October 7, the men had returned to Greenbrier County and camped at Muddy Creek, near Palestine, with the 37-man company of Captain P.W. Snyder at Meadow Bluff. Witcher returned with 400 horses, 200 cattle, and more than $5,000 taken from the Exchange Bank of Weston. His troops also captured and paroled 300 men. (3)

Attempting to deal with an ever-increasing number of refugees traveling north, the Confederate Department of Southwest Virginia and East Tennessee issued "General Orders No. 14." This order required all persons wanting to pass beyond the Confederate lines and into the Union lines to make application at the Dublin headquarters. Applicants were required to state their name, age, and sex, and give a description and value of any property they wanted to take with them. All persons granted permits were required to "present themselves in the town of Lewisburg...on the 14th day of October." Thus the village of Lewisburg, already subjected to four years of war, became a sort of clearing house for civilians fleeing the conflict. (4)

Having gone four months without enemy occupation of Lewisburg, the citizens were disturbed during the night of October 27 by the arrival of several hundred Yankee cavalry. These men were in search of Thurmond's Rangers or any other organized Rebel force. Discovering that enemy cavalry had gone to Giles and Tazewell County, the men remained a few hours and rode back into the Kanawha Valley.

A similar episode occurred during the night of November 11. Members of the Nicholas County Home Guard (Union), under Captain James Ramsey, raided Captain Amick's camp near Lewisburg. Taken by surprise, Amick's camp lost 50 horses and 10 men captured. They were able to regroup quickly, however, and in the pursuit retook the men and horses, also capturing five of Ramsey's men. (5)

In December, Federal forces under General George Stoneman

destroyed or damaged the Virginia and Tennessee Railroad, the Saltville salt works, and the lead mines in Wythe County. His forces did not enter Greenbrier County, though the presence of such a large force in the area caused considerable public anxiety.

Various losses, military and political, began to seriously erode public support for the Confederacy. Even some of the South's most stalwart defenders began to admit that it was growing less and less likely the South could gain its independence, but many remained hopeful. At Lewisburg, recovering from combat wounds on Christmas Day 1864, Lieutenant Thomas Feamster confided to his diary that "the news that greets us is bad and causes a gloom throughout our Confederacy." (6)

In January 1865, the 14th Virginia Cavalry was furloughed for 60 days. Their regimental headquarters was at White Sulphur Springs. McCausland's brigade spent much of the winter west of the Allegheny Mountains, with some companies of the 16th and 17th Virginia Cavalry camping in Greenbrier County, on picket and forage duty. General McCausland had his headquarters near Covington, with an observation post at White Sulphur Springs and pickets at Lewisburg.

According to a report received by Col. J.H. Oley at Charleston on January 9, there were only "about seventy rebels" at Lewisburg. Five days later, Col. Oley was told that some State scouts had gone within 20 miles of Lewisburg and heard of no enemy troops at or near the town. On January 18, deserters reported at Loup Creek, Fayette County (present Deepwater), that Meadow Bluff was occupied by Capt. John Halstead's company of Thurmond's Rangers. (7)

Capt. A.W. Mann wrote to Governor Boreman on January 19, requesting various supplies and equipment, as commander of the "Greenbrier County State Troops." Mann also stated that he had recently made a scout into Greenbrier County, from Nicholas County, and had captured five enemy soldiers and six horses. One of his prisoners was Joseph McMillion, who was "the worst man in our country…he is a bush whacker horse thief and murderer…" Another prisoner was William Hill, "a bad man." (8) Mr. Hill was a 19-year-old deserter from the 14th Virginia Cavalry. Sent to Camp Chase prison in Ohio, he acquired pneumonia and died there on March 20, 1865.

Gen. Echols assembled his brigade at Lewisburg on February 23, and delivered a patriotic speech. When these men came together, the fact was reported in the Kanawha Valley by scouts and deserters. Rumors led Federal authorities to believe that the enemy in Greenbrier County planned a raid into central West Virginia, but that was not the case. McCausland's brigade and the 34th Battalion Cavalry occupied Greenbrier County in late February and early March. McCausland's command subsequently moved to the Shenandoah Valley to oppose Gen. Philip Sheridan. Col. Witcher intended to combine his forces with McCausland's, but the swollen New River prevented it.

An order was sent out for members of the 14th Virginia Cavalry to assemble at Lewisburg on March 5, with instructions to proceed into eastern Virginia. Capt. Thomas Feamster noted in his diary that "many of the boys do not come up for some reason or the other, some have gone to the enemy. Quite a bad state of affairs." (9) Six days later, Col. John H. Oley reported from Charleston that Col. James Corns, of the 8th Virginia Cavalry, had surrendered. Corns stated that 200 of his men were in the mountains and would come in to surrender if they would not be sent away from their families. (10)

Gen. Lee surrendered his Army of Northern Virginia to Gen. U.S. Grant at Appomattox, Virginia, April 9, 1865. It took several days for word of Lee's surrender, unexpected by many, to reach the Greenbrier region. On Monday, April 17, Lt. Col. David S. Hounshell rode from Lewisburg to Mountain Cove (near present-day Ansted), Fayette County, to discuss surrender. Capt. J.M. Guion, commanding Federal forces at Gauley Bridge, reported meeting with the Rebel officer: "...I met Lt. Col. Hounshell with a flag of truce. He is commandant at Lewisburg, and desires a conference with Colonel Oley...for the purpose of putting an end to the present state of affairs in the Greenbrier district, as he expresses it; or, in plain English, surrendering his entire command on the terms given Lee by Grant, if possible. He is accompanied by his adjutant, one other commissioned officer, and an escort of eight unarmed men...." (11)

Lt. Col. Hounshell's surrender offer caused some question within the Federal government as to whether or not Grant's surrender terms allowed Confederate soldiers from loyal states to return to their homes. Gen. Winfield S. Hancock was in favor of allowing West Virginia Confederate veterans to go home: "These people have served in West Virginia, and probably nowhere else. Their homes generally are in counties never permanently occupied by us. Many Confederate officers and soldiers from Missouri and other loyal states are coming in, on their paroles, desiring to go to their homes....I will venture a suggestion, in consideration of the fact that there are many bands in West Virginia whose homes are there: It is that on surrendering and giving their paroles they should be permitted to go to their homes when they are in West Virginia. I believe it would be well to let them all go to their homes...." (12)

Another officer reported from Cumberland, Maryland, on April 18, that the citizens of Wheeling had "passed a resolution declaring that those [Rebel soldiers] from that place shall not return, and those that have already returned shall quit." (13) Thousands of Confederate veterans were eventually paroled in West Virginia. Some quietly returned home without giving their parole. Gen. W.H. Emory reported on April 20 that the mountains of West Virginia held "a great many stragglers, deserters, guerillas, and men on leave from the rebel army." (14)

Lt. Col. Hounshell was informed on April 20 that his surrender would be accepted on the same terms given Gen. Lee, and that his veterans would then be free to go home. Hounshell said his command in Greenbrier County was "about 400," with "other commands beyond." He stated that Gen. Echols disbanded his brigade and had gone south to unite with Gen. Johnston, leaving him in command of the Department of Western Virginia and East Tennessee. (15)

Col. Oley stated on April 26 that "Captain Rife is now at Lewisburg paroling all the forces in my front." (16) Captain Rife was back in Charleston on April 29, having paroled 39 officers and about 600 men at Lewisburg. He reported that he would return to Lewisburg on May 10. Rife said "the rebellion in that section has withered away. The people are tired of war and ready to quit." (17)

When the end came, Dr. John L. Ancrum was the Confederate physician in charge of the field infirmary at White Sulphur Springs. Without money or transportation, he was forced to walk to his home in South Carolina. He recalled his journey in the pages of *Confederate Veteran* magazine, in 1911: "When the war closed, I was stationed at the Greenbrier White Sulphur Springs,

Grave of Rose W. Fry, granddaughter of Rev. John McElhenny, in the graveyard of the Old Stone Church. *Photo by author, 2004*

without money. The paymaster had not been there for some time. My clothes were ragged, and I had only one suit at that. I could get no transportation, and started to walk the long distance to Charleston, S.C., and I did it. It was home under any conditions. The last I heard of my wife was that she had been sitting one night on a pile of furniture in a street of Columbia, S.C., with our child that I had never seen…while that city was burning….The farther I walked, the more anxious I became….I reached home at last, to find my child dead, but my wife awaiting me."

When peace returned, although it shone through darkness,
like stars on a clouded night, it was hailed by all
as the harbinger of an overcast dawn.

Rose W. Fry, 1893

The war was over, but true peace would not come to former Confederates and Southern sympathizers for several years. Greenbrier citizens found themselves residents of a new state, and, more ominously, a state dominated by Radical Republicans. Nearly two months prior to Gen. Lee's surrender, the West Virginia Legislature enacted a voters' test oath. This oath required each voter to swear that he had never borne arms against, nor held any office hostile to, the U.S. Government, the Restored Government of Virginia, or the new state of West Virginia. This act had the desired effect, in that it disfranchised thousands of former Confederates and their sympathizers. In counties such as Greenbrier the disfranchised accounted for so much of the electorate that civil government was seriously impaired without their participation.

West Virginia Governor Arthur I. Boreman declared in January 1866 that former Confederates would have no right to participate in government. He said men who had for four years sought to destroy the government now sought to participate in it, "as fully as if they had not so recently sought its destruction." Gov. Boreman realized that many former Confederates were attempting to "repossess themselves of place and power." He took particular notice of Samuel Price of Lewisburg, who had served as lieutenant governor of Virginia in the Confederacy. In October 1865, Price was elected judge of the Ninth Judicial Circuit, which included Greenbrier, Monroe, Pocahontas, and other counties. Declaring that Mr. Price could not take the test oath, Boreman said, "I cannot commission to so high and important an office one who has so recently been engaged in efforts to destroy the State and to overthrow the Government of the United States." In September 1865 Samuel Price had been approved for pardon by the United States Attorney General at Washington, D.C. Due to an unexplained delay in the paperwork being returned from the president, the pardon was not certified until the next year. Subsequent to receiving his pardon in July 1866, Mr. Price petitioned the court to be reinstated as an attorney in West Virginia. His appeal was denied on January 23, 1867. James Withrow, John W. Dunn, John A. Feamster, Alex Kearns, Samuel B. McClintic, and Joseph Beard, all of Greenbrier County, were included in the pardon. (18)

The West Virginia Senate also refused to seat Henry Mason Mathews, of Lewisburg, who won the Senate seat from the Ninth District in the same election. Mathews attempted to gain the seat by presenting a notarized oath stating that he would support the Constitution and faithfully perform his duties as state senator. This effort failed, and Mathews' seat was declared vacant. In October 1866, Dr. Charles A. Thatcher, a New York native and Lewisburg resident, won the seat in a special election.

On February 14, 1866, the Legislature imposed several new disabilities on former Confederates, including lawyers and teachers. It provided that no attorney could practice law unless he had taken an oath that he had not borne arms against the United States Government since June 20, 1863. It also passed a voters' registration law, under which the governor appointed a registrar for each county. The registrar would then appoint registrars for each township, with instructions to register only voters who took the test oath. Another law provided that court cases arising in pro-Confederate counties could be moved to neighboring counties loyal to the Union; and allowed tax collectors extra commissions for the collection of taxes in secessionist counties.

In Greenbrier County, Dr. J.F. Caldwell was made registrar and quickly seized the opportunity to punish the majority of the citizens in his district. Shortly after he became registrar, Dr. Caldwell made his sentiments known in the pages of the local newspaper: "Whereas, we have by rebellion, war and misrepresentation of our desires and interests, by gambling politicians and incompetent men, who pragmatically usurped the power to manage our political affairs, been much injured; be it therefore, resolved, that we will no longer confide in men who voluntarily participated in said rebellion against the Union." (19) Caldwell was said to have erased so many names from the voters' list that he reduced the number to seven-himself, his son, two Irishmen, and three Negroes. With as many as four-fifths of the voters disqualified in some counties, resistance to the registration law mounted steadily.

Editors of the *Greenbrier Independent* declared on June 21, 1866 that they would oppose test oaths and the registration system. The principles of the Radical Party were an "antagonism to the best interests of the country and of mankind," and they hoped to "discuss these questions in a spirit of fairness and candor." In an editorial several months later, they offered their opinion of Dr. Caldwell: "Ever since the close of the war, he has labored to make himself particularly odious to all right-thinking and right-feeling men…If ever man was universally detested by his neighbors and fellow-countrymen, he is that man….Whenever he appears in public-which is quite often, for he is totally insensible to shame-he becomes the object of universal comment of the most disparaging character…." (20)

Former Confederates were also subject to a Confiscation law that allowed claimants-Union veterans and citizens-to seize by way of court mandate the property of some former Confederates, military and civilian. Numerous court actions were pursued in West Virginia seeking to seize real estate and other property under this act. Of course all of these additional hardships only increased animosity between the former adversaries, and delayed true reconciliation. Many of Greenbrier's Confederate veterans were unwilling to suffer minority rule quietly. Col. B.H. Jones, past commander of the 60th Virginia Infantry, addressed all "Sufferers and Sympathizers," in the *Greenbrier Independent*, August 16, 1866. Jones said he was collecting information for two books he planned to write concerning the treatment of Southern soldiers and citizens. "My object," he said, "is not to stir up the elements of bitterness between sections, but to present, for our own vindication, a candid and dispassionate statement of FACTS—WELL AUTHENTICATED FACTS. Simple justice requires that this should be done. Heretofore we have had *ex parte* history; it is high time we were heard."

Two months later the newspapers editors echoed the opinion of Col. Jones. They claimed that true peace was impossible without majority rule: "The idea that 1,600 men will tamely submit to the tyranny of 100 or 150 is preposterous....the government of this county, and this district, and this State, is a tyranny of the most insufferable character....The government of West Virginia...is one of the most offensive and oppressive despotisms upon the face of the earth....We can have nothing but bitter wrangling and strife, which will finally lead to bloodshed..." (21)

A large number of Confederate veterans with ties to Greenbrier County were tried by jury for acts committed during the war. Captain Thurmond and several of his former rangers were sued and acquitted. A young Confederate veteran by the name of Cavendish was tried for murder, having killed a man in battle, and was also acquitted. James S. Cassady, a Union veteran, sued Gen. Alfred Beckley of Raleigh County and Col. James W. Davis of Greenbrier, for horses taken by them in their capacity as militia officers during the war. Cassady won a judgment of $600.00 against the two men. That amount is equivalent to more than $12,000 in 2004. At the November 1867 term of the Monroe County court, A.T. Caperton was ordered to pay Nicholas Martin $600.00 for having him jailed during the war. In his capacity as provost marshall, Caperton accused Martin of aiding Federal forces on a raid into Monroe County, and ordered him imprisoned at Richmond. A similar case was heard against General A.A. Chapman, of the Confederate militia, for his wartime detention of Grandison Landcraft. (22)

The *Wheeling Intelligencer* declared on November 27, 1866 that Rebels and their sympathizers were intimidating and harassing Union citizens of Greenbrier and Monroe Counties. It claimed that Allen T. Caperton, Samuel Price, Colonel D.S. Hounshell, H.M. Mathews, and others, had been "fomenting a recusant spirit among the masses by all sorts of incendiary harangues and utterances, and seem determined to make the country too hot to hold a single Union man...." Two weeks later the *Intelligencer* reported that Gen. Grant had ordered a small detachment of Federal troops into Monroe County to "suppress the outbreaks," among Rebel citizens there.

The editors of the Lewisburg paper replied to that article, stating that the idea of Federal troops in Monroe and Greenbrier was "one of the grandest humbugs of this most humbugable age!" (23) Several months later Col. Hounshell reported that he was leaving West Virginia because of the state's hostility to ex-Confederates. The infant State had "extinguished civil liberty," and allowed "legislative, executive, and judicial corruption [to] exude from every pore." (24)

In his January 1867 address to the Legislature, West Virginia Governor Arthur I. Boreman reported that the condition of the State as a whole was "gratifying," but in areas where the population had "participated in the rebellion" there was much discontent and dissatisfaction. Referring to the Federal troops keeping watch over Monroe and Greenbrier, he said "they will remain, no doubt, until order and security are restored."

At Lewisburg, concern for proper burial of their Confederate dead resulted in formation of the Ladies' Memorial Association in 1867. This organization solicited donations and volunteers to assist in removing the bodies of numerous Confederate veterans from the Old Stone Church, and other burial sites, to one large graveyard at the edge of town. The local newspaper reported the work on June 6, 1867: "The removal of the remains of the Confederate dead, buried in the Presbyterian Graveyard, in this place, was commenced last week, under the auspices of the Ladies' Memorial Association. The bodies are being transferred to the Soldier's Cemetery, near town, and the work is under the supervision of Capt. J.W. Branham." The next issue of the paper reported that a total of 269 bodies had been reburied: "The removal of the remains...has been completed. Capt. Branham, under whose supervision the work was conducted, informs us that 269 bodies have been removed to the soldiers cemetery, near town, and that the following states are represented: Georgia, Mississippi, Tennessee, Kentucky and Virginia." (25)

Responding to public pressure, the Legislature relaxed application of test oaths for lawyers and teachers in 1868. When the Legislature ratified the Fifteenth Amendment to the Constitution on March 3, 1869, it tied enfranchisement of former Confederates to the granting of the vote to Negroes. The idea of granting the vote to West Virginia's black citizens, while denying it to thousands of ex-Confederates, gave rise to considerable acrimonious debate on the suffrage question in 1869.

Liberal and Radical Republicans alike eventually found it expedient to move toward restoration of the vote to former Confederates. On January 18, 1870, Governor William E. Stevenson urged removal of political disabilities against former Confederates. Three weeks later, the Legislature eliminated test oaths for teachers and attorneys. More significantly, it also approved the Flick Amendment, conferring the right to vote on all males over the age of 21. In the elections of 1870, the Democratic candidate for governor, John J. Jacob, defeated Gov. Stevenson by 2,010 votes. The resurgent Democrats also won a majority of two in the Senate and 24 in the House of Delegates. Democrats also replaced Republicans in the state's congressional seats.

When the new Legislature convened on January 17, 1871, it began the removal of all political disabilities against ex-Confederates. On April 17, voters overwhelmingly approved the Flick Amendment, 23,546 to 6,323. On January 16, 1872, a constitutional convention assembled at Charleston, with Samuel Price as its president. Substantial changes were made in the legislative and judicial branches of government, and on August 22, the people of West Virginia ratified the new constitution. The era was hailed by many as the true end to the Civil War in West Virginia.

Capt. A.W. Mann's Company Greenbrier Scouts

This company of Union scouts from Greenbrier County was authorized in July 1864 and officially enrolled December 1, 1864. At first muster the company consisted of 29 men. On April 10, 1865 Captain Mann reported his company as being 50 strong. Although the State of West Virginia designated this organization a Greenbrier company, just 11 men in the original muster were citizens of Greenbrier County. The counties of Allegheny, Bath, Bedford, Floyd, Nicholas, and Pocahontas were also represented. Several members of Mann's Scouts were men who had deserted Confederate service late in the war. Their previous service included the 8th, 14th, and 19th, Virginia Cavalry, and the 22nd Virginia Infantry. Captain Mann was paid $50 monthly which increased to $60 after his first 90 days. Privates received $13 monthly that increased to $16, and sergeants were paid between $15 and $20 monthly.

Using Camp Drennen, Nicholas County, as their headquarters, supplies were hauled to the men under contract with Samuel J. Grose, a citizen of Nicholas County, who was paid $5 daily for this service. For several weeks after the end of the war Mann's Scouts apparently operated as some type of police force. Captain Mann reported on May 12, 1865 that in the previous 30 days his men had recovered a number of stolen horses and killed two men who had been "notorious bushwhackers and horse thieves since before the war."

This company disbanded at the end of July 1865. On August 4, Captain Mann returned to the State of West Virginia 40 rifles and muskets, along with a quantity of belts and other equipment. On August 7, the State of West Virginia paid Captain Mann $2,806.54 which he promised to pay to the officers and men formerly enrolled in his company. In 1901 Benjamin F. Williams, a veteran of Mann's Scouts, applied for compensation from the West Virginia State Service Commission, claiming he did not receive the amount due him at the close of the war. This information was compiled from various records in the manuscript collections of the State of West Virginia, Charleston.

Mann, Andrew W. Capt. 31
Anderson, John W. Pvt. 18
Baker, H.C. Pvt. 20
Blume, H.M. Pvt. 23
Boggs, A.V. Pvt. 24
Boggs, E.P. Pvt. 20
Boggs, J.B. Pvt. 21
Boggs, W.L. Pvt. 17
Boggs, W.H. Sgt. 22
Clutter, Stuart Pvt. 29
Collins, George L. Pvt. 18
Cox, G.A. Pvt. 31
Cox, G.H. Pvt. 25
Cox, W.H. Pvt. n/a
Crookshanks, T.H. Pvt. 22
Cutlip, J.T. Pvt. 28
Cutlip, S. Pvt. 25
Cutlip, Sam Pvt. 26
Cutlip, Tom W. Pvt.
Daner, I. Pvt. 18
Dean, Joseph B. Pvt. 17
Dean, W.M. Pvt. 18
Dean, Wm. Pvt. 19
Fisher, Wm H. Pvt. 32
Foley, Patrick Pvt. 23
Ford, A. Pvt. 21
Goins, T.F. Pvt. 19
Hanna, S. Pvt. (Silas C.?) 18
Holmes, D.K. Pvt. 19
Holons, Dan K. 18
Humes, D. Pvt. 37
Kellison, R.M. Pvt. 18
Kincaid, George R. Pvt. 18
Knox, Hilman H. Pvt. 27
Long, A. Pvt. 18
Long, Napolean B. Pvt. 18
McCoy, Austin Pvt. 41
McKeever, A. Pvt. n/a
McKewen, Allen Pvt. 22
McLaughlin, George W. Pvt. 20
McMillion, Wm R. Pvt. 17
Mann, Newton A. Pvt. 25
Mathews, H. Pvt. 27
Nicely, Wm J. Pvt. 24
Preas, C.W. Pvt. 26
Rader, B.L. Pvt. 35
Rader, J.M. Pvt. 24
Rader, M.L. Pvt. 29
Rightsman, J.H. Pvt. 16
Shackleford, C.R. Pvt. 18
Taylor, Sam W. Pvt. 17
Walton, Joseph Pvt. 32
Walton, W.C. Sgt. 19
Williams, A. Pvt. 35
Williams, Benj. F. Pvt. 18
Williams, Joe Pvt. 18
Williams, I.B. Sgt. 20
Williams, James M. Pvt. 19
Williams, Sam H. Sgt. 27
Williams, W.I. Pvt. 19

Appendix A
General Lee and Traveller

Thomas L. Broun wrote from Charleston, West Virginia to the Richmond, Virginia *Dispatch* of August 10, 1886, in regard to Gen. Lee's favorite war-horse, traveler:

Traveler was raised by Mr. Johnson, near the Blue Sulphur Springs, in Greenbrier County, Va. (now West Virginia); was of the "Gray Eagle" stock and as a colt took the first premium under the name of "Jeff Davis" at the Lewisburg fairs for the years 1859 and 1860. He was four years old in the spring of 1861. When the Wise Legion was encamped on Sewell Mountains, opposing the advance of the Federal army under Rosecrans, in the fall of 1861, I was a major of the Third Regiment of Infantry in that legion, and my brother, Capt. Joseph M. Broun, was quarter-master of the same regiment. I authorized my brother to purchase a good, serviceable horse of the Greenbrier stock for our use during the war. After much inquiry and search, he came across the horse above mentioned, and I purchased him for $175 (good value) in the fall of 1861, of Capt. J.W. Johnson, son of the Mr. Johnson first above mentioned. When the Wise Legion was encamped about Meadow Bluff and Big Sewell Mountains I rode this horse, which was greatly admired in camp for his rapid and springy walk, his high spirit, cold carriage, and muscular strength. He neither needed whip nor spur, and would walk his five or six miles an hour over the rough mountain roads of Western Virginia with his rider sitting firmly in the saddle and holding him in check by a tight rein, such vim and eagerness did he manifest to go right ahead as he was mounted.

When Gen. Lee took command of the Wise Legion and Floyd Brigade, which were encamped at and near Sewell Mountains in the fall of 1861, he first saw this horse, and took a great fancy to it. He called it his colt, and said he would need it before the war was over. Whenever the General saw my brother on this horse he had something pleasant to say to him about "my colt" as he designated him.

As the winter approached, the climate in the West Virginia mountains caused Rosecrans' army to abandon its position on Big Sewell and retreat westward. Gen. Lee was thereupon ordered to South Carolina. The third Regiment of the Wise Legion was subsequently detached from the army in Western Virginia and ordered to the South Carolina Coast, where it was known as the Sixtieth Virginia Regiment, under Col. Starke. Upon seeing my brother on this horse, near Pocotaligo, in South Carolina, Gen. Lee at once recognized the horse, and again inquired of him pleasantly about "his" colt. My brother then offered him the horse as a gift, which the General promptly declined, and at the same time remarked: "If you will willingly sell me the horse, I will gladly use it for a week or so, to learn its qualities." Thereupon my brother had the horse sent to Gen. Lee's stable. In about a month the horse was returned to my brother, with a note from Gen. Lee stating that the animal suited him, but that he could not longer use so valuable a horse in such times unless it were his own; that if he (my brother) would not sell, please to keep the horse, with many thanks. This was in February, 1862. At that time I was in Virginia on the sick list, from a long and severe attack of camp-fever contracted in the campaign on Big Sewell Mountains. My brother wrote me of Gen. Lee's desire to have the horse, and asked me what he should do. I replied at once: "If he will not accept it, then sell it to him at what it cost me." He then sold the horse to Gen. Lee for $200 in currency, the sum of $25 having been added by Gen. Lee to the price I gave for the horse in September, 1861, to make up for the depreciation in our currency from September, 1861, to February, 1862.

In 1868 Gen. Lee wrote to my brother, stating that this horse had survived the war, was known as "Traveller" (spelling the word with a double "l," in good English style), and asking for its pedigree, which was obtained as above mentioned, and sent by my brother to Gen. Lee.

General Lee and Traveller in 1866. *Courtesy Washington and Lee University*

Above: Jefferson Street (Route 219 south) going into Lewisburg. The large home on the left (Dr. John Montgomery home) was known as the Withrow House during the Civil War. Robert E. Lee was a guest here on August 3, 1867. *Photo by author*

Right: Born into slavery, Frank Page helped raise Traveller at Blue Sulphur Springs. This article was published in *Confederate Veteran* magazine in 1909.

TRAINER OF TRAVELER—FRANK PAGE.

The readers of the VETERAN are just now especially interested in Traveler, General Lee's war horse. A history of him has been published several times, but the first man who ever rode him has not yet been mentioned. The photograph here presented is a good likeness of Frank Page, as he was known to the people of Lewisburg, W. Va., when he was performing the duties of janitor at the school building and bank. He was born in 1846 a slave, the property of Mr. A. D. Johnston, near Blue Sulphur Springs, Va. (now West Virginia); and when quite a lad, he broke the colt "Jeff" which afterwards became the favorite Traveler of General Lee. This servant handled horses with much skill, and "breaking the colts" was his business. So he came to have the honor of being the first rider of Jeff (Traveler), and trained him for exhibition at the Lewisburg Fair in 1860.

Mr. Alexander Johnston writes in regard to this matter: "I secured the inclosed photograph shortly before the death of Frank Page especially for the VETERAN. The mounting and placing in position of the bones of Traveler reminds me of delay in sending this picture. I am a son of the Mr. A. D. Johnston mentioned, and know the facts in the case."

In March last the Richmond Times-Dispatch said: "The bones of Traveler, General Lee's favorite war horse, will soon be properly mounted and the skeleton placed on exhibition, most likely in the proposed Lee Museum at Lexington."

In that same paper the statement was made that arrangements had been completed for shipping the bones of the famous horse to a natural science concern for proper mounting. It is understood that the structure will be skeleton, and that the bones have been so well preserved as to appear white when mounted.

APPENDIX B

CONFEDERATE VETERANS RESIDING IN GREENBRIER COUNTY

AS OF JUNE 1ST 1903

This list was compiled by D.R. Thomas of Bryan's Battery Virginia Artillery in 1903. The roster includes veterans who enlisted in Greenbrier or "other points" and "now reside" in Greenbrier County. If an entry is followed by the name of a city or state, that is the location from which that veteran moved to Greenbrier County.

Austin, Sam H. Dr. 22 Va Infantry
Ayers, David Lt. 59 Va Infantry
Arbuckle, Andrew Virginia Military Institute Cadet
Arbuckle, John Davis 14 Va Cavalry
Arbuckle, Pearis Colorado, 14 Va Cavalry
Arbuckle, Robert P. Craig County, Va 14 Va Cavalry
Arbuckle, James H. Gilmer County, 14 Va Cavalry
Arbuckle, John H. California, 14 Va Cavalry
Alderson, J. Coleman Wheeling, 14 Va Cavalry
Alderson, Sampson 60 Va Infantry
Argabrite, James M. 14 Va Cavalry
Anderson, John Pocahontas County,
Alexander, Stephen
Ayers, Henry C. "56 years old" 37 Battalion Va Cavalry
Arbaugh, James D.

Ayers, J.M.
Arbaugh, R.M. 36 Battalion Va Cavalry
Adwell, Robert "deserter" 14 Va Cavalry "now drawing U.S. pension"
Adwell, W.T. 26 Battalion Va Infantry
Allen, Isaac 30 Battalion Va Sharpshooters
Brown, James Texas, 14 Va Cavalry
Brown, John C. Rev. 60 Va Infantry
Brown, John H. 60 Va Infantry
Bird? Joseph (Curly) 14 Va Cavalry
Bright, Charles M. 14 Va Cavalry
Bright, James K. 14 Va Cavalry
Buster, Charles B. Lt. 60 Va Infantry
Branham, George W. Bryan's Battery Va Artillery
Bell, David Henderson 27 Va Infantry
Burr, Bollar Lt. 14 Va Cavalry
Burr, J. Austin 14 Va Cavalry "died April 20, 1908"
Buster, Alexis M. Capt. 60 Va Infantry
Burns, Marshall 14 Va Cavalry
Bennett, Campbell 22 Va Infantry
Beard, Abraham 14 Va Cavalry
Beard, Joseph 14 Va Cavalry
Brinkley, Andrew Bath County Reserves
Brant, Mason
Bransford, Silas 60 Va Infantry "died"
Bryan, C.P. Dr. Bath Squadron Cavalry
Blankenship, Joseph 22 Va Infantry
Brannaman, John M. 26 Battalion Va Infantry
Bryant, Thomas 22 Va Infantry
Bolton, J.W. 14 Va Cavalry
Boothe, Wm Wallace 16 Va Cavalry "1st cousin to J. Wilkes Boothe"
Boice, Robert "died"
Burdette, John Lt. 36 Battalion Va Cavalry
Baker, Napolean 22 Va Infantry
Barker, J.E. Mosby's Command
Brown, J.A. 26 Battalion Va Infantry
Bransford, Thomas H. 19 Va Cavalry

Burdette, Frank C. Capt. St. Louis, Missouri 26 Battalion Va Infantry
Bennett, Wm 23 Battalion Va Infantry
Bennett, A.M. 26 Battalion Va Infantry
Bennett, Noah 26 Battalion Va Infantry
Bostick, Robert 26 Battalion Va Infantry
Baker, J.H. 26 Battalion Va Infantry
Burns, Michael
Byrd, V.W. 14 Va Cavalry
Bivens, A.C. Houndshells Battalion
Burgess, H.W. 14 Va Cavalry
Boone, H.L. 26 Battalion Va Infantry
Campbell, Thomas H. 60 Va Infantry
Campbell, G.W. 26 Battalion Va Infantry
Creigh, Joseph A. 14 Va Cavalry
Creigh, Cyrus H. 14 Va Cavalry
Creigh, Charles A. Ladonia, Missouri 14 Va Cavalry
Creigh, Fred Missouri, 14 Va Cavalry
Caraway, John H. Lt. 14 Va Cavalry
Cunningham, James M. 24 Va Infantry
Cullen, John A. 27 Va Infantry
Callison, Elisha F. Pocahontas County, 27 Va Infantry
Cary, George W. 26 Battalion Va Infantry
Correll, Wm 14 Va Cavalry
Cohenhour, Mason
Callison, Isaac 27 Va Infantry
Clingman, Addison 26 Battalion Va Infantry
Cart, Thomas 60 Va Infantry
Cackley, Wm H. 19 Va Cavalry
Cabell, Henry Clay 22 Va Infantry
Conner, John A. 26 Battalion Va Infantry
Cackley, James 26 Battalion Va Infantry
Callwell, Henry C.
Coughlin, Cornelius
Coffman, W.T. Overbrook, Kansas, Houndshell's Battalion
Campbell, John
Cavenaugh, Patrick

Cook, Alexander 45 Va Infantry
Childress, Clark L. 26 Battalion Va Infantry
Crone, John D. Philip Thurmond's Rangers
Curry, A.C. Atchison County, Missouri 26 Battalion Va Infantry
Campbell, Thomas B. 26 Battalion Va Infantry
Crookshanks, F.M. 26 Battalion Va Infantry
Crookshanks, T.H. 14 Va Cavalry
Comer, Wm 22 Va Infantry
Curry, George W. 26 Battalion Va Infantry
Corcoran, Michael 26 Battalion Va Infantry
Cox, John George 14 Va Cavalry
Creigh, Thomas 14 Va Cavalry "dead"
Creigh, Lewis 60 Va Infantry "dead"
Creigh, Wm H. 60 Va Infantry "dead"
Curry, Wm Newton
Davis, James W. Col. 27 Va Infantry "died"
Davis, Charles L. 27 Va Infantry
Dolan, Mark Bryan's Battery Va Artillery
Dennis, Thomas H. 14 Va Cavalry
Donnally, Hugh Wilson 14 Va Cavalry
Dunn, Henry C. 59 Va Infantry "died July 2, 1904"
Dunn, John Robert Va Military Institute Cadet
Dotson, Andrew Jackson Capt. Doyles Company
Dunbar, N.A. Bryan's Battery Va Artillery
Dolan, James E. 2 Va Cavalry
Dolan, Robert 2 Va Cavalry
Dolan, Lindsay C. Houndshell's Battalion
Duncan, Fleming
Dickson, Wm H. 14 Va Cavalry
Dickson, John
Dickson, Charles D. Chapman's Battery Va Artillery
Dickson, Henry Frazer 22 Va Infantry
Deshons, J.H. Dr. 14 Va Cavalry
Duncan, John Summers County, Thurmond's Rangers
Duncan, George Summers County, Thurmond's Rangers
Dawson, John 60 Va Infantry
Dotson, John D. 60 Va Infantry

Dameron, Charles L. Rev. 60 Va Infantry
Dysard, A.K. Pocahontas County, 26 Battalion Va Infantry
Dearing, Mason 60 Va Infantry
Davis, Lewellyn Capt. Amick's Company
Dean, John B. 14 Va Cavalry
Deal, R.L. Company C
Davis, Wm A. 26 Battalion Va Infantry
Dolan, Asbury Houndshell's Battalion
Dillion, Wm 26 Battalion Va Infantry "drummer"
Edgar, George M. Col. 26 Battalion Va Infantry
Edgar, A.M. 27 Va Infantry
Evans, Lewis S. 22 Va Infantry
Easter, Johnston 14 Va Cavalry
Easter, Charles 14 Va Cavalry
Erskine, G.W. 22 Va Infantry
Erwin, J.F. Caldwell County, Missouri 26 Battalion Va Infantry
Erwin, J.R. Caldwell County, Missouri 26 Battalion Va Infantry
Erwin, R.F. Atchison County, Missouri 26 Battalion Va Infantry
Erwin, Richard Dickson 26 Battalion Va Infantry
Elkins, E.C. 14 Va Cavalry
Fleshman, Thomas 22 Va Infantry "fifer"
Fleshman, Buoy 14 Va Cavalry
Fleshman, John Andy 14 Va Cavalry
Fleshman, Moses 60 Va Infantry
Fleshman, Charles H. Missouri, 60 Va Infantry
Frazier, Franklin M. Alabama, 14 Va Cavalry
Feamster, Thomas L. Lt. 14 Va Cavalry
Feamster, S.W. Newman Lt. 14 Va Cavalry
Feamster, Joseph A. 14 Va Cavalry
Feamster, John A. Lt. 14 Va Cavalry
Feamster, Wm A. Houndshell's Battalion
Feamster, John Fox
Foglesong, David Harvey 36 Battalion Va Cavalry
Freeman, W.L. Derrick's Battalion
Farrier, Martin P. 28 Va Infantry
Fisher, Christopher
Fisher, D.F. Ashby's Cavalry and 17 Va Infantry

Fox, George W. Missouri, 60 Va Infantry
Ford, Renick 60 Va Infantry
Fell, John P. 14 Va Cavalry
Fell, James 14 Va Cavalry
Falls, T.J. Anderson's Battery Botetourt Artillery
Fifer, Abraham 36 Battalion Va Infantry
Fifer, John 36 Battalion Va Infantry
Graham, Archibald Capt. Rockbridge Artillery
Graves, John W. Bryan's Battery Va Artillery
Gillilan, Charles W. 14 Va Cavalry
Gee, Robert W. 14 Va Cavalry
Gee, Joseph 60 Va Infantry
Gillispie, John
Gillispie, Wm
Gillispie, James
Gabbert, John L. 14 Va Cavalry
Gabbert, John T. 14 Va Cavalry
Gearing, John F.
George, Wm 36 Battalion Va Cavalry
George, John F. 22 Va Infantry
George, John A. 26 Battalion Va Infantry
George, Thomas Allen
Gwinn, Harrison 26 Va Infantry
Gwinn, Marion
Grimes, Wm S. Iowa, 26 Battalion Va Infantry
Grove, Alexander Chapman's Battery Va Artillery
Garing, Theodore 60 Va Infantry
Godwin, Thomas
Garten, Ed D. Capt. Wood's Albermale Cavalry "died Oct. 14, 1904"
Gibson, Thomas M. Laclide County, Missouri 26 Battalion Va Infantry
Gilbert, Charles L. 14 Va Cavalry
Gilbert, Arthur Lewis 14 Va Cavalry
Green, Zach 11 Va Cavalry
Groves, A.H. Chapman's Battery Va Artillery
Hunter, Henry F.

Handley, Alexander G. Capt. 22 Va Infantry
Handley, John A. 14 Va Cavalry
Hays, Christopher 14 Va Cavalry
Hays, John Sgt. 60 Va Infantry
Hays, Abe 14 Va Cavalry
Hunter, John H. Jackson's Battery 13 Battalion Va Artillery
Harris, John W. 19th Va Infantry
Harvest, Erasmus 26 Va Infantry
Hinkle, Richard M. 60 Va Infantry
Hinkle, Amos 60 Va Infantry
Holley, John 14 Va Cavalry
Honaker, Sty 26 Battalion Va Infantry
Hopper, Hanson W. 17 Va Infantry Pickett's Division
Hume, W.H.H. 14 Va Cavalry
Humphreys, Milton W. Sgt. Bryan's Battery Va Artillery
Humphrey's Mathew 22 Va Infantry
Humphreys, John M. 14 Va Cavalry
Humphreys, Alexander R. Lt. California, 26 Battalion Va Infantry
Humphreys, Robert R. 26 Battalion Va Infantry
Humphreys, M.N. 26 Battalion Va Infantry "drummer"
Hefner, R.H. 26 Battalion Va Infantry
Hefner, Alexander 26 Battalion Va Infantry
Hicks, Wm
Hefner, Rufus 26 Battalion Va Infantry
Hefner, Daniel Capt. 26 Battalion Va Infantry
Hannah, Samuel 14 Va Cavalry
Hannah, Clark 14 Va Cavalry
Hannah, Harvey 14 Va Cavalry
Hodson, H. Reese Florida, 26 Battalion Va Infantry
Hefner, Jacob Pocahontas County, 26 Battalion Va Infantry
Hefner, Lantz Z. 26 Battalion Va Infantry
Hull, Surber 26 Battalion Va Infantry
Holcomb, George 22 Va Infantry
Hoke, James H. Chapman's Battery Va Artillery
Henning, George W. 22 Va Infantry
Henning, Mason M. 22 Va Infantry
Hull, Crawford 60 Va Infantry

Hoylman, R.B. 26 Battalion Va Infantry
Hoylman, John H. 26 Battalion Va Infantry
Huddleston, D.Y.
Hull, J.S. 26 Battalion Va Infantry
Huffman, E.E.
Huffman, S.R. Thurmond's Rangers
Hartsook, John F. 14 Va Cavalry
Holley, Joel Independent Battalion
Hall, James B. 59 Va Infantry
Hall, T.A. 27 Va Infantry
Harvey, E.A. Verona, Missouri 26 Battalion Va Infantry
Harvey, Ellwood A. 36 Battalion Va Infantry "died Missouri, March 31, 1916"
Higginbotham, R.T. Lt. 22 Va Cavalry
Humphrey, C.W. 26 Battalion Va Infantry
Hillary, R.I. 25 Va Infantry
Haines, H.W. Houndshell's Battalion
Johnston, James W. Capt. 60 Va Infantry "raised Traveller, Gen. Lee's war-horse"
Johnston, John D. 26 Battalion Va Infantry
Johnston, Alexander A. 14 Va Cavalry
Johnson, Wm H. (peach) 14 Va Cavalry "died April 17, 1904 aged 70 years"
Johnson, M. Arbuckle 14 Va Cavalry
Johnson, John K. Highland County, 14 Va Cavalry
Johnston, Wm R. 14 Va Cavalry
Johnson, Green
Jack, Wm
Jackson, Andrew (Stonewall) 26 Battalion Va Infantry
Jameson, David 14 Va Cavalry "died April 4, 1904"
Jameson, Mason 14 Va Cavalry
Jarrett, Leonard 14 Va Cavalry
Jeffries, W.T. Houndshell's Battalion
Jones, David 26 Battalion Va Infantry
Jones, Caperton 14 Va Cavalry
Knight, James 14 Va Cavalry
Kirkpatrick, Thomas H. Lt. 26 Battalion Va Inf

Kirkpatrick, John 26 Battalion Va Infantry
Kirkpatrick, Wm Cpl. 26 Battalion Va Infantry
Kirkpatrick, F.H. 26 Battalion Va Infantry
Kincaid, George A. 26 Battalion Va Infantry
Kincaid, A.B.
Knapp, Charles Stuart 26 Battalion Va Infantry
Knapp, Joseph
Knapp, Samuel
Knapp, Charles
Kershner, James M.
Kershner, G.W. Ohio, 60 Va Infantry
Kershner, Roy 14 Va Cavalry
Kelly, John 14 Va Cavalry
King, Allen W. 22 Va Infantry
King, C.P. 26 Battalion Va Infantry
Keetley, J.H. 26 Battalion Va Infantry
Kerns, Robert 19 Va Infantry
Larue, Isaac H. Capt. 60 Va Infantry "died Sept. 29, 1904 near Pulaski, Va."
Lewis, C.I. Dr. Lt.Col. 8 Va Cavalry
Lewis, Thomas C. 60 Va Infantry
Lewis, John
Lewis, Clarke 22 Va Infantry
Ludington, Cavendish 14 Va Cavalry
Lipps, Joseph 22 Va Infantry
Lipps, Archibald 22 Va Infantry
Legg, John W. 14 Va Cavalry
Labban, John G.
Livesay, Jan 60 Va Infantry
Livesay, Washington 60 Va Infantry
Livesay, Robert F. 60 Va Infantry
Livesay, George W. 60 Va Infantry
Lowe, Wm P. Dr. Capt. Phil Snyder's Company Independent
Loudermilk, George 27 Va Infantry
Loudermilk, Wm F. 60 Va Infantry
Loudermilk, Hans 60 Va Infantry
Loudermilk, Josiah 22 Va Infantry

Loudermilk, David 22 Va Infantry
Loudermilk, Wm 26 Battalion Va Infantry
Landrum, Lewis 60 Va Infantry
Lemons, Houston 22 Va Infantry
Mastin, John A. Kansas, 22 Va Infantry
Masters, Wm 60 Va Infantry
Masters, George W. 26 Battalion Va Infantry
Mays, Jonathan Lt. 60 Va Infantry
Mathews, Alexander F.
Mathews, Joseph Wm Capt. 25 Va Infantry
Mathews, Henry Mason
Miles, Erastus 14 Va Cavalry
Miles, Tip 14 Va Cavalry
Miles, Reubin 14 Va Cavalry
Miles, John T. Thurmond's Rangers
McClung, Alpheus Pearis Capt. 14 Va Cavalry
McClung, Charles W. (Fox) 14 Va Cavalry
McClung, Thomas W. Va Military Institute Cadet
McClung, John A. (Hosey) 14 Va Cavalry
McClung, Wm (Grasshopper) 14 Va Cavalry
McClung, A.C. (Gus) 14 Va Cavalry
McClung, Wm H. Dr. 14 Va Cavalry
McClung, Steele 14 Va Cavalry
McClung, Joseph 14 Va Cavalry
McClung, John T. 14 Va Cavalry
McClung, Joe Bob 14 Va Cavalry
McClung, Wm Texas, 14 Va Cavalry
McClung, W.W. Houndshell's Battalion
McClung, Joseph A. 60 Va Infantry
McClung, Cyrus H. 14 Va Cavalry
Miller, T.J. Bryan's Battery Va Artillery
Miller, A.P. 27 Va Infantry
McDermott, James 26 Battalion Va Infantry
McClintic, Steele 60 Va Infantry
McDowell, Robert D. Bryan's Battery Va Artillery
McDowell, J. Washington Lt. 26 Battalion Va Infantry
McDowell, J. Wm 26 Battalion Va Infantry "drummer"

McKendree, George W. Major
McMillion, Robert Kansas,
McMillion, Nathan Georgia,
McMillion, James 60 Va Infantry
McCoy, James C. 14 Va Cavalry
McCoy, Wm 14 Va Cavalry
Martin, James E. "dead"
Martin, Thomas M. 14 Va Cavalry
Martin, Robert Monroe County, 14 Va Cavalry
Martin, Joseph Summers County, 22 Va Infantry
Munford, John 26 Battalion Va Infantry
Marrs, B.D. 29 Va Infantry
Morris, George H. 22 Va Infantry
McKorkle, Wm
Moorehead, Charles 60 Va Infantry
McNeer, John Thurmond's Rangers
Mansfield, Richard G. 26 Battalion Va Cavalry
May, Sam H. 26 Battalion Va Infantry
Mahan, L.A. Sgt. 60 Va Infantry
Mann, Wm H. 26 Battalion Va Infantry
McLaughlin, Andrew M. 18 Va Cavalry
McCleary, James 14 Va Cavalry
Morgan, G.C. 7 South Carolina Cavalry "56 years old"
Morgan, Albert 26 Battalion Va Infantry
Morgan, Charles M. 26 Battalion Va Infantry
Morgan, Joseph 26 Battalion Va Infantry
Morgan, E.H. 26 Battalion Va Infantry
Massie, Andrew 26 Battalion Va Infantry
Massie, Reuben 26 Battalion Va Infantry
Massie, Granville 26 Battalion Va Infantry
Neal, James H. 14 Va Cavalry
Nicholas, Michael 60 Va Infantry
Neal, John Felix 22 Va Infantry "died Nov. 8, 1905"
Nesmith, Wm H. 26 Battalion and 27 Va Infantry
Neff, J.W. 26 Battalion Va Infantry
Osborne, Wm A. 14 Va Cavalry
Osborne, Josephus

Preston, Walter Creigh Charlottesville Battery
Preston, John A. 14 Va Cavalry "56 years old"
Pollock, Wm 14 Va Cavalry
Pollock, Samuel 14 Va Cavalry
Pollock, Frank Sgt. 14 Va Cavalry
Patton, Edward 14 Va Cavalry
Patton, James M. 14 Va Cavalry
Peyton, Charles S. Lt. Col. 19 Va Infantry
Peyton, Lilburn S. 14 Va Cavalry
Parker, Preston Bryan's Battery Va Artillery
Pulliam, A. Dudley Lt. 60 Va Infantry
Pulliam, Thomas 60 Va Infantry
Piercy, Andrew Lt. Col. 1st Battalion Mississippi Cavalry
Price, J. Washington 60 Va Infantry
Price, John M. Sgt. Major 26 Battalion Va Infantry
Price, Robert A. Houndshell's Battalion
Perkins, Zebediah 26 Battalion Va Infantry
Perkins, Joseph A. Blue Sulphur Springs, 26 Battalion Va Infantry
Perkins, Joseph Pocahontas County,
Perry, John F. 26 Battalion Va Infantry
Perry, Wm G. 36 Battalion Va Cavalry
Pickering, John 10 Va Cavalry
Pickering, Reuben
Patterson, Thomas 1st Louisiana Infantry "gardener White S. Springs"
Rader, Archibald Hutchinson 60 Va Infantry
Raymond, E.F. Dr. 13 Battalion Va Artillery
Rutherford, John W. Kemper's Brigade Infantry
Riffe, Campbell B. 19 Va Cavalry
Relahan, Michael 27 Va Infantry
Rodgers, Nathan 14 Va Cavalry
Rodgers, J.W. 20 Va Cavalry
Rodgers, A.A. 26 Battalion Va Infantry
Rodgers, M.W. 26 Battalion Va Infantry
Rausbarger, Silas W. 14 Va Cavalry
Reynolds, Johnston California, orderly, 14 Va Cavalry
Reynolds, F.S. 36 Va Infantry

Richardson, James 60 Va Infantry
Reid, John P.
Rucker, Anderson
Ramsey, R.W. 26 Battalion Va Infantry
Rippetoe, J.J. 22 Va Infantry
Redfem, Charles 27 Va Infantry
Renick, Calvin B. 14 Va Cavalry
Robison, J.F. 26 Battalion Va Infantry
Robinson, Robert 36 Battalion Va Infantry
Robinson, Wm Phil Snyder's Independent Company
Sammons, W. Harvey 14 Va Cavalry
Sammons, A.A. Chapman's Battery Va Artillery
Sammons, Charles Jameson, Missouri 14 Va Cavalry
Scott, John 14 Va Cavalry
Scott, Rankin 14 Va Cavalry
Scott, Lanty K. 26 Battalion Va Infantry
Scott, Wm A. 26 Battalion Va Infantry
Scott, J.A. 26 Battalion Va Infantry
Suttle, James H. 14 Va Cavalry
Surber, Joseph 14 Va Cavalry
Skaggs, James M. 14 Va Cavalry
Skaggs, E. Clowney 14 Va Cavalry
Stuart, Wm R. 14 Va Cavalry
Stuart, Charles A. 14 Va Cavalry
Stuart, M.J. 26 Battalion Va Infantry
Strealy, Abraham H. 27 Va Infantry
Scudder, Fulton 26 Battalion Va Infantry
Snyder, Clinton 26 Battalion Va Infantry
Sullivan, John
Shaver, Wm 22 Va Infantry "fifer"
Squires, L.W. 19 Va Cavalry
Spencer, Wm 60 Va Infantry
Sharp, Joseph 14 Va Cavalry
Seward, Eli 22 Va Infantry
Sevy, George A. 26 Battalion Va Infantry
Sevy, Henry H. 26 Battalion Va Infantry
Syme, Samuel A.M.

Syme, Bernard C.
Simmons, John 60 Va Infantry
Sheppard, E.M. 60 Va Infantry
Sevy, A.R. Derrick's Battalion
Smith, Cyrus 60 Va Infantry
Smith, Wm M. 26 Battalion Va Infantry
Stevens, John Chapman's Battery Va Artillery
Smith, Wm M. 14 Va Cavalry
Smith, Thomas W. 14 Va Cavalry
Smith, G.E. 14 Va Cavalry
Smith, Charles T. 14 Va Cavalry
Stalnaker, D. Edward 27 Va Infantry
Stalnaker, A.G. Dr. 27 Va Infantry
Stalnaker, Randolph Jr. 27 Va Infantry
Stalnaker, John Wisconsin, 14 Va Cavalry
Sevy, Aaron R. 26 Battalion Va Infantry
Spitzer, Wm Irish Battalion Va Infantry
Stone, James M. 26 Battalion Va Infantry
Stevenson, Thomas T. 14 Va Cavalry
Sydenstricker, Isaac C. Marshall, Missouri 26 Battalion Va Infantry
Sydenstricker, Christopher C. Rev. 26 Battalion Va Infantry
Seldomridge, S.H.
Taylor, John W. (Trout)
Taylor, W.H. 24 Va Infantry "Irish Corner, died Dec. 4, 1906 color bearer"
Taylor, Charles R. 25 Va Infantry
Tyree, Sam F. 22 Va Infantry
Tuckwiller, John 60 Va Infantry
Thompson, D.J. 14 Va Cavalry
Thompson, Charles Roanoke, Va 14 Va Cavalry
Thompson, Isaac
Thompson, John W. 36 Battalion Va Infantry
Thompson, James 60 Va Infantry
Thompson, John B. Sgt. 26 Battalion Va Infantry
Thomas, James W. 22 Va Infantry
Thomas, G. Wash Bryan's Battery Va Artillery "died July 26, 1908"
Thomas, David Richard 14 Va Cavalry

Toothman, Charles A. 26 Battalion Va Infantry
Toothman, M.N. 14 Va Cavalry
Turner, S.H. 27 Va Infantry
Tinder, E.A. 6 Va Cavalry
Tritt, Isaac Thurmond's Rangers
Tigrette, J.W. 30 Battalion Va Sharpshooters
Vance, J.R. Chapman's Battery Va Artillery
Vineyard, Robert Gilmer County, 14 Va Cavalry
Woodard, Robert 14 Va Cavalry
Withrow, Edgar Dangerfield 14 Va Cavalry
Walkup, James 14 Va Cavalry
Walkup, Joseph A. 14 Va Cavalry
Walkup, Christopher R. 14 Va Cavalry
Walkup, W.H. Lt. 14 Va Cavalry
Walkup, Marshall 26 Battalion Va Infantry
Woods, John G. Indian Territory, 14 Va Cavalry
Woodson, Henry Col'd [colored?] (See)
Williams, George W. Bryan's Battery Va Artillery
Williams, Wm
Wilson, A.J.
Weakly, L.D. 10 Va Infantry "died April 19, 1908"
Womack, W.W. 60 Va Infantry
Woodard, W.L. Jr. Lt. Missouri, 60 Va Infantry
White, Richard D. 26 Battalion Va Infantry
White, Wm H. 26 Battalion Va Infantry
White, Harvey M. Anthony's Creek
Wade, Charles H. 26 Battalion Va Infantry
Wall, J.R. 45 North Carolina Infantry
Wyatt, W.H. 22 Va Infantry
Wickline, J.S. Rev. 26 Battalion Va Infantry
Watts, W.C. 14 Va Cavalry
Watts, C.C. 43 Battalion Va Cavalry Mosby's
Welch, Sam T. Sgt. 26 Battalion Va Infantry
Wilfong, John 31 Va Infantry
Wiley, P.B. 26 Battalion Va Infantry
West, Thomas I. 27 Va Infantry
Woddell, Thomas C. 11 Va Cavalry

Watson, James W. 26 Battalion Va Infantry
Wood, Wm D. 36 Va Infantry
Wickline, Jonathan 36 Va Infantry
Wheeler, Vincent W. 51 Va Infantry
Zimmerman, Wm 19 Va Cavalry

Courtesy, West Virginia and Regional History Collection, West Virginia University, Roy B. Cook papers.

D.R. Thomas, veteran of Bryan's Battery Virginia Artillery and compiler of the 1903 Greenbrier Confederate roster. *Courtesy Greenbrier County Historical Society*

APPENDIX C
THE BATTLE OF DRY CREEK

The following reminiscences of the Battle of White Sulphur Springs were written by Noyes Rand, and published in the *Monroe Watchman*, July 8, 1909. This is an abridged version of his original article.

In the closing days of August, or to be more exact, about the 23rd, grapevine messages began pouring into the District headquarters, then at Lewisburg, Va., to the effect that Averill, with a large force of cavalry and artillery, was advancing from the northwest, to raid the Virginia & Tennessee RR., which was one of the chief arteries for supplying the army of General Lee. To intercept and check this raid was of utmost importance to our cause, and the only troops relied upon for this important work consisted of the 22 and 45 Va. Vol. Infantry regiments; Edgar's, Darrick's, and Dunn's battalions of Infantry; Chapman's battery of Artillery, and a few companies, not exceeding four of the 8 Va. Cavalry.

Thurmond's and Halstead's Independent companies were scouting in the far off mountain wilds, but not available for a pitched battle, though rendering us good service as scouts. The force was certainly inadequate for the demands upon it, as in such a large scope of country, and with several avenues available to the enemy, two or three regiments of cavalry would have been requisite as a safe and proper advanced guard. To know for sure the road the enemy would take, and be prepared to meet him on favorable ground was the momentous question with our commanding officer. On the evening of the 25, and on a "grapevine telegram", the command made a forced march up Anthony Creek some fifteen miles, only to countermarch back towards Dry Creek (on another such telegram) and as rapidly as possible, and approached on the main pike leading over the Alleghenies, and on to the Ohio River called the James River and Kanawha Turnpike.

Skirmishing began at once. It was early in the morning, the enemy having formed his line of battle before our troops could get into line from their forced march during the previous night. Our line of battle was practically formed under a sharp fire of artillery and dismounted cavalry; but once formed, it was like a… "stone wall" of men and guns, which every effort of the enemy failed to break through or remove, though charge after charge was made to break through on every section of our line.

The battalion of gallant Edgar was in possession across the main pike except one company detached as skirmishers and on the hills to our right. Here it was that the enemy made a dashing charge with cavalry, only to meet a disastrous repulse by Edgar's brave men. The Commanding General (Patton) and his staff were at that juncture on the elevated ground to the right of the pike, as our army faced where a good view of the whole line could be had, and when Edgar's men had so handsomely repulsed this desperate charge of cavalry, Colonel Patton, exclaimed, "Glorious! Hurrah for the gallant Edgar!" and asked for someone of his staff to carry his compliments and thanks to Colonel Edgar and his men. Naturally, as Chief of Staff I started on this mission, but at the earnest solicitation of Colonel Hounshell, who was that day, acting as a voluntary aide de camp, he was permitted to convey the message, and rode deliberately across and towards the line of fire in a diagonal direction, as if on a dress parade. Edgar stood up to receive Hounshell's message, which was delivered with all the deliberation, peculiar to the man, as all who knew him were aware of the fact that he knew no fear. This scene occurred under a severe fire from the enemy, and none of us of the staff envied Edgar the ordeal of receiving a set speech under a rain of bullets.

The struggle continued all of the 26, and until the afternoon of the 27, when the enemy retreated, and we started in pursuit only to find we could make no headway, because of the mass of trees which were felled across the pike immediately behind Averill's rear guard. Evidently Averill's pioneer corps had been hard at work four hours before he began his retreat, in cutting great trees to such a point that one or two more strokes of the axe would cause them to fall across the pike, and the moment his rear guard passed, down they were thrown to impede our troops in the pursuit; and this object, it surely did accomplish to perfection. We soon found the utter futility of attempting to pursue cavalry with infantry, though such infantry as ours, which was known as "foot cavalry", from the rapidity of their marching, and the long stretches covered in an almost incredible space of time....Yet braver men never breathed the breath of life, and not even Sparta furnished their superiors. Scantily clad, badly shot, and scarcely ever with enough to eat, and that too, of the commonest and plainest food. History furnishes no parallel except possibly that of their Revolutionary ancestors in the war which gained our independence to the cheerful endurance of these privates of the Confederate Army....To Chapman's Battery, however, must be given the credit of holding back the enemy long enough to enable us to force our line of battle and perfect its alignment.

Two companies of the meager force of the 8 Cavalry were dismounted and took position in the Infantry line, and every man of all our forces acted the hero. Hence any one arrogating for himself special heroism is an egotist and unworthy of credence. The brave are the modest almost invariably.

In our short rush of pursuit we found a brass gun left by the enemy, which had been struck by one of our solid shot or shells square in the muzzle and put entirely "out of service". Next, we came to a small cottage situated on the sloping hillside below the pike, which had been used as the enemy's Field Hospital. The lower side of his cottage rested on posts about six or seven feet high to bring the floor level with the pike, and under the windows of same were great piles of amputated arms and legs, thrown out by the surgeons of the enemy in their rapid work. I, personally, saw several legs with the trousers and shoes or boots still on them, the surgeons evidently having no time to remove clothing before operating.

After pursuing the enemy a few miles and seeing the futility of endeavoring further pursuit over a road which their pioneers had so thoroughly blockaded, we were countermarched to the field of battle for a short rest, and to count up casualties, which were not a few, for our small force, and considerably more on the part of the enemy.

In this battle, the gallant Lieutenant Gay Carr, of the "Kanawha Riflemen", or Co. H. 22 Va., fell with a ball through his brain, and to whose memory I learn, a monument has been erected, either on the field where he laid down his life, or somewhere in the near vicinity, or it may be at Lewisburg, which was the "War Home" of the 22, Va. Regt., and where were many other brave and gallant men who fell victims of death on this severely contested field and whose memories deserve the richest plaudits of tongue and pen.

But after the lapse of forty-five years, and a wild pioneer life of much and thrilling excitement among the Indians, Mexicans, and Rustlers, or "bad men" of the far western border, my memory fails to recall their names though the best emotions of my heart go out to their memories, as well as to our surviving comrades.

So far as I am advised no one has ever written a detailed account of this glorious battle of Dry Creek, and I have appealed to Colonel Edgar to do this service for the benefit of our children and their descendants as well as those of us who were participants and yet living, and have written the foregoing reminiscences to submit to him for use as he may see fit in preparing his article. No man is better fitted for this work than he, and it is my earnest and sincere hope that he will do it in time for use at the Reunion on the old Battle Field on August 26 next. I am indebted to Captain and Comrade J.G. Stevens of Alderson, W. Va. For data which brought back to memory's tablet incidents connected with the Dry Creek Fight, which had almost become obliterated by time and the passing through such stirring events, in the "wild and woolly West", that served to cloud the characters engraved upon it in the long ago, when we were all faithful and true comrades in a glorious – even if lost cause.

My heart goes out to every comrade who participated in the Dry Creek Battle as if he was truly bound to me by closer ties than those of mere comradeship in arms; and this sentiment increases in strength as the years glide by, and our ranks are reduced to comparatively a limited few. And I also have a feeling of kindness, which I cannot describe in words, to all of those of our gallant foes, who contended so bravely and faithfully and desperately against us on that momentous occasion; and I trust that many of them will grace the Reunion with their presence, being assured in advance that the old-time hospitality of their Southern foes, then, Brothers, now, will be extended to them from a full heart and with a free hand.

It is almost an invariable fault with those attempting to give an accurate account of battles in which they were participants, to indulge too lavishly in the "Ego" to meet the requirements of exact history, and it is only natural that it should be the case. I have endeavored to evade this error in these recollections, and trust I have in great measure succeeded – though at the loss of some personal experience in the battle, which I know would interest my old comrades, but such must be left to the camp fire talks and swapping of reminiscences.

However, even at the risk of the charge of self laudation, where every man did his duty well, if not better than myself, I feel constrained to give one item of personal experience which was only known to a limited few of my associates in the army, including the members of our Staff and Colonel Patton (our brave and noble commander). Possibly the ludicrous in this event may shield me from unjust criticism from my surviving comrades, and this is all I care for, as I am not catering to the general public and hence am careless of its opinion.

At one point in the battle the writer was the victim of an amusing though somewhat rough personal experience. From the Commanding Officer's position at this juncture in the rear of our right center, it was necessary to carry an order to the extreme left flank of our line, and to do this I was compelled to ride diagonally across and towards the enemy's fire. Just as my horse was jumping a low tail fence in my route a shell from the enemy burst under him and he fell on his belly pitching me about ten feet in front of his head, where I landed on all fours. I thought of course he was killed outright, but as the order was very important, and I found I had no bones broken, I never stopped to even look at my horse but proceeded as fast as I could run on foot. On returning I found my horse grazing as if no battle was raging, and remounted and returned to my place with the staff. The horse had evidently struck his feet on the top fence rail at the very moment the shell burst under him, and so gave me a tumble. He was unhurt, but strange to say, I found on examination several bullets in my saddle, - when received God only knows, but one bullet went through my coat from side to side, leaving the back of my vest torn one side to the other, and another that tore the top of my right shoe and lodged midway in the wood stirrup. I trust I will be pardoned for mentioning this personal incident out of several which fell to my lot in those two days of constant and severe firing, the severity of which may be partially estimated when Averill's statement is considered, to the effect that his troops had to retreat from having exhausted his supply of ammunition to only a round or two to the man and none for his artillery.

The artillery contest was extraordinarily severe and at very close range. So also was the case with the firing of the men on both sides on the battle lines. Averill fought his men as infantry, they being dismounted, their horses left under guard beyond the line of fire in his rear. The same tactics were used by two of the companies of the 8 cavalry on our side. The cavalry charge on Edgar's battalion was made by men specially designated by Averill for the purpose, and who remounted in order to make same.

On that memorable occasion (speaking only to those surviving it), the writer only did his duty as he saw it (as did all his comrades faithfully and conscientiously do theirs), although possibly not so effectually as did some of his fellow officers, only to this extent, and on this account, does he crave the kind remembrance of his comrades. With all of us who participated in the Dry Creek Battle, the end is not far off for the final sound of "Taps". May it be well with us to march to another field of action.

To both comrades and erstwhile foes, a God Bless You for one and all, and good bye.

Noyes Rand,

Adj't 22 Va. Vol. Infantry, Acting A. A. F. of Confederate Forces at Battle of Dry Creek, August 26 & 27, 1863.

Noyes Rand, Adjutant of the 22nd Virginia Infantry. *Courtesy Greenbrier County Historical Society*

CHAPTER ONE NOTES

1. From Order Book of the Greenbrier County Court, 1861. Copy in the Greenbrier County Courthouse, Lewisburg.

2. James I. Robertson, ed., *Proceedings of the Advisory Council of the State of Virginia, April 21—June 19, 1861* (Richmond, Va.: Virginia State Library) p. 56, and p. 123.

3. United States War Department, *War of the Rebellion: A Compilation of the Official Records of the Union and Confederate Armies,* 70 vols. in 128 books, (Washington: Government Printing Office, 1881-1901), Series 1, Vol. 2, p. 808 and Vol. 51 Pt. 2, p. 76

4. Rose W. Fry, *Recollections of the Rev. John McElhenney, D.D.* (Richmond, Va.: Whittet & Shepperson, 1893), p. 170.

5. Official Records, Vol. 2, p. 633.

6. Fry, *Recollections of the Rev. John McElhenney,* p. 170-171.

7. Letters of Andrew Cook, 27th Virginia Infantry, in the possession of Mr. & Mrs. Lewis Crawford, Rupert, WV., letters of May 18, May 19, and May 21, 1861.

8. Lewisburg *Weekly Era,* May 25, 1861.

9. Cook letters, 27th Virginia Infantry, May, 26, 1861.

10. Robertson, ed., *Proceedings of the Advisory Council,* p. 123 and p. 128

11. Cook letters, May 31,1861.

12. Fry, *Recollections of the Rev. John McElhenney,* p. 176-177.

13. Greenbrier County Court Order Book, May 27, 1861.

14. "Diary of S.R. Houston," in Oren F. Morton, *A History of Monroe County, West Virginia* (Staunton, Va.: McClure Company, 1916; Baltimore: Regional Publishing Company, 1974) p. 170-171.

15. Official Records, Vol. 2, p. 906-909.

16. Ibid., p. 918-919.

17. Otis K. Rice, *A History of Greenbrier County,* (Parsons, WV McClain Publishing Co. 1986), p. 245.

18. Beuhring H. Jones, "My First Thirty Days Experience as a Captain" *Southern Literary Messenger,* Vol. 37, No. 2, 1863.

19. J.H. Cochran letter, June 17, 1861 manuscript collections of Virginia Tech, Blacksburg, Va.

20. Official Records, Vol. 2, p. 944

21. John S. Wise, *End of an Era,* (New York, A.S. Barnes & Co., 1965), p. 177.

22. National Archives and Records Administration, Record Group 109, *Records of the Army of the Kanawha,* letters sent by Gen. Henry A. Wise, June 1861-August 1864.

23. James Hamner papers, manuscript collections of the Virginia Historical Society, Richmond, Va.

24. NARA Record Group 109, Compiled Service Records of Confederate Soldiers From the State of Virginia, records of Col. St. George Croghan, 10th Virginia Cavalry.

25. Dinwiddie Family Papers, manuscript collections of the Virginia Historical Society, Richmond, Va.

CHAPTER TWO NOTES

1. United States War Department, *War of the Rebellion: A Compilation of the Official Records of the Union and Confederate Armies,* 70 vols. in 128 books, (Washington: Government Printing Office, 1881-1901), Series 1, Vol. 2, p. 995.

2. Ibid. p. 996

3. Official Records, Vol. 51 pt. 2, p. 178.

4. E. Morris Johnson, *A Year From Home*, published in the Journal of the Greenbrier Historical Society, Oct. 1966 p. 48.

5. James Hamner papers, in the manuscript collections of the Virginia Historical Society, Richmond, Va.

6. R. Lewis Scott papers, manuscript collections of the Virginia Historical Society, Richmond, Va.

7. Beuhring H. Jones, "My First Thirty Days Experience as a Captain" *Southern Literary Messenger,* Vol. 37, No. 2, 1863.

8. Official Records, Vol. 2, p. 1011-1012.

9. Ibid. Vol. 5, p. 552.

10. Official Records, Vol. 5, 553.

11. Ibid. p. 768.

12. Official Records, Vol. 51, pt. 2, p. 211.

13. Ibid. p. 213-214.

14. Official Records, Vol. 5, p. 768-771.

15. "Diary of S.R. Houston," in Oren F. Morton, *A History of Monroe County, West Virginia* (Staunton, Va.: McClure Company, 1916; Baltimore: Regional Publishing Company, 1974) p. 172.

16. Diary of A.B. Roler, in the manuscript collections of the Virginia Historical Society, Richmond, Va.

17. Diary of William Clark Reynolds, in the manuscript collections of the State of West Virginia, Charleston.

18. James Hamner papers, in the manuscript collections of the Virginia Historical Society, Richmond.

19. Henry Heth, (James I. Robertson, Jr. editor), "Memoirs of Henry Heth," *Civil War History*, Vol. 8, No. 1, p. 13. See also, Official Records, Vol. 5, p. 773.

20. Official Records, Vol. 5, p. 773-774.

21. Ibid. Vol. 51, pt. 2, p. 223-224.

22. Col. Charles Whittlesey, *War Memoranda: Cheat River to the Tennessee 1861-1862,* (Cleveland, Ohio, 1884) p. 26.

23. Official Records, Vol. 51, pt. 2, p. 218-219.

24. Ibid. p. 224-226.

25. Official Records, Vol. 5, p. 774, 778, 780.

26. Ibid. p. 781-782.

27. Official Records, Vol. 5, p. 789.

28. Joshua Horton & Solomon Teverbaugh, *History of the 11th Ohio Volunteer Infantry,* (Dayton, Ohio: W.J. Shuey, 1866), p. 38.

29. Official Records, Vol. 51, pt. 1, p. 448.

30. Ibid. Vol. 51, pt. 2, p. 236-237.

31. Joseph A. Brown, *The Memoirs of a Confederate Soldier,* (Abingdon, Va.: The Forum Press, 1940), p. 13.

32. Papers of Col. Albert G. Jenkins, in the manuscript collections of Marshall University, Huntington, WV.

33. Micajah Woods papers, in the manuscript collections of the University of Virginia, Charlottesville.

34. J.P. Sheffey papers, 8th Virginia Cavalry, in the manuscript collections of Virginia Tech, Blacksburg.

35. Letters of Andrew Cook, 27th Virginia Infantry, in the possession of Mr. and Mrs. Lewis Crawford, Rupert, WV.

36. William A. Smith papers, in the manuscript collections of Virginia Tech, Blacksburg.

Chapter Three Notes

1. Description of Gen. Wise from Walter H. Taylor, *Four Years With General Lee,* (Indiana University Press, reprint, 1962).

2. Troop positions and other material from Tim McKinney, *Robert E. Lee At Sewell Mountain: The West Virginia Campaign*, (Charleston, WV Pictorial Histories Publishing Co., 1990), p. 7.

3. United States War Department, *War of the Rebellion: A Compilation of the Official Records of the Union and Confederate Armies,* 70 vols. in 128 books, (Washington: Government Printing Office, 1881-1901), Series 1, Vol. 5, p. 575-577.

4. Ibid. Vol. 51, pt. 2, p. 243.

5. Official Records, Vol. 51, pt. 2, p. 246-247.

6. From the Southern Claims Commission case file of J.F. Caldwell. National Archives and Records Administration, RG 56, micropublication M87 *Records of the Commissioners of Claims, 1871-1880.* File published by Tim McKinney in *West Virginia Civil War Almanac Volume One,* (Charleston, WV Pictorial Histories Publishing Co., 1998) p. 540-547.

7. From a letter to the Richmond, Virginia newspapers, reprinted in the *Charleston Mercury,* Charleston, S.C., Sept. 2, 1861, letter by unidentified officer, dated at Lewisburg, Aug. 25, 1861.

8. Letters of Andrew Cook, 27th Virginia Infantry, in the possession of Mr. & Mrs. Lewis Crawford, Rupert, WV., letter dated Aug. 26, 1861.

9. William H. Jeffrey, *Richmond Prisons,* (St. Johnsbury, Vt., The Republican Press, 1893), p. 107.

10. W.R. Redding papers, 13th Georgia Infantry, in the manuscript collections of the University of North Carolina, Southern Historical Society Papers.

11. William A. Smith letters, in the manuscript collections of Virginia Tech, Blacksburg.

12. Micajah Woods papers, in the manuscript collections of the University of Virginia, Charlottesville.

13. Official Records, Vol. 51, pt. 2, p. 267-268.

14. E. Morris Johnson, *A Year From Home,* published in the Journal of the Greenbrier Historical Society, Oct. 1966, p. 41-54.

15. Official Records, Vol. 51, pt. 2, p. 270-271 and p. 287.

16. Ibid. p. 284-285.

17. Official Records, Vol. 5, p. 133.

18. James T. Hickey papers, in the manuscript collections of the Ohio Historical Society, Columbus. Also, Official Records, Vol. 5, p. 133.

19. From accounts in the Lytle and Lowe scrapbooks, Dayton-Montgomery County Library, Dayton, Ohio.

20. Robert W. Snead papers, in the manuscript collections of the Virginia Historical Society, Richmond, letter dated Sept. 10, 1861.

21. Col. St. George Croghan papers, in the manuscript collections of Perkins Library, Duke University.

22. National Archives and Records Administration, Record Group 109, *Records of the Army of the Kanawha,* chapter 2, vol. 94, Sept. 12, 1861.

23. Kenneth Swope, "Allegheny Blue Sulphur Springs," published in the *Journal of the Greenbrier Historical Society*, Vol. 2 No. 6, 1974, p. 38-70.
24. Official Records, Vol. 5, p. 599.

25. William Smith papers, in the manuscript collections of Virginia Tech, Blacksburg.

26. Official Records, Vol. 5, p. 861.

27. Ibid. p. 862.

28. Official Records, Vol. 5, p. 862-863.

29. National Archives, RG 109, *Records of the Army of the Kanawha*, chapter 2, vol. 318, letters sent by Gen. H.A. Wise, letter of Sept. 18, 1861.

30. Official Records, Vol. 51, pt. 2, p. 302.

31. Ibid. Vol. 5, p. 865-866.

32. Official Records, Vol. 5, p. 864.

CHAPTER FOUR NOTES

1. From the papers of George Alderson courtesy of Mrs. Kenneth Swope, Lewisburg, WV. Papers published in 1990 by Tim McKinney, see *Robert E. Lee at Sewell Mountain: the West Virginia Campaign*, (Charleston, WV Pictorial Histories Pub. Co.) p.25-26

2. National Archives and Records Administration, RG 109 *Records of the Army of the Kanawha*, Chapter 2, Vol. 323. Special Orders #228, Wise Legion, Sept. 22, 1861.

3. Diary of Micajah Woods, in the manuscript collections of the University of Virginia, Charlottesville.

4. National Archives, RG 109 Special Orders #111, Army of the Kanawha.

5. United States War Department, *War of the Rebellion: A Compilation of the Official Records of the Union and Confederate Armies,* 70 vols. in 128 books, (Washington: Government Printing Office, 1881-1901), Series 1, Vol. 5, p. 870.

6. Papers of Rev. G.G. Smith, Philips Legion Georgia Cavalry, in the manuscript collections of the University of North Carolina, Chapel Hill.

7. James H. Mays, Lee Mays, ed., *Four Years For Old Virginia*, (privately printed, 1972), p.17.

8. "General Lee on Sewell Mountain," from *The Southern Bivouac,* January 1883, number 5, p. 182.

9. Official Records, Vol. 5, p. 868

10. Ibid.

11. Official Records, Vol. 5, p. 873.

12. Ibid. p. 873-874.

13. Official Records, Vol. 5, p. 873-874.

14. Ibid. p. 878.

15. Official Records, Vol. 5, p. 878-879.

16. Ibid. Vol. 51, pt. 1, p. 486.

17. Letters of Jacob D. Cox, in the manuscript collections of Oberlin College, Oberlin, Ohio, letter dated Sept. 25, 1861.

18. From the papers of Robert E. Lee, in the manuscript collections of the Virginia Historical Society, Richmond, Va., letter of Sept. 24, 1861. Mss 31515b, film B55.

19. National Archives, RG 109 "Special and General Orders of the Army of the Kanawha," Chapter 2, Vol. 94.

20. *Southern Bivouac*, p. 182.

21. "A Virginian's Dilemma," The Civil War Diary of Isaac Noyes Smith, 22nd Virginia Infantry, Sept.—Nov. 1861, as printed in *West Virginia History*, April 1966, p. 184.

22. Official Records, Vol. 51, pt. 1, p. 487.

23. Ibid. p. 487-488.

24. Ibid.

25. Walter H. Taylor, *Four Years With General Lee,* (Indiana University Press, 1962 reprint), p. 33.

26. Official Records, Vol. 51, pt. 2, p. 312.

27. Ibid. Vol. 5, p. 879.

28. Ibid.

29. Official Records, Vol. 51, pt. 2, p. 313.

30. Diary of Micajah Woods, in the manuscript collections of the University of Virginia, Charlottesville.

31. W. Tate papers, in the manuscript collections of the University of Virginia, Charlottesville.

32. Official Records, Vol. 51, pt. 2, p. 312-313.

Chapter Five Notes

1. Rutherford B. Hayes, Charles R. Williams, ed., *Diary and Letters of Rutherford B. Hayes,* (Ohio State Archeological and Historical Society, 1922), p. 102-103.

2. Papers of Thomas Penn, in the manuscript collections of Duke University, Durham, North Carolina.

3. Letter of G.A. Cox, 8th Virginia Cavalry, Sept. 21, 1861, in the collection of Mr. John Alderman, Roanoke, Va.

4. Papers of Rev. G.G. Smith, Philips Legion Georgia Cavalry, in the manuscript collections of the University of North Carolina, Chapel Hill.

5. Ibid. Letter of A.J. Reese.

6. Hayes, p. 104.

7. Diary of C. Jenkins, 13th Georgia Infantry, in the manuscript collections of the Troup County Georgia Archives.

8. Sheffey papers, 8th Virginia Cavalry, in the manuscript collections of Virginia Tech, Blacksburg.

9. Papers of Lt. Col. St. George Croghan, 10th Virginia Cavalry, in the manuscript collections of Duke University.

10. United States War Department, *War of the Rebellion: A Compilation of the Official Records of the Union and Confederate Armies,* 70 vols. in 128 books, (Washington: Government Printing Office, 1881-1901), Series 1, Vol. 51, pt. 2, p. 321.

11. Ibid. p. 321-322.

12. Hayes, p. 103.

13. Sheffey papers, 8th Virginia Cavalry, in the manuscript collections of Virginia Tech, Blacksburg.

14. Stephen Adams, Adams Company Virginia Artillery, in the "Richmond Times Dispatch," Nov. 20, 1904.

15. Papers of Robert E. Lee, in the manuscript collections of the Virginia Historical Society, Richmond. Mss31515b film b55.

16. From a letter published in the "Wheeling Intelligencer," Wheeling, WV, Oct. 16, 1861.

17. Papers of R.N. Hewitt, 42nd Virginia Infantry, in the manuscript collections of Duke University.

18. William C. Workman letter, Oct. 5, 1861, in the manuscript collections of the Greenbrier County Historical Society, Lewisburg, WV.

19. Micajah Woods papers, in the manuscript collections of the University of Virginia, Charlottesville.

20. Robert E. Lee to his wife, Mary, letter of Oct. 7, 1861, published by Robert E. Lee, Jr., in *Recollections and Letters of Robert E. Lee,* (New York, 1904).

21. Lee papers, Va Historical Society.

22. Ibid. Letter of Dr. O.A. Krenshaw, Oct. 6, 1861.

23. William Smith papers, in the manuscript collections of Virginia Tech, Blacksburg.

24. Ibid. J.P. Sheffey papers.

25. Letter of W.D. Harris, Philips Legion Georgia Cavalry, in the manuscript collections of the University of North Carolina, Chapel Hill.

26. Charles Powell papers, in the manuscript collections of Duke University.

27. Letters and papers of the 14th North Carolina Infantry, in the manuscript collections of Duke University.

28. Rose W. Fry, *Recollections of the Rev. John McElhenney, D.D.* (Richmond, Va.: Whittet & Shepperson, 1893).

29. Official Records, Vol. 51, pt. 2, p. 347.

30. Ibid. p. 348-349.

31. Lee papers, Va Historical Society.

32. Official Records, Vol. 5, p. 908-909.

33. Lee papers, Va Historical Society.

34. Official Records, Vol. 5, p. 914, letter of Henry J. Fisher, civilian from Mason County, West Va.

Chapter Six Notes

1. Womack, Walter, ed., *The Civil War Diary of J.J. Womack Co. E 16th Tennessee Volunteers,* (McMinnville, TN: Womack Printing Company, 1961).

2. Papers of Robert E. Lee, in the manuscript collections of the Virginia Historical Society, Richmond. MSS 31515b film b55.

3. Letter of A.W. Johnson, 3rd Regiment Wise Legion, in the manuscript collections of West Virginia University, Morgantown.

4. Letter of Sergeant E.J. Humphries, Phillips Legion Georgia Cavalry, in the manuscript collections of Duke University.

5. Letter of William C. Workman, in the manuscript collections of the Greenbrier County Historical Society, Lewisburg, WV.

6. United States War Department, *War of the Rebellion: A Compilation of the Official Records of the Union and Confederate Armies,* 70 vols. in 128 books, (Washington: Government Printing Office, 1881-1901), Series 1, Vol. 5, p. 917-918.

7. Ibid. p. 924.

8. Official Records, Vol. 51, pt. 2, p. 360.

9. Ibid. p. 361-362.

10. Walter H. Taylor, *Four Years With General Lee,* (Indiana University Press, reprint, 1962). p. 34-35.

11. Official Records, Vol. 5, p. 951-952.

12. Ibid. Vol. 51, pt. 2, p. 385.

13. Official Records, Vol. 5, p. 657 and p. 662.

14. Ibid. p. 968.

15. James Booth papers, 36th Ohio Volunteer Infantry, in the manuscript collections of the Ohio Historical Society, Columbus.

16. Official Records, Vol. 51, pt. 2, p. 407.

17. Ibid. Vol. 5, p. 1000-1001.

18. Booth papers, OHS, and Official Records, Vol. 51, pt. 1, p. 54-56.

19. Ibid.

20. Official Records, Vol. 51, pt. 2, p. 415.

21. Ibid. Vol. 5, p. 1010-1011.

22. Letters of Andrew Cook, 27th Virginia Infantry, in the possession of Mr. & Mrs. Lewis Crawford, Rupert, WV.

CHAPTER SEVEN NOTES

1. Robert S. Conte, *The History of the Greenbrier: America's Resort,* (Charleston, West Va.: Pictorial Histories Publishing Company, 1989), p. 49-73.

2. Edmund Ruffin and Lewis Simpson, ed., *The Diary of Edmund Ruffin,* (Louisiana State University Press, 1972), volume 1, p. 330-334, 448-453.

3. Mary J. Windle, *Life at the White Sulphur Springs,* (Philadelphia, 1857), p. 41.

4. Morton–Halsey papers, letter of July 13, 1860, in the manuscript collections of the University of Virginia, Charlottesville.

5. Lewis Family papers, Elizabeth Noel to her daughter, Julia, Sept. 1, 1860, in the manuscript collections of the University of Virginia, Charlottesville.

6. Louisa Emerson papers, in the manuscript collections of the University of Virginia, Charlottesville. No date.

7. Papers of Lt. Col. St. George Croghan, 10th Virginia Cavalry, in the manuscript collections of Duke University.

8. Letter of Lt. John Guerrant, Floyd's Brigade, Sept. 21, 1861, in the manuscript collections of the Virginia Historical Society, Richmond.

9. "The Journal of a Soldier of 1861," published in *West Virginia Review,* Nov. 1930.

10. Letter of William H. Dobbins, Phillips Legion Georgia Cavalry, Sept. 29, 1861, and letter of Lt. Alex Erwin, in the manuscript collections of R.W. Woodruff Library, Emory University.

11. Dr. O.A. Krenshaw to R.E. Lee, Oct. 6, 1861, in the papers of Robert E. Lee, manuscript collections of the Virginia Historical Society, Richmond. Mss31515b film b55.

12. Letters of Lt. John D. Greever, 50th Virginia Infantry, Oct. 12, and 25, 1861, in the possession of Mr. Theodore C. Greever, 1990.

13. Memoir of Archibald Atkinson, in the manuscript collections of Virginia Tech, Blacksburg. See also, Emily Mason, *Memories of a Hospital Matron,* published in Atlantic Monthly Magazine, Sept. 1902, part one, p. 312.

14. Sister Mary D. Maher, *To Bind Up the Wounds,* (Westport, Ct.: Greenwood Press, Inc., 1989), p. 73, and "Bishop England's Sisterhood," unpublished dissertation by Sister M. Anne Francis Campbell, OLM, 1968 p. 96-98. Copy in the Archives of the Diocese of Charleston, Charleston, S.C., and Ellen Ryan Jolly, *Nuns of the Battlefield,* (Providence, R.I.: Providence Visitor Press, 1927), p. 293.

15. Letters Received by the Confederate Secretary of War, National Archives and Records Administration, Washington, D.C., RG 109, microcopy M437 Dec. 1861.

16. Sister De Sales to Bishop Lynch, original in the archives of the Diocese of Charleston, Charleston, S.C., letter of Dec. 31, 1861, as quoted on p. 104, of "Bishop England's Sisterhood," see note # 14.

17. Father O'Connell to Bishop Lynch, Jan. 11, 1862, archives of the Diocese of Charleston, Charleston, S.C.

18. Sister De Sales to Bishop Lynch, Jan. 26, 1862, archives of the Diocese of Charleston, Charleston, S.C.

19. Emily V. Mason, *Memories of a Hospital Matron,* Atlantic Monthly magazine, Sept. 1902, part one, p. 314.

20. Sister De Sales to "my dear Sister," March 11, 1862, archives of the Diocese of Charleston, Charleston, S.C.

21. Sister De Sales to Bishop Lynch, letters of April 4, 15, and 22, 1862, archives of the Diocese of Charleston, Charleston, S.C.

22. Father Corcoran to Bishop Lynch, archives of the Diocese of Charleston, Charleston, S.C., as quoted in "Bishop England's Sisterhood." See note # 14.

CHAPTER EIGHT NOTES

1. United States War Department, *War of the Rebellion: A Compilation of the Official Records of the Union and Confederate Armies,* 70 vols. in 128 books, (Washington: Government Printing Office, 1881-1901), Series 1, Vol. 51, pt. 2, p. 433.

2. Journal of William H. Bahlmann, in the manuscript collections of the State of West Virginia, Charleston, p. 13. See also, "Down in the Ranks," by William Bahlman, published in the *Journal of the Greenbrier Historical Society,* Oct. 1970.

3. Ibid. p. 12.

4. Official Records, Vol. 5, p. 1038, 1042.

5. Ibid. p. 1052, from A.T. Caperton to Col. William Jennifer.

6. George Crook, *General George Crook: His Autobiography,* ed. Martin F. Schmitt (Norman, Okla.: University of Oklahoma Press, 1986), p. 87-88. See also, Kenneth W. Noe, *Southwest Virginia's Railroad: Modernization and the Sectional Crisis* (University of Illinois Press, 1994), p. 120.

7. Official Records, Vol. 51, pt. 2, p. 463-464.

8. Letters of Captain A.R. Barbee, in the manuscript collections of the

Virginia Historical Society, Richmond. For "Heroes of America," see David Scott Turk, *The Union Hole: Unionist Activity & Local Conflict in Western Virginia*, (Bowie, MD: Heritage Books, 1994).

9. Official Records, Vol. 5, p. 1077-1078. Public sentiment concerning Heth's arrival is found in the *Richmond Dispatch*, Feb. 28, 1862, by an unidentified writer from Lewisburg. Letter also published in the *Pt. Pleasant Weekly Register,* March, 12, 1862.

10. Official Records, Vol. 51, pt. 2, p. 480.

11. Ibid. p. 494.

12. Official Records, Series 4, Vol. 1, p. 944-945, Feb. 17, 1862.

13. Ibid. Series 1, Vol. 5, p. 744-746.

14. From a letter published in the *Marietta Home News* (Ohio), April 4, 1862, letter from Summersville dated March 19, 1862.

15. Official Records, Vol. 51, pt. 2, p. 511.

16. J.W. Davis papers, in the manuscript collections of the Virginia Historical Society, Richmond. Letter dated March 12, 1862.

17. Official Records, Vol. 51, pt. 2, p. 511.

18. "Diary of S.R. Houston," in Oren F. Morton, *A History of Monroe County, West Virginia* (Staunton, Va.: McClure Company, 1916; Baltimore: Regional Publishing Company, 1974) p. 173.

19. Official Records, Vol. 12, pt. 3, p. 829-830.

20. Ibid. p. 834.

21. J.P. Sheffey papers, 8th Virginia Cavalry, in the manuscript collections of Virginia Tech, Blacksburg. Letter dated March 20, 1862.
22. Official Records, Vol. 12, pt. 3, p. 839.

23. Ibid. Vol. 51, pt. 2, p. 517.

24. Ibid. p. 526.

25. Official Records, Vol. 51, pt. 2, p. 531, for message to Fremont about the Rangers. See also, Kelley to Fremont, April 9, 1862, Vol. 12, pt. 3, p. 62 and R.H. Milroy to Fremont, April 12, 1862, Vol. 12, pt. 3, p. 71-72. See also, Jeff Weaver, *Thurmond's Rangers,* (Lynchburg: H.E. Howard Publishing Company, 1996) p. 11-12. See W.H. Flournoy, *Calendar of Virginia State Papers,* (Richmond, Va. 1893), p. 207-209.

26. Official Records, Vol. 12, pt. 3, p. 57.

27. "Incidents of a Long Life," by O.W. Kittenger, published in the *West Virginia Times,* Ronceverte, March 31, 1928 and reprinted in 1934.

28. Official Records, Series 4, Vol. 1, p. 1061-1062.

29. Ibid. Series 1, Vol. 12, pt. 3, p. 84-85.

CHAPTER NINE NOTES

1. Soldier's letter published in the *Springfield Republic,* (Ohio) May 26, 1862.

2. Ibid.

3. J.T. Booth papers, 36th Ohio Volunteer Infantry, in the manuscript collections of the Ohio Historical Society, Columbus. Quoting letter written by "WSS."

4. Houston, p. 174.

5. From correspondent "Zouave," in the *Springfield Republic,* (Ohio) June 6, 1862 letter dated May 23, 1862.

6. Booth, OHS.

7. Ibid.

8. J.J. Sutton, *History of the Second Regiment W.Va. Cavalry Volunteers,* (Portsmouth, Ohio 1892), p. 53.

9. Booth, OHS.

10. Letter by Captain Stough, 44th Ohio Infantry, published in the *Springfield Republic,* (Ohio) June 4, 1862.

11. Bahlmann papers.

12. Letter of Henry Mortimer in the *Gallipolis Journal* (Ohio), June 5, 1862.

13. From "Dane" in the *Richmond Daily Dispatch*, quoted by John Chapla in *50th Virginia Infantry*, (Lynchburg, Va.: H.E. Howard Pub. Co. 1997) p. 53.

14. Rose W. Fry, *Recollections of the Rev. John McElhenney, D.D.* (Richmond, Va.: Whittet & Shepperson, 1893) p. 180-181.

15. Booth papers, OHS.

16. Letter from "WSS," May 26, 1862, published in the *Marietta Home News* (Ohio), June 6, 1862.

17. Letter from "Zouave," in the *Springfield Republic* (Ohio), June 2, 1862.

18. Booth papers, OHS.

19. R. Byrd letter, 44th Ohio Vol. Infantry, in the Sydney Baker papers, manuscript collections of the Ohio Historical Society, Columbus.

20. E.H. Harman papers, 45th Va Infantry, in the manuscript collections of West Virginia University, Morgantown.

21. United States War Department, *War of the Rebellion: A Compilation of the Official Records of the Union and Confederate Armies*, 70 vols. in 128 books, (Washington: Government Printing Office, 1881-1901), Series 1, Vol. 12, pt. 1, p. 809.

22. Journal of William H. Bahlmann, manuscript collections of the State of West Virginia, Charleston. See also, "Down in the Ranks," by Wm Bahlmann, published in the *Journal of the Greenbrier Historical Society*, Oct. 1970.

23. Official Records, Vol. 12, pt. 1, p. 808.

24. Lt. W.A. Smith papers, 50th Va Infantry, in the manuscript collections of Virginia Tech, Blacksburg.

25. Joseph A. Brown, *The Memoirs of a Confederate Soldier,* (Abingdon, Va.: The Forum Press, 1940), p. 20.

26. Booth papers, OHS.

27. Letter of Alexander Welch Reynolds, May 23, 1862, in the Roy B. Cook papers, West Virginia University, Morgantown.

28. Official Records, Vol. 12, pt. 1, p. 812-813.

29. J.M. Clark, 36th Ohio Infantry, quoting an unidentified Confederate officer in the *Gallipolis Journal* (Ohio), June 5, 1862.

30. From a notice in the *Point Pleasant Register*, June 19, 1862.

31. Correspondent "L.B." of the 36th Ohio Infantry, in the *Marietta Home News* (Ohio), June 13, 1862. The 20-man crew sent out to burn the houses was led by Capt. Melvin C. True, 36th Ohio Inf.

32. By Editor of the *Marietta Home News* (Ohio), June 6, 1862.

33. Letter of Captain James Haddow, 36th Ohio Infantry, in the manuscript collections of the Greenbrier Historical Society, Lewisburg. Also, correspondent "L.B.," in the *Marietta Home News* (Ohio), June 13, 1862.

34. Booth papers, OHS.

35. Bahlmann journal, SWV.

36. George Jenvy, Second WV Cavalry, in the *Marietta Home News* (Ohio), June 6, 1862.

37. Letter of Captain Stough, 44th Ohio Infantry, published in the *Springfield Republic* (Ohio), June 4, 1862.

38. Booth papers, OHS.

39. From *Journal of the Greenbrier Historical Society,* Vol. 5, #5, 1991, and Vol. 4, #6, 1986.

40. Rose W. Fry, p.180.

41. From the papers of Samuel Harrison, 44th Ohio Infantry, in the manuscript collections of the Ohio Historical Society, Columbus. Quoted in "War in the Streets of Lewisburg," by James T. Siburt, published in *America's Civil War* magazine, Nov. 1998 p. 60.

Chapter Ten Notes

1. United States War Department, *War of the Rebellion: A Compilation of the Official Records of the Union and Confederate Armies*, 70 vols. in 128 books, (Washington: Government Printing Office, 1881-1901), Series 2, Vol. 2.

2. National Archives and Records Administration, microcopy M598 "Records of Prisoners of War at the Various Military Prisons." Information extracted from numerous individual rolls in this NARA series.

3. Official Records, Series 2, Vol. 2, p. 1420. Lt. Col. Peters to the CS Adjutant and Inspector General.

4. Various county genealogical and historical publications may reveal additional names. For an excellent review of partisan warfare in West Virginia and its impact on civilians, see Sean M. O'Brien, *Mountain Partisans: Guerrilla Warfare in the Southern Appalachians, 1861-1865* (Westport, Ct.: Praeger Publishing Co., 1999).

Chapter Eleven Notes

1. J.T. Booth papers, 36th Ohio Infantry, in the manuscript collections of the Ohio Historical Society, Columbus.

2. Correspondent "Zouave" (Lt. Evans) 44th Ohio Infantry, in the *Springfield Republic*, June 20, 1862.

3. From "The Yankee," a newspaper published at Lewisburg by U.S. forces, May 1862. Copy in the manuscript collections of the University of Virginia, Charlottesville.

4. The *Kanawha Republican* newspaper, as quoted in the *Point Pleasant Register*, June 5, 1862.

5. The *Gallipolis Journal* (Ohio), July 3, 1862.

6. United States War Department, *War of the Rebellion: A Compilation of the Official Records of the Union and Confederate Armies*, 70 vols. in 128 books, (Washington: Government Printing Office, 1881-1901), Series 1, Vol. 12, pt. 3, p. 320 and report to Lt. Fortescue, Second WV Cavalry, ibid., p. 360.

7. Official Records, Vol. 10 pt. 2, p. 603.
8. Ibid. Vol. 51, pt. 2, p. 584.

9. Quoting from Gen. Loring's letterbook, see James Raab, *W.W. Loring: Florida's Forgotten General* (Manhattan, Kansas: Sunflower University Press, 1996), p. 71. Heth claimed in his memoirs that he requested transfer. See Raab, p. 165.

10. From the "Record of Movements" Second West Va Cavalry, National Archives and Records Administration, microcopy M594 roll 194.

11. "John Maddy's Saltpeter Cave in Monroe County West Va," by Preston Green, published in the *Monroe Watchman*, April 9, 1914.

12. Official Records, Vol. 12, pt. 3, p. 430-431 and Crook's activities at Union in the Diary of S.R. Houston.

13. Official Records, Vol. 52, pt. 2, p. 327.

14. Ibid. p. 326.

15. Confederate account found in the papers of John Sheffey, 8th Va Cavalry, in the manuscript collections of Virginia Tech, Blacksburg. Union account published in the *Springfield Republic* (Ohio), July 25, 1862 by Lt. Evans, AKA "Zouave."

16. Official Records, Vol. 12, pt. 3, p. 471-472.

17. Story from the *Springfield Republic* (Ohio), July 28, 1862 by correspondent "G" on July 20, 1862.

18. The *Springfield Republic* (Ohio), July 25, 1862 by "Zouave" July 14, 1862.

19. Correspondent "H" 36th Ohio Inf. in the *Athens Messenger* (Ohio), July 31, 1862 letter written July 14, 1862.

20. Dickson family papers, in the manuscript collections of Virginia Tech, Blacksburg. Letter from E.L. Senters, June 15, 1862. Caldwell's letter is published in *Calendar of Virginia State Papers*, edited by H.W. Flournoy, (Richmond, Va. 1893), V. 11 p. 390-91.

21. Official Records, Vol. 12, pt. 3, p. 518-520.

22. Ibid. Vol. 12, pt. 2, p. 114-115.

23. Official Records, Vol. 12, pt. 3, p. 923-924, the second proclamation is on p. 947.

24. The *Springfield Republic* (Ohio), August 6, and August 11, 1862 by correspondents "Zouave" and "Justice."

25. J.P. Sheffey papers, Virginia Tech.

26. Official Records, Series 2, Vol. 4, p. 846, statement of Robinson dated July 10, 1862. For relevant documents see pages 845-847, 859-860.

27. Tim McKinney, *The Civil War in Fayette County West Virginia*, (Charleston, WV Pictorial Histories Pub. Co. 1988), p. 147-148.

28. Official Records, Vol. 12, pt. 3, p. 942.

29. Ibid. p. 943.

30. Official Records, Vol. 12, pt. 3, p. 946.

31. Mary D. Robertson, ed., *Lucy Breckinridge of Grove Hill: The Journal of a Virginia Girl*, (University of South Carolina Press, 1994), p. 51-52.

32. The *Staunton Spectator* (Virginia), Sept. 23, 1862 and June 30, 1863.

33. Official Records, Vol. 19, pt. 2, p. 625-626.

34. Ibid. p. 638.

35. Ibid. p. 656.

36. Official Records, Vol. 19, pt. 2, p. 666.

37. Ibid.

38. Ibid. p. 616-617. See also Raab, p. 79-85 (see note # 9 above)

39. Official Records, Series 1, Vol. 21, p. 1036.

40. Manuscript collections of the William R. Perkins Library, Duke University, quoted in Raab, p. 85 (see note # 9 above)

41. Official Records, Vol. 19, pt. 2, p. 690-691.

CHAPTER TWELVE NOTES

1. "Diary of S.R. Houston," in Oren F. Morton, *A History of Monroe County, West Virginia* (Staunton, Va.: McClure Company, 1916; Baltimore: Regional Publishing Company, 1974) p. 176.

2. United States War Department, *War of the Rebellion: A Compilation of the Official Records of the Union and Confederate Armies*, 70 vols. in 128 books, (Washington: Government Printing Office, 1881-1901), Series 1, Vol. 21, p. 1022-1023.

3. Ibid. p. 779-780.

4. Col. Powell's statement is in *Journal of the Greenbrier Historical Society*, Vol. 2, #5, 1973. "Greenbrier County and the Medal of Honor," by Kenneth D. Swope, p. 17-24.

5. Official Records, Vol. 21, p. 10-11, for Paxton's report; for Lane's report see p. 9-10.

6. From the *Gallipolis Journal* (Ohio), Dec. 4, 1862.

7. From the *Lexington Gazette* (Virginia), Dec. 4, 1862.

CHAPTER THIRTEEN NOTES

1. United States War Department, *War of the Rebellion: A Compilation of the Official Records of the Union and Confederate Armies*, 70 vols. in 128 books, (Washington: Government Printing Office, 1881-1901), Series 1, Vol. 21, p. 1058-1059.

2. Ibid. p. 1059.

3. Ibid. p. 1063-1064.

4. Ibid. p. 899.

5. Official Records, Vol. 20, pt. 2, p. 473-474.

6. Ibid. Vol. 18, p. 815-816.

7. Letter by George K. Jenvy, Second WV Cavalry, in the *Marietta Register* (Ohio), Jan. 23, 1863.

8. For Gen. Jones' complaint, see Official Records, Vol. 21, p.1093-1094. See also, *Journal of the Greenbrier Historical Society*, Vol. 2, #5, 1973, p. 23.

9. Official Records, Vol. 25, pt. 2, p. 85-86.

10. Randall Osborne and Jeff Weaver, *The Virginia State Rangers and State Line*, (Lynchburg, Va.: H.E. Howard Publishing Co. 1994) p. 114,119.

11. Official Records, Vol. 25, pt. 2, p. 199.

12. Ibid. p. 751.

13. Ibid. Vol. 25, pt. 1, p. 1100-1102. See also, *Journal of the Greenbrier Historical Society*, Vol 6, #2a, p. 9-15. Records transcribed by Mr. James E. Talbert.

14. Official Records, Vol. 25, pt. 2, p. 446. R.N. Sanders' story in the *Ironton Register* (Ohio), Jan. 12, 1888.

15. Official Records, Vol. 27, pt. 3, p. 957-959.

16. Ibid. Vol. 51, pt. 2, p. 735-736.

17. Ibid. Vol. 29, pt. 1, p. 38-40.

18. Official Records, Vol. 29, pt. 1, p. 40-43.

19. "Reminiscences of the Battle of Dry Creek," by Noyes Rand, published in the *Monroe Watchman*, July, 8, 1909.

20. Letters of Henry Carpenter, 45th Va Infantry, in the manuscript collections of Virginia Tech, Blacksburg.

21. "Battle of Dry Creek," by J.A. McNeel, published in the *Fayette Tribune*, 1907, exact date unknown.

22. Frank S. Reader, *History of the Fifth West Virginia Cavalry*, (New Brighton, Penn.: Daily News, 1890). Mark Crayon, *Life in the Irish Corner District During the Civil War.* (Union, WV: Monroe County Historical Society, 2001).

23. Ibid.

24. Darl L. Stephenson, *Headquarters in the Brush: Blazer's Independent Scouts*, (Athens, OH: Ohio University Press, 2001), p. 40-64. See also, Official Records, Vol. 29, pt. 2, p. 391 for raid at Blue Sulphur Springs.

25. Official Records, Vol. 29, pt. 1, p. 53-56 (Patton's report).

26. Mary D. Robertson, ed., *Lucy Breckinridge of Grove Hill: The Journal of a Virginia Girl*, (University of South Carolina Press, 1994), p. 144-145.

27. Charles Mestrezat papers, 14th Pennsylvania Cavalry, in the manuscript collections of West Virginia University, Morgantown.

28. Micajah Woods papers, in the manuscript collections of the University of Virginia, Charlottesville.

29. James Ireland papers, 12th Ohio Infantry, in the manuscript collections of the Ohio Historical Society, Columbus. See also, "The Letters of Mason Mathews," published in the *Journal of the Greenbrier Historical Society*, Vol. 5, #1, 1987, p. 21-22.

30. Miscellaneous State papers in the manuscript collections of the State of West Virginia, MSS 80-265.

31. Official Records, Vol. 29, pt. 2, p. 473.

32. Ibid. p. 517.

33. Ibid. p. 870-871. For description of ice storm and conditions in general, see W.S. Newton papers, 91st Ohio Infantry, in the manuscript collections of the Ohio Historical Society, Columbus. James Comly, 23rd Ohio Infantry, claimed that when they took Lewisburg on Dec. 12, 1863 they killed one enemy soldier, wounded "a few," and captured 13, with a loss of one wounded and four captured. See Letterbook of the 23rd Ohio Infantry, in the manuscript collections of the Ohio Historical Society.

34. Scammon moved back to Meadow Bluff, leaving there on Dec. 15, 1863. Official Records, Vol. 51, pt. 1, p. 1135. Scammon's scouts skirmished with Thurmond's Rangers on the Blue Sulphur Turnpike, Dec. 14, 1863. Official Records, Vol. 29, pt. 1, p. 940.

35. Official Records, Vol. 29, pt. 1, p. 935.

36. See - Darrell L. Collins, *General William W. Averell's Salem Raid*, (Shippensburg, Pa.: Burd Street Press, 1998). For Confederate attempts to

stop Averell's raid see Official Records, (Gen. Jones' report) Vol. 29, pt. 1, p. 943-945. Averell's report, Ibid., p. 924-925.

37. Captain A.R. Barbee, 22nd Va Infantry, as quoted in Terry Lowry, *22nd Virginia Infantry*, (Lynchburg, Va.: H.E. Howard Publishing Co. 1988), p. 55.

Chapter Fourteen Notes

1. Robert J. Driver, *Fourteenth Virginia Cavalry,* (Lynchburg, Va.: H.E. Howard Publishing Company, 1988) p. 31.

2. United States War Department, *War of the Rebellion: A Compilation of the Official Records of the Union and Confederate Armies,* 70 vols. in 128 books, (Washington: Government Printing Office, 1881-1901), Series 1, Vol. 33, p. 1106-1107.

3. Ibid. Series 2, Vol. 6, p. 875.

4. Ibid. Series 1, Vol. 33, p. 1155-1156.

5. Terry Lowry, *The Twenty Second Virginia Infantry,* (Lynchburg, Va.: H.E. Howard Publishing Company, 1988), p. 56-57.

6. The "Staunton Spectator," as quoted in *Fourteenth Virginia Cavalry*, Driver, p. 31.

7. Official Records, Vol. 33, p. 1236.

8. Ibid. p. 1323.

9. Official Records, Vol. 37, pt. 1, p. 41-42 (Averell's report) Ibid., p. 9-13, Crook's report.

10. Michael Egan, *The Flying Gray-Haired Yank,* (Edgewood Pub. Co., 1888) p. 180.

11. Official Records, Vol. 37, pt. 1, p. 500-501.

12. Ibid. p. 740-741.

13. C.J. Rawling, *History of the First Regiment (West) Virginia Infantry*, (Philadelphia: J.B. Lippincott, 1887) p. 189. Reprint, Quarrier Press, Charleston, WV 2002 with new material by Tim McKinney.

14. Diary of John V. Young in the Roy B. Cook papers, West Va University.

15. "Incidents of a Long Life," by O.W. Kittinger, published in the *Greenbrier Independent*, Feb. 1934.

16. Diary of James J. Wood, 34th Ohio Infantry, in the manuscript collections of Bowling Green State University, Ohio.

17. Henry A. Du Pont, *The Campaign of 1864 in the Valley of Virginia*, (New York, 1925), p. 44.

18. William Hewitt, *History of the Twelfth West Virginia Infantry,* (Twelfth WV Infantry Association, 1892), p. 141.

19. Official Records, Vol. 37 Pt. 1, p. 746.

20. Published in *Journal of the Greenbrier Historical Society*, Vol. 2 #5, 1973, p. 14-29, article by Kenneth D. Swope.

21. Official Records, Vol. 37 pt. 1, p. 145. Gen. Crook's part is Ibid p. 561.

22. Thomas F. Wildes, *Record of the 116th Ohio Volunteer Infantry*, (Sandusky, OH: I.F. Mack & Brothers, Printers, 1884), p. 91.

23. Journal of Sgt. Michael Ayers, 11th West Va Infantry, in the manuscript collections of West Virginia University, Morgantown.

24. Memoirs of Pvt. Mart Howe, 34th Ohio Infantry, published in the *National Tribune*, April 1, 1892.

25. William H. Armstrong, *Major McKinley: William McKinley and the Civil War,* (Kent State University Press, 2000), p. 67-68.

26. Ibid. p. 70, quoting from Murat Halstead, *The Illustrious Life of William McKinley,* N.p.: Murat Halstead, 1901.

27. Charles H. Lynch, *The Civil War Diary, 1862-1865, of Charles H. Lynch, 18th Conn. Volunteer's*, (Hartford, Ct.: Case, Lockwood & Brainard, 1915), p. 85-86.

28. "The Great Skedaddle," by William B. Stark, published in *Atlantic Monthly* magazine, vol. CLXII July-December, 1938, p. 91. The crossing

story is from William S. Lincoln, *Life With the 34th Massachusetts Infantry*, (Worcester, MA: Noyes, Snow & Co, 1879), p. 319.

29. Thomas J. Reed, *Tibbit's Boys: A History of the 21st New York Cavalry*, (Lanham, MD: University Press of America, 1997), p. 164-165.

30. William H. Beach, *The First New York Cavalry*, (NY: the Lincoln Cavalry Association, 1902), p. 381-382.

31. Samuel C. Farrar, *The Twenty Second Pennsylvania Cavalry and the Ringgold Battalion*, (Pittsburg, PA: the 22nd Penn. Cavalry Assoc., 1911), p. 249.

32. Cecil D. Eby, Jr. ed., *A Virginia Yankee in the Civil War: the Diary of David Hunter Strother*, (Chapel Hill, NC: UNC Press, 1961), p. 273-275.

33. Du Pont, p. 88-89.

34. Rose W. Fry, *Recollections of the Rev. John McElhenney, D.D.* (Richmond, Va.: Whittet & Shepperson, 1893), p. 182-183.

35. Lincoln, W.S., p. 319-321 – see note #28 above.

36. Stark, p. 92-93 – see note #28 above.

37. Diary of James Comly, 23rd Ohio Infantry, in the manuscript collections of the Ohio Historical Society, Columbus. Duffie's report is in the Official Records, Vol. 37, pt. 1, p. 143-145.

38. Reed, p. 166-167 – see note #29 above.

39. Hewitt, p. 152 – see note #18 above.

40. Official Records, Vol. 37, pt. 2, p. 291-293.

41. The Lexington, Va *Gazette* of July 29, 1864 quoted an article from the *Columbus Statesman* (Ohio), claiming that 27 men of the 12th OVI starved to death during the retreat. It also stated that more than 2,000 soldiers became barefooted. The *Cincinnati Commercial* of July 16, 1864 says 1,500 horses died on the march and that the burning of the library, governor's home, and similar non-military targets at Lexington was an "outrage." Similar articles appeared in the *Athens Messenger* (Ohio), July 7,14, 21, 1864; The *Gallipolis Journal* (Ohio), of July 7, 1864 lists the names of seven soldiers who died in the hospital there between June 30

and July 3. The deaths were caused by "The severity of the late raid under Hunter." An article appeared in the *Springfield Republic* (Ohio), July 15, 1864 reporting that Hunter's supplies never reached Meadow Bluff because Thurmond's Rangers attacked the column in Fayette County, destroying wagons, bags of oats, etc.

42. Official Records, Vol. 37, pt. 2, p. 105-106.

CHAPTER FIFTEEN NOTES

1. Clarence Shirley Donnelly, *David S. Creigh: the Greenbrier Martyr,* (privately printed, Oak Hill, WV 1950). The *Journal of the Greenbrier Historical Society,* Vol. 2, #2, 1970 p.15-38 reprints various documents relative to the hanging of Mr. Creigh. Especially valuable is the "Brief Sketch of the Life and Character of the Late David S. Creigh," originally published at Lewisburg in 1865.

2. *Journal,* p. 15-38. Creigh and Woods family papers, manuscript collections of the University of Virginia, Charlottesville, MSS 10279.

3. William Gilmore Beymer, *On Hazardous Service,* (New York: Harper & Brothers, 1912), p. 1-34.

4. United States War Department, *War of the Rebellion: A Compilation of the Official Records of the Union and Confederate Armies,* 70 vols. in 128 books, (Washington: Government Printing Office, 1881-1901), Series 2, Vol. 7, p. 473.

CHAPTER SIXTEEN NOTES

1. National Archives and Records Administration, RG 153, case file LL2540. This is the first time these records have been published. The author is indebted to DeAnne Blanton in "Old Military Reference" at the National Archives, for the recovery of this case file. Numerous historians have written over the years that Gen. Hunter ordered the hanging of Mr. Creigh against the advice of Generals Averell and Crook. To the contrary, both men signed the court martial documents indicating their approval of the sanction. It was simply in keeping with military regulations that Hunter's signature was the last one obtained.

Chapter Seventeen Notes

1. Special Orders published in the *Pt. Pleasant Register* (WV), July 21, 1864.

2. "Wartime Letters of Mason Mathews," published in the *Journal of the Greenbrier Historical Society*, Vol. 5 #1, 1987 p. 33, compiled by James T. Combs.

3. Scott Cole, *Thirty Fourth Battalion Virginia Cavalry*, (Lynchburg, Va.: H.E. Howard Publishing Co. 1993), p. 88-93. Jeff Weaver, *Thurmond's Partisan Rangers and Swann's Battalion Virginia Cavalry*, (Lynchburg, Va.: H.E. Howard Pub. Co., 1993), p. 48-54. Witcher's official report is in the Official Records, Vol. 43, pt. 2, p. 887-888.

4. Official Records, Vol. 43, pt. 2, p. 890.
5. Diary of Thomas L. Feamster, 14th Virginia Cavalry, in the manuscript collections of West Virginia University, Morgantown.

6. Ibid.

7. Official Records, Vol. 46, pt. 2, p 81,132-133,176.

8. A.W. Mann's letter is in the manuscript collections of the State of West Virginia, Charleston. Miscellaneous papers relating to West Virginia Home Guard and Militia.

9. Feamster diary.

10. Official Records, Vol. 46, pt. 2, p. 961.

11. Ibid. Vol. 46, pt. 3, p. 821.

12. Ibid. p. 828.

13. Ibid. p. 830.

14. Official Records, Vol. 46, pt. 3, p. 871-872.

15. Ibid. p. 873 – Echols disbanded his brigade at Christiansburg, Va., April 12, 1865.

16. Official Records, Vol. 46, pt. 3, p. 963.

17. Ibid. p. 1015.

18. Manuscript collections of the State of West Virginia, MS 79-83, file 15-083. See also, Applications of former Confederates for parole, National Archives and Records Administration, Washington, D.C.

19. From the *Greenbrier Independent*, August 23, 1866.

20. Ibid. Sept. 27, Nov. 8, 1866.

21. Ibid. Oct. 25, 1866.

22. From the *Greenbrier Independent*, December 13, 1866

23. Ibid. April 18, 1867.

24. Ibid. June 6, and 13, 1867.

25. Otis K. Rice and Stephen W. Brown, *West Virginia: A History*, (University Press of Kentucky, 1993), p. 159-161.

BIBLIOGRAPHY

BOOKS

Armstrong, William H. *Major McKinley: William McKinley and the Civil War.* Kent State University Press, 2000.

Beach, William H. *The First New York Cavalry.* NY: Lincoln Cavalry Association, 1902.

Benson, Evelyn A. *With the Army of West Virginia: Reminiscences & Letters of Lt. James Abraham, Pennsylvania Dragoons, First Regiment Virginia Cavalry.* Lancaster, Pa., privately printed, 1974.

Beymer, William G. *On Hazardous Service.* NY: Harper & Brothers, 1912.

Bodell, Dorothy H. *Montgomery White Sulphur Springs: A History of the Resort, Hospital, Cemeteries, Markers, & Monuments.* Blacksburg, Va.: Pocahontas Press, 1993.

Brown, Joseph A. *The Memoirs of a Confederate Soldier.* Abingdon, Va.: The Forum Press, 1940.

Chapla, John D. *50th Virginia Infantry.* Lynchburg, Va.: H.E. Howard Pub. Co. 1997.

Cole, Scott. *34th Battalion Virginia Cavalry.* Lynchburg, Va.: H.E. Howard Publishing Co., 1993.

Collins, Darrell L. *General William W. Averell's Salem Raid.* Shippensburg, PA: Burd Street Press, 1998.

Conte, Robert S. *The History of the Greenbrier: America's Resort.* Charleston, W.Va.: Pictorial Histories Publishing Co., 1989.

Crayon, Mark. [N.B. "Doc" McDowell] *Life in the Irish Corner District During the Civil War.* Copied and indexed by Mrs. Arravelva Humphries and Mrs. Reginald White. Union, WV: Monroe County Historical Society, 2001.

Crook, George. Martin F. Schmitt, ed. *General George Crook: His Autobiography.* Norman, OK: University of Oklahoma Press, 1986.

Cutchins, John A. *A Famous Command: The Richmond Light Infantry Blues.* Richmond, Va.: Garrett & Massie, 1934.

Dickinson, Jack. *The 8th Virginia Cavalry.* Lynchburg, Va.: H.E. Howard Publishing Co., 1986.

_____________. *Tattered Uniforms and Bright Bayonets: West Virginia's Confederate Soldiers.* Huntington, WV: Marshall University Library Associates, 1995.

Donnelly, Clarence Shirley. *David S. Creigh: The Greenbrier Martyr.* Oak Hill, WV: privately printed, 1950.

Driver, Robert J. *14th Virginia Cavalry.* Lynchburg, Va.: H.E. Howard Publishing Co., 1988.

Du Pont, Henry A. *The Campaign of 1864 in the Valley of Virginia.* NY: 1925.

Eby, Cecil D. jr. ed. *A Virginia Yankee in the Civil War: The Diary of David Hunter Strother.* Chapel Hill, NC: UNC Press, 1961.

Egan, Michael. *The Flying Gray-Haired Yank.* Edgewood Publishing Co., 1888.

Farrar, Samuel C. *The Twenty Second Pennsylvania Cavalry and the Ringgold Battalion.* Pittsburg, PA: the 22nd Penn. Cavalry Association, 1911.

Flournoy, W.H. *Calendar of Virginia State Papers.* Richmond, Va.: 1893.

Fry, Rose W. *Recollections of the Rev. John McElhenney D.D.* Richmond, Va.: Whittet & Shepperson, 1893.

Haga, Pauline. *Greenbrier County Wills, 1780-1865.* Crab Orchard, WV: privately printed, 1995?

Hayes, Rutherford B. Charles R. Williams, ed. *Diary and Letters of Rutherford B. Hayes.* Ohio State Archeological and Historical Society, 1922.

Hewitt, William. *History of the Twelfth West Virginia Infantry.* Twelfth West Va Infantry Association, 1892.

Horton, Joshua and Solomon Teverbaugh. *History of the 11th Ohio Volunteer Infantry.* Dayton, OH: W.J. Shuey, 1866.

Jeffrey, William H. *Richmond Prisons.* St. Johnsbury, VT: The Republican Press, 1893.

Jolly, Ellen Ryan. *Nuns of the Battlefield.* Providence, RI: Providence Visitor Press, 1927.

Lee, Robert E. Jr. *Recollections and Letters of Robert E. Lee.* NY: 1904.

Lincoln, William S. *Life With the 34th Massachusetts Infantry.* Worcester, MA: Noyes, Snow & Co., 1879.

Lowry, Terry. *The 22nd Virginia Infantry.* Lynchburg, Va.: H.E. Howard Publishing Co., 1988.

__________. *Last Sleep: The Battle of Droop Mountain.* Charleston, WV: Pictorial Histories Publishing Co., 1996.

Lynch, Charles H. *The Civil War Diary, 1862-1865 of Charles H. Lynch, 18th Conn. Volunteers.* Hartford, CT: Case, Lockwood, & Brainard, 1915

Maher, Mary D. *To Bind Up the Wounds.* Westport, CT: Greenwood Press, Inc., 1989.

Mays, James H. Lee Mays, ed. *Four Years For Old Virginia.* Privately printed, 1972.

McKinney, Tim. *The Civil War in Fayette County West Virginia.* Charleston, WV: Pictorial Histories Publishing Co., 1988.

____________. *Robert E. Lee at Sewell Mountain: The West Virginia Campaign.* Charleston, WV: Pictorial Histories Pub. Co., 1990.

_____________. *West Virginia Civil War Almanac* (in two vols.). Charleston, WV: Pictorial Histories Pub. Co. (v. 1) and Quarrier Press, (v. 2) 1998, 2000.

Morton, Oren F. *A History of Monroe County, West Virginia.* Staunton, Va.: McClure Company, 1916.

Noe, Kenneth W. *Southwest Virginia's Railroad: Modernization and the Sectional Crisis.* University of Illinois Press, 1994.

Norton, Chauncy S. *The Red Neck Ties: History of the 15th NY Cavalry.* NY: 1891.

O'Brien, Sean M. *Mountain Partisans: Guerrilla Warfare in the Southern Appalachian Mountains, 1861-1865.* Westport, CT: Praeger Publishing Co., 1999.

Ohio Roster Commission. *Official Roster of the Soldiers of the State of Ohio in the War of the Rebellion, 1861-1865.* Akron, OH: Werner Co., 1886-1895.

Osborne, Randall and Jeff Weaver. *The Virginia State Rangers and State Line.* Lynchburg, Va.: H.E. Howard Publishing Co., 1994.

Phillips, Edward L. *Lincoln's Bastile: The Atheneum, The Story of a Building, 1855-1868.* Privately printed, 1997.

_______________. *The Atheneum.* Privately printed, 1999.

Pollard, Edward A. *The Virginia Tourist: Sketches of the Springs and Mountains of Virginia.* Philadelphia, PA: J.B. Lippincott & Co., 1870.

Raab, James. *W.W. Loring: Florida's Forgotten General.* Manhattan, KS: Sunflower University Press, 1996.

Rawling, C.J. Tim McKinney, ed. Second edition. *History of the 1st Regiment (West) Virginia Infantry*. Philadelphia: J.B. Lippincott, 1887. Charleston, WV: Quarrier Press, 2002.

Reader, Frank S. *History of the 5th West Virginia Cavalry.* New Brighton, PA: Daily News, 1890.

Reed, Thomas J. *Tibbit's Boys: A History of the 21st New York Cavalry.* Lanham, MD: University Press of America, 1997.

Rice, Otis K. *A History of Greenbrier County.* Parsons, WV: McClain Publishing Co., 1986.

Rice, Otis K. and Stephen W. Brown. *West Virginia: A History.* University Press of Kentucky, 1993.

Robertson, James I. ed. *Proceedings of the Advisory Council of the State of Virginia, April 21-June 19, 1861.* Richmond, Va.: Virginia State Library.

Robertson, Mary D. ed. *Lucy Breckinridge of Grove Hill: The Journal of a Virginia Girl.* University of South Carolina Press, 1994.

Ruffin, Edmund. Lewis Simpson, ed. *The Diary of Edmund Ruffin.* Louisiana State University Press, 1972.

Shuck, Larry G. *Greenbrier County Marriages, 1782-1900.* Athens, GA: Iberian Publishing Company, 1991.

Stephenson, Darl L. *Headquarters in the Brush: Blazer's Independent Scouts.* Athens, OH: Ohio University Press, 2001.

Sutton, J.J. *History of the 2nd Regiment West Virginia Cavalry Volunteers.* Portsmouth, OH: 1892.

Taylor, Walter H. *Four Years With General Lee.* Indiana University Press, reprint, 1962.

Turk, David S. *The Union Hole: Unionists Activity and Local Conflict in Western Virginia.* Bowie, MD: Heritage Books, 1994.

United States War Department. *War of the Rebellion: A Compilation of the Official Records of the Union and Confederate Armies.* 70 vols. in 128 books. Washington: Government Printing Office, 1881-1901

Walls, R. Hal. *A History of the White Sulphur Rifles: Co. G, and the Scouts and Guides, Co. E, of Edgars 26th Virginia Battalion of Patton's Brigade.* Lewisburg, WV: Roadrunner Press, 1989.
Weaver, Jeff. *Thurmond's Rangers.* Lynchburg, Va.: H.E. Howard Publishing Co., 1996.

Whittlesey, Charles. *War Memoranda: Cheat River to the Tennessee 1861-1862.* Cleveland, OH: 1884.

Wildes, Thomas F. *Record of the 116th Ohio Volunteer Infantry.* Sandusky, OH: I.F. Mack & Brothers, printers, 1884.

Windle, Mary J. *Life at the White Sulphur Springs.* Philadelphia, 1857.

Wise, John S. *End of an Era.* NY: A.S. Barnes & Co., 1965.

Womack, Walter. ed. *The Civil War Diary of J.J. Womack Co. E. 16th Tennessee Volunteers.* McMinnville, TN: Womack Printing Co., 1961.

MAGAZINES AND JOURNALS

America's Civil War, Nov. 1998

Atlantic Monthly, Sept. 1902 – Vol. CLXII July-December 1938.

Confederate Veteran, Vol. 19, 1911 (417-418).

Journal of the Greenbrier Historical Society, Oct. 1966; Oct. 1970; Vol. 2 #5 1973; Vol. 2 #6 1974; Vol. 4 #6 1986; Vol. 5 #1 1987; Vol. 5 #5 1991; Vol. 6 #2.

The Southern Bivouac, Jan. 1883

Southern Literary Messenger, Vol. 37 #2 1863.

West Virginia History, April 1966.

West Virginia Review, Nov. 1930.

NEWSPAPERS

Athens Messenger (OH), July 31, 1862; July 7,14,21, 1864.

Beckley Post Herald (WV), Oct. 3, 1962; Dec. 8, 1964.

Charleston Gazette (WV), July 24, 1949.

Cincinnati Commercial (OH), July 16, 1864.

Columbus Statesman (OH), July 29, 1864.

Fayette Tribune (WV), Sept. 3, 1908; Jan. 22, 1920; May 16, 1928.

Gallipolis Journal (OH), June 5, 1862; July 3,7,16, 1862; Dec. 4, 1862; Feb. 18, 1864; July 7, 1864.

Greenbrier Independent (WV), June 21, 1866; Aug. 16,23, 1866; Dec. 13, 1866; Dec. 12, 1867; Aug. 8, 1867; various issues between 1867-1872.

Ironton Register (OH), July 28, 1887; Jan, 12, 1888.

Lewisburg Weekly Era (WV), May 25, 1861.

Lexington Gazette (VA), Dec. 4, 1862; July 19, 1864; July 29, 1864.

Marietta Home News (OH), June 6, 13, 1862.

Marietta Register (OH), Jan. 23, 1863; June 12, 1863.

Monroe Watchman (WV), July 8, 1909; April 9, 1914.

National Tribune, April 1, 1892.

Point Pleasant Register (WV), March 12, 1862; June 5, 1862; June 19, 1862; July 21, 1864.

Point Pleasant Weekly (WV), July 14, 28, 1864.

Richmond Daily Dispatch (VA), June 1862.

Springfield Republic (OH), 1862 dates: May 26; June 2,4,6,20; July 14,25,28; Aug. 6,11; July 15, 1864.

Staunton Spectator (VA), May 28, 1861; Sept. 23, 1862; June 30, 1863.

West Virginia Times, March 31, 1928.

Wheeling Intelligencer (WV), Oct. 16, 1861; May 30, 1862; July 18, 1864.

The Yankee, published at Lewisburg, WV May 29, 1862 by U.S. soldiers. Copy in the collections of the University of Virginia, Charlottesville.

MANUSCRIPTS

George Alderson papers in the collections of Francis Swope, Lewisburg, WV 1990.

Archibald Atkinson memoirs (10th Va Cavalry), in the manuscript collections of Virginia Tech, Blacksburg.

Michael Ayers journal (11th WV Infantry), in the manuscript collections of West Virginia University, Morgantown.

A.R. Barbee letters, in the manuscript collections of the Virginia Historical Society, Richmond.

J.T. Booth papers (36th Ohio Infantry), in the manuscript collections of the Ohio Historical Society, Columbus.

R. Byrd letters, in the Sydney Baker papers, manuscript collections of the Ohio Historical Society, Columbus.

Henry Carpenter letters (45th Va Infantry) in the manuscript collections of Virginia Tech, Blacksburg.

J.H. Cochran letters, in the manuscript collections of Virginia Tech, Blacksburg.

James Comly diary (23rd Ohio Vol. Infantry), in the manuscript collections of the Ohio Historical Society, Columbus.

Andrew Cook letters (27th Va Infantry), in the possession of Mr. & Mrs. Lewis Crawford, Rupert, WV.

Jacob D. Cox papers, in the manuscript collections of Oberlin College, Oberlin, Ohio.

G.A. Cox letters (8th Va Cavalry), in the collection of Mr. John Alderman, Roanoke, Va.

St. George Croghan papers (Wise Legion), in the manuscript collections of Perkins Library, Duke University.

J.W. Davis papers, in the manuscript collections of the Virginia Historical Society, Richmond.

Dickson Family papers, in the manuscript collections of Virginia Tech, Blacksburg.

Dinwiddie Family papers, in the manuscript collections of the Virginia Historical Society, Richmond.

Archives of the Diocese of Charleston, Charleston, S.C. including the letters of Sister De Sales, Father O'Connell, Bishop Lynch, and Father

Corcoran, 1861-1864 concerning work in the hospital at the Greenbrier White Sulphur Springs.

William H. Dobbins letters (Phillips Legion GA Cavalry), in the manuscript collections of the R.W. Woodruff Library, Emory University.

Louisa Emerson papers, in the manuscript collections of the University of Virginia, Charlottesville.

Alex Erwin papers (Phillips Legion GA Cavalry), in the manuscript collections of the R.W. Woodruff Library, Emory University.

Thomas L. Feamster diary (14th Va Cavalry), in the manuscript collections of West Virginia University, Morgantown.

Fourteenth NC Infantry letters and papers, various items in the manuscript collections of Duke University.

Greenbrier County Court Order Book, 1861-1865, at the Greenbrier County Courthouse, Lewisburg, WV.

John D. Greever letters (50th Va Infantry), in the possession of Mr. Theodore C. Greever, 1990.

John Guerrant letters (Floyd's Brigade), in the manuscript collections of the Virginia Historical Society, Richmond.

James Haddow letter (36th Ohio Infantry), in the manuscript collections of the Greenbrier Historical Society, Lewisburg, WV.

James Hamner papers, in the manuscript collections of the Virginia Historical Society, Richmond.

E.H. Harman papers (45th Va Infantry), in the manuscript collections of West Virginia University, Morgantwon.

W.D. Harris letter (Phillips Legion GA Cavalry), in the manuscript collections of the University of NC, Chapel Hill.

Samuel Harrison papers (44th Ohio Infantry), in the manuscript collections of the Ohio Historical Society, Columbus.

R.N. Hewitt papers (42nd Virginia Infantry), in the manuscript collections of Duke University.

James T. Hickey papers, in the manuscript collections of the Ohio Historical Society, Columbus.

E.J. Humphries letter (Phillips Legion Georgia Cavalry), in the manuscript collections of Duke University.

James Ireland papers (12th Ohio Infantry), in the manuscript collections of the Ohio Historical Society, Columbus.

Albert Gallatin Jenkins papers, in the manuscript collections of Marshall University, Huntington, WV.

C. Jenkins diary (13th Georgia Infantry), in the manuscript collections of the Troup County Georgia Archives.

A.W. Johnson letter (3rd Regiment Wise Legion), in the manuscript collections of West Virginia University, Morgantown.

Robert E. Lee papers, 1861, in the manuscript collections of the Virginia Historical Society, Richmond. Mss31515b film B55.

Lewis family papers, in the manuscript collections of the University of Virginia, Charlottesville.

A.W. Mann correspondence (Greenbrier Co. State Scouts, U.S.), various letters and documents relevant to U.S. scout and militia companies of West Virginia, in the manuscript collections of the State of West Virginia, Charleston.

Charles Mestrezat papers (14th Pennsylvania Cavalry), in the manuscript collections of West Virginia University, Morgantown.

Morton-Halsey papers, in the manuscript collections of the University of Virginia, Charlottesville.

National Archives and Records Administration, (NARA) RG 109, Records of the Army of the Kanawha, chapter 2, vol. 94, Aug-Sept. 1861; and chapter 2, volume 318, Sept. 1861. NARA Compiled Service Records of Confederate Soldiers from the State of Virginia; NARA RG 56, micropublication M87, Records of the Commissioners of Claims, Southern Claims Commission, 1871-1880. NARA M598 Records of Prisoners of War at the Various Military Prisons. NARA RG 153 Case File LL2540 (David Creigh).

W.S. Newton papers (91st Ohio Infantry), in the manuscript collections of the Ohio Historical Society, Columbus.

Thomas Penn papers (42nd Va Infantry), in the manuscript collections of Duke University, Durham, NC.
Charles Powell papers (14th NC Infantry), in the manuscript collections of Duke University.

W.R. Redding papers (13th GA Infantry), in the manuscript collections of the University of North Carolina, SHSP.

A.J. Reese letter (Phillips Legion GA Cavalry), in the manuscript collections of the University of North Carolina, Chapel Hill.

William Clark Reynolds diary, in the manuscript collections of the State of West Virginia, Charleston.

A.B. Roler diary (Wise Legion 1861), in the manuscript collections of the Virginia Historical Society, Richmond.

R.Lewis Scott papers, in the manuscript collections of the Virginia Historical Society, Richmond.

J.P. Sheffey letters (8th Va Cavalry), in the manuscript collections of Virginia Tech, Blacksburg.

William A. Smith papers, in the manuscript collections of Virginia Tech, Blacksburg.

Rev. G.G. Smith papers (Phillips Legion GA Cavalry), in the manuscript collections of the University of NC, Chapel Hill.

Robert W. Snead letters, in the manuscript collections of the Virginia Historical Society, Richmond.

State of West Virginia manuscript collections, MS 79-83, file 15-083. Applications from former Confederates to be reinstated as practicing attorneys in WV.

W.Tate papers, in the manuscript collections of the University of Virginia, Charlottesville.

James J. Wood diary (34th Ohio Infantry), in the manuscript collections of Bowling Green State University, Ohio.

Micajah Woods papers (Floyd's Brigade), in the manuscript collections of the University of Virginia, Charlottesville.

William C. Workman letter, in the manuscript collections of the Greenbrier Historical Society, Lewisburg, WV.

J.V. Young diary, in the Roy B. Cook collection, West Virginia University, Morgantown.

Left to right: Mr. Jim Talbert, archivist of the Greenbrier County Historical Society, Jason McKinney, and author Tim McKinney at "The Barracks" in Lewisburg, April 2003.

ABOUT THE AUTHOR

Tim McKinney is a member of the Greenbrier County Historical Society and is a past president of the West Virginia Historical Society. A 20-year staff employee of WVU Institute of Technology, Montgomery, this is McKinney's seventh publication on the Civil War in West Virginia. His other titles include *The Civil War in Fayette County West Virginia* and *West Virginia Civil War Almanac* in two volumes. Married, with one son, he resides with his family at Fayetteville, WV. Mr. McKinney may be written to at P.O. Box 157 Fayetteville, WV 25840.

INDEX

Frequently used names of people and places are not indexed in their entirety. Prisoner of war and other rosters are not included in this index.